*Nicaragua Must Survive*

VIOLENCE IN LATIN AMERICAN HISTORY

*Edited by Pablo Piccato, Federico Finchelstein, and Paul Gillingham*

# Nicaragua Must Survive

SANDINISTA REVOLUTIONARY
DIPLOMACY IN THE GLOBAL COLD WAR

*Eline van Ommen*

UNIVERSITY OF CALIFORNIA PRESS

University of California Press
Oakland, California

© 2024 by Eline van Ommen

Portions of chapter 1 were adapted from an essay originally published in *Latin America and the Global Cold War*, edited by Thomas C. Field Jr., Stella Krepp, and Vanni Pettinà. Copyright © 2020 by the University of North Carolina Press. Used by permission of the publisher. www.uncpress.org

Portions of the book have previously appeared in Eline van Ommen, "The Nicaraguan Revolution's Challenge to the Monroe Doctrine: Sandinistas and Western Europe, 1979–1990," *The Americas* 78, no. 4 (2021): 639–66.

Every reasonable effort has been made to supply complete and correct credits. If there are errors or omissions, please contact the University of California Press so that corrections can be addressed in any subsequent edition.

Cataloging-in-Publication data is on file at the Library of Congress.

ISBN 978-0-520-39074-4 (cloth)
ISBN 978-0-520-39076-8 (pbk.)
ISBN 978-0-520-39077-5 (ebook)

33  32  31  30  29  28  27  26  25  24
10  9  8  7  6  5  4  3  2  1

*For Joost*

# CONTENTS

# ILLUSTRATIONS

# ACKNOWLEDGMENTS

I am very lucky to have been supported by many people while researching and writing this book. First and foremost, I owe an enormous debt to my brilliant doctoral supervisor, mentor, and friend Tanya Harmer. From the moment I arrived at the London School of Economics (LSE) as a graduate student more than a decade ago, she has consistently provided me with encouragement, confidence, and inspiration. Her belief in me and my ability to complete this project is one of the main reasons this book exists. I am also incredibly grateful to my other doctoral supervisor, Piers Ludlow, for his kindness, support, and feedback on the European and transatlantic dimensions of the project. Thank you so much, Tanya and Piers.

As a student and teacher at the LSE, I benefited enormously from the expertise and feedback of those at the Department of International History, the journal *Cold War History*, and the Latin America and Caribbean Centre. I am particularly grateful to Megan Black, Anna Cant, Steven Casey, Vesselin Dimitrov, James Ellison, Matthew Jones, Paul Keenan, Pete Millwood, Sue Onslow, Anita Prazmowska, Taylor Sherman, and Vladislav Zubok. Significant portions of this book were written at Utrecht University, where I was fortunate to meet and work with dedicated and helpful colleagues. I would like to thank Eleni Braat, Liesbeth van de Grift, Erik de Lange, Jorrit Steehouder, Remco Raben, Lorena de Vita, Stefanie Massink, Frank Gerits, and Paschalis Pechlivanis. I am particularly indebted to Laurien Crump, for her mentorship and unwavering support, and Corina Mavrodin, who generously offered feedback, friendship, and excellent wine. I completed this book at the University of Leeds, where my colleagues at the School of History have been welcoming and supportive. I am grateful to Peter Anderson, Nir Arielli, Manuel Barcia, Sara Barker, Dhanveer Singh Brar, Sean Fear, Sarah Foster,

Simon Hall, Robert Hornsby, Elisabeth Leake, Joanna Philips, and Kimberley Thomas. I would like to thank Paulo Drinot, Alan McPherson, and Jussi Hanhimäki, who generously read and commented on earlier versions of the manuscript. For his support in the final stages of the writing process, I am also enormously thankful to Enrique Ochoa-Kaup at the University of California Press, whose concise feedback and knowledge of Latin American history helped me to improve the manuscript.

Researching everywhere, but especially in Nicaragua and Cuba, can be a daunting, exciting, and rewarding process, and I am grateful to all those who made it possible and enjoyable. In Managua, the staff at the Instituto de Historia de Nicaragua y Centroamérica deserve my thanks. And for their guidance, inspiration, and support, I am particularly indebted to Luis Caldera, Alejandro Bendaña, and Ángel Barrajón, as well as to all the interviewees who gave their time so generously. I am also immensely grateful to Friederike Apelt, Fernando Camacho Padilla, Kim Christiaens, David Johnson Lee, Hilary Francis, Christian Helm, Mateo Cayetano Jarquín, Michael William Schmidli, Gerardo Sánchez Nateras, Emily Snyder, and José Manuel Agreda Portero, who were kind enough to share their insights, contacts, and research experiences with me.

Throughout the years, I received a great deal of useful feedback from presenting at a number of workshops and conferences, such as the LSE International History Research Seminar in London, the New Diplomatic History Conference in Middelburg, the Summer School "Sandinista Culture in Nicaragua: Theories and Testimonials" in Wuppertal, the Cold War Research Network in Utrecht, and the first annual conference of historians of Latin America in the United Kingdom (UKLAH) in Bristol. Participating in the GWU-UCSB-LSE Graduate Conference on the Cold War in Santa Barbara was a particularly rewarding experience, and I would like to thank Thomas Field and Salim Yaqub for their feedback and advice. Many thanks also go out to Alexandre Moreli and Stella Krepp for inviting me to attend the second Latin America in a Global Context Workshop in Rio de Janeiro, where they provided a welcoming and friendly environment to discuss Latin American global history.

At the LSE and elsewhere, I was fortunate to be part of a wonderful and supportive community. I would especially like to thank Bastiaan Bouwman, Grace Carrington, Caroline Green, Cees Heere, Anne Irfan, Judith Jacob, Will King, Alex Mayhew, Tommaso Milani, Marral Shamshiri-Fard, and Max Skjönsberg for their company and friendship over the years. Long conversations, dinners, pub trips and—more recently—phone calls with Alexandre Dab made the past couple of years that much better. Thank you also to my brilliant academic sister Molly Avery, whose strength and bravery continue to inspire me.

Outside academia, I am forever grateful to my friends and family. Friends from Groningen and beyond deserve a special mention. Over the last decade, Rosa Deen, Freek Kilsdonk, Irene Krap, Floris Pas, Björn Quanjer, Annemarie Rullens, Bernard Slaa, Ruben Slagter, Eric Veldwiesch, Lisanne Verberkt, and Jeltsje van der Woude have been a constant source of laugher, strength, and support. Aside from reading draft chapters and visiting me in Managua, London, Leeds, and Utrecht, their friendship in itself sustained me. Certainly, this book would have never existed if it was not for the wonderful, strong, and fashionable Anne-Mette Hermans.

Special thanks go out to my parents, Christine Gutman and Gert van Ommen, for always stimulating me to read, travel, and learn about the world. You have taught me to be independent and believe in myself. Emma, Floris, and David, you are the best siblings I could have wished for. Thank you for being there when things were difficult, and for making me feel safe and happy. Klaas and Sinie Vogel, too, have always been amazingly supportive. I am lucky to be part of your family, too.

A lot has happened since I started writing this book. Most importantly and wonderfully, my two sons Robin and Daniel were born, teaching me about unconditional love, happiness, and selflessness in ways I could have never imagined. Having a toddler and baby in the house did not make writing, thinking, and meeting deadlines easier, though, and I have Joost Vogel to thank for always being there, making me laugh, and making sure everything turned out all right. Thank you, Joost; I could not have done this without you.

# ABBREVIATIONS

| | |
|---|---|
| AA | Auswärtiges Amt (Foreign Office) (West Germany) |
| AMLAE | Asociación de Mujeres Nicaragüense Luisa Amanda Espinoza (Luisa Amanda Espinoza Association of Nicaraguan Women) |
| ANN | Agencia Nueva Nicaragua |
| CAHRC | Central American Human Rights Committee (United Kingdom) |
| CDN | Coordinadora Democrática Nicaragüense (Democratic Coordinating Committee) |
| CDU | Christian Democratic Union (West Germany) |
| CNDS | Campaña Nicaragua Debe Sobrevivir (Nicaragua Must Survive Campaign) |
| CNSP | Comité Nicaragüense de Solidaridad con los Pueblos (Nicaraguan Committee for People's Solidarity) |
| CONIPAZ | Comité Nicaragüense por la Paz (Nicaraguan Peace Committee) |
| DRI | Departamento de Relaciones Internacionales (Nicaragua) |
| EC | European Community |
| EPC | European Political Cooperation |
| EPS | Ejército Popular Sandinista |
| FCO | Foreign and Commonwealth Office (United Kingdom) |

| | |
|---|---|
| FRG | Federal Republic of Germany |
| FMLN | Frente Farabundo Martí para la Liberación Nacional (Farabundo Martí National Liberation Front) |
| FSLN | Frente Sandinista de Liberación Nacional (Sandinista National Liberation Front) |
| GDR | German Democratic Republic |
| ICJ | International Court of Justice |
| IKV | Interkerkelijk Vredesberaad (Dutch Interchurch Peace Council) |
| IMF | International Monetary Fund |
| KKLA | Kultuur Kollectief Latijns Amerika (Latin American Cultural Collective) (Netherlands) |
| MDN | Movimiento Democrático Nicaragüense (Nicaraguan Democratic Movement) |
| MINEX | Ministerio del Exterior (Nicaragua) |
| MIR | Movimiento de Izquierda Revolucionaria (Revolutionary Left Movement) (Chile) |
| NAM | Non-Aligned Movement |
| NIEO | New International Economic Order |
| NKN | Nicaragua Komitee Nederland (Dutch Nicaragua Committee) |
| NSC | Nicaragua Solidarity Campaign (United Kingdom) |
| PvdA | Partij van de Arbeid (Labor Party) (Netherlands) |
| SI | Socialist International |
| SPD | Sozialdemokratische Partei Deutschlands (Social Democratic Party of Germany) |
| UNO | Unión Nacional Opositora (National Opposition Union) (Nicaragua) |

# Introduction

ALEJANDRO BENDAÑA CALLED ME the day before I was supposed to leave Nicaragua. He was inviting me to come by his Managua home to browse through some boxes with documents he had found. I had been in touch with Bendaña previously because I wanted to find out more about his work for the Nicaraguan foreign service after 19 July 1979, when the young revolutionaries of the Frente Sandinista de Liberación Nacional (Sandinista National Liberation Front, FSLN) toppled the anticommunist dictatorship of Anastasio Somoza Debayle, ushering in a decade of revolutionary change and regional upheaval. Tired, worried about bags that were still unpacked, and having already resigned myself to the impossibility of tracking down Nicaragua's foreign ministry archives, I hesitated for a moment. Then, I fortunately decided to make the journey to Bendaña's house, where he showed me the documents that are now at the heart of this book. Together with the other materials I had already collected, they helped me to understand why Bendaña believed that Nicaragua's political future was ultimately decided in the international arena. "Western public opinion was absolutely crucial to one small nation that was trying to defend its sovereignty, because we weren't going to win a major military conflict with the U.S. and wanted to avert it," Bendaña reflected in an interview he gave in July 1996. Indeed, he continued, despite the enormous human costs of the Nicaraguan civil war, the "real battle" over Nicaragua in the late 1970s and 1980s took place "in public opinion and in Congress, and with the Europeans."[1]

Like Bendaña, former participants in Nicaragua's revolutionary project often mention the international interventions, global trends, and transnational actors that transformed their country's history at the tail end of the Cold War. The Sandinista triumph over the Somoza regime on 19 July 1979 captured the imaginations of people around the globe. Thousands of sympathizers flocked to Nicaragua to experience firsthand how the revolution unfolded, and to help it fulfill its promises of radical social change, people's democracy, and national liberation. In the Americas and Europe, activists organized music festivals, staged protests, and sold posters to propagate the Sandinista cause, denounce its enemies, and raise funds for the FSLN's domestic programs. Famous intellectuals like Salman Rushdie, Régis Debray, Margaret Randall, Gabriel García Márquez, and Graham Greene praised and romanticized the young and ambitious Sandinistas. Foreign governments' reactions to the revolution largely depended on their outlook on the Cold War. Their responses either sought to support, restrain, or destroy the newly minted regime, all with significant consequences for how Nicaragua's revolutionary trajectory developed on the ground. Meanwhile, Sandinista diplomats navigated the shifting international landscape of the late Cold War, implementing an innovative foreign policy strategy that was designed to ensure the revolution's survival in the face of growing hostility from the anticommunist camp. This dense web of contacts between Nicaragua and the outside world unraveled when the FSLN lost the elections held on 25 February 1990, effectively ending the country's revolutionary experiment and its place in the international limelight.

But why did the revolution have such a massive global impact? And why did transnational actors and foreign policies have such immediate consequences for how the revolution developed on the ground? None of this was inevitable, automatic, or even logical, considering Nicaragua's lack of valuable resources to export, its small size, and its location in what had historically been considered the "back yard" of the United States. The answer to both these questions, I argue, can be found in the Sandinistas' unique, ambitious, yet pragmatic diplomatic campaign, which blended grassroots organizing with traditional foreign policy. Indeed, the Sandinistas' revolutionary diplomacy was not just concerned with managing relations between states. Like Cuban attempts in earlier decades, the FSLN sought to construct a new international order that would benefit the countries of the Global South: a "revolutionary world" in which the Nicaraguan Revolution could triumph, survive, and ultimately thrive.[2] This radical objective required a different and much more creative set of diplomatic relationships and practices than those employed by nonrevolutionary states. Inspired by examples from Vietnam, Cuba, and Algeria, the FSLN's revolutionary diplomacy targeted government leaders and diplomats, but also musicians, feminists, guerrillas, teachers, journalists, priests, peace activists, town councillors, and human rights campaigners from around the world. Recognizing that public perceptions and non-state actors mattered for the revolution's future, the Sandinistas combined state-level diplomacy with a unique mix of culture, propaganda, and personal relationships. The Sandinistas' efforts resulted in a transnational network of solidarity activists who carried out crucial tasks for the FSLN's foreign policy, albeit with varying levels of success and enthusiasm.

*Nicaragua Must Survive* tells the story of the FSLN's revolutionary diplomacy, the people who gave it substance and meaning, and how it helped to shape Nicaragua's domestic history. Twenty years after Fidel Castro and his band of guerrillas triumphed in Cuba, and six years after the violent overthrow of Latin America's first democratically elected socialist president, Salvador Allende, in Chile, the victory of the Nicaraguan revolutionaries over the Somoza dictatorship in July 1979 remains an understudied moment of profound change in Cold War Latin America. In Central America, the revolution served as fresh inspiration for the armed Left and it further radicalized the anticommunist Right, resulting in genocidal violence in Guatemala and a brutal civil war in El Salvador.[3] Beyond the isthmus, the FSLN triumph encouraged conflicting state and non-state intervention from Cuba, Chile, Argentina, Mexico, the United States and others, with foreign powers either seeking to fight Cold War battles or offering negotiated diplomatic solutions purporting to transcend Cold War binaries. More than an anomaly or afterthought in Latin America's Cold War, as general overviews of this period tend to portray the civil wars of the 1980s, the Revolución Popular Sandinista ensured that Central America became the principal arena in which local, regional, and international actors determined whether, when, and how Latin America's Cold War struggles could be ended.[4]

The Sandinistas were pivotal in determining how this ideological battle unfolded. Even before they came to power, the FSLN managed to mobilize a transnational pro-Sandinista network dedicated to the overthrow of the Somoza dictatorship. Employing the language of human rights, anti-imperialism, and social justice, Sandinista ambassadors and their non-state allies convinced politicians in the Americas and Europe that Nicaragua mattered, that Somoza had to go, and that the FSLN represented a legitimate alternative. After the revolution's triumph on 19 July 1979, Sandinista revolutionary diplomacy was crucial in raising funds for ambitious domestic programs such as the literacy crusade, health care initiatives, and cultural projects. For a moment after their victory, though, the Sandinistas considered abandoning—or at the very least reducing—their connections with the transnational solidarity movement in favor of a more traditional foreign policy. After all, they had achieved their primary objective of taking charge of the Nicaraguan state.

However, the 4 November 1980 U.S. electoral victory of the Republican Ronald Reagan, who made no secret of his hostility to the Sandinistas, changed their minds. The Reagan administration, convinced that interference from Cuba and the Soviet Union was responsible for the Sandinista victory and the revolutionary wars in El Salvador and Guatemala, employed various tactics to "roll back" communism in Central America. Throughout most of the 1980s, U.S. officials worked to weaken the Nicaraguan economy, isolate the country diplomatically, and provide Nicaraguan insurgents—also known as Contras (after *contrarrevolucionarios*, or counterrevolutionaries)—with money, military training, and weapons. The human costs of the U.S.-funded Contra war were enormous; around fifty thousand people died, a hundred thousand were wounded, and many more were displaced.[5] The U.S. government did not work alone, collaborating with allies from around the world to achieve its Cold War objectives, including the Argentine and Chilean military dictatorships and a range of anticommunist private organizations and individuals.[6] To protect the revolution from attacks by a much more powerful opponent, the Sandinistas took the battle to the international arena once more, successfully mobilizing public opinion, governments, and non-state actors to support the Nicaraguan Revolution's survival.

Intriguingly, considering Reagan's Cold War rhetoric, the primary targets of the FSLN's revolutionary diplomacy were not the ideological enemies of the United States, such as Cuba, the Soviet Union, or even the members of the Non-Aligned Movement (NAM). While these countries mattered for the revolution's survival, *Nicaragua Must Survive* contends that Western Europe was at the heart of the Sandinistas' revolutionary diplomacy. From the late 1970s until their electoral loss in February 1990, Sandinistas and pro-FSLN solidarity activists encouraged Western European governments to become involved in Central American affairs. The Sandinistas' policy toward Western Europe was specifically designed to weaken the resolve and limit the possibilities of the United States and its allies for defeating the Nicaraguan Revolution. Specifically, by pushing Western Europeans to launch an alternative diplomatic campaign toward Central America and—ideally—channel developmental aid to Nicaragua, the FSLN sought to shift the inter-American balance of power in their favor. Western European involvement, the

Sandinistas pragmatically calculated, would counter the infamous 1823 Monroe Doctrine that envisaged U.S. dominance over the Western Hemisphere, and which, Nicaraguan revolutionaries believed, still determined U.S. foreign policy and perceptions of Central America.[7] Western European involvement, even if not directly supportive of the revolutionaries, would undermine the United States' regional hegemony. Moreover, it would provide the FSLN with a significant propaganda victory. After all, the Western Europeans were generally seen as the United States' close—but perhaps more restrained—Cold War allies and their independent involvement in Central America would be a blow to the Reagan administration's global credibility. The Sandinistas' outreach to Western Europe hence serves as an important example of how the FSLN's revolutionary diplomacy creatively constructed opportunities to benefit the revolution's survival and reshape international affairs.

Even so, the Sandinista Revolution was not immune to, and would ultimately be consumed by, wider changes in the international system. In the early years of the revolution, the FSLN and its allies managed to use the charged atmosphere of the late Cold War to their advantage by claiming that *la guerra fría* had nothing to do with what was happening in Nicaragua. This was an appealing argument to Western European activists and politicians who were frustrated by Reagan's dangerous obsession with fighting communism. It was precisely because Western European governments believed that the European Community (EC)—in collaboration with Latin American states—could prevent Central America from turning into a Cold War hotspot that they decided to become involved in the region in the first place. Moreover, at a time when millions of peace activists demonstrated against the placement of North Atlantic Treaty Organization (NATO) missiles on Western European soil, the FSLN's claims that Reagan was a dangerous leader fell onto fertile ground. Yet, in the late 1980s, with Cold War tensions in decline and the Soviet Union retreating from the Global South, these once powerful ideas lost their urgency, and the Sandinistas were unable to come up with an effective response beyond making further concessions to their ideological enemies. To be sure, the FSLN's electoral loss in February 1990 was as much a domestic as an international event, but the refusal of Western Europeans to prop up Nicaragua's faltering economy and the decline in public sympathy for the Sandinista cause undoubtedly played a part in convincing Nicaraguans to vote for the U.S.-backed opposition. As Western Europe turned its gaze away from Central America, the inter-American balance was—albeit not fully restored in favor of the United States—no longer as beneficial to the Sandinista revolutionaries as it had been in the late 1970s and early 1980s.

· · ·

Through the history of the Sandinistas' revolutionary diplomacy, *Nicaragua Must Survive* aims to make four significant contributions. First, it traces the ability of a small revolutionary movement, and later a government, to use the international environment to its own advantage. What opportunities did the Sandinistas have—or create for themselves—as they faced an opponent that was significantly more powerful in terms of resources, size, and military strength? Similar to the David and Goliath narrative that the FSLN presented to international audiences in the 1980s, diplomatic historians studying Nicaragua's relations with the United States often portray the Sandinistas as relatively powerless victims of the Reagan administration's aggressive and illegal campaign against the revolution.[8] Yet, despite the fact that U.S. foreign policy toward Nicaragua was well-funded, Reagan never succeeded in achieving his primary objective of removing the Sandinistas from power. To be sure, as one would expect, the United States had a significant degree of influence over how the Central American civil wars unfolded, and the Nicaraguan Revolution was significantly debilitated because of U.S. anti-communist policy. Nevertheless, it was only during the presidency of George H. W. Bush, a Republican who was more reluctant than Reagan to pursue the military option against Nicaragua, that the FSLN was *voted* out of office.

To make sense of the FSLN's ability to use the international environment for the revolution's survival, it is worth first briefly reflecting on the concept of power in international relations. As the Sandinistas' diplomacy shows, power is more than obtaining "the outcomes you want through threats, violence, and coercion."[9] Indeed, as Tom Long demonstrated in a recent study on international relations in the Western Hemisphere, Latin American countries had "autonomy and influence" over the United States despite their relative lack of "military and economic resources."[10] That is because smaller states are forced to rely on different—but not necessarily less influential— sources of power to pursue their goals. They use and create "margins for maneuver" for themselves in the international arena by adopting creative and sometimes unconventional strategies.[11] Using multilateralism, public diplomacy, and transnational relationships, governments can "co-opt ... rather than coerce" people to work toward intended outcomes.[12] For this so-called "soft power" strategy to work, though, governments need to project a positive image of themselves to international audiences, for instance through cultural expression, relationships with non-state groups, and cultivating appealing narratives.[13] If they do so effectively, seemingly weaker states can achieve their objectives and build an international environment that works in their favor, even though they—like all governments—do not always manage to shape outcomes.

Building on the idea that public opinion, culture, and perceptions are powerful tools in international relations, *Nicaragua Must Survive* thus explains why the Sandinistas managed to build and maintain a revolutionary state over a significant amount of time. In the period leading up to Somoza's fall in July 1979, the Sandinistas' revolutionary diplomacy shared many similarities with—and was undoubtedly inspired by—the successful transnational strategies employed by the Vietnamese revolutionaries, the Palestine Liberation Organization, and the Algerian National Liberation Front.[14] The revolution's triumph, as well as the shifting international landscape the Sandinistas encountered following their victory, necessitated a new global strategy. After all, implementing and defending the revolution's promises came with a different set of foreign policy challenges than mounting an armed insurgency. For the FSLN, it required reaching out to Western Europe for financial aid, making concessions to avoid international isolation and, crucially, a transnational campaign to make the revolution appear attractive. Throughout much of the 1980s, to the frustration of U.S. officials, the FSLN and its allies presented international audiences with a powerful narrative of a young, romantic, and adventurous revolutionary project that was under attack by a powerful imperial state with a long history of bloody interventions, including in Vietnam, Chile, and, from 1983 onwards, Grenada.

Yet, as it turns out, narratives, perceptions, and ideas are complex and unpredictable. States can use them to their own advantage and sometimes do so effectively; ultimately, however, they are difficult to influence. Indeed, as Daniel Sargent argues, the "resources on which power depends are myriad, and they are specific to context."[15] Forces more powerful than states, including nationalism, anti-imperialism, socialism, and globalization changed world politics and as they did so states, including superpowers, could do little more than improvise and adapt. The Reagan administration's well-funded propaganda campaign failed to convince European audiences that the anti-communist Contras were, in fact, "freedom fighters," serving as a powerful demonstration of the limits of propaganda and, by extension, state power.[16] For the Sandinistas, the decline of Cold War tensions in the late 1980s meant that their revolutionary diplomacy no longer fell on fertile ground; the ideas on which their foreign policy depended were no longer as powerful as they once had been. And while the FSLN tried to adapt to the new global context, after more than a decade of economic hardship and civil war the revolutionaries were no longer up to the task.

The FSLN's reliance on international goodwill and sympathy brings us to the second contribution of this book, namely the study of solidarity activism and what it can tell us about North-South relations in the Cold War. There has been ample scholarship on the history of transnational movements, Third World activism, and left-wing student protest.[17] And while much of the literature remains focused on what was happening in Western Europe and the United States during the so-called "Global Sixties," recent studies by Aldo Marchesi, Jessica Stites Mor, Katie Marino, Heather Vrana, and others have expanded the geographic and temporal scope to the Global South and the late Cold War.[18] This integration of new actors and regions into histories of protest not only enriches the literature; it also sheds new light on the forces that drove processes of mobilization in Europe and the Americas. In West Germany, as Quinn Slobodian points out, "proximate interactions" with foreign students and other "members of the Third World" had a crucial influence on the politics of the emerging New Left.[19] Similarly, rather than spontaneous outbursts of Western European solidarity, many of the protest groups that denounced the human rights abuses of the Chilean and Argentine dictatorships in the 1970s and early 1980s were backed by Latin American exiles.[20]

For all its insistence on recognizing the agency of Third World actors, however, there is still a tendency in the literature to romanticize solidarity activism. In the Nicaraguan case, the emerging body of scholarship that details the activities of pro-FSLN groups in Western Europe and the Americas acknowledges the central role Sandinistas played in coordinating the transnational solidarity movement.[21] Yet little attention is paid to how fluctuating power dynamics, tensions, and hierarchies infused the relationships between European activists and revolutionary politicians. The collaboration between Sandinistas and international activists was not always as smooth as it appeared to be on the surface. Overall, solidarity activists were generally well-intentioned and genuine in their desire to contribute to the Nicaraguan Revolution's success, but, as Agnieszka Sobocinska reminds us, "good intentions can be misguided" if the needs of "recipient communities" are not taken into sufficient account.[22] Solidarity activists, disillusioned with the lack of revolutionary progress in their own countries, projected their hopes, dreams, and political ambitions onto Nicaragua. More than contributing to the revolution, solidarity activists wanted to participate in it; they wanted to feel part of a project that was ultimately not their own.

To be sure, the FSLN encouraged this sentiment and often managed to harness it for the revolution's benefit, inviting thousands of Western volunteers—or *brigadistas*—to Nicaragua for coffee-picking, construction projects, or fact-finding missions with high propagandistic value.[23] Yet, in other instances, activists' individual ambitions were directly at odds with the needs of the Nicaraguan people. Developmental aid, for instance, was a key priority for the Sandinistas, who struggled to raise the country's standard of living, but fundraising was simply not an appealing task to the Western activists, who preferred so-called "political" work over "humanitarian" campaigns. Efforts by the FSLN to centralize the solidarity movement to make it more effective and easier to coordinate were also actively resisted by activists, who opted instead for more intimate relationships in the form of so-called sister bonds with Nicaraguan cities, schools, and labor unions. Ultimately, as *Nicaragua Must Survive* demonstrates, these contests about what solidarity entails, how the movement should operate, and who was allowed to make decisions about its functioning, limited the effectiveness of transnational solidarity work and, as such, the ability of the FSLN to implement its revolutionary diplomacy.

The rise and decline of the pro-Sandinista solidarity movement also helps us understand the process through which solidarity activism became increasingly deradicalized—at least on the surface—as the Cold War came to an end. First strategically, but later out of necessity, solidarity activists embraced the ostensibly universal language of human rights, development, democracy, and humanitarianism. This allowed activists to deflect accusations of political bias, as well as to mobilize financial and political support for the Nicaraguan Revolution from organizations across the political spectrum. In the late 1970s and early 1980s, these concepts were relatively fluid and open to contestation. Within human rights language, for instance, there was space for an explicit emphasis on social and economic rights. Democracy could refer to popular participation, neighborhood committees, and grassroots political initiatives. And development was not necessarily synonymous with capitalism and so-called free market economics. By appealing to universal and politically neutral values that appeared to transcend Cold War politics,

Western European solidarity activists transformed the Nicaraguan Revolution into a popular and relatively uncontroversial cause.

Yet, as Alyssa Bowen shows in relation to the Chile solidarity movement, the "politics of anti-politics" had unintended consequences for the Left.[24] It assisted the creation of a culture in Western Europe and the United States in which politics became somewhat of a dirty word: a culture with little space for concepts such as anti-imperialism, national liberation, and social justice. Moreover, in the 1980s, Ronald Reagan and Margaret Thatcher successfully promoted an articulation of human rights as "rooted in anti-communism, democracy promotion, and free-market fundamentalism."[25] The triumph of neoliberal human rights over the politics of social justice had serious and devastating consequences for the solidarity groups, as Nicaragua simply did not fit the new model. Indeed, as the 1980s progressed and global disenchantment with state socialism in Eastern Europe grew, pro-FSLN activists struggled to answer critical questions about press freedom, human rights, and democracy in Nicaragua, resulting in intense debates about strategy and the future directions of the movement. In the run-up to the 1990 elections, solidarity groups in the Netherlands even considered breaking ties with the FSLN, and some switched to a more general policy of backing Nicaragua's democratic *process* instead. Swept up by the "neoliberal maelstrom" that characterized the end of the Cold War, the solidarity movement thus lost much of its previous radicalism, which impacted its ability to support the increasingly isolated Nicaraguan revolutionaries.[26]

The Sandinistas' interactions with the world beyond the Americas, as well as the Nicaraguan Revolution's intimate connections to global processes of change, are central to this book's third contribution. By including the voices of actors from outside the inter-American system, the book brings us closer to a more nuanced understanding of the *global* Cold War and Latin America's place within it. This is a much-needed intervention, as scholars of contemporary Latin America have yet to incorporate the region fully into a global framework.[27] Indeed, as Tanya Harmer and Alberto Martín Álvarez lament, historians have "only really begun to scratch the surface when it comes to understanding Latin America's relationship with the wider world in the twentieth century."[28] In the case of Nicaragua, recent international histories of the country's revolutionary decade, although no longer obsessed with debating the rights and wrongs of U.S. foreign policy, have not yet managed to break down the historiographical barrier that separates the Western Hemisphere from the rest of the world.[29] Important steps have been made toward uncovering the inter-American dynamics of the Nicaraguan Revolution, but we still know very little about the revolution's global dimensions, repercussions, and reception.[30] The point of telling the story of the Sandinistas' outreach to Western Europe, then, is to examine how people, ideas, and events originating in Latin America traveled across borders and came to transform the character and dynamics of the global Cold War, and vice versa.

Perhaps one of the more surprising consequences of the Central American civil wars was their contribution to the revival of Western Europe as a global power acting independently from—although mostly in collaboration with—the United States on the world stage. To be sure, this process was already underway before the Sandinistas' revolutionary victory, but concerns that the Central American "pawn" could be used by the Soviet Union to weaken Western Europe's position in the "international game of chess" certainly helped to convince European leaders, particularly the West Germans, that they had to play a more active international role.[31] Concerned that Reagan's obsession with fighting Central American guerrillas would divert his attention away from the European theater, the EC member states set out to prevent further military escalation in Central America. Insisting that social and economic inequalities—and not Soviet and Cuban intervention—were driving the revolutionary struggles, the Europeans publicly dismissed Reagan's Cold War narrative. They also refused to exclude Nicaragua from regional aid packages to mitigate these inequalities, calculating that this would only make the Sandinistas more reliant on Cuba and the Eastern bloc. The European initiative was thus a clear rejection of the Reagan administration's methods of fighting the Cold War, but behind the scenes the transatlantic allies shared the goal of eroding the appeal of socialism.

This European initiative, analyzed for the first time in *Nicaragua Must Survive*, would not have taken place if it was not for the efforts of Latin Americans who developed the regional peace initiatives—first the Contadora and later the Esquipulas process—that the EC ended up supporting.[32] Indeed, as the 1980s progressed, Nicaraguan claims that Western Europe should play a more active role in Central America were increasingly backed up by a chorus of powerful voices from Mexico, Costa Rica, Guatemala, Cuba, Colombia, Venezuela, and others. While not all these countries sympathized with—indeed, in some instances they even actively despised—the Nicaraguan revolutionaries, their leaders all agreed that it should no longer be up to the United States alone to determine the outcomes of Latin

America's political, social, and economic crises. Like the Sandinistas, these governments believed that Western European engagement could strengthen their multilateral diplomacy and prevent regional initiatives toward Central America from being blocked by the U.S. administration. And ultimately, as Mateo Jarquín points out, it was Latin America and not the United States that "won the wider war of ideas" regarding how to respond to the Central American crises.[33] Despite various attempts by the United States to exclude the Sandinistas from regional peace initiatives, the Esquipulas process—with European support and Nicaragua's participation—brought the Central American conflicts to a negotiated solution. The influence of Latin America on the global Cold War, then, should not be underestimated; not only did actors from the region shape European foreign policies, but the collaboration between the EC and various Latin American coalitions also highlights the multipolarity of the late Cold War, and how this formed a challenge to U.S. hegemony in Central America.

On a more personal level, the story of the Sandinistas' revolutionary diplomacy also helps us understand the various ways that individuals experienced the global Cold War. What was it like to live through and participate in the struggle over Nicaragua's ideological future? Who participated in this struggle? What can this teach us about the human dimension of the Cold War? Greg Grandin and Gilbert Joseph have argued that "the internationalization and politicization of everyday life" was at the heart of the Latin America's Cold War experience."[34] To an extent, the same can be said about the Cold War in Western Europe, even though Europeans obviously did not have to deal with the same levels of violence as many Latin Americans. Nevertheless, the Nicaraguan Revolution, and the ideological Cold War struggle that accompanied it, transformed individual lives, local politics, and grassroots activism, not just in the Americas but also in other areas of the world. As councillors in British town halls engaged in heated debates about the legitimacy of Sandinista rule, schoolchildren in the Netherlands listened to Nicaraguan music, and West German solidarity activists befriended Nicaraguan campesinos they otherwise would not have met, the ideas at the heart of the Cold War battle over the Sandinista Revolution were increasingly part of Western Europeans' everyday lives. It is only by situating the human dimension of the Sandinistas' global outreach into the "broader geopolitical and institutional narratives" of the twentieth century that we come to understand the intimate connections between the local, the transnational, and the global during the Cold War era.[35]

For all its significance for the outside world, the Sandinistas' revolutionary diplomacy was ultimately about Nicaragua, which brings us to this book's fourth contribution. By analyzing the revolution's transnational and international dimensions, we gain new insight into the character and trajectory of the Nicaraguan Revolution, as well as the hopes, insecurities, and strategies of the Sandinista revolutionaries. Conversations between Nicaraguan representatives and international actors shed light on how the FSLN wanted to be perceived by potential allies, supporters, and enemies. Perhaps unsurprisingly, comments and promises made by Sandinistas in Cuba and the Eastern bloc contrasted sharply with the picture Nicaraguan officials presented to Western journalists, politicians, and academics. In Europe, Sandinista diplomats carefully presented the revolution as fundamentally different from other revolutionary states, most notably Cuba. Arguing that the revolution was neither socialist nor hostile to the West, the FSLN asked for developmental aid to end the poverty, injustice, and exploitation that had characterized the Somoza era. By contrast, in the Eastern bloc, Sandinistas admitted that claims that the revolution was moderate and democratic were mostly for show, as the FSLN could not yet afford to lose the support of the West or of Nicaragua's domestic elites. From the socialist perspective, then, the Sandinistas were not different from other revolutionaries, but simply more pragmatic and conscious of the global environment's opportunities and restrictions.

So, what was the real character of the Nicaraguan Revolution? Until we have access to the Sandinista leadership's archive, this question remains difficult to answer, although that does not mean we should not try. An important point to make here is that the revolution meant different things to different people. Especially in the years leading up to Somoza's fall, the Nicaraguan revolutionaries managed to bring together a diverse ideological coalition under the Sandinista banner, including social democrats, Marxist-Leninists, liberation theologians, and nationalists. After 19 July 1979, the revolution's plurality came under pressure as the FSLN set out to consolidate its power and their highly centralized approach often clashed with the various needs, ideas, and ambitions of Nicaragua's local populations. The Sandinista elites who are central to this book, though, primarily looked toward socialist Cuba for inspiration and advice. Drawing on the memory of Augusto César Sandino, a peasant leader and member of the Liberal Party who fought against the U.S. occupation of Nicaragua between 1927 and 1933, the Sandinistas believed that their country's national sovereignty was best served by more anti-imperialist revolutions in the Global South. And in this global struggle against imperialism, they considered the Soviet Union to be a natural ally. Despite declarations that *sandinismo* transcended the Cold War, then, the ideas at the heart of the Sandinistas' revolutionary vision were very much part of the global ideological struggle between capitalism and socialism.

An international lens allows us to make sense of the domestic trajectory of the Nicaraguan Revolution. For one, Sandinista revolutionary diplomacy was designed to benefit the revolution, so by assessing its impact, we gain a better understanding of the Sandinistas' ability to defend the revolution, at least until 1990. Moreover, crucial FSLN policy decisions were often made in response to shifts in the international system. In the 1980s, the revolutionaries used domestic reforms and concessions toward political opponents to obtain support, legitimacy, and popularity on the world stage. The 1984 election, for instance, was as much about proving Nicaragua's democratic credentials in Europe and the Americas as it was about obtaining popular support at home. Similarly, the decision to negotiate with the Contras as part of the Esquipulas peace process in the late 1980s can only be understood in the context of the FSLN's growing international isolation, which pushed them toward making further concessions. This is not to suggest that the Nicaraguan Revolution can only be studied as an international phenomenon. To make sense of its history, we require a strong grasp of its local and national dimensions and, thankfully, there exists a rich body of scholarship to draw on.[36] However, the Sandinistas' diplomacy illuminates a key part of what revolutionary states do to survive and why they opt for particular choices. And as such, transnational and international dimensions must be taken into consideration when explaining the revolution's initial triumph, character, longevity, and eventual demise.

. . .

Writing a multilayered international history of the Nicaraguan Revolution comes with a set of conceptual and methodological challenges. The Sandinistas' revolutionary diplomacy blurs the conventional boundaries between diplomacy, transnational activism, and domestic politics. Of course, the idea that governments take domestic trends into account when developing foreign policy is hardly new. Government leaders and policymakers, concerned with winning elections, public opinion, and business interests, let domestic phenomena influence their relationships with the rest of the world.[37] Sandinista leaders, too, kept developments "on the ground" in Nicaragua in mind as they formulated their international strategy. But there was more to it. The Sandinista leadership calculated that if foreign policy—at least to a certain extent—was a continuation of national affairs, it only made sense to also target the populations of the countries whose foreign policies they sought to shape, such as the United States, Mexico, West Germany, the Netherlands, and the United Kingdom. And to do this effectively, the FSLN relied on thousands of grassroots actors who had deep knowledge of their own societies and cultures to carry out important aspects of Nicaragua's revolutionary diplomacy. We do have to make a distinction here between the activists who were part of the transnational solidarity movement that received direct instructions from the Nicaraguan government and maintained close relationships with the FSLN, and those campaigners that supported the revolution in a more indirect manner, for instance the human rights activists, church groups, and other non-governmental organizations (NGOs) that provided humanitarian and developmental aid to Nicaragua in the late 1970s and 1980s. All these foreign activists were volunteers and operated outside of the formal parameters of the state, but the work of the transnational solidarity movement breaks down the traditional distinction between state and non-state actors in the international arena.

To do justice to the breadth and depth of the Sandinistas' revolutionary diplomacy, *Nicaragua Must Survive* adopts a methodology that blends diplomatic and international history with transnational history. In the book, I use the term *transnational* to refer to the connections between the FSLN and non-state actors, the term *diplomacy* to talk about state-to-state relations, and the term *international* to talk about the Sandinistas' relationship to "international society" more in general.[38] Taking the Sandinistas' revolutionary diplomacy as its starting point, this hybrid approach allows me to trace the rise and fall of the Nicaraguan Revolution through an international lens: its impact on the personal lives of those living thousands of miles away; the responses of Western European governments to the Central American civil wars; and, crucially, the dwindling but nonetheless impressive ability of the FSLN to use multilateral diplomacy and the international landscape of the late Cold War for the benefit of the Revolución Popular Sandinista.

The book's methodology also helped me to overcome some of the difficulties that come with studying the Sandinistas' foreign policy in the late Cold War. In Nicaragua, written materials from the revolutionary period are difficult to come by. There is no national archive that systematically collects, catalogues, and declassifies the records of Nicaragua's Ministerio del Exterior (MINEX). Meanwhile, the archives from the FSLN's Departamento de Relaciones Internacionales (DRI) are located at an unknown—at least to me—location, if they have not been destroyed. To assemble a full picture of the FSLN's revolutionary diplomacy, I had to be creative. A range of detailed interviews conducted with former Sandinista leaders, diplomats, and government officials, combined with published memoirs and private collections in Nicaragua, provided crucial insight into the FSLN's international objectives. In some instances, interviews resulted in exclusive access to the personal papers of former diplomats, such as the already-mentioned private archives of Alejandro Bendaña and the papers of Ángel Barrajón, the Sandinistas' representative in Western Europe. Of course, like all primary source material, interviews and written memories need to be critically analyzed and cross-referenced to be useful to historians. In the story that follows, oral histories and memoirs are complemented with archival collections, newspapers, magazines, and extensive online sources from Cuba, the United States, Nicaragua, the United Kingdom, Germany, and the Netherlands. Crucially, the transnational methodology employed in this work brought me to archives not frequently visited by diplomatic historians. The archival collections of solidarity groups, scattered across multiple social history archives in Europe such as the International Institute of Social History in Amsterdam, contain a plethora of letters from the FSLN, detailed correspondence, and records of meetings with Sandinista representatives. Together, these materials shed light on the FSLN's global outreach and its impact on Western European governments and societies.

In scope, the analysis that follows is attentive to the global trends and international politics that shaped, and were shaped by, the Sandinista Revolution and its allies. At its heart, this story is part of the ideological struggle between capitalism and communism that famously characterized the Cold War, particularly in the so-called Global South.[39] Yet this book does not claim to be a complete international history of the Nicaraguan Revolution. Rather, it is a close study of the FSLN's revolutionary diplomacy and its shifting impact on Western European governments, societies, and individual activists. Within Western Europe, three countries stand out in my analysis. I chose to focus on the Netherlands, as the headquarters of the Western European solidarity movement was located there. Moreover, to the frustration of U.S. officials, the Dutch government provided the new

Nicaraguan government with significant financial assistance. By zooming in on the Federal Republic of Germany (FRG), the book also shows the centrality of the West German Auswärtiges Amt (Foreign Office, AA) in the development of a European foreign policy toward Central America. The United Kingdom was also central to the FSLN's revolutionary diplomacy. Not only did the British Nicaragua Solidarity Campaign (NSC) have a permanent office in Managua, but the Nicaraguans also believed—albeit overly optimistically—that the United Kingdom's "special relationship" with the United States could work in their favor.

This is not to suggest that other countries in Europe or indeed the world beyond Europe did not matter for the Sandinistas. On the contrary, the FSLN's revolutionary diplomacy was global in scope. As future historians will undoubtedly explore in more detail, the Soviet Union, Cuba, and the countries of the Global South—and particularly Latin America—were of vital importance in both financial, military, and diplomatic terms. Obviously, the United States played an oversized role, both in the minds of the Sandinista revolutionaries, and on the ground through its hostile foreign policies. And as scholars such as Roger Peace have documented, the FSLN considered the domestic opposition movement in the United States, which campaigned and lobbied fervently against Reagan's violent Central America policy, to be a crucial component of its transnational solidarity network.[40] In fact, combining newly declassified archival sources with the ever-expanding body of literature that explores U.S. state and non-state relations with the Nicaraguan Revolution, this book incorporates U.S. perspectives to assess the effectiveness of the FSLN's diplomacy. It maintains, however, that we should decenter the United States if we want to understand how the Sandinistas used revolutionary diplomacy for the revolution's survival. And whether it was to tip the inter-American balance in favor of the Sandinistas, challenge U.S. influence in Central America, or as an alternative to financial dependency on the Soviet Union, the story that follows shows that the survival of the Nicaraguan Revolution seemed increasingly to hinge on Western Europe as the 1980s progressed.

We begin with an investigation of the Sandinistas' international campaign to isolate the Somoza dictatorship in the years prior to the dictator's fall. It shows how the FSLN developed its own brand of revolutionary diplomacy from 1977 onwards, targeting individuals, organizations, and governments from across the political spectrum. Chapter 2 turns to the remarkable process of remaking the Nicaraguan state and society in the aftermath of the revolution's triumph. After coming to power, the Sandinista leaders pursued dual-track diplomacy, setting out to change the world while at the same time adopting a pragmatic attitude to the international system as they found it. Chapter 3 analyzes the response of the Nicaraguan revolutionaries to the election of Ronald Reagan, whose anticommunist rhetoric prompted fears of a military intervention. In this context, the Sandinistas struggled to strike a balance between, on the one hand, not antagonizing their enemies and, on the other hand, preparing for an attack by obtaining weapons in the East. Chapter 4 opens in April 1983, with the hugely successful Concierto por la paz en Centroamérica (Central American Peace Concert) at Managua's Plaza de la Revolución. As regional tensions intensified, the Sandinistas attached growing importance to these and similar expressions of solidarity. In chapter 5, I explain how Sandinista hopes that an electoral victory would lead to better times were dashed by a series of setbacks and miscalculations. Desperate for financial support, the FSLN organized a centralized fundraising campaign entitled Nicaragua Debe Sobrevivir (Nicaragua Must Survive) to collect money and luxury goods to keep the economy going. The final chapter zooms in on the revolution's end, analyzing the participation of the Sandinista government in the Central American peace processes, which resulted in a devastating electoral loss for the FSLN in February 1990. But before delving into the revolution's tragic demise, let us first turn toward its triumphant beginnings.

# ONE

## Internationalizing Struggle, 1977–1979

ON 30 OCTOBER 1978, the Central American Human Rights Committee (CAHRC), recently founded by a group of Latin American students based in the United Kingdom, hosted a public lecture on the revolutionary war in Nicaragua at the London School of Economics (LSE). The priest and historian Álvaro Arguello Hurtado opened the session with a brief history of Nicaragua, describing how the Somoza family—with the support of the United States—had maintained "control of the country" since the early 1930s. It was only through "violent struggle," the Nicaraguan speaker announced, that the people "could rid themselves of Somoza." The program continued with a half-hour film on the Nicaraguan civil war created by the British journalist Jonathan Dimbleby, who had recently returned from Managua. Then Ángel Barrajón, a Spanish priest and spokesperson for the FSLN in Western Europe, gave a passionate speech, describing the crimes of the dictatorship in vivid detail and calling for "moral, economic, and material assistance to enable the Nicaraguan people to continue their armed struggle against the Somoza regime." Barrajón, who had lived in Nicaragua for several years before being forced to return to Western Europe by the dictatorship, asked the two hundred people in the audience to donate money to the FSLN, reminding them that "only those who had the most and best arms" would be the victors in Nicaragua. His "revolutionary rhetoric" was concerning to a critical observer from the British Foreign and Commonwealth Office (FCO), who later reported that Barrajón appeared to blame "North American imperialism ... for all Nicaragua's present trouble."[1] In a press release, the CAHRC adopted a more pacifist tone than Barrajón, highlighting that "international pressure" could prevent "further bloodshed ... and restore freedom and democracy to Nicaragua."[2]

This public lecture in London was just one of the many events the Nicaraguan revolutionaries and their allies organized in the tumultuous period leading up to the collapse of the Somoza regime on 19 July 1979. From 1977 onwards, the FSLN successfully broadcast its message of Third World revolution and national liberation to thousands of politicians, feminists, priests, solidarity activists, students, journalists, human rights campaigners, and business leaders in the Americas, Europe, and beyond. By building connections—both real and imagined—to audiences outside of Nicaragua, the FSLN strengthened its international standing and obtained material support for its armed struggle against the regime. At the heart of the Sandinistas' revolutionary diplomacy in the years leading up to Somoza's fall was a transnational network of solidarity committees that functioned as a counterweight to the Nicaraguan government's official network of embassies and diplomats. Many solidarity groups were founded spontaneously, but the FSLN played a key role in coordinating their campaigns. In Western Europe, Sandinista representatives such as Barrajón and Enrique Schmidt Cuadra, a Nicaraguan exile who lived in the West German city of Cologne in the 1970s, provided activists with propaganda material and encouraged local solidarity committees to collaborate on a Western European scale. The Sandinistas' global outreach in the late 1970s represented a turning point in the revolutionary struggle, isolating the dictator in the international arena and convincing anticommunist politicians in Europe and the Americas that the participation of the FSLN in Nicaragua's new government was a reasonable alternative to the Somoza dynasty.

The key to the Sandinistas' successful targeting of international audiences in the two years leading up to the revolution's triumph was their apparent ideological flexibility and pragmatism. Extending its domestic strategy of building alliances with other anti-Somoza groups to the international arena, the FSLN connected with individuals, governments, and organizations from across the political spectrum. This strategy was remarkably effective, leading to the formation of an international anti-Somoza alliance including church groups, social democrats, and Third World activists. Intimately related to this success story was the new image—or rather images—the FSLN adopted to mobilize supporters for its cause. Sandinista representatives consciously tailored their message to fit their audiences' preferences, but there was a notable attempt to counter the idea that the FSLN was merely another group of Cuban-backed Marxist guerrillas. Rather, they presented the FSLN as the legitimate representative of a nationalist struggle for democracy and social justice in which Nicaraguans from all political and socioeconomic backgrounds participated. By arguing that the civil war in Nicaragua could not be framed as a conflict between East and West, the revolutionaries consciously placed themselves outside of the Cold War context and inside the long tradition of Third World national liberation movements. This strategy of moving beyond the Cold War resonated with audiences in Western Europe, where many citizens and politicians were frustrated by the United States' tendency to frame international affairs solely in terms of the superpower conflict.

An exploration of the Sandinistas' revolutionary diplomacy prior to Somoza's fall and of how this played out on the ground in Western Europe helps us understand how revolutions are made. They are, as Claudia Rueda reminds us, not "explosive events" but the result of years of hard work, setbacks, and an uneven process "through which society comes to accept the legitimacy of armed uprising."[3] In Nicaragua, the project of building a revolution took place in the mountains, the countryside, and in urban areas, where guerrillas and their sympathizers took enormous personal risks to share their message of national liberation with the people they claimed to represent. Yet, as this chapter shows, the struggle against Somoza also took place in the international arena, as Sandinistas roamed the globe in search of material support and attempted to convince foreign audiences of the validity of their armed struggle. In other words, the road to the Sandinista triumph on 19 July 1979 was what George Lawson described as a "transboundary" process in which the international, transnational, and domestic interacted with one another.[4] And similar to the "painstaking way" that Nicaraguans created a "culture of insurrection" within their country, the internationalization of the anti-Somoza struggle was a laborious process that took place at the grassroots level as much as in organizations such as the United Nations (UN) and the Organization of American States. Indeed, it was only by building meaningful personal, cultural, and political connections to local activists in Europe and the Americas that the Sandinistas could create a transnational revolutionary family dedicated to the overthrow of the Somoza regime.

## FROM ISOLATION TO STRENGTH

Things moved quickly for the Sandinistas in the late 1970s but before that, it took the FSLN more than fifteen years of trial and error to develop the pragmatic strategy that—in combination with beneficial domestic and international circumstances—would ultimately come to topple the Somoza dynasty. Throughout much of the 1960s, the guerrillas were militarily weak, unpopular, and isolated from the people they claimed to represent.

Founded in the wake of the Cuban Revolution, the FSLN initially consisted of a small and radical group of students, peasant leaders, and working-class youth such as Carlos Fonseca Amador, José Santos López, Tomás Borge Martínez, Germán Pomares Ordóñez, and Silvio Mayorga Moreno.[5] They named their movement after the Nicaraguan revolutionary Augusto César Sandino, who led a rebel army against the U.S. Marines occupying his country in the late 1920s and early 1930s. In 1934, Sandino was murdered by the Guardia Nacional (National Guard) at the orders of Anastasio Somoza García, the father of Anastasio Somoza Debayle, who ruled Nicaragua in the late 1960s and 1970s.[6] The freshly minted Sandinistas, Borge recalls in his memoirs, attempted to unify all anti-Somoza forces in an "anti-imperialist" movement, led by an armed vanguard. Yet, he admits, this was no more than a mirage; the only base of support inside Nicaragua the young guerrillas could count on existed in their "imagination and desire."[7]

While this was a slight exaggeration, Borge was mostly right. The FSLN might have been inspired by Cuba's revolutionary example and the principles of Marxism, but many socially conscious Nicaraguans in the 1960s were unconvinced by the Sandinistas' radical politics and believed that change through electoral politics was still a valid option for their country. The relatively tolerant attitude of the Nicaraguan government under the brief presidency of René Schick Gutiérrez—a Somoza ally—strengthened this perception of democratic opportunity, undermining the FSLN's core belief that armed struggle was necessary for social change.[8] Two Sandinista operations at Río Coco y Bocay in 1963 and Pancasán in 1967, where the guerrillas did not succeed in applying the Argentine revolutionary Ernesto "Che" Guevara's foco theory, only served to highlight their inability to build meaningful connections with the local population.[9] The Pancasán operation, moreover, resulted in the death of many FSLN fighters, including Mayorga and his entire guerrilla column, who walked into an ambush by the National Guard.[10]

These disastrous episodes were followed by a period of critical reflection and internal debate, which largely took place outside of Nicaragua. Fonseca, the most prominent intellectual leader of the FSLN, spent much of the early 1970s in Havana, where he was joined by Sandinista leaders Humberto

Ortega Saavedra, Eduardo Contreras Escobar, and later Jaime Wheelock Román, who had previously been studying abroad in Salvador Allende's Chile and the German Democratic Republic (GDR).[11] In Cuba, Fonseca expressed his reservations about the FSLN's rural guerrilla strategy, which had clearly failed to achieve its objectives. Sandinista comandante Víctor Tirado López, too, shared Fonseca's doubts about the "guevarista foquismo" strategy. Instead of burying "the heart of the enemy in the mountains," he later commented on the FSLN's misfortunes in the 1960s, "the enemy [had] buried *us* in the mountains."[12]

If the leadership agreed that things had gone wrong in the past, they could not agree on a new strategy. To be sure, the FSLN remained committed to armed struggle and—despite critical questions from journalists—did not seriously believe that Salvador Allende's peaceful and democratic road to socialism in Chile was an option for Nicaragua. The overthrow of Allende in a violent coup in 1973 only strengthened the guerrillas in this conviction.[13] Beyond these general sentiments, though, the comandantes failed to maintain a united front. An increasingly heated debate about revolutionary theory and practice—inspired by the works of Mao Zedong (China), Ho Chi Minh (Vietnam), Guevara (Cuba), Ahmed Ben Bella (Algeria), and Emilio Lussu (Italy)—ultimately resulted in the formation of three Sandinista factions.[14] The first, the Tendencia Guerra Prolongada Popular (Prolonged People's War Tendency), led by Henry Ruiz and Borge (who were both based in Nicaragua), argued that the FSLN, before the conditions of an urban insurrection could be met, should first focus on the slow accumulation of forces in the countryside.[15] The Tendencia Proletaria (Proletarian Tendency) disagreed, arguing that the political and economic reality in Nicaragua demanded a stronger focus on (urban) workers, the so-called proletariat. In an interview, Wheelock pointed out that, according to his faction, Sandinismo was "more than simply a guerrilla force or an organization of more or less radicalized university students, but the vanguard organization of the working class."[16] The third tendency—more commonly known as the terceristas—was the Insurrectional Tendency, which primarily targeted the urban areas, where they organized "spectacular" military actions meant to provoke a popular insurrection. Tirado and the brothers Humberto and Daniel Ortega led this more pragmatic and ultimately more powerful faction, focusing on—besides military successes—political legitimacy and strategic alliances with other opposition groups.[17]

Meanwhile, in Nicaragua, the situation had changed quite dramatically since Fonseca and his comrades were forced to leave the country in the aftermath of the Pancasán defeat. The governing style of Anastasio Somoza Debayle, who officially became president in 1967, became increasingly repressive and violent, demonstrating to many Nicaraguans that social and political change could only be realized through radical means, including armed struggle. The government's corruption and abuse of foreign aid in the aftermath of the devastating 1972 earthquake that effectively destroyed the country's capital Managua further eroded state legitimacy. At universities, student leaders who sympathized with the Sandinistas and "embraced revolution" finally started to defeat moderates in elections.[18] Horrifying testimonials of survivors of massacres by the National Guard resulted in a "clear surge in Sandinista support" among campesinos and indigenous peoples living in the country's impoverished rural areas.[19] Disillusioned by the National Guard's brutality and inspired by the rise of liberation theology, many Catholics embraced struggles for social justice and joined the anti-Somoza movement.[20] Nicaraguan conservative elites, such as intellectual and politician Pablo Antonio Cuadra, and Pedro Joaquín Chamorro, the editor of opposition newspaper *La Prensa*, also became more vocal in their critique of the regime, flirting openly with the idea of a nationalist revolution, albeit not necessarily one led by the FSLN.[21] Predominantly as a result of the dictators' uncompromising politics and state violence, more and more Nicaraguans opposed the regime and contemplated armed revolution.

In this context of growing disillusionment and radicalization, the FSLN emerged as the leader of a broad anti-Somoza coalition. The tercerista strategy of combining pragmatic alliances with the bourgeoisie with spectacular guerrilla raids was crucial, resulting in increased levels of sympathy for the FSLN as well as many new Sandinista recruits. In January 1975, U.S. ambassador Thomas Shelton reported that a Sandinista raid of the house of a Somocista businessman, where the FSLN took prominent hostages and managed to secure the release of several political prisoners, was "received with surprisingly widespread approval" in Nicaragua.[22] Even more spectacular was the occupation of the National Palace in August 1978, where a small group of Sandinistas dressed as members of the National Guard successfully took more than one thousand members of the National Congress hostage. In exchange for the return of the hostages, Somoza agreed to release political prisoners, aired a pro-FSLN message on the national radio, and paid the guerrillas $500,000. The famous novelist Gabriel García Márquez described the raid in lyrical terms in a 1978 edition of the *New Left Review*, transforming the responsible comandantes Edén Pastora, Dora María Téllez, and Hugo

Torrez Jiménez into youthful heroes.[23] More than a military action, Téllez later explained, the raid was a successful "political maneuver" to create an insurrectional culture within Nicaragua, convincing many to align themselves with the Sandinista cause.[24]

Despite their avoidance of radical language as to not alienate potential allies, the tercerista leaders remained committed to a Marxist revolution. While playing down their connections to Cuba, the revolutionary island remained an inspiration and source of practical—albeit rather limited—assistance for the tercerista guerrillas, as the Cubans provided them with propaganda support, training, sanctuary, and passports. After being recruited by the FSLN in 1974, for instance, Téllez traveled to Cuba to study "military" medicine, learning how to treat gunshot wounds and cure tropical diseases in Havana's hospitals.[25] Daniel Ortega spelled out the tercerista strategy in an interview with the journal *Latin American Perspectives* in 1979, commenting that they aimed to "join together all the anti-Somoza sectors and mass organizations of the country, including sectors of the opposition bourgeoisie." In doing so, he continued, "we seek to conserve the political hegemony of the FSLN and ... avoid the possibility of the bourgeoisie becoming the political leader of an anti-Somoza front."[26] Humberto Ortega made similar comments in a secret letter to his comrades on 7 January 1979. The alliance with the "bourgeoisie" was simply a means to an end, he wrote. Despite their collaboration with opposition politicians, the FSLN was not planning to impose a "social democratic capitalist style of development" in Nicaragua. Rather, to "make a leap" toward popular power and the construction of a socialist revolutionary state, the bourgeoise's participation in the struggle against Somoza was—at least for the time being—simply necessary.[27]

By 1977, then, the anti-Somoza movement had grown substantially, and the dictator's position was significantly weakened. Nevertheless, a Sandinista triumph was by no means inevitable. Somoza—still supported by the powerful National Guard—refused to give up power and, as U.S. officials speculated, preferred a continued war with the guerrillas to a negotiated solution with "moderate" opposition figures such as Chamorro. Somoza opted for further polarization, a U.S. State Department official commented in October 1978, as he believed that "we will have no choice but to support him" if it comes to a "Somoza vs. Marxists" situation.[28] Somoza was not entirely wrong. The administration of Jimmy Carter did worry about a radical Cuban-backed government in Central America, even considering a military intervention to keep the Sandinistas out of power.[29] Within the anti-Somoza movement, too, there were significant challenges to the Sandinistas' revolutionary ambitions. The "elite" and "bourgeois" opposition, for instance, as historian David Johnson Lee points out, wanted to maintain the National Guard, collaborated with the Carter administration, and was willing to "maintain the institutions of the Somoza government even if Somoza himself stepped down."[30] The Sandinistas, however, fiercely rejected this so-called "Somocismo without Somoza."[31] They continued to aim for the dictator's military overthrow and, by extension, FSLN leadership over the anti-Somoza struggle and the future transformation of Nicaragua. To achieve this objective, the Sandinistas complemented their domestic strategy with an ambitious international component, projecting a powerful image of the FSLN as the legitimate representative of Nicaraguan people to the outside world.

### SANDINISTAS GO GLOBAL

In the late 1970s, the tercerista strategy of building a diverse anti-Somoza alliance was thus extended to the international arena, where the FSLN looked for donors other than Fidel Castro for financial aid, logistical support, and political backing. Inspired by the global resonance of the Vietnam War protests and the Chile solidarity movement, the Sandinistas and their allies organized lectures, encouraged the formation of solidarity groups, and presented pro-FSLN arguments to a range of audiences. In these early days, the FSLN's revolutionary diplomacy was still rather unorganized and Sandinista representatives did not always receive clear directions or relevant information from their leadership. The fact that the FSLN itself was divided also made it difficult to convey a coherent message to the international community. Nevertheless, Sandinistas around the globe had a solid idea about what their organization needed: material support, political legitimacy, and the isolation of Somoza.

Crucial to this international outreach was the work of the Grupo de los Doce (Group of Twelve), a group of Nicaraguan intellectuals, priests, and business leaders who functioned as the political arm and public face of the FSLN. The Twelve aimed to make the radical Sandinistas—and the idea of an armed insurrection—more palatable to Nicaragua's elites, as well as to government leaders, politicians, and journalists in the Americas and Europe. A group of "respectable" Nicaraguan citizens, the Sandinista priest Fernando Cardenal remembers, was much more likely to be "received by Latin

American political leaders who were skeptical of guerrilla groups" than the Sandinista comandantes themselves.[32] On 18 October 1977, citing the "repressive apparatus" and "irrational violence" of the Somoza regime, the Twelve publicly endorsed the FSLN's armed struggle on the radio and in Nicaragua's main opposition newspaper *La Prensa*.[33] This open declaration of support from prominent Nicaraguans for the guerrillas initially caused "confusion and commotion," the document's author, Sergio Ramírez Mercado, recalled. A frustrated Somoza immediately ordered the "prosecution" of the statement's signatories, who included Carlos Tünnerman Bernheim, the rector of the National Autonomous University; Miguel d'Escoto Brockmann, a Maryknoll priest based in the United States; Emilio Baltodano Pallais, a well-known lawyer; and Fernando Cardenal's brother Ernesto, also a priest, liberation theologian, and writer.[34]

After these initial moments of confusion, though, the Grupo de los Doce became increasingly popular and visible, both within Nicaragua and abroad. Members traveled around the world as Sandinista ambassadors, skillfully using their prestige and international network to give the FSLN's revolutionary war momentum, legitimacy, and press coverage. Ramírez, for instance, taking advantage of his contacts with famous writers such as García Márquez and Julio Cortázar, was able to get in touch with several sympathetic Latin American leaders and convince them of the "moderate tendencies in the Sandinistas."[35] Ramírez also tried to persuade the skeptical Carter administration that the FSLN was not as radical as was generally believed. At a meeting in Managua in 1978, Ramírez, Baltodano, and d'Escoto told Richard Feinberg, a policy planner at the U.S. State Department, that the group's new manifesto was in fact quite "moderate."[36]

Next to raising international awareness about the Sandinista struggle, the work of the Twelve had a direct impact on the terceristas' military capabilities. The abovementioned 1978 attack on the National Palace had a clear international component. To prepare the guerrilla operation's escape plan, Tünnermann went on a mission to Caracas, where he asked the social democratic president Carlos Andrés Pérez for a plane to escort the released political prisoners out of Nicaragua. Despite Andrés Pérez's positive response, the prisoners did not end up in Venezuela, which highlights the somewhat chaotic communication between the Sandinista leadership and its international representatives in the late 1970s. Indeed, Tünnermann recalls in his memoirs, when Borge decided to direct the prisoners to Cuba instead, it was up to him to "suffer the anger" of a dejected Andrés Pérez, who fortunately calmed down quickly when Edén Pastora and Dora María Téllez gifted him with the Nicaraguan flag that they had taken from the palace.[37]

Beyond the Twelve, Sandinista revolutionary ambassadors were predominantly male Nicaraguans from elite or middle-class backgrounds. In some cases, non-Nicaraguans, such as the Spanish priest Ángel Barrajón, could also act as FSLN representatives.[38] Nicaraguans who already lived abroad, including students, exiles, and expats, were perfect candidates to become Sandinista spokespeople. Not only was this a cheap and convenient option for the FSLN, but Nicaraguans living abroad also tended to have significant networks and in-depth knowledge of the customs, languages, and politics of other countries, increasing their potential effectiveness as ambassadors. The student Tomás Arguello Chamorro, for example, became one of the representatives of the FSLN in Western Europe after he had a secret meeting with Rogelio Ramírez (the brother of Sergio Ramírez), who was passing through London on his way back from the Soviet Union. The two revolutionaries were able to recognize each other at Heathrow Airport, Arguello Chamorro remembers fondly, because each carried a copy of *La Prensa* under his arm. As a Sandinista representative based in the United Kingdom, Arguello Chamorro tried to raise public awareness about the revolutionary war and, together with exiled Salvadoran politician Rubén Zamora, he also co-founded the CAHRC.[39]

Building on the revolutionary culture the Sandinistas and their allies had already created in Nicaragua, artists and intellectuals also contributed to the FSLN's revolutionary diplomacy by presenting audiences with a romanticized image of the war.[40] For example, the exiled Sandinista poet Gioconda Belli campaigned against Somoza from Mexico and Costa Rica by, among other things, drafting press releases on the human rights violations in Nicaragua, working with the Costa Rican Committee for Solidarity with Nicaragua, and publishing the award-winning poetry collection *Linea De Fuego* in 1978, which glorifies motherhood, revolution, and guerrilla warfare.[41] Sergio Ramírez's novel *¿Te dio miedo la sangre?* (also published in English under the title *To Bury Our Fathers*), written in West Berlin between 1973 and 1975, was a particularly important "piece of cultural capital" for the Sandinista guerrillas.[42] In this unique novel, first published in Caracas in 1977, Ramírez paints a powerful picture of Nicaraguan history as a continuous struggle for national sovereignty against U.S. imperialism (represented by the Somoza dynasty), initially carried out by Sandino and later by the FSLN. The book appeared in multiple languages and editions, further propelling Nicaragua into the international limelight. Similarly, the poet-priest

Ernesto Cardenal used his literary network and religious credentials to denounce the Somoza regime's human rights violations, legitimizing the FSLN's armed struggle. Cardenal was a particularly well-known figure in literary circles in the Americas and Europe, and his books on liberation theology, revolution, and Nicaraguan history were published in Spanish, German, French, English, Italian, and Dutch. One of his first journeys for the FSLN, Cardenal recalls, was a trip to West Germany, where he met the editor Hermann Schulz of the Peter Hammer Publishing House in Wuppertal, known for its translations of literature from Latin America and Africa. Schulz, who had already visited Nicaragua on multiple occasions, translated and published several of Cardenal's works in German, including *En Cuba* and *El Evangelio en Solentiname* (The Gospel in Solentiname).[43]

Beyond cultural diplomacy, the FSLN employed several arguments and tactics. First, they argued passionately against Somoza's claim that the only two options for Nicaragua were "himself or the communists."[44] Correctly assessing that many politicians in Europe and the Americas would look at events in Nicaragua primarily through a Cold War lens, the FSLN sought to assuage fears that the country would become a second Cuba—isolated, dependent on the Soviet Union, and a source of regional instability. Downplaying their connections to Cuba or the Eastern bloc, Sandinista representatives presented the FSLN as a national liberation movement that fought against a brutal dictatorship and believed in social justice and political pluralism. On 28 June 1979, Daniel Ortega went "out of his way to stress the moderate, democratic orientation of the frente" and their "desire to get rid of Somoza" in a meeting with the U.S. ambassador to Panama, Ambler Moss.[45] And on 29 June 1979, Arguello Chamorro told British officials in London "that it was quite untrue that the only alternative to Somoza or Somocismo was the extreme left and that it had been untrue for many years." Urging the British government to "break diplomatic relations" with Somoza as soon as possible, the young Nicaraguan promised the revolutionary junta would implement "moderate policies."[46] Pragmatically ignoring the FSLN's historical origins, the Sandinistas also rejected comparisons with Latin America's armed Left. One tercerista was quoted in *The Washington Post* pointing out that "while other revolutionaries enter banks to assault them, we were just received in Ecuador by the president of the central bank."[47] And Pastora, now famous under his nom de guerre Comandante Cero, vehemently denied claims that Cuba was funding and influencing the FSLN. Describing the raid of the National Palace, where he earned his nickname, to foreign journalists,

Pastora declared that the Sandinistas "did not need anyone" as "we are intelligent, we are capable, and we are revolutionaries."[48]

As alluded to above, however, the Cubans continued to play a crucial role in the Nicaraguan struggle in the months leading up to Somoza's fall. Fidel Castro used his prestige and negotiating skills—as well as the promise of a substantial increase of Cuban military support—to ease the tension between the three competing FSLN factions, which contributed to their official unification on 8 March 1979.[49] Moreover, Castro and Manuel Piñeiro Losada, the head of the Cuban Communist Party's prestigious Departamento América, responsible for Havana's relations with Latin American left-wing organizations, lobbied the governments of Costa Rica, Panama, Colombia, and Venezuela on behalf of the Sandinistas, encouraging them to provide Sandinista militants with arms, safe havens, and political support.[50] The Cuban Ministerio de Relaciones Exteriores (Ministry of Foreign Relations), too, developed a strategy to support the struggle of the young revolutionaries against the Somoza dictatorship, which deputy foreign minister René Anillo Capote described as the most "Made in the USA" regime in the world. Convinced by effectiveness of the tercerista strategy of building a strategic anti-Somoza alliance, Cuban officials denounced Somoza's human rights violations in international organizations such as the United Nations.[51] Cuba also contributed to the Sandinistas' revolutionary diplomacy by printing, designing, and disseminating propaganda materials, such as posters and news bulletins about guerrilla victories in Nicaragua. Pastora's claims, while convenient for the FSLN's revolutionary diplomacy, were thus far from accurate.

While playing down their connections with Cuba and international communism so as not to provoke opposition from anticommunists, the FSLN simultaneously highlighted the dependency of the Somoza regime on the United States. When unidentified gunmen in Managua murdered the popular editor Pedro Joaquín Chamorro on 10 January 1978, for instance, Ernesto Cardenal accused Carter of trying to cover up Chamorro's murder, declaring publicly "Somoza knows who killed Chamorro and if Somoza knows, Carter knows, and if he doesn't know he has not wanted to ask."[52] Invoking memories of the early twentieth century, when U.S. marines had occupied Nicaragua for several years, the FSLN also repeatedly warned the international community of the possibility of another "North American military intervention in Nicaragua" to prevent the Sandinistas from taking power.[53] In private meetings with U.S. government officials stationed in Managua, who could no longer deny the Sandinistas' growing military power and domestic popularity, FSLN negotiators toned down their anti-imperialist rhetoric, even going so far as to admit that Carter's efforts to mediate between the dictator and the opposition were "being distorted by Somoza and the media."[54] Indeed, Ramírez and d'Escoto told Feinberg in August 1978, "the Sandinistas were not anti-U.S," pointing out that in the recently released FSLN manifesto "one of the references to the U.S. was favorable." They did, however, stress the United States' responsibility for Somoza's continued hold onto power, stating "the U.S. could remove him if it wanted."[55]

While there was a general tendency to move beyond Cold War rhetoric, the arguments Sandinista ambassadors used to mobilize support varied greatly depending on their audience and location. When talking to potential supporters in Western Europe, the Sandinista campaign strategy was to "avoid political discussions" and instead "look for common ground."[56] For example, if an organization or individual was deemed unlikely to back the military struggle but could perhaps be persuaded to denounce the human rights violations of the Somoza regime, the conversation focused on the latter. In meetings with Western European officials, Sandinista ambassadors did not ask them to recognize the FSLN as the "diplomatic representative of Nicaragua." Instead, they focused on the human rights violations and dictatorial character of the Somoza dynasty, asking Western European governments to "break off diplomatic relations" with the regime.[57] During a visit to the West German capital Bonn, for instance, Ernesto Cardenal called for "a suspension of all German investment and credits" in Nicaragua, arguing all aid would end up in "the pockets of the Somoza family."[58]

To mobilize the public, Sandinista representatives consciously adapted the style of their campaigns to suit the domestic situation in the countries they targeted. In 1978, Barrajón commented to a comrade that, unlike the Spanish, British people had little "sympathy for armed movements." Therefore, he recommended that fundraising campaigns in the United Kingdom should have a "humanitarian" instead of a revolutionary and political character.[59] In letters to the FCO and the Nicaraguan embassy, the CAHRC accordingly focused on human rights violations. They accused Somoza—with good reason—of "imprisoning, torturing, and killing" and denounced the "atrocities perpetuated by the National Guard against ordinary people."[60] On their flyers, the CAHRC wrote that any money they received at fundraising events would be used "for immediate relief work" and "items such as beds, blood, blankets, field hospitals etc."[61] Most likely, however, this this was another example of tactical mobilization of support; the money was probably used for military means.

The new strategy the Sandinistas launched in the late 1970s was remarkably effective, as the FSLN was increasingly seen as the vanguard of the anti-Somoza movement, mobilized a range of people for its cause, and managed to obtain financial and political support from new sources.[62] Based in the Costa Rican capital of San José, Gioconda Belli observed that the "level of solidarity was so great we could scarcely deal with it. Journalists from all over the world flooded to the city to interview the Sandinistas. Revolutionaries from across the continent joined the Nicaraguan struggle: Chileans, Spaniards, Argentineans, Colombians, North Americans."[63] Latin American governments were supportive of the FSLN, with significant consequences for the guerrillas' military effectiveness.[64] Indeed, as Dirk Kruijt writes, "it was only in 1978 and 1979 . . . that a sufficiently regular flow of arms and money reached the Sandinista Frente in Nicaragua."[65] Moreover, by repeatedly asking the Carter administration when the United States "would be getting rid of Somoza," these governments contributed to Somoza's political isolation.[66]

All of this had consequences for the FSLN's position within Nicaragua, where a growing number of people came to associate opposition against the repressive dictatorship with support for the Sandinistas. An insurrectional culture rapidly took hold in the country, and spontaneous (or loosely organized) mass protests, demonstrations, and violent confrontations between members of Somoza's National Guard and Sandinista fighters were an increasingly common sight. Hoping to capitalize on the Sandinistas' growing domestic and international popularity, in September 1978 the tercerista leadership launched a "final offensive," calling for a nation-wide insurrection and seeking to take control of cities such as Managua, León, Chinandega, Estelí, Masaya, Diriamba, Jinotepe, and Rivas. Thousands of Nicaraguans responded to this call to arms, and guerrillas briefly took control of several important cities, including León and Masaya. Yet, through extreme violence that included aerial bombings, summarily executing people for living in pro-Sandinista neighborhoods, and torturing opponents, the National Guard managed to repress the Nicaraguan uprising.[67]

Ultimately, however, the Somoza government's brutal response only increased support for the revolutionaries, ensuring that there could be no solution to Nicaragua's political crisis without the participation of the FSLN. Indeed, other Nicaraguan opposition groups, such as the Frente Amplio Opositor (Broad Opposition Front), which mostly represented the country's middle and upper classes, worried about the growing popularity of the FSLN, both within Nicaragua and abroad. In May 1979, one FAO representative reported to the Dutch foreign ministry that his group was currently "sandwiched" between Somoza's National Guard on the one hand and the increasingly powerful Sandinista guerrillas on the other.[68] Somoza, too, noticed this trend, and complained to the U.S. ambassador in Nicaragua, Mauricio Solaún, about the "new legitimization of the FSLN," adding that there was clearly "a problem with the growing respectability of the Communists."[69] By early 1979, as the U.S. embassy in Managua reported, there were "two poles of strength in Nicaragua, the GON [Somoza] and the FSLN."[70]

To understand why, how, and with what results the FSLN attracted such an impressive amount of international support and attention in the late 1970s, it is crucial to look at how the Sandinistas' revolutionary diplomacy played out and was experienced on the ground. Just as the FSLN had intended, individuals, political parties, and governments in Western Europe responded to its diplomatic offensive in different ways, choosing to support the revolutionaries for a range of reasons. Moreover, as the next sections demonstrate, the Sandinistas were lucky that their representatives encountered unusually receptive Western European audiences, as solidarity activists were growing disillusioned with the Chile movement and the Socialist International developed an interest in the Global South.

## BUILDING A SOLIDARITY MOVEMENT

A key aspect of the FSLN's revolutionary diplomacy was the coordination of a transnational network of activists. Solidarity committees in the Americas and Europe cooperated with the Sandinistas to collect money, disseminate information about the situation in Nicaragua, and pressure governments into breaking off relations with the Somoza regime. And while the FSLN determined the general direction of its revolutionary diplomacy, it was up to solidarity activists to translate the Sandinista message of national liberation into posters, festivals, and other activities that attracted attention and money (figure 1). In the years before the revolution's triumph, the network of Western European solidarity activists was still small, especially when compared to the 1980s, when hundreds of committees worked to defend the Nicaraguan Revolution from attacks. Nevertheless, this was the crucial period when the solidarity movement came into being, and its origins would continue to shape its future trajectory.

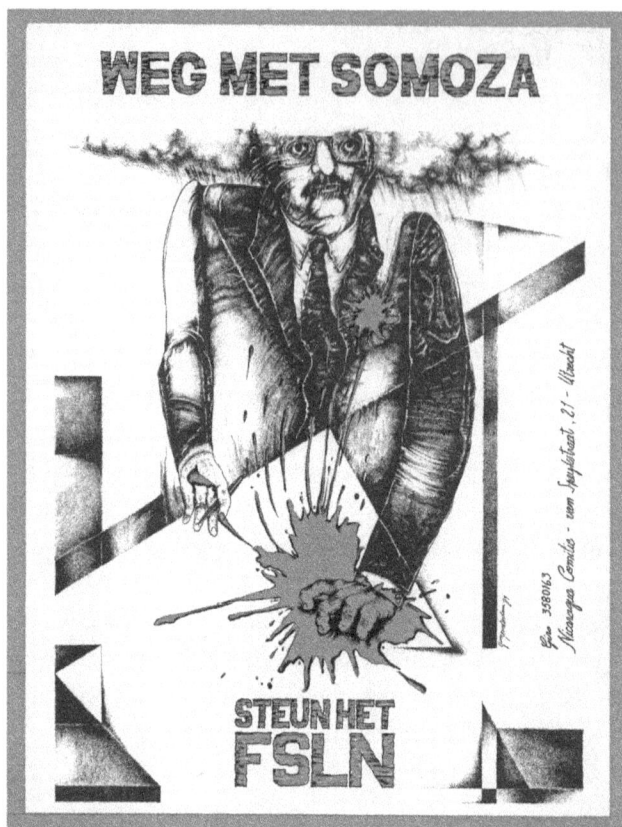

FIGURE 1. In the late 1970s, the FSLN successfully positioned itself as the leader of a broad anti-Somoza movement. This poster, produced by the Dutch Nicaragua Committee, located at the Van Speijkstraat in Utrecht, calls on those who reject Somoza—portrayed as a bloodthirsty businessman—to "support the FSLN." Photo: Nicaragua Komitee Nederland, International Institute of Social History, Amsterdam.

As noted above, Ernesto Cardenal visited Western Europe regularly to promote the Sandinista message. The charismatic priest gave television interviews, sold translated copies of his books, and was regularly quoted in newspapers.[71] These visits, however, had a purpose that went beyond mere publicity; he also collected money for weapons, gave messages and instructions to exiled Nicaraguans, and encouraged Western European activists to set up solidarity committees. In this vein, Cardenal established contacts with grassroots organizations in the United Kingdom, West Germany, the Netherlands, and beyond. The abovementioned CAHRC flyer, for example, called on the people of the United Kingdom to raise funds for the Nicaraguan people and send them "to the account of Father Ernesto Cardenal."[72]

Due to the nature of his work, Cardenal was never in one place long enough to become the official FSLN representative in Western Europe. To effectively coordinate the Western European network of solidarity activists, the FSLN needed ambassadors that were permanently based in the region. Therefore, Nicaraguan expatriates, particularly those who had fled the Somoza regime, ended up playing an important part in uniting and coordinating the solidarity movement. Unable to fight within Nicaragua, these individuals continued to work for the revolution from abroad. A key figure in Western Europe was Ángel Barrajón, who lived in Madrid and was responsible for the solidarity movement in Southern Europe and the United Kingdom.[73] The other representative was a Nicaraguan of German descent named Enrique Schmidt Cuadra, who was responsible for the functioning of the solidarity movement in Northern and Central Europe. Born in the Nicaraguan town of Chinandega in 1949, Schmidt moved to West Germany in the late 1960s to study at the University of Cologne. Unlike Barrajón, Schmidt had experience with solidarity activism in West Germany, as he had been a member of the Chile solidarity movement after the violent overthrow of Salvador Allende's socialist government in 1973. Schmidt briefly returned to Nicaragua between 1974 and 1977, where he fought with the FSLN until he was captured and imprisoned by the regime. Upon his release in 1977, he returned to West Germany to mobilize as many solidarity committees for the Sandinista cause as possible.[74]

As Sandinista representatives, Barrajón and Schmidt received monthly faxes from the FSLN's international section, based in Costa Rica, providing them with instructions, advice, and the latest news about the armed struggle. Within the FSLN's international section, Gioconda Belli and Melania Agüero were responsible for communication with the transnational solidarity movement.[75] The information they provided was then passed on to the solidarity committees, who used it to raise awareness, sympathy, and funds. To reach the Sandinistas, the money collected by solidarity groups had to be smuggled into Central America. In 1978 and 1979, Barrajón and Schmidt traveled multiple times to Costa Rica, carrying with them what Barrajón described decades later as suitcases filled with "thousands of dollars."[76] Moreover, the two Sandinista ambassadors pushed activists to incorporate all the individual solidarity committees into a functionally transnational structure. To that end, the FSLN organized two solidarity conferences in

1978, in Madrid and Utrecht, each attracting hundreds of activists from across Western Europe.

At these conferences, practical decisions were made regarding the structure of the movement. The activists decided that, in addition to local solidarity groups, each country needed a national committee (often called a coordinating committee) to be able to coordinate events and communicate more effectively with the FSLN. These national committees, in turn, were represented by a secretariat that could organize events and distribute information on a Western European scale. The secretariat's members were in touch with prominent Sandinistas, such as Ramírez and Ernesto Cardenal, as well as with Schmidt and Barrajón, and they passed on information from the FSLN's international section to the national coordinating committees. Throughout most of the 1970s, the office of the Nicaragua Komitee Nederland (Dutch Nicaragua Committee, NKN) located at the Van Speijkstraat in Utrecht—which also housed several Dutch activists and Latin American exiles—simultaneously functioned as the headquarters of the Western European solidarity movement.[77]

The Western European secretariat consisted of Klaas Wellinga and Hans Langenberg, from the Netherlands, and Hermann Schulz, from West Germany. What attracted these three activists to the Sandinista cause was a fascination with Latin American politics, culture, and particularly literature. Wellinga, who joined Utrecht University in 1969 as a lecturer in Latin American Studies, developed an interest in the region through the works of Cortázar and García Márquez. Together with his former pupil Langenberg, as well as Jannie van den Berg, another central figure in the solidarity movement, Wellinga was a member of the Latin American Cultural Collective (Kultuur Kollectief Latijns Amerika, KKLA), a nonprofit organization that translated and distributed Latin American literature and music in the Netherlands.[78] In the late 1970s, the Dutch activists used the KKLA for the Nicaraguan revolutionaries' benefit when they translated and published a collection of poems from Ernesto Cardenal. The book's introduction, Langenberg recalls, provided readers with a highly "political" account of the many heroic ways Nicaraguans were resisting the Somoza dictatorship.[79] Schulz, as director of Peter Hammer Publishing House, was similarly attracted to Latin American literature, although his interest in Nicaragua preceded that of the Dutch activists. Indeed, Schulz had become enamored with Nicaraguan literature after reading two poems by Ernesto Cardenal in a Swiss newspaper in the late 1960s, which prompted him to do further research into the history and politics of this relatively unknown Central American country. After traveling to Nicaragua for the first time in 1972, he obtained the rights to publish works by Sergio Ramírez, Gioconda Belli, and Ernesto Cardenal.[80]

By 1979, the solidarity movement had become a significant cultural and political force. In West Germany, dozens of solidarity committees campaigned for the Sandinista cause in cities including Munster, Berlin, Wuppertal, Göttingen, Frankfurt, München, Hamburg, Bremen, and Tübingen. In most Dutch university cities, too, such as Groningen, Nijmegen, Utrecht, and Wageningen, local activists—most of them students—managed to set up active Nicaragua solidarity committees.[81] In the United Kingdom, Nicaragua groups operated in at least twenty cities, such as Birmingham, Bristol, Leeds, Bath, and Oxford.[82] Nevertheless, as the FCO noted, "despite two very disturbing television documentaries" about the violent situation in Nicaragua, "the campaign . . . failed to capture much public interest" in the United Kingdom.[83] Solidarity activists such as John Bevan, a prominent activist in the British solidarity committee, and Barrajón admitted that the movement in the United Kingdom had a slow start, but pointed out that the British network became increasingly skilled at raising money for the Sandinistas during the 1980s, as we shall see in later chapters.[84]

Before the revolution, therefore, with regard to Western Europe, the FSLN predominantly relied on committees in the Netherlands and West Germany, where the Nicaraguan solidarity groups were bigger and better organized.[85] In these countries, the movement succeeded in building an anti-Somoza alliance by establishing ties with human rights organizations, church groups, political parties, labor unions, and charities. The NKN, for instance, offered a petition to the Nicaraguan consul in Rotterdam, stressing the right to "self-determination" of the Nicaraguan people. Political parties across the political spectrum had signed this petition—not only the Partij van de Arbeid (Labor Party, PvdA) and the Dutch Communist Party, but also the center-right Volkspartij voor Vrijheid en Democratie (People's Party for Freedom and Democracy) and the conservative Christen-Democratisch Appél (Christian Democratic Appeal).[86] In West Germany, committees also succeeded in creating a broad opposition front, as they had a good relationship with the Sozialdemokratische Partei Deutschlands (Social Democratic Party of Germany, SPD) and received support from politicians in the Green and Communist parties, as well as from Christian groups inspired by the work of Sandinista liberation theologians such as Cardenal.[87] By contrast, the solidarity movement in the United Kingdom was not able to bridge the political divide in the country, and received only support from the Labour Party, not the Conservatives.[88]

In some rare cases, the competition and distrust between the leaders of the three Sandinista tendencies before the FSLN's official reunification in March 1979 spilled over to Western Europe. In November 1978, a German solidarity committee based in Göttingen wrote a circular letter stating its members did not recognize the authority of Enrique Schmidt, and refused to accept the solidarity committee in Wuppertal as their national representative. One reason the Göttingen committee gave was that Schmidt gave favorable treatment to his "friends from the proletarian tendency" of the FSLN.[89] This was, however, an isolated incident and the FSLN largely succeeded in preventing Nicaraguan divisions from having a negative impact on the functioning of the transnational solidarity network. Indeed, George Black, one of the founders of the British solidarity movement, wrote to the FSLN that the movement in the United Kingdom was "pluralist" and had been able to "avoid ideological conflict."[90] At solidarity conferences, FSLN representatives also spoke openly about the ideological differences that existed between the three tendencies but took care to stress that they all worked together to overthrow Somoza.[91] Barrajón summed up the FSLN's position clearly in a letter written to his friend Miguel Castañeda, another Sandinista, in February 1979: "The struggle against the dictatorship is just more important than problems between the tendencies, particularly when this endangers the solidarity movement."[92] Within Nicaragua, too, the divisions between the different Sandinista factions had lost much of their importance by early 1979, as many of the young women and men who were recruited into the FSLN were more interested in toppling Somoza than in internal debates about revolutionary theory and strategies. As the FSLN transformed from a small group of guerrillas into a massive popular movement, many of its new members chose to simply ignore differences between the factions.[93]

Undoubtedly, the solidarity activists' personal determination to avoid ideological disputes was inspired by their earlier experiences with the Chilean solidarity movement, which started to disintegrate in the late 1970s. Since the overthrow of Allende in 1973, Chilean exiles had worked hard to isolate the dictatorship of Augusto Pinochet, denouncing his crimes and illegitimacy. The Chile movement, however, was split between the radical

Movimiento de Izquierda Revolucionaria (Revolutionary Left Movement, MIR), the Chilean Communist Party, and the Chilean Socialist Party. In Western Europe, the inability of these parties to overcome their differences prevented them from working effectively for their cause. Furthermore, the movement was increasingly split between exiles and activists who continued to believe in the value of armed struggle and those who advocated the human rights narrative as a more effective strategy to overthrow Pinochet.[94] The internal divisions and debates within their network frustrated Chilean exiles and left many of their Western European and Latin American supporters confused and disenchanted.[95] Nicaraguan exiles, and particularly Schmidt, who had participated in the Chile solidarity campaign in Germany, did not want history to repeat itself, consciously structuring the Nicaragua solidarity movement as a broad anti-Somoza alliance.

Although not wanting to repeat the Chileans' divisions, the FSLN did successfully target the radical flank of the Chile solidarity movement. When the Sandinistas looked toward Western Europe for political and financial support, they encountered many disillusioned activists with a strong interest in Latin America's radical Left. In particular, as armed revolution in Chile seemed increasingly unlikely and human rights language became the dominant narrative, those Latin American exiles and solidarity activists advocating armed struggle, such as the supporters of the MIR, ended up isolated and without financial resources.[96] In the late 1970s, these activists were the most likely to take up the Sandinista cause since, after many years of fruitless solidarity activism against the anticommunist dictatorships of the Southern Cone, they—to put it crudely—wanted a win. When the Sandinista guerrillas grew stronger and gained popularity and legitimacy, the situation in Nicaragua was therefore interpreted as proof that guerrilla warfare was still a valuable and admirable strategy. Wellinga, for example, was the Dutch representative of the MIR before he became a founding member of the NKN.[97] George Black and John Bevan, too, remember that Chilean exiles from the MIR and other militant groups played a key role in the early British mobilization for the armed struggle in Nicaragua.[98] The Sandinistas' revolutionary diplomacy, then, was flexible enough to mobilize the radical Left as well as more moderate groups.

Solidarity activists were not attracted to armed struggle alone. Like Wellinga, Schulz, and Langenberg, many were drawn to Nicaragua due to a combination of cultural and political reasons. Here, too, the FSLN was able to build on the work of Southern Cone exiles and solidarity groups. Indeed, in the 1970s, Latin American activists in the United Kingdom, the Netherlands, and West Germany organized many cultural events, such as concerts, art exhibitions, film showings, and literary nights. In the Netherlands, the abovementioned KKLA translated and distributed Latin American literature, poetry, and music.[99] These cultural events had a strong political undertone. For example, most musicians who played at the solidarity concerts were part of the popular Latin American Nueva Canción (New Song) movement. Returning to a more traditional folkloric style, these musicians, such as the Uruguayans Héctor Numa Moraes Rosa and José Carbajal, addressed social tensions in their region and delivered political messages to their audiences.[100]

The Nicaragua solidarity movement thus successfully continued the familiar strategy of linking political messages to cultural entertainment, legitimizing and popularizing the Sandinistas' armed struggle. Beyond translating and disseminating the work of Nicaraguan authors, they organized art shows and movie nights, and invited Central American artists to perform at concerts. Nicaragua solidarity committees also sold copies of the Costa Rican-made movie *Nicaragua: Patria Libre o Morir* (1979), which chronicled the FSLN's heroic military struggle against Somoza.[101] The Nicaraguan singers Carlos and Luis Enrique Mejía Godoy were particularly popular. In their songs, the Godoy brothers spoke about social issues and romanticized guerrilla warfare. In "Guitarra Armada," for instance, they explain how to make explosives, handle small arms, and disassemble and reassemble an M1 carbine, a weapon commonly used by Somoza's National Guard. By telling personal stories about the lives of ordinary Nicaraguans, their music also functioned as a sort of testimonio, a powerful "narrative performance" of life under and resistance to the Somoza dictatorship.[102] In the song "Venancia," for example, Luis Enrique Godoy told the story of a young female guerrilla from the mountains whose brother was murdered by the army for joining a labor union.

The high participation of women in the Sandinista struggle also attracted the attention of Western European women and feminist activists.[103] To many, the FSLN seemed particularly progressive since, in their 1969 "historic program," the Sandinistas had already vowed to "abolish the odious discrimination that women have been subjected to compared to men."[104] Moreover, as historian Friederike Apelt writes, the FSLN actively engaged in constructing and spreading "emancipatory gender images" all over the world, thereby mobilizing many women for the Sandinista cause.[105] The participation of the guerrilla commander Dora Maria Téllez (also known as Comandante Dos)

FIGURE 2. A Sandinista fighter in September 1978 in Estelí, a city 150 kilometers north of Managua. There were many women fighting for the FSLN in the late 1970s. Besides their military significance, these women contributed to the Sandinistas' revolutionary diplomacy by helping the movement build connections to feminist organizations and women's groups in Europe and the Americas. Photo: John Giannini/Sygma via Getty Images.

in the occupation of the National Palace turned her into an international symbol of the FSLN's revolutionary feminism, creating a powerful image of Nicaraguan women putting down their "kitchen pots" to take up arms against an oppressive regime, laying claim to power as wielded by the barrel of a gun (figure 2).[106] Building on this rejection of gender discrimination, Sandinistas and their supporters presented the FSLN as a movement in favor of gender equality and female empowerment.

By connecting to existing networks of solidarity committees and smartly playing into the political agendas and cultural interests of Western European activists, the FSLN was thus able to bring together a diverse range of supporters. Through revolutionary diplomacy, the Sandinistas not only turned their small and relatively unknown Central American country into a topic of interest for Western Europeans, but also succeeded in presenting the war as a noble struggle for national liberation against a violent dictatorship. This clearly frustrated Somoza's ambassadors in Western Europe, who tried to counter the Sandinistas' propaganda by writing angry letters to the media. Florencio Mendoza, the Nicaraguan ambassador in West Germany, for instance, accused the editors of left-wing magazine *Stern* of misrepresenting the situation in Nicaragua in a recent article. The Sandinistas were not freedom fighters, Mendoza argued in a letter to the journal's editorial team, but rather violent "communists" who killed everyone who disagreed with them.[107] But the FSLN's successful diplomacy meant that such accusations did not stick. In addition to outwitting the anticommunist narrative of the Somoza regime's officials, the Sandinistas' diplomacy, as the section below further demonstrates, also brought the revolutionaries into contact with Western European social democrats.

## SOCIAL DEMOCRATS AND THE SANDINISTAS

Sandinista leaders considered Western European politicians an important diplomatic target, as they believed Western European government policy could pressure the United States into changing its approach toward Somoza. Although not particularly involved in Central America throughout most of the Cold War period, Western European politicians and activists slowly began to pay more attention to developments in Nicaragua in the late 1970s. Key in this context was the role and network of the Socialist International (SI), through which the FSLN established contacts with prominent Western European social democrats, such as François Mitterrand (France), Joop den Uyl (the Netherlands), Olof Palme (Sweden), Mário Soares (Portugal), and Felipe González (Spain). The charismatic leadership of the SPD's Willy Brandt also mattered. Brandt, who was elected president of the Socialist International on a platform of human rights and North-South cooperation in 1976, shifted the focus of the association toward Latin America.[108]

The SI, founded in 1951, was an influential international organization bringing together Western European socialist, labor, and social democratic parties. It aimed to challenge the bipolarity of the Cold War by presenting social democracy as a "third way"—a suitable alternative to both Soviet communism and U.S. capitalism.[109] In the 1960s and 70s, the SI's principal focus had been on Southern Europe and the organization played an important role in the democratic transitions in Spain, Greece, and Portugal. Under Brandt's leadership, it rapidly grew in membership and scope. Stressing the need for greater economic cooperation between the world's rich and poor countries, the organization started to develop activities outside of Europe, and these initiatives were particularly well received in Latin America.[110] In the 1970s, prominent Latin American leaders including Carlos Andrés Pérez (Venezuela), José Francisco Peña Gomez (Dominican Republic), and Daniel Oduber Quirós (Costa Rica) became active and influential members of the SI. Others, such as Omar Torrijos Hererra (Panama) and Leonel Brizola (Brazil) regularly attended SI meetings and conferences.[111]

The growing interest of the SI in Latin America was excellent news for the Nicaraguan revolutionaries. As we have seen above, because of their international campaign, Sandinistas had already managed to establish friendly and constructive relationships with, among others, Pérez, Torrijos, and Oduber. These connections with Latin American socialists and social democrats provided the FSLN with an opportunity to put the Nicaraguan civil war on the SI's agenda, thereby increasing international pressure on Somoza. In 1978, Ernesto Cardenal and several other Sandinista representatives were invited to speak at a Socialist International conference in Vancouver, Canada, where they received a standing ovation.[112] In the conference's final resolution, the SI called for international solidarity with the Nicaraguan struggle against the dictatorship and, implicitly referring to the United States, urged all governments "which have so long maintained the Somoza regime in power" to end their support for the regime.[113] Furthermore, the social democrats adopted concrete plans to assist the Nicaraguan revolutionaries with financial and material aid, medical assistance, and political training.[114]

Because of the Socialist International's position, developments in Central America increasingly shaped political debates in Western Europe. Not only did left-wing politicians voice their concerns about the Somoza dictatorship in national parliaments, urging their governments to break ties with the U.S.-backed regime, some also endorsed the FSLN as the legitimate representative of the Nicaraguan struggle for social justice, democracy, and nonalignment.[115] On 20 December 1978, the British Labour Party passed a resolution extending "their warmest support to all the democratic opposition forces and particularly the Sandinista National Liberation Front." Echoing the Sandinista claim that their struggle transcended Cold War politics, Labour firmly rejected "the idea that the only alternative to Somoza is communist takeover in Nicaragua."[116] The PvdA, too, promoted the cause of the FSLN in the Netherlands, criticizing the Somoza dictatorship, U.S. foreign policy, and Israeli arms shipments to Nicaragua.[117] The Dutch Labor leader Joop den Uyl, emphasizing the "responsibility" of the Carter administration for Somoza's violence, urged his government to express "sympathy" for the struggle in Nicaragua.[118] The PvdA also called on the public to financially support the

FSLN, pointing out that "you have to help the Frente, and not the dictator Somoza."[119] Finally, in West Germany, the SPD and its associated political foundation the Friedrich Ebert Stiftung actively backed the guerrillas, providing the FSLN revolutionaries with money, training, and political support.[120]

Through its connections with left-wing politicians, the FSLN could lobby Western European governments more directly. The Nicaraguan brothers Tomás and Humberto Arguello Chamorro, for instance, arranged a meeting with Louise Croll from the FCO, set up "through a British intermediary" from the Labour Party.[121] In this secret meeting on 29 June 1979, which took place outside Whitehall, the Chamorro brothers asked the British government to break off relations with the Somoza regime and recognize the new Junta de Gobierno de Reconstrucción Nacional (Junta of National Reconstruction), a provisional government that the FSLN, in cooperation with other opposition groups, had established to give the military struggle a civilian and moderate face. The revolutionary junta, they stressed, represented "a broad spectrum of opinion in Nicaragua" and was committed to "restoring confidence in democracy" and creating "a mixed economy." Smartly playing into what they perceived as the political ideology of Margaret Thatcher's new conservative government, the Chamorro brothers also argued that "private property would be respected" and that several members of the junta were "businessmen and landowners."[122]

Again, the international strategy of the Sandinista revolutionaries was effective. In less than two years, the FSLN had transformed from a marginalized group of guerrillas into an organization with connections to a respectable and influential network of Latin American and Western European politicians. To be sure, the FSLN was lucky to encounter an unusually receptive Socialist International, eager to be convinced by the Sandinistas' argument that their revolutionary project would transcend the bipolar Cold War order. Yet the FSLN's ability to attract the support of social democrats was unique. As historian Bernd Rother points out, "never before had the International taken the side of a revolutionary movement so unequivocally as in the case of the Sandinistas."[123] Apart from giving the Sandinistas an international platform to voice their concerns, the growing support of Western European social democrats for the FSLN inevitably had an impact on government policy. In the late 1970s, the political Left in Western Europe was particularly strong, making this a propitious time for the FSLN to obtain the movement's support. Left-wing parties were in power in the United Kingdom (until 1979) and West Germany (until 1982), and the PvdA—albeit in opposition—was the largest political party in the Netherlands. In Greece and France, too, the Left would soon win power in elections. As the final section of this chapter demonstrates, then, this forced Western European governments in the late 1970s to engage with Nicaragua, a country where they historically had few direct economic or political interests.

## WESTERN EUROPEAN GOVERNMENTS AND SOMOZA

As developments in Nicaragua captured the public's attention and the Sandinistas' military strength grew, Western European governments became increasingly critical of Somoza. The general sentiment in the region was that Somoza's dictatorial behavior was unacceptable, and that Nicaragua deserved democracy and social justice. On 29 June 1979, the foreign ministers of the nine member states of the European Community—an economic and political association of Western European countries that played an increasingly prominent role on the international stage in the 1970s and 1980s—joined the public debate by issuing a statement declaring "their very grave concern over the disturbing developments in Nicaragua and the steadily worsening sufferings being inflicted upon the Nicaraguan people." The Nine, as the EC member states were called, demanded "an immediate halt to the conflict" so that "free elections can be held without delay."[124]

This was the first time the Nine had issued a joint statement on a Central American country; it was a region of little strategic importance, as it was considered to be firmly within the United States' sphere of influence. The United Kingdom and the Netherlands did not have embassies in Managua and depended on their ambassadors in Costa Rica, Mexico, and Panama for relevant information on the revolutionary war in Nicaragua. And while this irritated the British ambassador in Costa Rica, who noted during the insurrection of September 1978 that "under the inefficient system of non-resident representation we tend to be two jumps behind events," the FCO did not feel the need to change these arrangements.[125] John Shakespeare, for example, the head of the British Mexico and Caribbean Department (MACD), stated in November 1978 that Central America was an area where the United Kingdom "could close down all our missions without serious harm to the national interest."[126] West Germany did have an embassy in Managua and, according to the British ambassador, "relatively big commercial interests" in Nicaragua.[127] Nevertheless, the German AA did not feel the need to become actively involved in the region. In fact, at an Anglo-German meeting to discuss foreign policy in 1978, the German representative noted that West Germany "had no active policy toward Latin America."[128]

It is therefore remarkable that, a year later, despite this lack of direct interests, Western European governments became openly opposed to the continuation of Somoza's regime and issued a joint statement.[129] What is more, the governments of West Germany, the United Kingdom, and the Netherlands urged the International Monetary Fund (IMF) to refuse the Nicaraguan government any new loans.[130] And although the EC countries had little power to put pressure on Somoza, the British Secretary of State David Owen (a member of the Labour Party) took the symbolic measure of not accrediting the new British ambassador in Costa Rica to Nicaragua.[131] Also, he urged the United States in February 1979 to "pull the props out from under Somoza," even suggesting that the United Kingdom could take "a lead in the EC in support of any U.S. action against Somoza."[132]

The swiftly rising level of Western European governmental interest in Nicaragua is evidence of the impact of Sandinista revolutionary diplomacy. Certainly, diplomats were aware of the public's interest in Nicaragua and took this into account when making foreign policy decisions regarding Central America.[133] The MACD, for instance, recommended that Owen make the U.S. administration aware of the "strong opposition to the Somoza regime within the Labour Party and amongst liberal and human rights groups in the UK."[134] Surely, the memorandum continued, there would be "parliamentary and public criticism of the U.S. if, in spite of Somoza's rejection of the mediation proposals, they were to continue to give him any support."[135] Furthermore, as parliamentarians and the public pressured governments into a more proactive foreign policy, Western European officials simply could no longer remain neutral. Even if they disagreed with public opinion and disliked the Sandinistas, EC leaders had to come up with a response to justify this. To give one example, West German officials had to write responses to letters by solidarity committees, church groups, and human rights activists who asked foreign minister Hans-Dietrich Genscher why his government was still supporting the "feudalist-dictatorial" Somoza dictatorship.[136] Owen, too, received dozens of letters asking the British government to support the "development of a democratic government in Nicaragua."[137] These letters were sent by a range of organizations, including the Council of Churches, constituency Labour Parties, War on Want, the Justice and Peace Group for Prisoners of Conscience, and several student unions.[138] In the late 1970s, although initially reluctant to get involved in the region at all, Western European governments had to rethink their approach to the upheavals in Central America.

Nevertheless, to understand how Western European foreign policy toward Nicaragua was subsequently shaped, we need to take note of another—more powerful—actor that pressured Western Europe to get involved in the Nicaraguan conflict. In June 1979, several Western European governments, including the United Kingdom, West Germany, and the Netherlands, received a secret letter from the United States' president Jimmy Carter asking for support for his "general objectives" in Central America, most notably "a reduction of violence and the restoration of peace in Nicaragua."[139] Carter was clearly worried about the rapid military advances the FSLN was making since the revolutionaries had called for another mass insurrection on 4 June 1979 and asked his allies to embargo "arms shipments to both sides in the Nicaragua conflict."[140] Specifically, the letter reflected the U.S. administration's fear of a Castroite takeover in Nicaragua, stating that "Western democracies less directly involved in Central America than the United States may have special advantages in helping to develop and strengthen centrist political forces in these countries."[141]

The initial Western European response to Carter's letter varied from passive to negative. British diplomat Anthony Parsons, the UK's Permanent Representative to the United Nations, summarized the situation as follows: "The Americans have got rather a nerve. Since the 19th century they have treated the countries of Central America like a private estate and have resolutely discouraged any other powers from developing their interests on any significant scale there. Now the structure is coming apart and they are turning to us and presumably others for help."[142] The Dutch were equally unimpressed and concluded that the Carter administration was "relatively powerless" since an "old school intervention" was no longer politically acceptable. They also rejected Carter's suggestion that they could directly assist "moderate political groups" in Nicaragua since they considered this a task for political parties, not governments.[143]

The reluctance of Western European governments to support Carter's objectives does not necessarily mean that they were entirely convinced by the FSLN's argument that their revolutionary struggle had nothing to do with the Cold War. Although Western European officials wanted Somoza out as soon as possible, they certainly shared some of the United States' concerns regarding the possibility of growing Cuban and Soviet influence in Central

America. West German diplomat Andreas Meyer-Landrut, for instance, informed his government on 10 July 1979 about the "increasingly active involvement" of the Cubans in the Nicaraguan struggle, warning that Fidel Castro's government supported the Sandinistas with arms and military training.[144] The British ambassador in Costa Rica, rather speculatively, noted that the Costa Rican security service had discovered Sandinista propaganda and arms in a house in San José "not far from the Soviet Embassy."[145] Furthermore, in November 1978 a representative from the Overseas Information Department (OID), an obscure propaganda branch of the FCO which had ties to the British intelligence services, secretly attended the Nicaragua solidarity event at the LSE. In a letter to the FCO, the OID compared Barrajón's speech to the language of the Cuban revolutionaries and concluded that it was "not clear" whether the FSLN "would follow Cuba's pro-Soviet" line.[146] Finally, the Dutch also admitted that the United States' fears "for escalation" and the "increase of Cuban/Marxist influence" in Central America were largely justified.[147] Overall, then, Western European diplomats agreed with Carter that it was in the interest of the West to bolster the moderates in Nicaragua in order to prevent a communist takeover.

Rather, the negative response in London, Bonn, and The Hague to Carter's letter needs to be placed in the wider context of transatlantic relations and the heightening of Cold War tensions in the late 1970s.[148] To summarize, transatlantic relations were extremely tense during the Carter presidency; Western European leaders were irritated by Carter's foreign and trade policies toward the Middle East, the Soviet Union, and East Asia, which they saw as inconsistent, demonstrative of a lack of concern for the transatlantic alliance, and inconsiderate of Western European Cold War interests.[149] West German Chancellor Helmut Schmidt, in particular, was known to disagree with Carter on a wide variety of issues, most notably the correct response to the global economic crisis and nuclear arms control.[150] Additionally, as old rivalries intensified and relations between the United States and the Soviet Union crumbled once again, Western Europeans were reluctant to start a new phase of the Cold War and remained committed to the continuation of détente.[151]The reaction to Carter's letter, therefore, is reflective of the increasing frustration of Western European governments with his administration. With regard to Nicaragua, Carter's refusal to push the repressive dictator Somoza out of office, which contrasted sharply with his earlier focus on human rights, only confirmed what many Western Europeans leaders already believed, namely that Carter's foreign policies were vague, inconsistent, and contradictory. Indeed, when the Carter administration showed itself unable to integrate human rights and Cold War concerns into a coherent and effective foreign policy toward Nicaragua, the United States alienated its Western European allies. Meyer-Landrut, for instance, concluded that Carter's policy toward the Nicaraguan crisis was not "credible" because it lacked a clear "political conception" combining regional stability with a decline in support for Somoza.[152] The British ambassador in Costa Rica was even more disapproving, noting that "the all-important United States are still obsessed with the fear of a second Cuba and have reluctantly concluded that Somoza is the only figure who can effectively subserve their desire to keep the region quiet."[153] The British ambassador in Washington, too, aired his frustration with what he saw as the irrational underpinnings of Carter's foreign policy, lamenting that the United States was once again "haunted by the memory of the Cuban Revolution."[154]

Of course, despite these tensions, the Europeans recognized that, in the Cold War, they were on the same side as the U.S. Indeed, Parsons concluded his note by writing that there was "no point in rubbing salt in the Americans' wound" since "we all share the same objectives."[155] Rather, the main point of disagreement between the United States and its European partners was about the right methods for achieving these goals in Central America. Crucially, Western European officials believed that Carter's reluctance to push Somoza out only worsened the situation, as this would bolster the radicals and leave less room for a negotiated—and what they perceived as moderate—solution to the crisis. The nine EC member states thus wanted Somoza to leave Nicaragua as soon as possible and were frustrated with Carter's hesitation to increase pressure on the dictator. At its heart, this perception was based on the calculation that "the longer Somoza remains, the greater the chance of the extreme leftwing controlling the next government of Nicaragua and of it coming under Cuban influence."[156] The best strategy to keep Nicaragua away from Cuba and the Soviet Union, the Western Europeans argued, was to make sure the revolutionaries felt appreciated and welcomed by the West.[157]

The situation in Nicaragua soon outpaced the development of the foreign policies of both Western Europe and the United States. The offensive launched in early June was successful, and the revolutionaries quickly took control of major cities and towns. On 19 July 1979, Sandinista guerrillas entered Managua, succeeding in overthrowing the Somoza regime, and together with the opposition coalition they assembled, installed a new revolutionary government. How Western European involvement might have developed had this not happened is unclear. By 1979, one thing was certain: at the level of the state, the FSLN's international campaign, initiated two years earlier, combined with pressure from the Carter administration, put Nicaraguan developments on the Western European political agenda. As they did, these governments agreed with the Sandinistas that Somoza's regime should be ended. Although Western European governments were not entirely convinced of the FSLN's declared intentions to move beyond the Cold War, they were even more frustrated by the apparent complacency of the United States.

## CONCLUSION

The late 1970s were a transformative period in the Sandinistas' long struggle against the Somoza dynasty. After more than a decade of hardship and military setbacks, the revolutionaries launched a new strategy, building a broad movement through cultural outreach, toning down radical rhetoric, and staging spectacular guerrilla raids. Applying this strategy to the international arena, the Sandinistas' revolutionary diplomacy had an enormous impact, mobilizing a wide range of audiences for their cause. As they publicly distanced themselves from their traditional association with Latin America's armed Left, the guerrillas presented the FSLN as a broad movement for democracy and social justice that fought against an oppressive dictatorship. Realizing that significant parts of the world were tired of Cold War narratives and bloodshed, it also made the conscious choice to transcend the bipolarity of the global Cold War and place itself in the long tradition of Third World national liberation movements.

Responding to the Sandinistas' pragmatic international campaign, Western European activists and politicians had many reasons to support Nicaraguan's revolutionary war, varying from anti-imperialist ideology to feminism. Cultural appeal was crucial, and the literature and music of Nicaraguan artists—previously unknown to most Western Europeans—was at the heart of the transnational anti-Somoza movement that put the FSLN into the international limelight in the late 1970s. In Western Europe, the Sandinistas were lucky that their revolutionary diplomacy fell onto fertile ground, as the guerrillas and their allies could build on the work done by existing solidarity networks and organizations dedicated to Latin American culture and politics. The Socialist International, attracted to the Sandinistas' claim that their movement was a unique ideological and political project, was also exceptionally keen to take up the revolutionaries' cause.

In this favorable international context, the impact of the Sandinistas' revolutionary diplomacy on government policy was clear. Because of public interest and Sandinista pressure, Western European officials were forced to engage with a region they had comfortably ignored in the previous decades. To be sure, Western European foreign policy in the late 1970s was incoherent and fundamentally shaped by Cold War concerns. Moreover, the EC member states did not coordinate their approach to the region besides a joint statement denouncing Somoza. Yet, the insistence of Western European governments that Somoza should go provided the FSLN with legitimacy and contributed to the isolation of the dictatorship.

As we shall see in the chapters that follow, the tactical maneuvers and ideological flexibility demonstrated by the Sandinistas to secure international and domestic support in the years leading up to Somoza's fall would continue to shape the revolution's trajectory. Crucially, their revolutionary diplomacy created expectations about Nicaragua's future that were often conflicting and utopian. These expectations shaped how governments, politicians, and activists around the world engaged with the Sandinistas and responded to their policies. Indeed, soon after the dictators' fall the FSLN was faced with the seemingly impossible task of marrying all these contrasting images it had helped to create with the reality on the ground in Nicaragua. In short, the Sandinistas' revolutionary diplomacy of the late 1970s set the stage for the tumultuous decade of the 1980s.

# TWO

# Triumph and Consolidation, 1979–1980

ON 19 JULY 1979, triumphant FSLN guerrillas poured into the Nicaraguan capital of Managua. It was a transformative moment; for the first time since the 1959 Cuban Revolution, armed left-wing revolutionaries in Latin America had succeeded in toppling a U.S.-backed anticommunist regime. Moreover, as we saw in the previous chapter, the Sandinista comandantes did so with widespread domestic and international support. Journalists in Europe and the Americas reported on the "liberation" of Nicaragua in jubilant terms, as they described how "thousands of cheering people" welcomed the new revolutionary junta to Managua and expressed relief that Anastasio Somoza and his abusive National Guard were at last defeated by the "kind, courteous, and cordial" Sandinista guerrillas.[1] In Western European capitals, solidarity activists celebrated the victory by enthusiastically occupying Nicaraguan embassies in Bonn, Brussels, Madrid, and Paris, making sure that Somoza's ambassadors were no longer in a position to represent the Nicaraguan government.[2]

The end of the Somoza dynasty, however, was only the beginning of the Nicaraguan Revolution. After years of armed struggle, economic devastation, and a massive earthquake that virtually destroyed Managua in 1972, the daunting process of building a new and—hopefully—better Nicaragua had just begun. And it was this remarkable process of remaking the Nicaraguan state and society in the aftermath of 19 July 1979, rather than the successful insurrection against Somoza itself, that determined the nature, impact, and future of the Nicaraguan Revolution. Indeed, as Forrest D. Colburn writes, "the violent replacement of governors . . . gives a birthday to the revolution, but it is in the ensuing revamping of society . . . that the character and the consequences of the revolution are defined."[3] This was particularly true in the

Nicaraguan case because the revolution took place at a specific juncture of the Cold War, when the U.S. administration's view of the world moved away from détente and toward renewed confrontation with international communism and the Soviet Union. In this context, the political significance and impact of the revolutionaries' political statements, policy choices, and alliances, both at a domestic and international level, were severely heightened.

Even so, historians and political scientists have largely ignored this foundational period of the revolution's history, focusing instead on its trajectory during the Ronald Reagan presidency in 1981–88, when the U.S. government launched a secret campaign to overthrow the Sandinista government. Historians of U.S. foreign relations, albeit with some exceptions, have also predominantly focused on Reagan's foreign policy toward Central America, largely overlooking the Carter period.[4] Similarly, historians writing about the Sandinista solidarity movement have paid little attention to the early revolutionary years, giving prominence to American and Western European protests against the Reagan's Central America policies in the mid-1980s.[5] Overall, our knowledge of the early revolutionary period remains patchy, and we still know little about the objectives of Sandinista revolutionary diplomacy, the importance of transnational activism, and the revolutionaries' relations with the wider world.

This chapter, then, aims to shed light on the history of Nicaragua's revolutionary trajectory in the months following Somoza's fall on 19 July 1979. It demonstrates that FSLN officials used revolutionary diplomacy to build a strong and internationally recognized government. By showing a degree of political pluralism and ideological flexibility to the outside world, this new government succeeded in obtaining much-needed financial aid and material assistance from the Americas, Europe, and sympathetic states in the Global South. Despite presenting a different picture of the revolution to audiences in Europe and the United States, the Sandinistas did not intend to create a Western-style democratic and pluralistic state in Nicaragua. Behind the scenes, the Sandinista leaders slowly but unquestionably consolidated their power over the country's institutions and foreign relations. To be sure, the FSLN had widespread popular support and was largely successful in keeping together the broad coalition that it had forged to overthrow Somoza, incorporating different sectors of the population into a relatively pluralistic revolutionary process. The revolutionaries also implemented an ambitious domestic reform program, drastically improving health care, education, and access to food.[6] The Sandinista movement was in charge, but—despite claims from its anticommunist critics—Nicaragua was far from a Soviet-style dictatorship.

In the months following the triumph, the Revolución Popular Sandinista (Sandinista People's Revolution) captured the imaginations of thousands of activists, teachers, musicians, writers, social democrats, priests, and students around the world. As Nicaraguan guerrillas enthusiastically embarked on the next phase of the FSLN's revolutionary project, their determination, youth, and idealism were vividly pictured in the international press. The Sandinistas were able to capitalize on their popularity financially and politically by encouraging a powerful sense that activists could also be part of the revolution. The National Literacy Crusade, an ambitious education project implemented in the countryside and poor urban areas between March and August 1980, provided the FSLN with a particularly useful tool to connect Western European states and peoples to its revolutionary program.

Nevertheless, Western European support for the revolutionary junta should not solely be understood as the result of the Sandinistas' international popularity and diplomatic skills. Western policy was, to a significant extent, shaped by Cold War concerns, as European Community leaders were apprehensive about the possibility that Nicaragua would drift toward the Eastern bloc if it did not receive sufficient support from the West. While many Western European politicians adopted a genuinely friendly attitude toward the Nicaraguan Revolution, concerns existed about the Sandinistas' intentions and ideological convictions, most notably regarding promises to implement a democratic, nonaligned, and pluralist system. These anxieties increased in the months following the revolution's triumph, as several prominent leaders resigned from the revolutionary junta in April 1980. Moreover, EC leaders watched the changing attitude of U.S. president Jimmy Carter with concern. Initially, the Carter administration adopted a cautiously positive approach to the revolution, offering Nicaragua a $75 million aid package that primarily benefited the country's private sector and other nongovernmental and independent organizations, such as the newspaper *La Prensa*.[7] Yet relations between the United States and the FSLN quickly deteriorated when Carter accused the Nicaraguan government of providing weapons and logistical support to the Frente Farabundo Martí para la Liberación Nacional (Farabundo Martí National Liberation Front, FMLN), a guerrilla movement in neighboring El Salvador that maintained close ties to the Sandinistas.

Ironically, in the first months following Somoza's fall, the revolutionary victory also created problems for the Sandinistas' relationship with the solidarity movement. Now that the task of supporting the armed struggle against the Somoza regime was completed, Western European solidarity activists had to reevaluate the purpose and nature of their work, as well as their relationship with the FSLN. This turned out to be a difficult process, as the priority of the Sandinistas in the months following the revolution was not the solidarity movement, but rather the implementation of its revolutionary program and the creation of a functioning diplomatic service at the level of the state. As the revolutionaries made it clear to solidarity activists that they were no longer equals in the international arena, the activists accused their Nicaraguan compañeros of neglect. Indeed, from the perspective of solidarity activists, the Sandinistas did not sufficiently appreciate the crucial importance of transnational activism for the survival of the Nicaraguan Revolution. Solidarity activism, they believed, would be vital in protecting the FSLN from anticommunist propaganda, as well as economic and political pressure from Western governments. The result was that, in the period from July 1979 until November 1980, it was Western European activists—convinced of their continued relevance to developments in a country thousands of miles away—who were the driving forces behind the transnational solidarity movement.

## A NEW FOREIGN POLICY

The weeks following the victory of the Nicaraguan revolutionaries on 19 July 1979 were marked by chaos, optimism, and spontaneity. Sandinista comandantes, newly appointed cabinet ministers, diplomats, and junta members operated without central coordination, making decisions based on common sense, impromptu meetings, and promises made by FSLN guerrillas in pamphlets and speeches. Diplomacy was largely the result of judgment calls and improvisation, as communication with the outside world was difficult and, more importantly, a functioning foreign ministry did not yet exist. Nevertheless, the FSLN leadership, conscious that the international community would play a decisive role in determining the country's future, moved quickly to develop an international strategy, take control of the country's state institutions, and create an effective foreign policy apparatus.

For the FSLN, it was obvious that Nicaragua's foreign policy after 1979 would have to be radically different from the past, when Somoza had implemented what Sandinistas described as a "policy of submission to Yankee imperialism."[8] Alejandro Bendaña, the General Secretary of Nicaragua's

Ministerio del Exterior, reflected in 1989 that Somoza had been the "most faithful ally" of the United States, and his foreign policy had been a "colonial" policy, dictated by North American economic interests and ideological preferences rather than by the needs of the Nicaraguan people.[9] Similarly, Sergio Ramírez writes in his memoirs that, throughout the twentieth century, his nation was "held hostage" by the Somoza dynasty, which allowed the United States to plunder Nicaragua's "national resources."[10]

Anti-imperialism was thus at the heart of the FSLN's struggle for national liberation, and this fight did not end with the dictator's overthrow. On the contrary, Sandinista revolutionaries understood their triumph in the context of a global struggle of Third World national liberation movements against Western—and more specifically North American—imperialism. In its historic program, the FSLN vowed to support the common fight of "the peoples of Asia, Africa, and Latin America" against "Yankee imperialism" through a "foreign policy of absolute national independence."[11] And to Sandinista revolutionaries, imbued with the hubris of having just won power at the end of the 1970s, the efforts of the Third World to challenge the imperialist world order seemed to be going remarkably well. With a Marxist revolution in Ethiopia, the defeat of U.S. forces in Vietnam, the rise to power of Maurice Bishop's New Jewel Movement in Grenada, and the decision of several African governments, such as Angola, to adopt Marxist-Leninism as an official state ideology, the FSLN leaders operated under the—overly optimistic—assumption that they were on the winning side of the global anti-imperialist struggle.[12] Adding to this impression, the Sandinistas also predicted that the FMLN would take power in El Salvador. Hoping for another revolutionary triumph in Central America, the FSLN backed the FMLN with military and political support and provided exiled Salvadoran guerrillas with a safe haven.[13]

Intimately related to the Sandinistas' identification with the Third World was the Nicaraguan government's decision to send a large delegation to the Sixth Conference of Heads of State of the Non-Aligned in Havana from 3 to 9 September 1979, which was presided over by Fidel Castro.[14] By joining the NAM, foreign ministry official Ernesto Alomá Sánchez wrote in September 1979, Nicaragua became part of a powerful organization that held a majority in all major international institutions. Nicaragua's future proposals in the United Nations, he predicted, could count on the support of a "solid majority [of] brother countries." In addition, Alomá Sánchez underlined the nonaligned countries' ability to help the FSLN solve Nicaragua's troubling financial problems. Specifically, he pointed out, the Sandinistas had inherited an external debt of more than $1.5 billion, which was impossible to pay off since it far exceeded the value of the country's yearly exports. As the "standard bearer" for the New International Economic Order (NIEO), which aimed to replace the "global capitalist economic order" with a more fair and equal system, the NAM could back up the Nicaraguan claim that they could not be expected to pay off Somoza's debts. So, Alomá Sánchez concluded, through the solidarity of the NAM, the Sandinistas could strengthen the Nicaraguan Revolution's international standing and overcome future financial obstacles.[15] Interestingly, then, the Nicaraguan revolutionaries continued to attach importance and hope to the values of NAM and the NIEO at a time when—most historians now agree—these political and economic projects had already lost most of their momentum.[16]

With regard to the Cold War competition, the Sandinista leaders certainly sympathized more with the socialist bloc than with the Western world.[17] In August 1979, FSLN comandante Bayardo Arce argued at Managua's Universidad Centroamericana (UCA) that the Soviet Union was simply not an "imperialist" country, because "imperialism" and "capitalism" were two intertwined processes.[18] Alomá Sanchez made a similar point in September 1979, commenting that socialist countries were significantly more supportive of Third World liberation movements than Western Europe and the United States. Indeed, he added, for their own economic benefit, the capitalist countries consistently obstructed the proposals and ambitions of the "underdeveloped" world.[19]

Taking the Sandinistas' worldview and hopes for the future into consideration, then, the plans of the Nicaraguan revolutionaries to have good relations with the West might appear somewhat contradictory. Yet the FSLN was faced with the economic and political reality of having inherited a poor, war-torn, and unequal country that was almost entirely dependent on aid and trade with the much more powerful United States.[20] The insurgent war against Somoza had slowed down the country's production of meat, coffee, and cotton, making it difficult for the FSLN to generate income through exports.[21] The state of the country's health care and food provision system was also abysmal. Before the revolution, more than 50 percent of Nicaraguan children were malnourished and "one in every eight infants died in their first year" due to diseases such as measles, pneumonia, and polio.[22] Similarly, land distribution was highly unequal, as the countryside was dominated by the "rural bourgeoisie" and small farmers were not given the same amount of access to credits as the "big agro-export landowners."[23] The illiteracy rate, too, was high, as approximately 50 percent of Nicaraguans could not read or write.[24] If the Sandinistas were determined to provide Nicaraguans with equal and improved access to land, health, food, and education, they had to be pragmatic and cast their net wide.

In addition, in the years leading up to the revolution's triumph, the Sandinistas had built fruitful alliances with governments and mainstream political forces in Western Europe and the Americas, such as the Socialist International and the governments of Panama, Venezuela, and Mexico. The FSLN had done so by presenting the war against Somoza as a nationalist struggle for social justice, democracy, and nonalignment in the global Cold War. Changing tactics and adopting a hostile attitude to the capitalist world immediately after victory, the Sandinista leaders understood, would not only undo the positive results of the FSLN's revolutionary diplomacy in the late 1970s, but could also ruin Nicaragua's chances of obtaining desperately needed financial assistance. Based on the assumption that the United States and its European allies—hoping that Nicaragua would stay in the Western camp—would be willing to provide the country's new government with financial aid and technical assistance, the FSLN leaders deemed it necessary for the revolution's survival to initially adopt a cautious and cooperative attitude to the West.

This outreach to the West was also meant to weaken the Sandinistas' ideological enemies. Despite their willingness to cooperate with the Western world, the FSLN did prepare for the possibility of an anticommunist counterrevolution. When Bayardo Arce underlined the importance of an "extremely careful" foreign policy at the UCA, for instance, he explained that the Sandinistas were also making sure that, if the "imperialist powers" ever decided to intervene against the Nicaraguan Revolution, they could not convincingly argue that Nicaraguans had somehow "provoked this aggression." When the revolution is attacked, Arce argued, the international community will be confronted with the truth, namely that Cuban exiles, United States Marines, and Somoza's former guardsmen were forced to "drop their mask" to defend their "imperialist economic interests."[25]

In this vein, the Sandinistas presented the Nicaraguan Revolution in a nonthreatening way to potential enemies, both at home and abroad. Critically, to assuage fears about the revolution's radical nature, Sandinista officials downplayed the extent of their power. The official face of the Nicaraguan Revolution, for example, was not the FSLN leadership, but the Junta de Gobierno de Reconstrucción Nacional, a body that represented

FIGURE 3. The Nicaraguan junta swears in members of the new cabinet on 25 July 1979. The official face of the revolution, the junta represented the ideological diversity of the anti-Somoza movement. From left to right: Sergio Ramírez, Daniel Ortega, Violeta Chamorro, Alfonso Robelo, Moisés Hassan. Photo: Bettmann via Getty Images.

the ideological and political diversity of the anti-Somoza alliance (figure 3). It had five members, all of whom had actively contributed to the fall of the Somoza dynasty. Violeta Chamorro, widow of the murdered *La Prensa* editor Pedro Joaquín Chamorro, was the only woman on the junta. After Pedro Joaquín's assassination on 10 January 1978, Chamorro continued to run *La Prensa*, and as a junta member she represented the Union Democrática de Liberación (Democratic Liberation Union), a diverse opposition coalition including socialists and social Christian organizations that had opposed Somoza since 1974. Alfonso Robelo was a businessman who founded the Movimiento Democrático Nicaragüense (Nicaraguan Democratic Movement, MDN), another anti-Somoza opposition party. Moisés Hassan, a guerrilla and politician of Palestinian heritage, represented the Movimiento del Pueblo Unido (United People's Movement), a grassroots organization closely aligned to the FSLN. Sergio Ramírez represented the group of twelve anti-Somoza intellectuals known as the Grupo de los Doce, discussed in the previous chapter. The fifth and last member was Daniel Ortega, the only known Sandinista on the junta and one of the nine FSLN comandantes. The revolutionary cabinet was also not dominated by Sandinista guerrillas. Most of the new ministers came from the Grupo de los Doce, including the new foreign minister Miguel d'Escoto, a Sandinista priest educated in the United States.

Despite appearances and claims to the contrary, however, real power in Nicaragua lay with the Sandinista movement and, more specifically, with the nine comandantes—all former guerrilla leaders—of the FSLN's Dirección Nacional (National Directorate).[26] Soon after the revolution, the other junta members found out that, apart from Daniel Ortega, Ramírez and Hassan, too, were Sandinista militants, meaning that three of the five members voted in favor of FSLN proposals. As Ramírez writes in his memoirs, the Sandinistas' tercerista tendency had previously kept his FSLN membership "secret" because Ramírez's role "as the head of the Grupo de los Doce demanded an illusion of independence."[27] Since the FSLN held a firm majority on the junta, which ruled Nicaragua by decree, Sandinista leaders could push through their policy proposals with ease. Aside from dominating the junta, Sandinista representatives also held the majority on the Council of State, which was presided over by comandante Carlos Nuñez. Within the FSLN party structure, key decisions were made by the nine comandantes who formed the Dirección Nacional, namely Daniel Ortega, Humberto Ortega, Tomás Borge, Bayardo Arce, Jaime Wheelock, Victor Tirado, Carlos Nuñez, Henry Ruiz, and Luis Carrión. The fact that these nine men essentially controlled Nicaragua after Somoza's downfall meant that, even though dictatorship had been destroyed, people in Nicaragua had not been able to escape, in the words of Ramírez, "their authoritarian faith."[28]

The country's foreign policy, too, was determined by a small team of six or five Sandinistas, who had weekly meetings to analyze global politics, discuss problems, and make key decisions. This foreign affairs committee consisted of three FSLN comandantes, namely Arce, who also supervised the FSLN's DRI, junta member Daniel Ortega, and—if necessary—his brother Humberto Ortega, who presided over the newly established Sandinista army, the Ejército Popular Sandinista (EPS). The other three members of the group were Miguel d'Escoto, his vice minister Victor Hugo Tinoco Fonseca, and the head of the DRI, a position first held by ex-guerrilla Doris Tijerino until Julio López Campos replaced her in September 1980. Two newly created institutions, namely the Ministerio del Exterior, part of the government, and the DRI, which belonged to the FSLN, implemented the decisions and recommendations of the commission. According to Tinoco, the members of

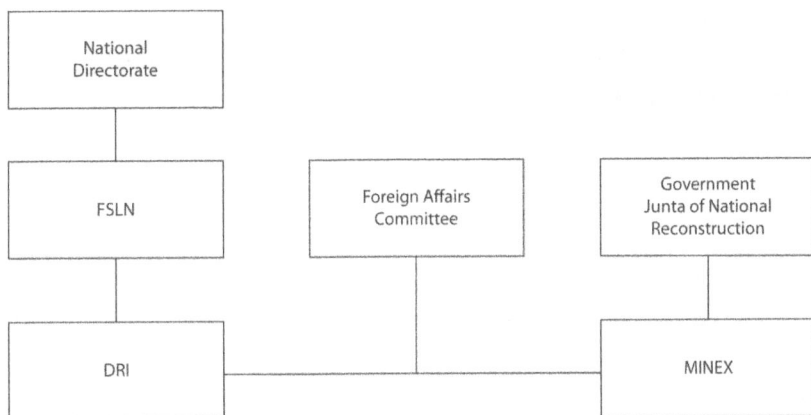

FIGURE 4. This chart gives an overview of how the Nicaraguan government's foreign policy apparatus functioned after the revolution's triumph. Both the DRI (responsible for the FSLN's relations with political parties, the solidarity committees, and national liberation movements) and MINEX (responsible for Nicaragua's relations with national governments and international organizations) received directions from the Foreign Affairs Committee.

this commission treated each other as equals, and decisions about the country's foreign policy were made as a collective (figure 4).[29]

In the first months following the overthrow of Somoza, Nicaraguan diplomats used the pluralistic composition of the junta to the revolution's advantage. In meetings with Western diplomats, Nicaraguan leaders constantly underlined the moderate nature of the revolution, while at the same time making clear that future democratic development depended on the arrival of sufficient economic and technical aid to rebuild the country. Indeed, Ramírez reflects in his memoirs, "the game consisted of denying the identity of the FSLN as a Marxist-Leninist party to both friends and enemies."[30] In that vein, on 21 July 1979, comandante Tomás Borge—who was known as a staunch communist—greeted U.S. ambassador Lawrence Pezzullo at the airport. The decision of the revolutionary regime to send Borge, Pezzullo explained to the State Department, was a "significant gesture" since the Sandinistas had clearly selected the individual "most suspect to [the U.S.] and had him carry the olive branch."[31] Moreover, when Borge asked the United States for technical and military aid, he told Pezzullo that the Nicaraguan government "shared the democratic principles valued by the U.S."[32] In Western Europe, too, Eduardo Kühl, who traveled through the region to represent the revolutionary government in July and August 1979, explained several times that "all political orientations were represented in the junta."[33]

And to further assuage Western European concerns about the possibility of radicalization, Kühl promised there would be "no revenge on the Iranian pattern" and stressed that Nicaraguans would "not seek to export their revolution" to their neighboring countries.[34] Conscious that Western officials would draw comparisons between Nicaragua and other revolutionary transformations in the Global South—which often had significant international and Cold War implications—the FSLN thus underlined its singularity. Accordingly, the Sandinistas distanced themselves from Iran, where tribunals had ordered the execution of thousands of alleged enemies of the 1979 revolution. In Nicaragua, members of the National Guard were imprisoned or fled the country, but no mass executions took place, and indeed the FSLN abolished the death penalty in August 1979.

Sandinista revolutionaries were also in no hurry to establish diplomatic relations with the Soviet Union, which had done virtually "nothing" to contribute to the Sandinista victory.[35] True, Leonid Brezhnev warmly welcomed the Sandinista victory in a celebratory speech on 20 July 1979, but the two states only established official relations on 19 October, three months after the revolution's triumph. Moreover, while all five members of the Nicaraguan junta visited the White House on 24 September 1979, the revolutionaries waited until March 1980 to send an official—and smaller—delegation to the Eastern bloc. In the highly polarized Cold War context, this was a cautious maneuver. The Sandinistas' attitude of distance toward the Soviet bloc was more than a tactical move to avoid criticism, though. Financially, there was also little to gain in the Soviet Union, as Brezhnev was reluctant to provide Nicaragua with large amounts of aid. Indeed, as historian Danuta Paszyn argues, Moscow initially took a "cautious approach towards revolutionary Nicaragua [since] one Cuba in Latin America was enough for the USSR."[36]

Behind the scenes, the Cuban government played a prominent role in helping the new revolutionary state manage its relations with the Western world.[37] Notably, Ernesto Alomá Sánchez, who as noted pushed Nicaragua to join the NAM, was a Cuban national who had joined the Nicaraguan foreign ministry in July 1979. Moreover, on the advice of Fidel Castro, the FSLN appointed Bernardino Larios Montiel, a former officer in Somoza's National Guard, as the country's new defense minister. Larios had deserted from the Nicaraguan military in the months leading up to Somoza's fall, and his appointment served as a demonstration of the FSLN's commitment to political pluralism, as well as its willingness to cooperate with their former enemies. However, as Raúl Castro explained to the Soviet ambassador in

Cuba, Vitaly Vorotnikov, on 1 September 1979, Montiel's role was "mostly for show" since "all real power in this area" belonged to Sandinista comandante Humberto Ortega, and the EPS was "being built without [Larios's] knowledge."[38] Larios's participation in the new Nicaraguan government did not last long, as he was imprisoned several months later, accused of conspiring against the revolution. He was officially replaced by Humberto Ortega.

Moreover, Raúl Castro told Vorotnikov, the National Directorate, following the advice of Fidel Castro, appointed several popular religious figures to Nicaragua's revolutionary cabinet, such as foreign minister Miguel d'Escoto—who Raúl described as one of the few "red priests" in Latin America—and minister of culture Ernesto Cardenal, the liberation theologian who had traveled extensively through Western Europe prior to Somoza's fall.[39] The Cuban ambassador to Sweden, Quintin Pino Machado, too, according to Eduardo Kühl, urged the Sandinistas on 20 July 1979 to be extremely cautious while implementing their revolutionary plans, stressing the need to prevent foreign intervention and isolation, as had happened to his own country.[40] By assisting the Sandinistas, then, deputy foreign minister Pelegrín Torras told Bayardo Arce on 6 February 1980, the Cuban government hoped to prevent the FSLN from making "the same mistakes" that they had made in the first years after Fidel Castro's triumph.[41] Memories of what had happened to Cuba in the early 1960s, and ideas about how this could have been prevented, thus had a significant impact on the Sandinistas' revolutionary diplomacy.

In sum, the Sandinistas' revolutionary diplomacy mixed optimism about a new global order with a pragmatic assessment of the international system as they found it. On the one hand, the FLSN tried to maintain the image it had created for itself during the struggle against Somoza, hoping to obtain economic aid, win hearts and minds in the Western world, and not give potential enemies a reason to threaten the Nicaraguan Revolution. On the other hand, Sandinista leaders clearly operated under the assumption that Third World national liberation movements were on the rise and that, in the long run, a conflict with the imperialists could simply not be avoided. We might have "tranquility" now, Bayardo Arce predicted soon after Somoza's fall, but this situation could not "last forever" because, at some point in the future, the "sovereignty" of Nicaraguan people would certainly clash with the demands of the capitalist system.[42] Before such a clash could occur, however, the FSLN comandantes first needed to consolidate power and build an effective state. And for this purpose, the international community and its response to the revolutionary regime were deemed pivotal.

On 19 July 1979, when the Sandinistas entered Managua, Eduardo Ramón Kühl was already on his way to Sweden to attend a Socialist International conference. His invitation to the meeting, Kühl recalls, was arranged by West German social democrats, who were interested in the young Nicaraguan because of his German heritage and affiliation with the anti-Somoza movement.[43] The mission in Stockholm was simple: to mobilize support for the armed struggle against Somoza and to push for international recognition of the junta. It was only upon his arrival at the airport that an exhausted Kühl received the news of the revolution's victory, as jubilant delegates Olof Palme (former Swedish prime minister and leader of the country's social democratic party) and François Mitterrand (leader of the French socialist party) greeted him with celebratory bottles of champagne.[44] In the days that followed, the fall of the Somoza regime and the victory of the Sandinista revolutionaries dominated the proceedings. Kühl remembers fondly, for instance, how the delegates wanted to congratulate him and hear stories about the revolutionary victory.[45] Kühl's speech at the opening session was the "high point" of the conference, U.S. diplomat Paul Canney reported back to the State Department, describing how the "special ambassador" of the revolutionary junta "unfurled a Nicaraguan flag and was greeted by the warmest applause of the day."[46]

By pure coincidence, then, Eduardo Kühl became the first official face of the Nicaraguan Revolution in Western Europe. In July and August 1979, to take control of his country's embassies and drum up financial and political support for the new revolutionary government, he traveled to Bonn, Brussels, Oslo, Paris, and Madrid. It is worth pointing out that the first ambassador of the revolution in Western Europe was not a Sandinista. A young upper-class Nicaraguan, Kühl was more closely aligned to Robelo's MDN. "I have always been a capitalist," the coffee planter later commented in an interview with Nicaraguan newspaper *El Nuevo Diario*, "but definitely one with a strong sense of social responsibility."[47] However, in the months leading up to Somoza's fall, these political differences did not matter as much as they would in later years. Toppling the dictatorship was the key objective, Kühl remembers, and he had supported the Sandinista struggle by providing guerrillas with shelter and a place to hold their meetings.[48]

Due to the chaotic situation in Nicaragua in July and August 1979, it was difficult for the young ambassador to communicate directly with the newly installed government in Managua. To prepare for meetings and interviews,

Kühl relied on the junta's revolutionary program, the advice of Cuban ambassador Quintin Pino Machado, and, in some cases, his own creativity. According to Dutch newspaper *De Volkskrant*, Kühl proposed enthusiastically to the Socialist International conference that each Western European country could fund the construction of "a little city," including churches, schools, and hospitals. These cities would then be named after their donors, he explained, so there would be towns called "Sweden, Italy, and Holland" in Nicaragua.[49] While this was clearly not a seriously thought-out proposal, it nevertheless indicated the welcome and open embrace that the Sandinistas and their allies extended to Western Europeans after the revolution triumphed, and their invitation—albeit not yet centrally directed—to play a role in their country's future.

Kühl was a popular figure, as Western European students, diplomats, activists, politicians, and journalists were all in search of up-to-date information about the situation in Nicaragua. Government officials also kept a close eye on him, as they were anxiously trying to figure out how to respond to the revolution's triumph. True, Western European leaders welcomed the departure of Somoza, but they were concerned about the ideological path the revolutionaries wanted to follow. Due to the strong leftist orientation of many of the guerrillas, Western European politicians and civil servants had little doubt that the Soviet bloc and Cuba saw the Sandinistas' triumph as an opportunity to expand their influence in Latin America and embarrass the United States. On 18 September 1979, for example, a representative of the West German foreign office shared his view on the Nicaraguan Revolution with his EC colleagues, noting that "the prime objective of Cuba and the Eastern bloc is no doubt ... to neutralize and discredit U.S. influence in Central America."[50] Moreover, on 24 and 25 July 1979 in Dublin, at a political directors' meeting of the European Community's foreign policy arm (European Political Cooperation, EPC) concerns about growing Soviet bloc influence in Central America formed the backdrop to a discussion about the correct way of dealing with Nicaragua's revolutionary junta. Dutch official Charles Rutten, for instance, noted that "East European countries were moving to establish relations with the new Nicaraguan regime more quickly than the West."[51] In that same meeting, British political director Julian Bullard expressed concerns about the future of the revolution, arguing that the congratulatory language used by Brezhnev with regard to the overthrow of Somoza "was ominous."[52] The priority of Western European officials, then, was to make sure that Nicaragua would not drift toward Cuba and the

Eastern bloc and cause instability to the international system. Despite the Soviet Union's reluctance to become financially and politically involved in Central America, as we have seen above, the Cold War remained the dominant frame through which Western officials understood the Nicaraguan Revolution.

Despite these concerns, Kühl's comments and Sandinista assurances regarding the pluralist, democratic, and moderate nature of the revolutionary junta assured Western Europeans that the political situation in Nicaragua was, at the very least, still fluid. Optimistically, British diplomat Stephen Wall commented to Prime Minister Margaret Thatcher that the new government was "a generally moderate, broad-based team with, so far, only one Sandinista member."[53] Based on this assumption, a consensus soon emerged among Western European officials that, through friendly diplomatic relations and economic assistance, they could influence the trajectory of the revolution and keep Nicaragua out of the Soviet sphere of influence. Conscious of the popular argument that Fidel Castro's Cuba had only turned toward the Soviet Union after the West gave him the cold shoulder, European officials argued that, in the Nicaraguan case, they could prevent history from repeating itself.[54] Cuba, and readings of what had happened to it after 1959, thus provided a frame of reference both for the new Nicaraguan government and those it wished to court, inclining them to work together in the FSLN's favor.

West Germany was particularly supportive of giving further aid to Nicaragua, pushing its European allies to give generous financial support to the revolutionary junta. In a preparatory telegram for the EPC's Latin America Working Group in September 1979, the AA announced that "Germany [was] convinced that the political development of Nicaragua [was] essentially dependent on the West providing swift and effective assistance."[55] By contributing to the reconstruction effort of the Nicaraguan junta, the West German officials argued, the West could "strengthen the moderate forces in Nicaragua and increase the possibility of a more pragmatic and less ideological outlook among the forces tending towards the Left."[56] The Latin America Working Group largely adopted the position of the AA, as it recommended that the European Commission—an independent body that represented the EC as a whole, rather than the individual member states—and the nine individual EC member states should provide Nicaragua with technical, humanitarian, and economic aid, because this would "foster a political development as pluralist as possible and, in particular, less closely linked to Cuba and the Soviet Union."[57]

In addition to Cold War concerns, another reason for Helmut Schmidt's government to have an active policy toward Nicaragua, West German diplomat Herbert Limmer told U.S. officials in Bonn, was that it was seen as uncontroversial within West Germany itself. There were simply "no political groups in Germany opposing help to Nicaragua," Limmer explained, and therefore it was an "easy decision for the politicians in the cabinet to make."[58] Undoubtedly, the West German attitude toward the Nicaraguan Revolution should be seen in the context of the FSLN's revolutionary diplomacy before Somoza's fall, which mobilized thousands of activists and social democrats for the Sandinista cause. The Socialist International, for example, called on the United States and Western Europe to "urgently" send aid to the new revolutionary junta, pointing out that Nicaragua was on the brink of a humanitarian disaster.[59] Indeed, Dutch Labor Party chairman Max van den Berg announced, there was "a massive lack of medication and food" in Nicaragua, most notably "because Somoza had destroyed the entire harvest."[60] Grassroots mobilization and pro-Sandinista public opinion, then, impacted how states developed their foreign policy toward the new Nicaraguan regime.

To maintain friendly relations with the new Nicaraguan junta, the European Commission and EC member states moved quickly to make significant amounts of financial and material aid available. Less than a week after Somoza's fall, on 25 July 1979, Wilhelm Haferkampf, the vice president of the European Commission, welcomed Eduardo Kühl to Brussels, expressed support for "the economic and democratic reconstruction" of Nicaragua, and informed him of the Commission's decision to grant the country emergency aid of $270,000.[61] This was only the first of many Western European donations to the revolutionaries, as the Commission transferred around $9 million in reconstruction aid to Nicaragua in 1979, almost half of its budget for Latin America.[62] According to records of the Central Intelligence Agency, in the months following Somoza's fall West Germany was the biggest Western European donor, providing the junta with around $17 million in economic aid.[63] The Netherlands and Sweden, too, made significant contributions to the reconstruction effort, donating respectively $6.4 and $8.1 million. The British government, due to "cuts in the aid programme" under Thatcher's Conservative government, did not provide Nicaragua with bilateral aid, but contributed around $2.9 million through multilateral institutions, such as the World Bank, the Inter-American Development Bank, and the European Community.[64] In 1979, therefore, as British diplomat Alan Payne proudly concluded on 7 February 1980, the aid of "Western donors [to Nicaragua was] greater than that provided by the Eastern Bloc," a claim that was later backed up by U.S. intelligence officials.[65]

SOLIDARITY ACTIVISTS AND THE
SANDINISTA TRIUMPH

At the same time as policymakers debated the correct way of responding to the revolution's triumph, solidarity activists and exiles in Western Europe celebrated victory by organizing concerts, parties, and demonstrations marking "the liberation of Nicaragua."[66] Unsurprisingly, activists and Nicaraguan exiles were elated, as they had been working with the FSLN to isolate and overthrow the Somoza regime for years. On behalf of the Sandinistas, the Dutch Nicaragua Committee published several advertisements thanking the Dutch people for their financial assistance to the FSLN's armed struggle.[67] Excited to contribute to the revolution's success, solidarity activists announced that "their work was not yet finished."[68] After a Western European solidarity conference in Vienna, the movement announced it would now dedicate itself to spreading positive information about the Nicaraguan Revolution and, if necessary, it would "defend the revolution" from, among others, the U.S. administration, Nicaraguan opposition groups, and critical mainstream media.[69] Immediately after Somoza's overthrow, then, local solidarity committees started calling on the international community to contribute financial and material aid for the reconstruction effort. Activists Eve Hall and George Black—one of the founders of the British Nicaragua Solidarity Campaign— wrote a piece for *The Guardian* with the headline "a bleak inheritance for the teenage guerrillas" in Nicaragua. Hall and Black urged the United States and Western European countries to be more forthcoming, announcing that "the need for aid" in Nicaragua was desperate, but due to the reluctance of "Western industrialized countries and international agencies" to send "aid or even emergency supplies," these were "slow in coming."[70] Turning away from their previous focus on armed struggle and Somoza's human rights violations, activists now zoomed in on reconstruction and development.

In the months following Somoza's fall, the solidarity movement flourished. Now that the violent struggle in Nicaragua was over, political parties, newspapers, and humanitarian organizations no longer had to worry about the ethical implications of supporting an armed movement. The number of solidarity committees grew exponentially, as many Western Europeans were inspired by the Sandinistas' victory and message of national liberation, nona-lignment, and social justice.[71] Dutch solidarity committees, in cooperation with the Labor Party and the socialist television broadcaster VARA, col-lected approximately $350,000 with the purpose of "rebuilding Nicaragua" in the months after the revolution.[72] Western European politicians and jour-nalists also contributed to the popularity of the revolutionaries, describing the FSLN in positive terms. In the Netherlands, newspapers published pic-tures of FSLN fighters hugging their children "with tears of happiness" in their eyes and images of laughing Nicaraguans who were "finally free to read other newspapers than Somoza's *Novedades*."[73] Echoing the solidarity activ-ists' claims, journalists and politicians highlighted the fact that Nicaragua was in desperate need of financial and material aid. West German news magazine *Der Spiegel*, for instance, argued that the war against the dictator-ship had "left such deep wounds" that the country simply could not recover "without outside help."[74] The media, then, amplified the message of the soli-darity committees, thereby contributing to the success of the FSLN's revolu-tionary diplomacy in the months following Somoza's fall.

Yet, below the surface, the revolution's victory in Nicaragua also signified a difficult period of reorientation, discussion, and frustration. Crucially, most Nicaraguan exiles and Sandinista representatives in Western Europe returned to Nicaragua after Somoza's fall, including Enrique Schmidt Cuadra, his wife María Victoria Urquíjo Nuño, and Ángel Barrajón. Those who decided to stay behind often took up diplomatic posts for the new government and con-sequently had less time for solidarity work. For instance, the Sandinista rep-resentative in the United Kingdom, Tomás Arguello Chamorro, became the chargé d'affaires of the Nicaraguan embassy in London.[75] The departure of many Nicaraguan exiles, combined with the absence of direct lines of communication with Managua, meant that the movement existed in what solidarity activists described as "a vacuum" in the weeks following the revolu-tion.[76] Indeed, Klaas Wellinga, Hermann Schulz, and William Agudelo (a Colombian poet and friend of Ernesto Cardenal) wrote to the representatives of national solidarity committees on 1 August 1979 that it was unclear what "type of support" the Sandinistas needed now that Somoza was out of the picture. Therefore, they recommended, Western European solidarity activists simply had to improvise and wait until their compañeros in Nicaragua pro-vided them with more detailed information.[77]

Another issue that the solidarity movement confronted was the question of how the FSLN victory would change the nature of their work. Overall, activists agreed that solidarity activism was much more "political" than the work of developmental and human rights organizations, and therefore solidarity committees wanted to do more than simply help with the financial aspects of reconstruction.[78] In West Germany, Ernesto Medina, a Nicaraguan doctoral student based in Göttingen, stressed that solidarity activism was not about "progressive forces" sending "developmental aid" to an oppressed people. Rather, he argued, solidarity between West Germany and Nicaragua should be an equal "partnership" with a "common objective."[79] It was, however, not always clear what this partnership should look like now that the Sandinistas were in power. Did this mean support for the FSLN, the revolutionary junta, or the Nicaraguan people as a whole? Should solidarity committees start assisting guerrilla movements in neighboring Central American countries, such as El Salvador, or should they focus on changing the political situation in Western Europe, too?

Some committees wanted to focus on the latter, such as the Wageningen committee in the Netherlands, which believed that the priority of solidarity activists should be to raise "political awareness" among the Dutch population. These activists from Wageningen, however, were a minority, heavily criticized for their "lack of loyalty" to the Sandinistas.[80] In fact, most solidarity activists agreed with Ernesto Medina, who argued strongly in favor of a close relationship with the FSLN, noting that a "large majority of the people" in Nicaragua "support" and "trust" the Sandinista leaders. Solidarity with the Nicaraguan Revolution, Medina pointed out, meant that committees should "support and respect" the decisions and leadership of the Sandinista comandantes.[81] After some weeks of discussion, therefore, the Western European solidarity movement decided that it would "unconditionally" support the FSLN by, among other things, publishing propaganda, defending the revolution from "bourgeois" attacks, and fundraising for Sandinista reconstruction projects.[82]

In practice, it turned out that these decisions were difficult to implement. As Bayardo Arce told Hans Langenberg during a visit to the Netherlands in March 1980, the FSLN was in a different position than prior to Somoza's fall. Now that they were in power, Arce explained, it was crucial for Sandinistas to build connections with Western European politicians and governments, and the collaboration between the solidarity movement and the Sandinistas could simply not continue "on [an] equal footing."[83] Arce felt the need to point this out as he was disappointed by the welcome the Nicaraguan delegation received from the Dutch solidarity activists who had been tasked with organizing the visit. Arce had hoped for the solidarity committee to have arranged meetings with high-ranking Dutch government officials. They had largely failed to do so, however, focusing instead on small-scale events with Third World activists and other grassroots organizations. Moreover, the Nicaraguans were dissatisfied with the Dutch activists' proposal that junta member Sergio Ramírez, who was also part of the delegation, could travel to The Hague, the Dutch seat of government, in Langenberg's private car, a red Peugeot 304. A black Mercedes-Benz, the Nicaraguans believed, would have been much more appropriate in this situation.

While the revolutionaries were hoping for more formality, then, the Dutch were expecting a continuation of the intimate relationship between solidarity groups and FSLN representatives that had existed prior to the revolution's triumph. In the end, the Nicaraguans and activists reached a compromise, and they rented a black Ford Taurus. Moreover, after finding out about the visit, the Dutch government spontaneously reached out to the Sandinista delegation, and Arce and Ramírez spoke with development minister Jan de Koning about the country's financial needs.[84] Next to demonstrating the FSLN's new priorities after the revolution's triumph, stories like these also highlight the extent to which the Sandinistas' revolutionary diplomacy was improvised in the revolution's early months. In the future, the FSLN would not repeat the mistake of leaving a solidarity group in charge of organizing such an important visit.

Unsurprising as Arce's abovementioned comments to Langenberg might have been considering the enormous challenge that the FSLN faced at home and in the international arena, Western European activists soon became irritated with what they perceived as the Sandinistas' lack of interest in the solidarity movement. The FSLN leadership, the activists believed, did not fully understand how important the solidarity movement remained for the revolution's future success and consolidation. In particular, solidarity groups were convinced that they could play a vital role presenting the FSLN in a positive light to Western audiences, as well as raise substantial funding from non-governmental sources. In October 1979, George Black wrote to Doris Tijerino, the head of the DRI, and told her that it was currently impossible for British committees to defend the revolution against the increasingly critical Western press. The solidarity magazine *Nicaragua Libre*, he explained, could only communicate the "true facts" about the Sandinista Revolution to the British people if the FSLN provided the committees with regular updates and Nicaraguan newspapers, such as the Sandinista newspaper *Barricada*.[85] Moreover, on 28 September 1979, at the first Western European conference since the revolution's triumph, solidarity activists constantly criticized what they saw as the FSLN's passive attitude toward the movement. On several occasions, European representatives asked Silvia McEwan and María Victoria Urquíjo, the two Sandinista diplomats who had traveled from Managua to the West German town of Herdecke for the conference, if the FSLN leaders even considered the solidarity movement to be "important" for the revolution's future.[86] And while the Nicaraguans answered affirmatively, the lack of communication from the FSLN toward the solidarity committees in the months that followed suggested that the Sandinistas did, in fact, have other priorities.

In sum, the overthrow of Somoza opened a new realm of possibilities for the FSLN in Western Europe. News of the Sandinista triumph turned Nicaragua into front page news, the Socialist International was keen to contribute to the success of the revolution, and Western European governments provided the new government with money, advice, and material aid. Unsurprisingly, this influx of international interest and support for Nicaragua also meant that Sandinista revolutionaries had less time for and interest in solidarity activism. Confronted with the enormous task of creating a strong and legitimate revolutionary state, the Nicaraguan revolutionaries considered building fruitful alliances with governments and political parties to be more important than providing solidarity activists with information on the inner workings of their government. This change in the FSLN's position after a period of close cooperation between the Sandinistas and the solidarity movement in the period leading up to Somoza's fall frustrated the activists, who remained convinced of their own political significance. Yet, at a time when the Nicaraguan government was in desperate need of financial aid to rebuild the country after years of revolutionary war, the Sandinistas' focus on state relations made sense; governments and international institutions could simply offer much more money.

## THE LITERACY CRUSADE

If international legitimacy and popularity mattered for the new regime, the FSLN was primarily interested in consolidating the revolution at home, seeking to implement its political program as soon as possible. Less than one month after Somoza's fall, the Nicaraguan junta appointed Jesuit priest and liberation theologian Fernando Cardenal as the coordinator of the Cruzada Nacional de Alfabetización (National Literacy Crusade), a highly successful campaign that radically transformed the country's political and educational culture, mobilizing many young Nicaraguans for the revolution. Echoing Cuba's own literacy campaign two decades before, from March to August 1980 somewhere between sixty and a hundred thousand Nicaraguan teenagers traveled to the countryside to teach around four hundred thousand Nicaraguans to read and to write in Spanish. These young brigadistas, according to official estimations, reduced the illiteracy rate from 50.35 percent to 12.96 percent.[87]

For the Nicaraguan revolutionaries, the literacy campaign was part of the process of national liberation. Already in 1969, when the FSLN's historic program was first published, Sandinista guerrillas promised that the Revolución Popular Sandinista would "push forward a massive campaign to immediately wipe out illiteracy."[88] Teaching Nicaraguan people to read and write, campaign coordinator Fernando Cardenal writes in his memoirs, was in itself a revolutionary act because under the Somoza regime "literacy was subversive and communist" and therefore discouraged.[89] In revolutionary Nicaragua, by contrast, education would be part of a process that transformed people's lives, raised political consciousness, and encouraged campesinos to become active participants in the reconstruction of the country. Bayardo Arce described the crusade as "a strategic task to consolidate our revolution."[90] The aim of the literacy crusade, then, was not only to fight illiteracy, but also to teach Nicaraguan campesinos how to "read their reality" and involve them in the revolutionary process.[91] Through education, Fernando Cardenal explains, the Nicaraguan people would lose their ignorance and understand that poverty was not "produced by nature, but [by] the actions of human beings, that is, those who have economic and political power."[92]

The plan for a literacy crusade was not new. To a significant extent, the Sandinista project was shaped by the ideas of Brazilian education scholar Paulo Freire, who wrote his famous *Pedagogy of the Oppressed* based on his own experiences teaching adults in Brazil.[93] According to Freire, rather than simply transferring "knowledge" to marginalized communities, education should encourage oppressed people to become independent thinkers, "critically conscious" of their environment, and therefore able to change the societal structures of oppression. In October 1979, at the invitation of Fernando Cardenal, Freire, who also worked as special adviser for the World Council of Churches, went to Nicaragua to assist the Sandinistas, and encouraged them to approach the nationwide education project as a political event with pedagogical implications, rather than the other way around.[94] Moreover, the revolutionaries' resolve to wage a literacy crusade in Nicaragua was shaped by their impressions of Fidel Castro's successful campaign of 1961, when a hundred thousand young Cubans reduced the country's illiteracy rate to 3.9 percent and, as historian Lillian Guerra writes, "lifted the prestige of the revolution to unprecedented levels."[95] The Cuban literacy project, Fernando Cardenal remembers, "struck great admiration and enthusiasm in me."[96] Hoping to learn from the Cuban example, Cardenal traveled to Cuba in September 1979, where he spoke to literacy experts and conducted research in the archives of the Museo Nacional de la Alfabetización. At Cardenal's request, several Cuban experts such as Raúl Ferrer, the Cuban vice minister of education, visited Nicaragua to provide the campaign organizers with technical and strategic support.[97]

The literacy crusade was an expensive and ambitious endeavor, even though most of the teachers were volunteers. Teaching brigades needed clothing, pens, backpacks, hammocks, medicine, books, food, transport, and training. In addition, the campaign coordinators needed money to cover administrative costs, arrange transportation, and set up an emergency response system. Overall, the organizers calculated that around $20 million was necessary to fund the entire literacy crusade. To cover these costs, the Nicaraguan government launched a fundraising and publicity campaign. In Nicaraguan cities and towns, Sandinista groups organized parades, debates, raffles, music festivals, and poster sales to generate interest and funding for the literacy crusade.[98]

The appalling financial situation in which Nicaragua found itself, however, meant that most of the money had to come from abroad. The international community, the FSLN realized, was needed to make the literacy crusade a success. In the months leading up to the crusade, Sandinista diplomats, ministers, junta members, and comandantes traveled extensively around Europe and the Americas to raise funds and material contributions, meeting with government officials, solidarity activists, unions, church groups, and journalists. Crucially, in February and March 1980, a Nicaraguan delegation consisting of Sandinista comandante Omar Cabezas, church representative Edwin Maradiaga, and literacy crusade coordinator Francisco Lacayo spent thirty days in Western Europe in search of international support. This publicity journey, Fernando Cardenal remembers, turned out "to be key because they returned with enough money to cover the remaining expenses of the campaign."[99]

To mobilize as many groups, institutions, and governments as possible for the crusade, the Nicaraguan government and its allies employed a range of arguments and strategies. Once again, Sandinistas used Cold War rivalries for the revolution's benefit. In March 1980, the Nicaraguan government simultaneously sent representatives to both sides of the Iron Curtain. At the same time as Sergio Ramírez and Bayardo Arce visited Belgium, the Netherlands, Austria, and West Germany, comandante Tomás Borge and junta member Moisés Hassan spoke to politicians in East Germany, the Soviet Union, Czechoslovakia, and Bulgaria. By so doing, the FSLN reinforced the rivalry that existed between East and West, creating a sense that both capitalist and socialist countries could influence the future course of the revolution through donations and assistance. As a steering brief from the British FCO noted in 1980, the Nicaraguans "often remarked that if they could not find the necessary resources in the West, they would be forced to look to the East."[100] Undoubtedly, this was a smart strategy, as one of the primary motivations for Western European governments to support the literacy crusade was to "compete" with the Cubans and Soviets over influence in Nicaragua.[101] The European Community, for instance, financed the participation of two hundred Costa Rican teachers in the literacy crusade because this would contribute "to the general desire not to leave the effort entirely to the Cubans."[102]

By requesting financial and material aid from Cuba, the Soviet Union, the United States, Venezuela, Mexico, the Nordic countries, and the EC member states, the Sandinista government not only obtained significant amounts of financial support, but also strengthened its international image as a nonaligned state whose revolution transcended the bipolarity and polarization of the Cold War conflict. In speeches and interviews, the Nicaraguan revolutionaries pointed out that the literacy campaign had obtained aid and support from governments from across the political spectrum, and that it had received a prestigious UNESCO literacy award. Sergio Ramírez, during the celebratory closing ceremony of the crusade in Managua on August 1980, highlighted that it had been supported by a wide range of governments, including Mexico, the Netherlands, Cuba, Spain, the Soviet Union, the Federal Republic of Germany, and the German Democratic Republic.[103] Educators and volunteers from all around the world, Ramírez stressed, came to Nicaragua to reduce illiteracy, including from Canada, West Germany, Mexico, Peru, and Czechoslovakia.[104] That Rodrigo Carazo, the Costa Rican president, was the guest of honor at the closing ceremony also served as a powerful demonstration that the Nicaraguan Revolution had the support of its Central American neighbors.[105]

To make the crusade appear attractive and uncontroversial to Western European peoples and governments, representatives of the Nicaraguan government generally presented it as a humanitarian project that needed practical assistance. When Nicaraguan organizers realized that many older campesinos were unable to participate in the campaign due to visual impairments, for instance, they mobilized the solidarity movement to organize collections for second-hand glasses.[106] The Nicaraguan embassy in London, too, published flyers and sent out letters asking for donations, noting that £2.50 would provide students with a classroom, £5.00 with a school desk, and £80 would "finance a literacy teacher in the countryside."[107] The "ability to read and write," the flyers pointed out in a rather paternalistic manner, was "taken for granted in a developed Western country like Britain" but unfortunately was "a privilege of the few in Latin America."[108] Similarly, on 26 February 1980, Tomás Arguello Chamorro and Edwin Maradiaga argued to British officials that, in addition to increasing literacy, the crusade would improve the country's health care and agricultural production. By contributing to the crusade, the Nicaraguan representatives stressed, the United Kingdom "would be helping maintain and develop human rights in Nicaragua, as well as helping the country's social and economic reconstruction."[109] Finally, in the Netherlands, Francisco Lacayo told reporters that, in addition to teaching the campesinos to read and write in Spanish, the young volunteer teachers—also known as brigadistas—would contribute to the fight against malaria in the countryside.[110] By cloaking the literacy campaign in the universal and seemingly apolitical language of development and human rights, then, the FSLN managed to appeal to a wide range of audiences.

What is more, the Sandinista effort to present the literacy campaign as part of the larger reconstruction effort after Somoza's fall functioned as a counterweight to accusations that the campaign was being used for ideological indoctrination. On 10 December 1979, the *Daily Telegraph* in the United Kingdom announced that Cuba was sending "scores of intelligence agents and hundreds of Communist ideological cadres" to revolutionary Nicaragua. While the "ostensible purpose is to help Nicaragua carry out a crash literacy drive," the newspaper commented, it is clear "that the teachers will be more concerned with political indoctrination."[111] Some politicians and government officials in Western Europe, too, expressed concerns about the content of the teaching materials and the Cuban involvement in the crusade, noting for example that the literacy campaign's reader *El Amanecer del Pueblo* (Dawn of the People) focused too heavily on the revolution's heroes Augusto

Sandino and Carlos Fonseca, the agrarian reform program, and the FSLN's vanguard position. Nicaraguan representatives, however, fiercely denied these claims, even though there was a clear political component to their campaign, as we have seen above. Edwin Maradiaga told British officials in London that "ideological indoctrination" was simply not the crusade's purpose and that "reports in the *Daily Telegraph* to this effect were quite false."[112] Fernando Cardenal, too, lamented that the "enemies of the revolution" had falsely accused the Cubans of "brainwashing Nicaraguan children."[113]

Despite these minor setbacks, the literacy crusade mobilized a wide range of actors for the Sandinista project. On 29 March 1980, at the first British solidarity conference for Nicaragua, which focused on literacy, several organizations with diverging—but still mostly leftist—political orientations spoke out in support of the revolution, including the national Labour Party, War on Want, Oxfam, the World University Service, Christian Aid, and the Chile Solidarity Campaign. Several labor union councils and local political groups also sent delegates, such as the Chilean far left party the Movimiento de Izquierda Revolucionaria, the Hackney Teachers' Association, and the Northampton Labour Party.[114] Indeed, Western European organizations from across the political spectrum were jubilant about the literacy drive. Christian Aid, for example, a developmental agency of around forty Irish and British churches that contributed £30,000, commented in its newsletters that there "was enormous enthusiasm for the crusade" to "fight ignorance" in Nicaragua, noting that "even the matchboxes and beer bottle tops carried words and letters for the people to learn!"[115] Solidarity committees, too, dedicated themselves to the crusade by, among other things, encouraging Western Europeans to organize information evenings and providing volunteers with movies, slides, and booklets on the literacy project.[116]

Yet the Sandinistas' portrayal of the crusade as a humanitarian project does not fully explain why it succeeded in mobilizing such a broad range of actors for the Nicaraguan Revolution. Rather, the key to the success of the Sandinista literacy campaign among Western European solidarity activists and grassroots organizations was the fact that it allowed for a variety of interpretations of the Nicaraguan Revolution and its objectives. Different organizations were able to frame and understand the crusade in such a way that it matched their own interests and ideologies. For example, solidarity committees and church groups had different political agendas, but both found convincing reasons to support the Sandinistas' educational project. Church organizations were more interested in the religious and social justice components of the literacy crusade and the Nicaraguan Revolution. Christian Aid, for example, published a booklet on the contribution of the church to "Nicaragua libre." Instead of focusing on militancy, class struggle, and the FSLN comandantes, it quoted Ernesto Cardenal as saying that the Nicaraguan Revolution was a "human revolution" that carried "a deep sign of Christian love." Church groups in Nicaragua, the booklet pointed out, "are now in a position to make an important contribution to the transformation of society."[117] Solidarity committees, on the other hand, largely ignored the religious aspects of the literacy drive, including the fact that it was called a crusade, a word with clear Christian connotations. Instead, they focused on the political context and "military model" of the literacy crusade, analyzing the many parallels between the guerrilla struggle against the Somoza regime in the past, and the work of "literacy militias" in the "war against ignorance" in the present.[118] The primary goal of the literacy crusade, in the eyes of the Sandinistas' Western European allies, was to mobilize the campesinos for the Sandinista Revolution, thereby strengthening the domestic position of the FSLN (figure 5). In his 1981 book *Triumph of the People*, for example, George Black argued that the literacy campaign helped to consolidate the revolution, as it united the FSLN with the country's young urban elites as well as with the people living in the countryside.[119]

Overall, the Nicaraguan effort to use the international community for the literacy crusade's success went well. The revolutionaries mobilized a wide range of international actors for their cause, such as UNESCO, the solidarity movement, the World Council of Churches, and various governments from the Americas and Europe. As Nicaraguan education minister Carlos Tünnermann Bernheim announced in September 1980, a high percentage of the total costs of the literacy campaign was "financed with donations [from] the international community."[120] Indeed, on 7 March 1980, European Commissioner Claude Cheysson assured Sergio Ramírez and Bayardo Arce that the European Community would contribute $2.6 million, to be used for teaching materials and food aid (rice and red beans).[121] And on 11 March 1980, at a pro-Sandinista concert at the Vredenburg music hall in Utrecht, representatives of the Dutch Nicaragua Committee presented Sergio Ramírez with a check for $250,000 to fund the literacy campaign.[122] Even the British government, despite massive cuts to the international development budget under Thatcher, contributed to the campaign by purchasing £20,000 worth of first aid kits for Nicaraguan schools.[123] The British public, however, was less keen to contribute to the crusade. On 9 June 1980, Tomás Arguello

FIGURE 5. A poster produced by the NKN promotes an event to celebrate the Nicaraguan literacy campaign in Utrecht. Showing two young Nicaraguans carrying pencils (as opposed to guns), the poster describes the campaign as the "second war of liberation from the Somoza legacy" and mentions it will bring "awareness and real democracy" to Nicaragua. Highlighting how much importance the FSLN attached to the campaign's international dimensions, the event in the Netherlands was attended by junta member Sergio Ramírez, comandante Bayardo Arce, and the singer Carlos Mejía Godoy with his band Los de Palagcaguïna. Photo: Nicaragua Komitee Nederland, International Institute of Social History, Amsterdam.

Chamorro told FCO official Geoffrey Cowling that the British campaign to raise money had "produced only £800" in the last three or four months, which was a "fairly low" sum, especially "when compared to the money raised by his counterparts in other parts of Europe."[124] While it is difficult to trace the exact reasons for this apparent lack of British generosity, it is worth noting here that the British solidarity movement (until 1983) was significantly smaller and less centralized than the Dutch and German organizations, which might have limited the NSC's ability to raise money.

### THE ANTI-SOMOZA MOVEMENT BREAKS APART

The literacy crusade succeeded in mobilizing the Nicaraguan population and the international community for the revolution, but the FSLN could not keep together the broad and politically diverse coalition that had caused Somoza's departure. Ultimately, different visions about what the revolution should look like, how it should be carried out, and who its allies were caused tensions between the Sandinistas and their former allies from the country's elite families. In April 1980, Violeta Chamorro and Alfonso Robelo, the two junta members who represented the private sector, stepped down. While Chamorro cited health reasons for her resignation, Robelo openly accused FSLN leaders of violating their promises on democracy and argued that the Sandinistas were turning Nicaragua into a Marxist state. After his resignation, Robelo became a well-known spokesperson for the anti-Sandinista cause, traveling to cities in the Americas and Western Europe to speak about the "Marxist-Leninist influence which came from the Sandinista Directorate."[125] On 14 May 1980, Robelo told British official Geoffrey Cowling, who was visiting Managua, that the Sandinistas had turned Nicaragua into "a battleground for superpower ideology." Indeed, Cowling reported back to the FCO, Robelo was "depressed at the injection of class hatred into internal politics by the Directorate, something they had never had in Nicaragua, even in Somoza's time."[126] In April 1980, Eduardo Kühl, who had returned to northern Nicaragua to manage his coffee farm after the revolution's triumph, also encouraged Western European officials to remind the FSLN that efforts to "suppress other viewpoints would place in jeopardy the economic support which, for example, the European Community had given."[127] In addition, members of the clergy started to speak out against the Sandinista movement using anticommunist language, such as the Catholic archbishop of Managua, Miguel Obando y Bravo, who accused the Sandinistas of waging "a Marxist ideological campaign."[128] Finally, the newspaper *La Prensa*, which had played a crucial role in the struggle against the Somoza regime but had started to criticize the revolution soon after the Sandinista triumph, closed down for a couple days in April 1980, blaming "government intimidation."[129]

The revolutionaries' response to growing polarization in Nicaragua had two somewhat contradictory components. On the one hand, FSLN comandantes and the Sandinista newspaper *Barricada* spoke in harsh terms about Obando y Bravo and Robelo, describing opposition figures as *vendepatrias* (traitors) and counterrevolutionaries. Publicly, the Sandinistas and their allies linked Robelo and the MDN to Somoza, international capital, and U.S. imperialism. The Nicaraguan ambassador in London, Gonzalo Murillo Romero, described the MDN as a "conservative party made up of privileged groups who had accrued wealth under Somoza."[130] Western European activists, too, considered accusations against the Sandinistas as a predictable response of conservative and reactionary groups to the "consolidation of the revolution" and the "intensification of the class struggle" in Nicaragua.[131] In journals and pamphlets published by solidarity committees, opposition figures were portrayed as enemies of the revolution. In *Nicaragua Today*, for instance, the NSC accused opposition parties, such as the MDN, the Democratic Conservative Party, and the Social Christian Party, of undermining "unity" in Nicaragua by using "their influence in local right-wing media to slander the Sandinistas" and getting business supporters to "block production and further undermine the country's economic recovery."[132] Robelo's movement, the NSC added, had only "recently been formed with U.S. guidance and finance."[133] Together with development organization Novib, the Dutch solidarity movement, too, funded a Nicaraguan comic book on the popular struggle against U.S. imperialism. In this comic—entitled *The Militia in Action*—opposition figures carrying signs calling for elections were described as "traitorous" and "friends of international imperialism."[134]

On the other hand, Sandinista comandantes showed a degree of willingness to cooperate with representatives from Nicaragua's business and religious sectors, as the FSLN needed their support for domestic stability, international legitimacy, and economic development. The National Directorate appointed two "moderate" members to replace Robelo and Chamorro on the junta, namely Arturo Cruz, the director of Nicaragua's Central Bank, and Rafael Córdova Rivas, a conservative lawyer. These appointments, the

Nicaraguan embassy in the United States announced, once again demonstrated the Sandinistas' commitment to "political pluralism" and a "policy of alliances" with a variety of "political entities" as well as "the private sector."[135] Alfonso Robelo's resignation, the Nicaraguan ambassador to the United States Rafael Solís announced in a communiqué, was "motivated by his own political ambitions" and not by the lack of political freedom in Nicaragua. Regarding composition of the Council of State, Solís continued, this "reflects the minimal control exercised by the FSLN" as it only had a 51 percent majority, which is "not a source of astonishment in Nicaragua since it is evident that the organization enjoys massive support."[136]

Sandinista diplomats tried to stop the growing domestic polarization from spilling over to Western Europe and negatively impacting the financial and political support of EC member states for the Nicaraguan Revolution. They attempted to downplay Robelo's accusations that the FSLN was turning Nicaragua into a Cold War battleground by highlighting the revolution's unique character and political pluralism. In August 1980, Nicaraguan foreign minister Miguel d'Escoto visited West Germany, where he met with FRG foreign minister Hans-Dietrich Genscher, Bundespräsident Karl Carstens, and representatives of political foundations such as the Friedrich Ebert Stiftung (linked to the SPD), the Friedrich Naumann Stiftung für die Freiheit (linked to the Free Democratic Party), and the Konrad Adenauer Foundation (linked to the Christian Democratic Union, CDU).[137] The unique revolutionary ideology of Sandinismo, d'Escoto told Genscher on 28 August 1980, was not for sale on "the international market of ideologies." Indeed, he added, unlike the "dogmatism" of previous revolutions, the Sandinista Revolution was "pluralist, moderate, and pragmatic."[139]

Nicaraguan diplomats also highlighted the importance of active Western European involvement in Central America, warning that there was a real danger that the struggle of Central American liberation movements for national self-determination would become swept up by the Cold War. Realizing that the Western Europeans had disagreed with their U.S. allies about the Vietnam War, d'Escoto warned Genscher about the possibility of the so-called "Vietnamization" of Central America. If the United States continued to "intervene" unilaterally in the region, most notably by supporting anticommunist forces in El Salvador and Guatemala, d'Escoto told Genscher, the history of the Vietnam War might repeat itself, albeit in a different part of the world. The Western Europeans could help prevent military escalation, he argued, by actively supporting the "right for self-determination" and the quest for "nonalignment" of the Central American people.[141] Strategically playing into Western European concerns about further Cold War escalations in the Global South, the Sandinistas hoped to challenge U.S. dominance in Central America.

To be sure, accusations by Sandinista comandantes and solidarity activists that armed groups and foreign powers were trying to undermine the revolutionaries' hold on power were not wrong. Immediately after the revolution's triumph, anticommunist and conservative groups in the Americas and Europe had started to channel arms and funds to the anti-Sandinista opposition. As historian Ariel C. Armony demonstrates, Argentine and Israeli intelligence officers assisted former members of Somoza's National Guard with the creation of a counterrevolutionary force in Honduras, which would later be known as the Contras.[142] In addition, the Carter administration approved $750,000 in funding to finance and assist "moderate" newspapers, political parties, and labor unions to resist attempts by "Cuban-supported and other Marxist groups to consolidate their power" over Nicaragua.[143] Undoubtedly, these foreign threats to the revolution led to increasing polarization and a hardening of positions within Nicaragua. As a U.S. intelligence daily concluded on 26 April 1980, the FSLN National Directorate had become more "intransigent" because "armed groups opposed to their rule [were] becoming increasingly active."[144]

Growing regional tensions and Cold War insecurities notwithstanding, the Sandinistas' revolutionary diplomacy convinced Western European governments that they could push the Nicaraguan junta toward establishing a nonaligned revolutionary state. On 28 February 1980, ambassador Efrain Jonckheer, who was assigned to Nicaragua, wrote to the Dutch Ministry of Foreign Affairs about what he perceived as the growing influence of the Soviet Union in the country and the decline in press freedom. While Jonckheer was not "overly optimistic" about the future trajectory of the revolution, the ambassador nevertheless recommended that the Ministry of Foreign Affairs should provide the Nicaraguan junta with aid, noting that this could be used to "carefully push" the revolutionaries toward a "more pluralist and democratic" mode of governance.[145] West German officials, too, maintained that financial support was the "only political tool" available to prevent closer alignment between Nicaragua and the Soviet bloc. As such, despite some pressure from opposition politicians, the West German cabinet did not reverse its policy of "cooperation and aid" with the Sandinista revolutionaries.[146]

D'Escoto's visit to Bonn appears to have had a particularly positive impact on the West German position. Indeed, after meeting his Nicaraguan colleague on 4 September 1980, Genscher wrote to U.S. Secretary of State Edmund Muskie about his conversations, which he said took place in a "pleasant atmosphere."[147] Concerned about a breakdown in relations between the Sandinistas and the United States, Genscher argued that the Western countries should support those forces in Nicaragua that are working for a "nonaligned" foreign policy and, he added optimistically, "Padre d'Escoto" was one of those people.[148] By this time, however, Carter was already severely disillusioned with the Sandinistas, as he had been receiving multiple reports about the FSLN's military support for the Salvadoran guerrillas. Just before leaving office in January 1981, Carter suspended all U.S. economic assistance to the Nicaraguan revolutionaries.[149] Already during the Carter years, then, Western European and U.S. foreign policies toward Nicaragua started to diverge.

Despite their efforts, the Sandinistas could not stop the growing polarization among Nicaraguan elites from affecting certain sections of Western European public opinion, as conservative officials, journalists, and politicians started to express concern at "the slide towards one party dictatorship" in Nicaragua, as well as the growing Cuban and Soviet influence in the region.[150] On 24 April 1980, Dutch newspaper *Het Parool* responded to the departure of "moderate" junta member Alfonso Robelo by publishing an article on the "rapid Cubanization" of Nicaragua.[151] In particular, Christian Democratic parties who sympathized with Robelo and opposition newspaper *La Prensa* started to use Cold War rhetoric to denounce the Nicaraguan revolutionaries.[152] On 23 September 1980, Ottfried Hennig, a prominent West German politician from the CDU, accused Genscher of "uncritically accepting the antidemocratic and Marxist-revolutionary" Sandinista government.[153] Another example is the London celebration of the anniversary of the revolution on 19 July 1980, when the NSC organized a music and poetry event at Logan Hall, University of London, which was attended by around two thousand people. Among others, the organizers had invited Tomás Arguello Chamorro, British labor organizor Arthur Scargill, Labour MP Stan Newness, representatives from Cuba, Grenada, Mexico, and Vietnam, and the poets Lynton Kwesi Johnson and Eduardo Embry.[154] FCO official Francis Trew, who attended the event, described the evening as "frightening" and "poisonous." Indeed, Trew added, he was shocked by the "revolutionary hysteria of the audience" and "sincerely hoped the Security Service" was covering the occasion "as it provided a naked glimpse of the enemy within." For Trew, this "enemy within" was the "very left wing" British and Latin American audience and particularly Arthur Scargill, who called for "a British revolution in emulation of Nicaragua's."[155] Despite attempts to stress the Nicaraguan Revolution's singularity, then, Cold War concerns—and exaggerated anxieties about armed revolution in Western Europe—increasingly shaped the way Western officials perceived the Sandinistas and their allies.

Moreover, Western European supporters of the FSLN found it difficult to explain Robelo's resignation to the Western media. In June 1980, Dutch solidarity activists Ted van Hees and Hans Langenberg concluded that Robelo's resignation had diminished the support of Christian Democratic parties for the Nicaraguan Revolution. Moreover, when the NKN sent a telex to Nicaragua to ask for more information about the political crisis, they never received a response.[156] This was a concerning development, the Dutch activists warned, particularly since in the future, right-wing parties would certainly wage a more "intensive campaign against the revolutionary process." To defend Nicaragua from any new propaganda attacks, they repeated to the Sandinistas, the FSLN should start paying more attention to the solidarity movement. Specifically, the solidarity activists wanted insider information about the decision-making processes within the Nicaraguan government, which they could use to convincingly defend these decisions to Western audiences.[157] Still, the FSLN did not seem to attach much importance to these and similar warnings from activists and continued to ignore their requests for more information and collaboration. Irritated by the Sandinistas' attitude, in March 1980 Klaas Wellinga and Hans Langenberg decided to travel to Nicaragua to convince the Sandinista leadership of their continued importance. In Managua, Bayardo Arce promised to send them a definitive answer "within two weeks" about the future role of solidarity activism. However, to the frustration of the activists—some of whom suggested they might as well "stop with solidarity work altogether"—Wellinga and Langenberg never received an answer.[158] Moreover, even though Sandinista representative Erick Blandón was traveling through Switzerland in June 1980, the FSLN did not send any representative to attend the solidarity conference in Vienna, which took place that same month.[159] The solidarity movement was at a critical juncture, and developments in the international arena in the months that followed—and the Sandinista response to them—would determine its future.

# CONCLUSION

In the months following Somoza's fall, the Sandinistas and their allies enthusiastically launched the next phase of the revolution, seeking to transform everyday life in Nicaragua by improving access to health care, food, and education, as well as building a strong and popular revolutionary state. For the FSLN, this project of national liberation was simultaneously national *and* international. The revolutionaries sought to liberate Nicaraguan campesinos through the literacy crusade, but they also understood their victory as part of a global struggle against Western imperialism, hence their support for the FMLN and collaboration with Cuba, Algeria, and the NAM. In this context, the FSLN's outreach to Western European states and people was a strategic move designed to raise much-needed funds and neutralize—at least for the time being—potential enemies. Smartly playing with East-West and North-South dynamics, the Sandinistas obtained significant amounts of financial aid and political legitimacy, as well as mobilizing a range of non-state actors for the revolution, varying from local church groups to large international organizations such as UNESCO.

In this brief but intense period following Somoza's fall, when the FSLN was busy setting up a new government and reshaping their country's domestic and international affairs, solidarity activists struggled with the Sandinistas' new set of priorities and changing attitude toward the solidarity movement. If Sandinistas and activists had cooperated on relatively equal footing before 19 July 1979, this relationship—much to the chagrin of solidarity groups—changed when the revolutionaries took charge of the Nicaraguan state. When the Sandinistas made clear that they would not provide committees with regular updates on the revolution's internal dynamics and decision-making processes, many activists—who often saw themselves as personal friends and allies of the revolutionaries—were dismayed. Driven by their own self-importance, enthusiasm, and ideological convictions, solidarity groups appeared unwilling to seriously consider the needs and priorities of the people they claimed to support, continuing to push the FSLN for recognition and attention. And while Sandinistas certainly did not ignore the activists, frustration and disillusionment within the solidarity movement was clearly growing, which only serves to highlight the crucial importance of Nicaraguan input for its continued functioning and survival. Thankfully for the activists, as the next chapter shows, the Nicaraguans changed their minds about the importance of solidarity activism after the Republican candidate Ronald Reagan won the U.S. elections in November 1980.

The FSLN's revolutionary diplomacy in the months following Somoza's fall challenges the traditional timeline that is used to make sense of the revolution's trajectory. While traditional scholarship on U.S.-Nicaraguan relations might have us believe otherwise, the Cold War was not something that Reagan imposed on the Nicaraguan Revolution after he assumed the presidency in January 1980. Before the U.S. administration changed its position on what it perceived to be the rise of communism in Central America, Sandinistas and their opponents were already engaged in domestic and international battles for hearts and minds, accusing their opponents of being either communist hardliners or imperialist aggressors. Even the literacy crusade, albeit highly popular, could not fully transcend the Cold War framework. Western European politicians, too, interpreted events in Nicaragua largely through a Cold War lens, making connections to other world-historical events with significant international consequences, such as the Cuban and Iranian revolutions and the Vietnam War. Indeed, what becomes clear from studying this transformative period in the revolution's history is that Nicaragua entered the global stage months before Reagan's ambassador to the United Nations, Jeane Kirkpatrick, declared that "Central America [was] the most important place in the world."[160] Nevertheless, as we shall see in the next chapter, the consequences of Reagan's presidency were significant, prompting the Sandinistas to develop a new and more ambitious international strategy.

# THREE

# The Revolution under Attack, 1981–1982

ON 26 JANUARY 1981, hundreds of activists and politicians from Europe and the Americas arrived in Managua to attend the First International Conference in Solidarity with Nicaragua. For the delegates, it was an impressive conference; they were received with great extravagance by the nine Sandinista comandantes of the National Directorate, who went out of their way to make the activists feel welcome, appreciated, and relevant.[1] This "remarkable political event," British solidarity magazine *Nicaragua Today* reported, was of "equal importance" to the first anniversary celebrations of the revolution's triumph.[2] The only other occasion where the entire FSLN National Directorate had come together to greet a foreign delegation, another internacionalista noted proudly, was when Fidel Castro visited Managua on 19 July 1980.[3] Raúl Guerra, the new Sandinista coordinator for the Western European solidarity movement, was quick to reject proposals of his predecessor Erick Blandón, who had wanted to transform solidarity committees into mere "cultural groups." From now on, Guerra promised, solidarity groups would be treated as if they were "big political parties."[4] More than a celebration of solidarity activism, the conference was also a call to arms. In their speeches, Sandinista officials called on activists to defend the Nicaraguan Revolution against the growing threat of imperialist aggression. Because "we are concerned about the new currents that are emerging in today's world," Sandinista comandante Bayardo Arce warned, the meeting constituted "a work session, a planning session for defense, a broad complex organization for the defense of revolutions."[5]

The solidarity conference in Managua in January 1981 marked the beginning of a more intense and violent phase in the international struggle for Nicaragua's future. In sharp contrast to what the Nicaraguan guerrillas had envisaged after the revolution's triumph, Third World countries' ambitions and aspirations to radically transform the international economic and political system lost their momentum, prestige, and persuasive power in the early 1980s.[6] Hopes for the implementation of the New International Economic Order disappeared almost entirely in August 1982 when the Mexican government, which had previously supported the revolutionaries with generous financial and material aid, defaulted on its external debt obligations and Latin America descended into a decade-long financial crisis, also known as La Década Perdida (the Lost Decade).[7] Meanwhile, the rise to power of Cold War hardliner Ronald Reagan in the United States emboldened Latin America's anticommunist regimes and threatened the survival of left-wing governments and revolutionary movements, including the Nicaraguan government and the guerrillas of the FMLN in El Salvador. Determined to "draw the line" against the spread of communism in the Western Hemisphere, the Reagan administration used military aid, financial assistance, and anticommunist propaganda to bolster the Salvadoran regime and destabilize the Nicaraguan Revolution.[8] This strong pivot in U.S. domestic politics, as this chapter demonstrates, had significant implications for the FSLN and its relations with the wider world, including Western Europe, Central America, and the Eastern bloc.

Not unrelated to these changes in the international environment was the increasingly tense, politicized, and violent situation on the ground in Nicaragua. As we have seen in the previous chapter, in 1980 the FSLN had already lost the support of several prominent anti-Somoza opposition leaders who criticized the Sandinista leadership for its alleged totalitarian tendencies. In 1981, open conflict also erupted between the FSLN and several indigenous communities living on the country's Atlantic Coast, who rejected government programs such as the literacy campaign (since there was initially no attention for indigenous languages, only Spanish) and the agrarian reform program launched in July 1981 (which ignored indigenous land claims). In this context of racial prejudices, mutual misunderstanding, and growing distrust, there were "at least 25 instances of armed combat" between Sandinista soldiers and Miskito Indian fighters between September 1981 and January 1982, as well as multiple cases of extreme violence against indigenous civilians.[9] In addition, Nicaraguan exiles based in Honduras and Miami (most of them former Somoza guardsmen) also embarked on armed opposition against the FSLN with the active backing of Honduras, Argentina, and the United States.[10] In the spring of 1982, these so-called Contra insurgents launched their first major military attack on Nicaraguan soil, blowing up several bridges near the Honduran border on 15 March 1982.[11] The Sandinistas responded by cracking down on their political opponents and declaring a state of emergency that suspended civil liberties, such as press freedom and the right to strike.[12] This, of course, provided critics of the Sandinistas, both inside and outside Nicaragua, with new evidence that the FSLN was, in fact, becoming increasingly authoritarian.

In this precarious context of growing domestic tensions and foreign intervention, the FSLN reoriented its revolutionary diplomacy. Notably, after a period of relative neglect, the Sandinistas looked toward the solidarity committees, calling on activists to build a transnational movement to defend the revolution against the threat of U.S. intervention. This so-called anti-intervention movement was an enormous success in Western Europe, where the FSLN and its allies capitalized on anti-Reagan sentiment among European audiences, most notably in the peace movement.[13] The Socialist International was also concerned about Reagan's anticommunist ambitions and set up a committee to protect the Nicaraguan Revolution from external aggression. In the early 1980s, Sandinistas successfully mobilized Western European audiences for the revolution by presenting a convincing narrative of a small Central American country seeking to defend its sovereignty against a powerful empire.

At the state level, Nicaragua continued to receive financial aid from individual Western European governments, most notably the Netherlands and France. After Reagan assumed the presidency on 20 January 1981, however, the Western European consensus regarding the right approach to the Nicaraguan Revolution broke down. While some EC leaders continued to adhere to the idea that foreign aid could keep the Sandinistas away from the Soviet bloc, others considered Nicaragua a lost cause and refused to provide the government with extra aid. French and West German attempts to solve these disagreements by proposing a regional foreign policy framework toward Central America also failed to have much of an impact, as individual EC member states disagreed on which countries should profit from any regional aid package. In addition, Central America was certainly not on the top of the European Community's priority list this period, as politicians juggled constructive responses to the Polish crisis, the deteriorating situation in the Middle East, and preparations for the upcoming follow-up Conference on Security and Cooperation in Europe in Madrid.[14] So, while Western European governments were certainly concerned that the growing unrest in Central America would transform the region into a Cold War battlefield, they could—at least for the time being—not agree on a common foreign policy to decrease tensions, nor did they share the activists' sympathy for Central American revolutionaries.

## THE RISE OF REAGAN

The Sandinistas followed the 1980 presidential campaign in the United States with great interest, as it was clear that the outcome of the election would have an enormous impact on the future of the region.[15] In campaign speeches, Ronald Reagan argued passionately that the Nicaraguan Revolution and the guerrilla struggles in El Salvador and Guatemala were examples of growing Soviet and Cuban influence in the Western Hemisphere and therefore a threat to U.S. national security. While "the Soviets and their friends are advancing" in Africa, Asia, and Latin America, Reagan told an audience of veterans on 18 August 1980, Jimmy Carter's administration remained "totally oblivious" to the fact that American power was in decline.[16] To stop the spread of communism in Central America, Republicans and their allies asserted, the United States should immediately cancel all economic aid to Nicaragua, abandon Carter's human rights principles, and drastically increase military assistance to anticommunist regimes in El Salvador, Guatemala, Argentina, and Chile.[17]

Unsurprisingly, then, Reagan's electoral victory on 4 November 1980 alarmed the Sandinistas, who believed the president-elect was a dangerous radical, incapable of adopting a nuanced approach to their revolution. On 9 January 1981, political adviser Michael Clark (the nephew of Nicaraguan foreign minister Miguel d'Escoto) sent a long memorandum on Reagan's perception of Central American affairs to Rita Delia Casco, the Nicaraguan ambassador to the Organization of American States. Reagan and his neoconservative friends, Clark asserted, believed the United States was "locked in an undeclared mortal combat" with the Soviet Union and its allies. And unlike the Carter administration, these new policymakers saw the Nicaraguan Revolution as evidence of the growing "power of the Soviet Union" in the United States' sphere of influence.[18] Francisco d'Escoto, the FSLN's temporary ambassador in Washington and Miguel d'Escoto's brother, presented a similar analysis of Reagan's thinking to the Nicaraguan foreign ministry on 17 February 1981. Diplomacy and international relations were black-and-white issues to the new administration, d'Escoto explained, and the neoconservatives' primary foreign policy objective was to halt the global "expansion of communism." The United States' president, in particular, based his foreign policy decisions on a simple slogan: "if you are not with us, you are against us." As a result of this binary Cold War thinking, d'Escoto concluded, the new administration falsely perceived Nicaragua as "a Soviet and Cuban satellite" and "a communist spearhead in Central America."[19] The Sandinistas realized that Reagan's worldview, which left no room for ideas of nonalignment and ideological pluralism, nor for the strategy of simultaneously appealing to both sides of the Iron Curtain, would have problematic implications for the FSLN's revolutionary diplomacy.

Sandinista diplomats also cautioned that Reagan's electoral victory was representative of a broader shift to the right in the inter-American system, further threatening the Nicaraguan Revolution. After participating in a session of the OAS on 19–27 November 1980, Sandinista representatives Casimero Sotelo, Saúl Arana, and Ramón Meneses warned MINEX that the "present political conjuncture" in Latin America was highly "unfavorable" for countries with socialist governments, most notably Nicaragua and Grenada, the small Caribbean island where Maurice Bishop had recently installed a left-wing government, and they predicted that "1981 will be a difficult year for our revolution." The electoral defeats of Jimmy Carter in the United States and Michael Manley (a democratic socialist) in Jamaica, they observed, "have strengthened the reactionary positions [of] fascist governments" in Latin America, such as the military regimes in Bolivia and Argentina. Further underlining that the international environment was becoming more hostile, the diplomats noted that the growing confidence of anticommunists weakened the regional standing of other "progressive" countries that had previously adopted a friendly attitude towards the Nicaraguan Revolution, such as Mexico, Ecuador and Panama.[20]

Even though Nicaraguan officials were concerned about the impact of Reagan's election, they also understood that details of U.S. foreign policy were still being formulated and, consequently, could be influenced. Undoubtedly, Clark admitted to Casco on 9 January 1981, the new president would refuse "to supply any additional bilateral aid to Nicaragua." Yet, there was an important distinction to be made between "active and passive" hostility. Indeed, Clark continued, the Reagan administration's options ranged from "a simple hands-off approach [to] covert, and perhaps overt, support for group seeking to overthrow the Sandinista-led government." Nicaragua's revolutionary diplomacy could steer the United States toward the first option, he believed, if it ensured that "no direct connection can be drawn between the foreign policy of the Soviet Union and that of Nicaragua." Moreover, Reagan should know about the massive international and domestic "backlash" against a direct U.S. intervention in Central America.[21] Francisco d'Escoto adopted a similar position, encouraging the government to propagate the revolution's message of mixed economy, democratic pluralism, and nonalignment to "seek the solidarity of the peoples of the world."[22] Sotelo, Arana, and Meneses, too, argued for a more "concrete" effort to build an international coalition in support of the revolution, stressing that this could "block the interventionist and destabilizing plans of imperialism and its allies."[23] Reagan's rise to power thus prompted the revolutionaries to reevaluate their international strategy, attaching renewed importance to solidarity activism and propaganda. The hostile campaign rhetoric in the 1980 elections, Luis Caldera from the FSLN's DRI remembers, was a reminder that activists were "important allies" in the international arena, who could help derail the United States' plans for Central America.[24]

It was in this context that Sandinista leaders presented their new international strategy and plans to undermine the United States' "campaign of economic, military, and ideological aggression" at the Managua conference in January 1981.[25] To ensure the revolution's survival in this increasingly hostile international environment, the FSLN called on solidarity committees to "channel the maximum possible material assistance" to Nicaragua so that reconstruction effort could continue. It also encouraged solidarity committees to "publish widely" the achievements and advances of the Nicaraguan revolutionaries to counteract the "lies and falsehoods" spread by "transnational press agencies and North American imperialism."[26] Finally, the Sandinistas called for the establishment of a transnational anti-intervention movement. Solidarity groups would form the backbone of the anti-intervention front, but the objective was to form alliances and build a broad network including church groups, the peace movement, labor unions, left-wing political parties, and human rights organizations.[27]

The Nicaraguan revolutionaries developed up several new initiatives to influence international public opinion in 1981. The Sandinista news agency Agencia Nueva Nicaragua (ANN), which was linked to the DRI, provided solidarity committees, politicians, and journalists with updates about the latest developments in Nicaragua.[28] Moreover, on 5 July 1981, the FSLN published the first issue of *Barricada Internacional*, a newspaper that specifically targeted solidarity committees in Europe and the Americas, and was published in both Spanish and English. The purpose of *Barricada Internacional*, the editors explained in the first edition, was to provide solidarity committees with a new "weapon" to defend the revolution against the U.S.-coordinated "campaign of misinformation and misrepresentation."[29] Finally, the Jesuit Instituto Histórico Centroamericano (Central American Historical Institute) in Managua, which targeted audiences in Europe and the Americas, published a monthly bulletin called *Revista Envío* that carried in-depth analyses of the "political, social, and economic situation" in Nicaragua.[30] These publications went a considerable way to addressing the lack of information solidarity groups had faced the previous year. However, despite these significant improvements, activists in Europe remained critical of the quality of the materials they received. In November 1981, West German and Dutch activists told Luis Caldera that the rather superficial and propagandistic *Barricada* was of "limited usefulness." It certainly did not meet the "requirements" for effective solidarity work, as committees needed extensive and multisided information to mobilize Western European audiences. In addition to ANN and *Barricada Internacional*, therefore, activists demanded copies of *El Nuevo Diario*, which they believed had a more analytical approach to the revolutionary process, as well as opposition newspaper *La Prensa*.[31]

The Sandinistas never managed to solve all communication problems with the activists, who continued to complain about receiving insufficient information from the FSLN throughout the decade. As such, solidarity activists took it upon themselves to improve the flow of information, benefiting from the fact that several solidarity activists settled in Nicaragua on a more permanent basis following the revolution's triumph. These individuals—who sometimes combined solidarity activism with work for NGOs or volunteered with grassroots Nicaraguan organizations—provided their counterparts in Western Europe with extra material, including newspapers, pamphlets and observations about everyday life under the revolution. Some national solidarity groups set up a permanent office in Managua, which greatly strengthened the lines of communication between Nicaragua and Western Europe. The Dutch committee, for instance, created an official "dependance" in Managua, which communicated with the headquarters in Utrecht via telex (a network of teleprinters that was replaced by the fax machine later in the 1980s). Depending on availability and the committee's financial situation, one or two salaried staff members worked at the Managua branch, which also helped to manage visits by Dutch politicians and, as we will see in the next chapter, assisted with the coordination of brigades and study tours to Nicaragua.[32]

Reagan's electoral victory also pushed the FSLN toward further strengthening its bilateral ties with other regional guerrilla movements, most notably the FMLN. At the same time as they were criticizing foreign intervention in Central America, then, Sandinista comandantes and solidarity activists used the Managua meeting in January 1981 to publicly align themselves with the armed struggle of the Salvadoran guerrillas. Highlighting the importance of a quick FMLN victory for the Sandinista cause, the conference's official slogan was "El Salvador Vencerá" (El Salvador shall triumph).[33] In his opening speech, Bayardo Arce emphasized the similarities between the struggles in Nicaragua and El Salvador. The people of these two Central American countries were fighting the same battle, the comandante argued, even though Nicaragua was at a more advanced stage of its revolutionary process.[34] In the final resolution, all participants declared their "unrestricted support and recognition of the just and heroic struggle being waged today by the people of El Salvador to win their freedom" and condemned the efforts of U.S. imperialism to frustrate "the legitimate aspirations of our Salvadoran brothers and sisters."[35]

The focus on El Salvador during the solidarity conference is representative of the Sandinistas' conviction that, despite the importance of diplomacy and transnational activism for the revolution's survival, Nicaragua would be best served by a second revolutionary triumph in Central America. Behind the scenes, as recent scholarship shows, Sandinista support for the FMLN went much further than declarations of solidarity. Sandinista leaders at the time denied that the Nicaraguan government was providing the Salvadoran guerrillas with arms and political support, but it is now clear that the Sandinistas helped with the preparations for what was supposed to be the final battle against the anticommunist regime, which the FMLN launched on the eve of Reagan's inauguration on 10 January 1981. With that objective, between October 1980 and January 1981, weapons from Vietnam, Ethiopia, Angola, and the Eastern bloc were shipped clandestinely via Cuba and Nicaragua to the Salvadoran insurgents.[36]

The FSLN's support for the FMLN was more than a calculated move. There was also a real sense of solidarity with the Salvadoran guerrillas and genuine concern about the human rights abuses being committed by the regime and anticommunist death squads. Following Reagan's electoral victory, violence in El Salvador had reached unprecedented heights. The

Salvadoran extreme Right, as Molly Avery points out, embarked on a "renewed campaign of terror" in this period, which included assassinations of left-wing political leaders and the murder of Catholic missionaries from the United States.[37] In addition, the left-wing insurgents in El Salvador had also assisted the anti-Somoza struggle in 1979 by sending "money and fighters" to Nicaragua, ensuring the Sandinistas "felt a moral debt to their revolutionary counterparts."[38] Referring to Ronald Reagan's military support for the Salvadoran armed forces, therefore, Arce told solidarity activists in Managua that "an individual who claims to be a defender of human rights has just donated 10 million dollars' worth of weapons to the mass killers in El Salvador who last year put to death over 15,000 Salvadorean brothers."[39] The FSLN's support for the FMLN was thus motivated by a mixture of ideological, moral, and pragmatic reasoning.

In hindsight, the Sandinistas' clandestine support for the FMLN might appear like a miscalculation. Not only did the final offensive in January 1981 fail to bring about revolutionary change before the Reagan administration started to channel massive amounts of military aid to the Salvadoran government, but it also provided Reagan and his allies with an excuse to launch a counterrevolutionary campaign against the Nicaraguan government and cut off economic aid. Yet, at a time when regional anticommunists were growing more confident and powerful, this was a gamble the FSLN was willing to make. Sandinista comandante Jaime Wheelock, for example, told Western European solidarity activists in Managua that the position of the Nicaraguan Revolution would be much stronger once the situation in El Salvador was "resolved in favor of the revolutionaries," predicting that El Salvador would become Nicaragua's most important regional partner.[40]

Similarly, despite initially adopting a cautious attitude toward the Soviet Union, the Sandinistas refused to keep their distance from the Eastern bloc, even though they knew this would provide the Reagan administration with another reason to destabilize the Nicaraguan Revolution. In part, the Sandinistas' decision to openly collaborate with socialist countries stemmed from a desire to demonstrate Nicaragua's independence from the United States. The U.S. administration could "no longer dictate" Nicaraguan foreign policy, Alejandro Bendaña reflected in an interview with magazine *Revista Envío* in 1989, and it was "an expression of our sovereignty" to establish diplomatic relations with the socialist bloc after the revolution's triumph.[41] As we have seen in the previous chapter, though, the relationship between Nicaragua and the Soviet Union during the Carter years had little substance besides friendly political declarations, and the Sandinista government received virtually no financial and military support from the USSR and its allies.[42]

The rise to power of Ronald Reagan was a turning point in this regard, as it convinced Sandinista leaders that Nicaragua needed Soviet arms to defend itself against a forthcoming military intervention. According to Luis Caldera, the FSLN saw Reagan's campaign rhetoric as a prelude to a U.S.-coordinated military campaign against the Nicaraguan Revolution.[43] Sergio Ramírez, too, remembers that Reagan's hostile language convinced the FSLN that "we had to prepare for the worst" and "preparing for the worst meant assuming risks in advance."[44] Thus, despite the obvious risks attached to cooperating with the Soviet Union, the Nicaraguan government—realizing that Western Europe was unlikely to satisfy its need for weaponry—saw no other option than to turn to the Soviets and their allies for increased military assistance. And since Soviet leaders shared the Sandinistas' concern regarding the growing power of "imperialist and other reactionary circles," as East German officials reported in 1981, they responded positively to the Nicaraguan request, agreeing "to supply weapons and other military equipment to the armed forces of Nicaragua."[45]

To prevent international isolation, Managua and Moscow were careful to hide the full extent of the Soviet Union's assistance to Nicaragua, making sure weapons were predominantly delivered by third countries.[46] In 1981, Algeria transported Soviet weaponry to Nicaragua, including tanks, ammunition, and rifles. For the Sandinistas' international image, obtaining military equipment from a nonaligned country like Algeria was much less controversial than receiving weapons directly from the Soviet Union.[47] Indeed, on 19 July 1981, Christopher Dickey from *The Washington Post* speculated that military aid from Arab states such as Algeria and Libya "may help [Nicaragua] survive without aligning with either of the superpowers."[48] Unfortunately for the Sandinistas, they lost this advantage in 1982 when the Algerian government, possibly due to U.S. pressure, refused to ship any additional arms to Nicaragua and Moscow asked the German Democratic Republic—obviously not a nonaligned state—to take over this "precarious task."[49]

In sum, as the international environment grew more hostile in late 1980 and early 1981, Sandinista leaders tried to strike a balance between, on the one hand, not antagonizing potential enemies and, on the other hand, preemptively strengthening the revolution. The obvious problem was, of course, that the steps that needed to be taken to defend the revolution, such as obtaining Soviet arms and supporting Salvadoran guerrillas, played right into the hands of the revolution's adversaries, who were looking for reasons to discredit the Nicaraguan regime. To prevent regional anticommunists from using Nicaraguan ties to the FMLN and the Eastern bloc as an excuse to intervene, the FSLN therefore proposed the creation of a transnational anti-intervention movement. This network of solidarity activists, left-wing politicians, and progressive organizations, as the next section demonstrates, delegitimized U.S. foreign policy toward Central America by presenting the revolutionary wars in Central America as a David and Goliath situation, with young and idealistic Nicaraguan and Salvadoran guerrillas fighting against a powerful and aggressive United States. In doing so, the FSLN altered the power balance between the two adversaries, strengthening the position of the Sandinista government in the face of an isolated Reagan administration.

## THE ANTI-INTERVENTION MOVEMENT

The solidarity conference in Managua on 26–31 January 1981 achieved its objectives by convincing Western European activists that the Sandinista Revolution was under attack. Nicaragua was "a country under siege, with a people committed to defend the gains of the revolution at all costs against foreign and domestic aggression," delegates from the London-based Nicaragua Solidarity Campaign reported upon their return.[50] In addition to citing hostile actions by the incoming Reagan administration, which refused to release the remaining $15 million of Jimmy Carter's $75 million aid package to Nicaragua, British activists were shocked to notice that the number of "border attacks" by former members of Somoza's National Guard had "escalated frighteningly" since September 1980.[51] Dutch participants made similar observations, noting that Europeans had wrongly assumed that the Sandinista Revolution "was safe" because the United States considered its existence "a fait accompli." In Managua, the Dutch delegation wrote, it had learned that the opposite was true; Nicaraguans were rightly worried about United States' hostility, specifically the "threat of a direct invasion" and the "possibility of an economic boycott."[52]

Inspired by the grandeur and political message of the Managua conference, solidarity activists responded enthusiastically to the Sandinistas' call for a broad anti-intervention front. At the fifth Western European solidarity conference, which took place in Paris in April 1981, representatives from national committees compared experiences and coordinated future campaign strategies with Raúl Guerra. The key objective of the anti-intervention movement, they agreed, should be to alert Western European audiences and governments to the danger of U.S. military interference. This meant that the public narrative of the Nicaragua solidarity movement had to change. Instead of focusing on the revolution's domestic accomplishments, such as literacy campaigns and health care reforms, solidarity committees would now primarily concentrate on foreign policy. In campaign material, they discussed the long and violent history of U.S. interventions in Central America and the Caribbean, demonstrating that Reagan's foreign policy toward the Nicaraguan Revolution should be understood in the context of U.S. imperialism, which could be traced back all the way to the early twentieth century. To bring this message across effectively, the solidarity movement decided to collaborate more closely with Salvadoran and Guatemalan solidarity groups, aiming to unite the individual Central America committees into a transnational anti-intervention network.[53]

To some extent, the decision to join forces with other Central America committees was motivated by Sandinista ambivalence about the growing strength of the El Salvador movement in Western Europe. Even though the FSLN and FMLN were allies in the Central American context, as we have seen above, there was also an element of rivalry to their relationship since the two revolutionary organizations competed for public recognition and sympathy in the international arena. At a time when the Salvadoran civil war received extensive media coverage, the FSLN and its allies struggled to hold the attention of Western European audiences. In February 1982, West German solidarity activists noted with concern that the guerrilla war in El Salvador had caused people to lose interest in the Nicaraguan Revolution. It was simply more exciting, one activist concluded, to join a solidarity movement supporting "people still fighting for their freedom" than to work for a committee supporting revolutionaries who were already in power.[54] A similar issue was discussed at a meeting of several Central America solidarity groups in London, where NSC representatives expressed concern that the Nicaraguan revolutionaries would be forgotten since the struggle in El Salvador was constantly "in the headlines."[55] At the Paris conference, Raúl Guerra, too, emphasized that activists should keep working for Nicaragua alone, and not switch allegiance to "other committees."[56] The best way to assist national liberation movements, Guerra insisted, was by "defending and publishing information" about the Sandinista process.[57] By explicitly linking the survival of revolutionary Nicaragua to the struggle in El Salvador, then, the FSLN and solidarity activists were doing more than expressing genuine support; they were simultaneously making a move to harness the media focus on El Salvador for their own purposes. Meanwhile, activists largely ignored the situation in Guatemala, where government forces and anticommunist death squads engaged in widescale repression and genocide against the country's indigenous population, which they accused of supporting the guerrillas.[58]

For the FSLN, the new strategy worked remarkably well. Central America solidarity groups set up a wide range of anti-intervention events, such as concerts, lecture series, demonstrations, art shows, and charity runs. On 9 April 1981, more than seven hundred solidarity activists gathered in front of the U.S. embassy in London to protest against the visit of U.S. Secretary of State Alexander Haig.[59] And in West Germany, activists set up a successful campaign that called on people to boycott coffee produced by big "transnational companies" in El Salvador and buy Nicaraguan coffee instead.[60] Solidarity committees also published monthly newsletters, powerful posters, translations of Sandinista speeches, and books on the history of U.S. interventionism in Central America, such as the magazine *Nicaragua Aktuell* and a book entitled *Reagan, Haig, and the Destabilisation of Nicaragua*.[61]

Moreover, at the initiative of Klaas Wellinga and Hans Langenberg from the Nicaragua Komitee Nederland, in the spring of 1982 a group of Sandinista officials, representatives of the Salvadoran and Guatemalan guerrilla movements, and the Nicaraguan band El Pancasán toured thirteen Western European countries, visiting cities such as Utrecht, Paris, Rome, London, Frankfurt, Vienna, Copenhagen, and Madrid. In these cities, the revolutionary diplomats of the so-called "anti-intervention caravan" were hosted by local solidarity activists, who were also tasked with organizing public programs of exhibitions, parades, and demonstrations.[62] The committees in Spain and Belgium did a particularly good job, Wellinga reported, noting that at least seven thousand people participated in the demonstration in Bilbao and more than three hundred cars joined the anti-intervention caravan when it drove past parliament in Brussels.[63]

From the perspective of the FSLN and its Western European allies, domestic opponents of the FSLN, such as former junta member Alfonso Robelo and perennial opposition newspaper *La Prensa*, were accomplices of U.S. imperialism. As Raúl Guerra explained to European activists in April 1981, it was "no coincidence" that from the moment Reagan assumed office,

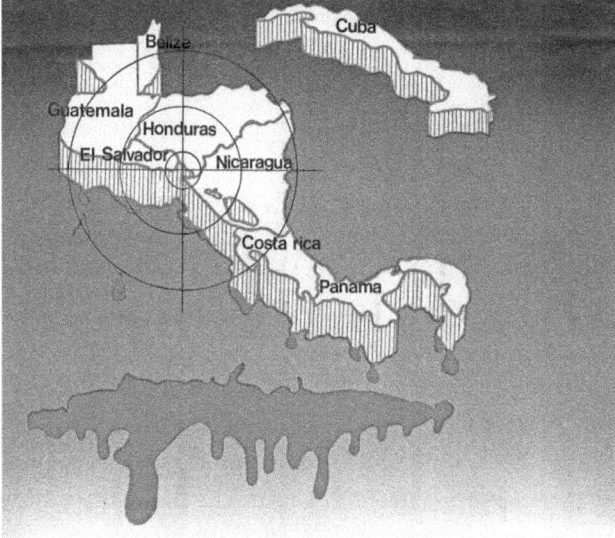

FIGURE 6. This poster, produced by Central America committees in the Netherlands, calls upon people to participate in an "anti-intervention week." Seeking to isolate the Reagan administration and delegitimize its foreign policy towards Central America, the poster warns audiences that Central America should not become a "second Vietnam." Photo: Nicaragua Komitee Nederland, International Institute of Social History, Amsterdam.

domestic opposition forces in Nicaragua began to grow more successful in their campaign to "destabilize, boycott, and sabotage" the revolutionary process. The opposition strikes and other manifestations of discontent were all examples of "external" aggression, Guerra asserted, and the Nicaraguan people would simply not accept these—or any other—types of attacks against the revolution.[64] As the revolution came under increasing pressure, the FSLN and their allies presented Western European audiences with a simplistic narrative in which you could either side with the Nicaraguan Revolution or with the Reagan administration, largely ignoring complexities on the ground in Nicaragua itself.

From the Sandinista perspective, this was an excellent strategy since few Western Europeans wanted to be associated with Ronald Reagan, or U.S. foreign policy more generally. Less than ten years after the last U.S. combat troops left Vietnam, it did not take a lot of effort to convince European audiences that Reagan's anticommunist approach to Central American affairs—if unchecked—would result in a devastating war. As such, solidarity activists' warnings that Central America could become a "second Vietnam" struck a chord in Western Europe (figure 6). Indeed, to a significant extent the success of the anti-intervention movement was due to the ability of the FSLN and its allies to capitalize on the strong anti-Reagan sentiment that existed in Western European countries at the time.[65] In the early 1980s, many Western Europeans saw Reagan as a reckless, hawkish, and arrogant president, willing to risk a nuclear war and sacrifice global security for the purpose of defeating the Soviet Union.[66] The planned stationing of cruise and Pershing missiles in Western European countries, in particular, was opposed by large numbers of activists, students, church groups, and politicians. Millions of members of these antinuclear groups united in a transnational peace movement demanding that Western European governments halt the deployment of new missiles, calling for nuclear disarmament, and attacking the U.S. administration for fanning the flames of the Cold War. Nicaragua solidarity activists smartly played on these sentiments by arguing that the militarization of Western Europe and U.S. foreign policy toward Central America were two sides of the same coin.[67]

Yet, depending on the country, the domestic context was not always favorable for anti-intervention activism. The United Kingdom was considered a particularly difficult place for solidarity work at the start of the 1980s. At the 1981 Paris conference, the NSC reported that the "British population does not seem very interested in Latin America" and that, therefore, Nicaragua solidarity committees consisted predominantly of Latin Americans.[68] The visit of the anti-intervention caravan to the United Kingdom, too, was considered a disappointment, as the NSC had shifted all responsibility for the organization to a local committee in Sheffield, which simply did not manage to attract large crowds or provide acceptable housing for the Central American representatives.[69] The NSC came up with several explanations for the lack of British interest in Central American solidarity activism, citing unemployment and financial crises, factionalism and splits within the Labour Party, as well as Margaret Thatcher's radical conservativism and alliance with the United States.[70] One year later, however, the situation had slightly improved. As one British diplomat noted on 1 April 1982, "public interest here in Nicaragua continues to grow, although it remains overshadowed by the extensive media coverage given to bloodshed in El Salvador."[71]

The relative weakness of the Labour Party, which underwent a period of intense rivalry and internal splits following Thatcher's election in 1979, might well have contributed to the difficulties of the British solidarity movement. Elsewhere, the strength of Western European social democrats and their support for the Nicaraguan Revolution provided the FSLN with visibility, political backing, and legitimacy. In particular, the Socialist International, by founding the so-called International Committee for the Defense of the Nicaraguan Revolution, endorsed the Sandinista argument that the revolution was under siege. This committee was established at an SI congress in November 1980, after European and Latin American social democrats expressed concern that Reagan's election would cause further instability, civil war, and polarization in Central America. The goals of the new "Nicaragua Solidarity Committee," the SI announced in a press release in December 1980, were "to avert foreign intervention in Nicaragua's internal affairs" and "to spread information about the country and its democratization process."[72] Its members were prominent socialists and social democrats from Europe and Latin America, such as Mario Soares (Portugal), Willy Brandt (FRG), Olof Palme (Sweden), Carlos Andres Perez (Venezuela), Joop den Uyl (the Netherlands), François Mitterrand (France), Bruno Kreisky (Austria), and Felipe González (Spain), the chairman.[73] Michael Foot, who was elected British Labour leader on 10 November 1980, also agreed to join the committee in March 1981, after a fruitful meeting with Miguel d'Escoto in London.[74]

The social democrats did not try to hide their disdain for Reagan's approach to the Cold War and the Central American crises. On 6 December 1980, during a meeting in Washington, Swedish politician Pierre Schori told Sandinista representatives Miguel d'Escoto and Julio López Campos that the

SI was trying to "get the Americans to learn to live with revolutionaries and national liberation movements."[75] And in a press release, the SI expressed its "concern with the growing tensions" in Central America, which were greatly intensified by "North American declarations about a possible intervention."[76] When the Reagan administration cut off aid to Nicaragua in January 1981, Bernt Carlsson, the Secretary-General of the Socialist International, described it as an act that "illustrates the linkage of the new U.S. administration with the extreme rightwing forces in Latin America."[77]

The Sandinistas greatly valued the support of the Socialist International. The fact that the world's most prominent social democrats had created an official committee to defend the Sandinista Revolution strengthened Nicaragua's image as a democratic and nonaligned country and, by extension, delegitimized the foreign policy objectives and Cold War narrative of the Reagan administration. Economically, the FSLN could also benefit, as Western European social democrats lobbied governments to provide the Nicaraguan revolutionaries with more financial and material aid. It was thus no surprise that the headline of the first issue of *Barricada Internacional* was "Internacional Socialista: Nicaragua; esperanza para América Latina" (Socialist International: Nicaragua; hope for Latin America) (figure 7).[78]

Behind the scenes, however, the alliance between Sandinistas and social democrats was not as harmonious as it appeared at the time. While the FSLN and the Socialist International were both highly critical of the Reagan administration, the two organizations did not fully trust one another. On the one hand, Sandinista leaders, as Sergio Ramírez writes in his memoirs, always kept social democratic parties at a certain distance since they considered them to be part of the capitalist, and therefore U.S.-dominated, system. At the end of the day, the FSLN believed, the Socialist International would always align itself with the United States.[79] On the other hand, in the early 1980s, Western European social democrats grew increasingly suspicious of Sandinista claims that they were dedicated to democracy.[80] Schori, for instance, told López and d'Escoto that he hoped that national liberation movements such as the FSLN would "learn to live with an opposition."[81] Willy Brandt, too, feared that the Sandinistas were using their relationship with the SI to publicly justify controversial domestic policies, such as the "dismantling of pluralism and the rule of law," as well as the imprisoning of opposition figures, such as the journalist Guillermo Treminio.[82] They were particularly concerned about the Sandinistas' treatment of the opposition party led by former junta member Alfonso Robelo, who was harassed by

FIGURE 7. On 5 July 1981, on the cover of the first *Barricada Internacional*, a Sandinista newspaper specifically targeted towards international audiences, Sandinista comandantes are seen working with members of the Socialist International's Committee for the Defense of the Nicaraguan Revolution. The article's headline quotes the SI's description of Nicaragua as a country of "hope for Latin America." Photo: International Institute of Social History, Amsterdam.

Sandinista youth groups and banned from holding a demonstration on 9 November 1980.[83] "I believe it cannot be acceptable for our friends from Nicaragua to claim sanction by way of our association for everything which they deem to be appropriate in their country," Brandt wrote to González on 8 June 1981, urging his Spanish colleague to make clear that the Socialist International's commitment was dependent on how "the leadership of the FSLN in Nicaragua defines its continuing political direction."[84]

Despite differing visions about the Nicaraguan Revolution's future, however, the FSLN succeeded in mobilizing a range of Western Europeans for its defense, precisely because they were asking for defensive support rather than potentially more controversial backing for their program and political aims. Ultimately, what united Western Europeans in the early 1980s was not necessarily sympathy for the Nicaraguan revolutionaries—although that was certainly a part of it—but rather their shared dislike of the newly elected U.S. president and his foreign policy. Somewhat ironically, then, Reagan's election provided the solidarity movement with a new window of opportunity after a period of relative neglect and frustration.

It was relatively easy for the Sandinista comandantes to convince their Western European supporters of the necessity of an anti-intervention movement, but they were still confronted with the more difficult task of influencing state policy. The position of Western European governments, Sandinistas believed, could be a "crucial counterweight" to the Reagan administration's dangerous plans for Central America.[85] Indeed, they calculated, Reagan was unlikely to launch a military intervention against the Nicaraguan Revolution without the support of his Western European allies. Demonstrating that the U.S. administration had no Western European support, then, was considered vital for the Nicaraguan Revolution's survival. In that vein, Ramírez told Dutch journalists from *Het Vrije Volk* that Reagan was virtually isolated, since it was "obvious that Europe is pursuing an independent foreign policy with regard to Central American and the Caribbean."[86] Maintaining good relations with Western Europe would undermine the United States' position, Sandinistas realized, as it challenged its Cold War framing of the Central American civil wars. In *Barricada Internacional*, therefore, Sergio Ramírez's trip to Sweden, the Netherlands, Austria, and Spain in April and May 1982 was described as an example of "the willingness of the Sandinista People's Revolution to maintain good relations with all those countries that respect our sovereignty and independence."[87]

A key objective of the FSLN was to convince policymakers in Western Europe to pursue a foreign policy toward Central America that neutralized Reagan's anticommunist offensive in the region. To persuade Western European countries to become involved in Central American affairs, the FSLN strategically played on what they—correctly—perceived as the ambition of EC leaders to be more present on the global stage and, more specifically, the desire of Western Europeans to move beyond the Cold War conflict and focus instead on the socioeconomic causes of Central America's revolutionary upheaval. In meetings with diplomats and politicians, Nicaraguan officials continued to push the argument that the Western Europeans, due to their close relationship with the United States, could prevent Central America from being swept up by Cold War dynamics.[88] Francisco d'Escoto, for instance, told British officials on 13 January 1982 that Reagan was causing regional instability as he tried to "weaken" the Nicaraguan government by "restricting credit" and allowing "hostile" anticommunist groups to "train on U.S. soil."[89] Due to its "considerable influence" on U.S. foreign policy, d'Escoto claimed, the United Kingdom could "ensure there was no aggression against Nicaragua."[90] Miguel d'Escoto presented a similar narrative to the West German foreign minister Hans-Dietrich Genscher on 2 March 1981, contrasting the militaristic Central America policy of the U.S. administration, which he described as a "political fantasy," to the much more constructive and reasonable position of the West German government.[91]

In addition to flattering Western European leaders by telling them that they had the power, skills, and responsibility to restrain the Reagan administration in Central America—and at the same time as they were exploring the possibility of securing more assistance in military equipment from the Soviet bloc—Sandinista leaders continued to encourage the view that Western European political and financial support could keep the FSLN nonaligned and the Soviet Union at bay. During a visit to Paris in July 1982, Sandinista comandante Daniel Ortega argued that "true nonalignment depended on the aid and support nonaligned countries could get from the West."[92] Indeed, Francisco d'Escoto explained, it "would be absurd" for Nicaragua to rely on the Eastern bloc if they received "financial credits" from the EC.[93] Similarly, on 13 May 1982, Nicaraguan labor minister Virgilio Godoy Reyes warned Genscher that "growing pessimism" in Western Europe about the revolution could "drive Nicaragua into the arms of communism." For example, when Chancellor Helmut Schmidt did not have time to meet with Sergio Ramírez in April 1982, it "immediately rained invitations from the East."[94] Western European visitors to Nicaragua, too, such as Bundestag representative Manfred Coppik (a member of the Green Party) in August 1981, left the country with the impression that the Sandinista government greatly valued Western European support, since it ensured that Nicaragua could remain independent from both of the Cold War superpowers.[95]

The Sandinistas achieved several diplomatic successes in Western Europe in the early 1980s, most notably in France and the Netherlands. In July 1982, Daniel Ortega visited Paris, where he was warmly welcomed by the new socialist president Mitterrand, who had assumed office on 5 May 1981, and his new foreign minister Claude Cheysson. The worst error France could make, Cheysson reportedly said after the meeting, was to "follow the policy adopted by the United States of trying to isolate Nicaragua."[96] Crucially, in Paris, the Sandinistas entered secret negotiations with Mitterrand's government about possible arm supplies to Nicaragua. When Le Monde broke the story in January 1982, the French government declared that its decision to provide Nicaragua with "non-offensive" weapons was motivated by the desire to not let "third-world countries become too exclusively dependent on the Soviet bloc."[97] Moreover, in April 1982, the Dutch authorities gave a warm welcome to Sergio Ramírez and his delegation. In addition to being invited to dinner with Queen Beatrix, the Nicaraguan representatives had conversations with Prime Minister Dries van Agt, Foreign Minister Max van der Stoel, and labor politician Joop den Uyl.[98]

Despite these propaganda victories, the Sandinistas quickly realized that they were no longer the only ones actively trying to shape Western European public opinion and foreign policy toward Central America.[99] On 11 February 1981, at a National Security Council meeting, Reagan's Secretary of State Alexander Haig complained that "few, especially in Europe" seemed to grasp the high levels of Cuban "involvement" in Nicaragua's revolutionary process.[100] Immediately after assuming power, therefore, Reagan and his allies, frustrated with what they perceived as the misguided views of Western Europeans, started to wage a similar battle for their hearts and minds, albeit on the opposite side. Like the Sandinistas, U.S. officials calculated that the position of Western European governments, politicians, and public opinion could tilt the international balance in favor of either the revolutionaries or the Reagan administration. This was not only the case due to the high levels of Western European financial support for Nicaragua, which allowed the FSLN to enact its domestic program and stay in power, but also because Western European voices could provide the Reagan administration with the legitimacy it needed to launch a military intervention, and possibly even sway congressional votes. Caspar Weinberger, the Secretary of Defense, summed it up clearly when he concluded that "we must get to the Europeans and especially the Germans."[101]

To bring the European allies in line, on 16 February 1981 Reagan's Assistant Secretary of State for European Affairs Lawrence Eagleburger departed on a mission to several Western European cities, including The Hague, London, Bonn, Paris, and Brussels.[102] In meetings with officials, Eagleburger showed them "evidence of high-level Nicaraguan involvement in the delivery of arms and other forms of support to guerrillas in El Salvador."[103] These weapons, Eagleburger stressed, came from the Soviet Union, Cuba, and Vietnam, which implied that the revolutionary war in El Salvador was not, as many Western Europeans believed, a struggle for social justice but rather a Cold War conflict, and consequently a threat to U.S. security.[104] When Thatcher visited the White House on 26 February 1981, Reagan made a similar point, noting that "Central and South America had become part of the predominant international problem facing the West today" and that the

Soviet Union—"the villain in this area"—was responsible.[105] To fight Soviet and Cuban interventionism in Central America, the U.S. administration specifically asked EC leaders to *publicly* align with Reagan's position. Indeed, Eagleburger asked the British government for "public support for American efforts to back the Salvador Government, . . . some public indication of UK disapproval of clandestine arms supplies to the insurgents, [and] public support for U.S. endeavors to bring arms supply to a halt."[106] In Bonn, too, Eagleburger requested from Genscher "a public condemnation by the FRG of the weapon transfers to El Salvador," as well as an acknowledgment of the "involvement" of the Eastern bloc in the region.[107]

While the prevention of a revolutionary victory in El Salvador was at the center of Reagan's foreign policy agenda, he also tried to prevent Nicaragua from receiving financial, political, and military support from Western European countries. Reagan's meetings with Mitterrand in March and June 1982, Haig noted with delight, resulted in "a delay in French arms shipments to Nicaragua" that might continue "indefinitely."[108] Haig's predictions were too optimistic, though, and on 13 July 1982, *The New York Times* reported that France was resisting U.S. pressure and had started to fulfill its $13 million weapons contract with Nicaragua, which included helicopters, patrol boats, and rocket launchers.[109] The newspaper's claims were later backed up by the CIA, which admitted in 1983 that "Paris will probably fulfill its 1981 arms contract with Nicaragua."[110] To convince EC leaders to cut off aid to Nicaragua, U.S. diplomats portrayed the country as a Cuban-style dystopia: a one-party state that was financed by the Soviet Union and sought to export its revolution to neighboring countries, specifically El Salvador.[111] Nicaragua "was getting more totalitarian all the time," Haig told British Foreign Secretary Peter Carrington on 21 September 1981, adding that "arms were coming in at a level far beyond legitimate defense needs."[112] U.S. diplomats also accused the Nicaraguan regime of committing gross human rights violations, going as far as to describe the Sandinistas' forced resettlement of the indigenous populations on the Atlantic Coast as an "example of genocide."[113] George Shultz, too, who replaced Haig as U.S. Secretary of State, told Genscher on 7 December 1982 that El Salvador "clearly" had a much better human rights record than Nicaragua, a statement that could not have been farther from the truth.[114]

As a result of Reagan's propaganda campaign, Nicaraguan officials in Western Europe increasingly found themselves on the defensive. Instead of discussing the danger of a U.S. military intervention or the possibility of receiving extra financial aid from EC countries, Sandinista officials had to respond to accusations that they were violating human rights, supporting the FMLN, and creating a one-party state. "How can we export revolution, when we don't have the money, or the arms, or the men—even if we want to!," the Nicaraguan ambassador to the United Nations, Javier Chamorro Mora, exclaimed.[115] Nicaragua was not providing any military assistance to FMLN guerrillas, Daniel Ortega—falsely—told his Spanish hosts in July 1982, even though the FSLN had a lot of "sympathy" for the Salvadoran struggle.[116] Regarding the harsh treatment of the Miskito Indians, Sergio Ramírez correctly pointed out that the photo of burning bodies that the U.S. ambassador to the United Nations Jeane Kirkpatrick had presented as evidence was in fact taken during Somoza's rule.[117] Nicaraguan diplomats also dismissed their government's alleged "totalitarian" tendencies and dependency on Cuba, noting to Western European officials that Nicaragua simply had "no democratic tradition" and that the number of Cuban advisors was much smaller than generally believed.[118] Nevertheless, as the next sections shows, Sandinista efforts to counter accusations against the Nicaraguan Revolution were not enough to alleviate the concerns of a number of Western European leaders, who started to consider the Sandinistas a lost cause.

## WESTERN EUROPEAN DISAGREEMENTS

In a context of heightening tensions and accusations, the consensus among EC leaders that financial and political support could keep the Sandinistas in the Western camp, or at the very least nonaligned, broke down. To be sure, most Western European countries, particularly those with social democratic and socialist leaders, continued to side with the Nicaraguan revolutionaries, but the conservative and Christian Democratic governments of the United Kingdom and—albeit in a less extreme fashion—West Germany broke ranks and cut aid to the Nicaraguan state. The Thatcher government was the first to decide that Nicaragua was a lost cause. Like the Reagan administration, British officials looked at the Sandinista Revolution through a Cold War lens. Nicaragua followed "the style of its Cuban mentor," the British ambassador in Costa Rica, Michael Brown, wrote to the Foreign and Commonwealth Office on 9 January 1982, noting that its "one-party state" engaged in "repression at home and subversion abroad." The only reason opposition parties were tolerated by the FSLN, Brown added, was to keep up the "façade" of political pluralism to the outside world.[119] Citing the "military build-up" and "increasingly pro-Soviet stance being adopted" by the nine Sandinista comandantes, the British government not only refused to provide the Nicaraguan revolutionaries with economic aid but also resolved to "oppose loans to Nicaragua from international financial institutions," such as the International Monetary Fund, the Inter-American Development Bank, and the World Bank.[120] There was not a lot of internal discussion about these decisions among British policymakers. In the eyes of British officials, it was simply not worth antagonizing the Reagan administration over the Nicaraguan Revolution. Central America was "a peripheral region" for the United Kingdom, the FCO concluded, but it was of "paramount importance and emotional content for the present U.S. administration."[121] The shift in the British position, though, was more of a political than an economic blow to the Sandinista government, as the United Kingdom had never been among the larger Western European sources of aid.

West Germany, unlike the United Kingdom, continued to provide Nicaragua with some bilateral support, but the levels of West German aid declined from $13.3 and $14.1 million in 1980 and 1981 to $8.5 and $6.9 million in 1982 and 1983.[122] The Sandinistas blamed the decrease in West German aid on "Reagan's new ally" in Western Europe, namely Helmut Kohl, a Christian Democrat who replaced Helmut Schmidt as chancellor on 1 October 1982. The views of Christian Democratic groups in West Germany, the editors of Revista Envío wrote in 1982, did "not benefit Nicaraguan or other struggling peoples of the area" since they, like the Reagan administration, used the "framework of an East-West conflict" to understand Central America's problems.[123] While Kohl was undoubtedly more skeptical of the FSLN than Schmidt, a social democrat, the position of the West German government had, in fact, already started to shift several months before he took power. On 12 January 1982, West German officials, citing the Sandinistas' close relations with the Soviet bloc, agreed that financial aid to Nicaragua should be reduced. Clearly, they were no longer confident that future developments in revolutionary Nicaragua could be influenced through financial assistance. Genscher, for instance, despite several invitations from Sandinista diplomats, decided not to add Nicaragua to the itinerary of his forthcoming trip to Latin America after Volker Haak, the West German ambassador in Managua, argued that such a visit would "benefit the regime more than the opposition" and that the possibilities to "influence" the Sandinistas were small.[124]

In contrast, the levels of Dutch and French development aid to Nicaragua increased significantly in the early 1980s. The Netherlands was the biggest

Western European donor; in 1981 and 1982, the Sandinista government received $15.1 and $23.9 million in bilateral aid, respectively. And although the levels of French aid to Nicaragua were much lower, it was an important political gesture that Mitterrand, in another act of open defiance of the Reagan administration's policy, increased the size of its Nicaragua aid program from $1.4 million in 1981 to $8.5 in 1982. In addition, Western European countries who were not members of the European Community also made considerable financial contributions to Nicaragua's reconstruction process. Sweden and Austria, for example, both allocated around $9 million to Nicaragua in 1982.[125] Unlike West Germany and the United Kingdom, therefore, these countries continued to support the Sandinista government and held out hope that, through financial aid, Western Europe could encourage the creation of a "democratic and pluralist" society in Nicaragua. Isolating and threatening the Sandinista leaders, French and Dutch officials believed, would only foster more polarization, instability, and radicalization in Central America.[126]

Notwithstanding disagreements about the character of the Nicaraguan Revolution, the member states of the European Community (now ten strong with the addition of Greece on 1 January 1981) agreed that the U.S. administration's approach to Central American affairs was dangerous. Reagan's anticommunist crusade against national liberation movements, EC leaders feared, threatened to damage the transatlantic alliance, created divisions within the European Community, and destabilized the international Cold War system.[127] British diplomat Geoffrey Cowling, for instance, warned that Reagan's desire to "squash an irritating Nicaragua . . . could develop into a world issue with the major powers on opposite sides." Western European governments and peoples would almost unanimously reject a military intervention against the Sandinista regime, Cowling predicted, noting that "Nicaragua has a significant sympathetic following," because the Germans, Greeks, Irish, and Belgians were generally "critical of U.S. action" and the Danes, French, and Dutch were in a very "anti-U.S. mood."[128] Genscher, too, told Shultz on 7 December 1982 that the United States would be wise to adopt a more cautious approach. Not only was there a lot of "anti-Americanism" in West Germany as a result of the United States' behavior in Central America, Genscher warned, but there also existed the danger that the Soviet Union would try to use the region as a "pressure point" in the Cold War, which could threaten regional security in Western Europe. Invoking memories of the 1962 Cuban missile crisis, when the United States dismantled missiles in Turkey in exchange for the Soviet removal of nuclear weapons from Cuba, Genscher pointed out that the Soviet Union could try something similar with the Central American crises. It was crucial, he believed, that the Soviet Union not be allowed to use its support for revolutionary movements in Central America—including the Sandinistas—as a tool to prevent the stationing of new cruise and Pershing missiles Western Europe.[129] Further highlighting how concerned the West Germans were about the global implications of Reagan's foreign policy toward the isthmus, Genscher urged his U.S. colleague on another occasion that "in the international game of chess, the Central American pawn must not be used against Europe."[130]

The reluctance of Western European leaders to support Reagan's plans for Central America was not solely based on strategic concerns. It should also be placed in the context of the appalling human rights record of the Salvadoran regime, which many Western Europeans perceived as a U.S. puppet state. When four Dutch journalists were killed by the Salvadoran army on 17 March 1982, journalists and activists in the Netherlands were convinced that, behind the scenes, the Reagan administration was responsible for the murders. Protesters organized vigils, attacked the U.S. consulate in Amsterdam, and destroyed a miniature of the White House in theme park Madurodam.[131] Dutch cabinet ministers agreed with the demonstrators that the United States' foreign policy was, to a significant extent, responsible for the journalists' deaths, but they were unsure how to respond. After some deliberation, the government canceled a visit of education minister Jos van Kemenade, who was to have celebrated two hundred years of American-Dutch relations in Washington, but decided that the Netherlands could not deliver a "formal protest" to the American ambassador in The Hague, as it had no concrete evidence of direct U.S. involvement.[132] Unsurprisingly, though, after this incident Dutch leaders were even more disinclined to side with the Reagan administration, either publicly or privately.

Concerns about U.S. foreign policy and the rising tensions in Central America prompted the EC member states to work toward a coordinated response to the region's crises, despite their ideological differences regarding the right approach to the Nicaraguan Revolution. At a meeting of the European Community's foreign policy arm, the EPC, on 23 March 1982, Genscher, Cheysson, and Emilio Colombo, the Italian foreign minister, all agreed with Max van der Stoel that—"in spite of U.S. sensitivities"—the question of increasing European Community aid to "assist stabilization" in Central America should be discussed at the next European Council summit in Brussels on 29 and 30 March.[133] West Germany and France, in particular, pushed for a more active EC role in the region. By increasing the levels of Western European economic aid to the Central American region, West German diplomats argued on 16 February 1982, the EC could tackle the underlying causes of Central America's revolutionary upheaval, which were primarily socioeconomic and not, as the Reagan administration believed, the result of Soviet and Cuban expansionism.[134] Jacques Dupont, a French diplomat, presented a similar analysis at a meeting with Western European diplomats on 19 January 1982. The European Community should increase economic aid to Central America, Dupont argued, since "this was an explosive region whose root problems were social and economic."[135]

In Brussels, the EC member states formally agreed that "they could not remain indifferent" to the growing crisis in Central America but they quarreled over the best way for Western Europe to get involved. In particular, the Thatcher government, already loath to needlessly antagonize the Reagan administration, lobbied actively against the proposed increase in financial and material aid to the region. As a result, the financial—as opposed to the political—aspects of the European Council's conclusions on 30 March 1982 were cautiously phrased. On the one hand, the Western Europeans openly dismissed Reagan's position that the region's revolutionary upheaval should be understood in Cold War terms, declaring instead that "grave economic problems and social inequalities [caused] the tensions and conflicts ravaging Central America." On the other hand, they were vague about the exact contribution that the EC countries could make to bring an end to these inequalities, announcing that aid for the development of Central America would only be increased "within the limits of their possibilities."[136]

In the months following the Council's decision, Western European officials engaged in heated debates about how much money the EC should spend on the region and, crucially, which countries should be allowed to profit from the new aid package. France and West Germany were adamant that, for a regional foreign policy to be effective, no Central American country should be excluded, as this would only lead to more polarization. The United Kingdom, the Netherlands, Greece, and Denmark, on the other hand, argued that political and human rights considerations should be taken into account when allocating aid. To create a consensus, it was decided that each member state had a veto and "no proposals would be made for any country on which reservations were entered."[137] Unfortunately, this compromise also created a problem, as it resulted in the exclusion of exactly those countries that were suffering most from inequality and civil war. While the

Netherlands, Denmark, and Greece refused to provide El Salvador with any money, the United Kingdom rejected Nicaragua and Guatemala (due to its border conflict with former British colony Belize, not because of anticommunist violence and genocide).[138]

Since the British government was the only one to object to Nicaragua, it was under a lot of pressure to change its position. Dutch and French officials lobbied actively in favor of Nicaragua's inclusion. The country "fully meets the set criteria" of the special aid package and its exclusion would be a "purely political decision," Kees van Dijk, the Dutch minister for development, lamented in October 1982.[139] French diplomats went even further, threatening to "veto the whole program" if Nicaragua was excluded.[140] Moreover, when journalists from *The Observer* disclosed to the public that the United Kingdom was preventing Nicaragua from receiving aid, the Sandinistas and their allies launched a campaign to get the FCO to reconsider its position. Sandinista diplomats, solidarity committees, human rights organizations, politicians, and church groups wrote letters accusing the British government of supporting the U.S. administration's "systematic program of destabilization" in Nicaragua, contrasting the British position to "that of other European countries whose governments have praised the enormous achievements of the revolution."[141] On 4 October 1982, in an official statement, the Nicaraguan embassy in London announced that the United Kingdom's decision "to discriminate against Nicaragua" went "against the spirit of the Community's special aid programme for Central America as a whole."[142]

Unfortunately for the Nicaraguan revolutionaries, the British government did not change its mind. At the Foreign Affairs Council on 22 November, the EC ministers decided that only Honduras, the Dominican Republic, and Costa Rica would be allowed to benefit from the new aid package of 30 mecu (around $28 million).[143] Nevertheless, while this decision was undoubtedly damaging to the international reputation of the Sandinista Revolution, the economic consequences for Nicaragua were small. True, Nicaragua could not profit from this specific aid package, but EC foreign ministers also agreed that the country could still receive an "unspecified sum from existing aid funds."[144] This worked in the Sandinistas' favor, as the European Commission—the EC's executive arm, whose members represented the interests of the Community as a whole, rather than the individual member states' interests– used this loophole to put forward several new aid projects for Nicaragua.[145] Specifically, the Community wanted to contribute financially to the implementation of the Sandinistas' agrarian reform law (distributing land and equipment to small farmers), the "integrated develop-ment" of the remote Waslala region (building a road network, improving health care and education, and assisting farmers), as well as the reconstruc-tion of three bridges on the main road between Nicaragua and Honduras that had been destroyed by floods in early 1982. The total value of these pro-posed projects, British officials noted with "horror" in December 1982, was 16.5 mecu ($15 million), which was more than the 10 mecu ($9 million) that Costa Rica, Honduras, and the Dominican Republic would each receive under the special aid program.[146] And since the United Kingdom could only object on "technical grounds" and wanted to avoid "any mention of political misgivings regarding aid to Nicaragua," there was little the FCO could do to prevent the Nicaraguan junta from receiving this generous sum of EC aid.[147]

Despite their shared frustration with Reagan's militaristic foreign policy, Western European governments were therefore unable to overcome their ideological differences and develop a coordinated foreign policy toward Central America during the first two years of the Reagan presidency. The Sandinistas did not suffer major financial losses in Western Europe, but the failure of EC leaders to agree on a common approach that would potentially undermine Reagan's military support for the Contras and the Salvadoran regime was bad news. Not only could the FSLN leaders no longer claim that the EC was united in its support for the Nicaraguan Revolution, but a divided Western Europe also meant that there was no powerful counter-weight to Reagan's foreign policy in Central America. More broadly, the limited results of the Sandinistas' revolutionary diplomacy in Western Europe highlight the difficulties—if not impossibilities—of pursuing a nonaligned foreign policy in a world that was once again swept up by bipolar Cold War thinking. In this context, the FSLN's strategy of appealing to both the East and the West—while at the same time implementing a radical revo-lutionary program at home—was no longer enough to appease Western Europe's conservative and Christian Democratic government leaders.

CONCLUSION

Reagan's election, and the broader shifts in the international system that came with it, signified a turning point in the Sandinistas' revolutionary diplomacy. Having previously used its relations to the wider world to imple-ment its ambitious political program at home, the FSLN now found itself primarily focused on the revolution's survival in the international arena. Confronted with a significantly less favorable global environment, the Sandinistas decided to be careful, but ambitious. On the one hand, they proactively prepared for military confrontation by reaching out to the Soviet Union for military support and strengthening relations with other Third World liberation movements, most notably the Salvadoran guerrillas. On the other hand, they developed a creative international campaign to make a military intervention—at least in political terms—very damaging for their opponents. In this context, transnational activism and public opinion were once again powerful tools for the Sandinistas, which they effectively used to isolate the Reagan administration and delegitimize its foreign policy.

As the Nicaraguan government competed with Reagan's diplomats for the hearts and minds of Western European peoples, moreover, the struggle to determine Nicaragua's future took on a distinctly international character. Two contrasting narratives were at play. On the one hand, Sandinistas and their allies presented audiences with a picture of a small and brave Central American country fighting for social justice, equality, and independence from U.S. hegemony. On the other hand, the Reagan administration portrayed Nicaragua as a Cold War troublemaker, depicting the nine Sandinista comandantes as already having transformed the country into a dystopian and heavily armed Soviet satellite, threatening regional security and stability. Of course, the FSLN was not wrong when they accused Reagan and the CIA of trying to destabilize the Sandinista government by secretly funding the Contras and launching an international propaganda campaign. Yet, contrary to what the FSLN told Western European solidarity activists, not all international criticism and domestic opposition to the Revolución Popular Sandinista was somehow the result of external intervention or U.S. pressure. Rather, the increasingly violent and tense situation on the ground in Nicaragua was the result of a complex interplay of factors, as grassroots grievances intersected with the dynamics of the global Cold War. By publicly focusing on defense and foreign intervention, however, the FSLN succeeded in distracting international audiences from these domestic troubles and miscalculations.

While certainly not the only player in the international struggle over Nicaragua's future, Western Europe was a crucial region. Both the Reagan administration and the Sandinistas worked hard to reach out to Western European governments and audiences, believing that public opinion and the foreign policies of EC countries could influence the future trajectory of the Nicaraguan Revolution. Western European financial assistance for revolutionary Nicaragua was considered particularly important, not just because the Sandinistas needed money for their domestic programs, but also because it validated the FSLN's claim that the country pursued a nonaligned foreign policy. Similarly, the Reagan administration sought to change the public positions of EC governments, realizing that a shift in Western Europe's attitude could lend credibility and legitimacy to Reagan's foreign policy. Interestingly, then, the FSLN and the United States both operated on the assumption that, with regard to Central American affairs, the voices and policies of Western Europeans carried great political value.

By the end of 1982, having successfully capitalized on the anti-Reagan sentiment that existed in Western Europe at the time, Sandinista revolutionaries and their allies clearly had the upper hand in this fight for Western European public opinion. Any overt attempts to destroy the Nicaraguan Revolution, politicians knew, would result in a massive international public outcry, anti-intervention demonstrations, and heavy pressure on EC leaders to break with U.S. foreign policy. At the level of the state, however, Western European leaders were no longer able to agree on a collective approach to the region. While social democrats continued to side with the FSLN revolutionaries, conservatives and an increasing number of Christian Democrats lost faith in the ability of the West to keep Nicaragua out of the Soviet camp. From 1982 onwards, therefore, notwithstanding efforts by Sandinistas and their allies to present the Nicaraguan Revolution as democratic and nonaligned in the Cold War, the international struggle for the country's future would increasingly be fought along ideological lines.

# FOUR

# *Creative Defense, 1983–1984*

IN APRIL 1983, THE NICARAGUAN state-affiliated Comité Nicaragüense por la Paz (Nicaraguan Peace Committee, CONIPAZ) organized an international music festival in Managua, entitled Concierto por la paz en Centroamérica (Central American Peace Concert). The concert, staged at the Plaza de la Revolución, was a massive success for the FSLN and its allies; it attracted around five hundred thousand visitors from the Americas and Europe and put the Sandinistas' revolutionary cause in the international spotlight, demonstrating to the world that the Revolución Popular Sandinista could still count on the international community's solidarity. More than 150 artists traveled to Managua to perform, including famous folk singers and popular symbols of the Latin American left such as Amparo Ochoa from Mexico, Daniel Viglietti from Uruguay, Mercedes Sosa from Argentina, Alí Primera from Venezuela, and Silvio Rodríguez from Cuba. The Nicaraguan brothers Carlos and Luis Enrique Mejía Godoy, composers of what Sophie Esch describes as the "soundtrack" of the Sandinista Revolution, performed their famous songs "Yo soy de un pueblo sencillo" and "Nicaragua Nicaragüita."[1] Western European solidarity activists played a prominent role in the concert's organization, too, raising funds and ensuring that a selection of the best performances was made into a record, entitled *April in Managua* (figure 8), which was later sold to raise money for the FSLN.[2] Jan Kees de Rooy, one of the Dutch organizers of the Concierto, fondly remembers the festival as the "Woodstock" of Central America.[3]

Building on the Sandinistas' long history of using music, poetry, and art for revolutionary purposes, this kind of cultural solidarity became increasingly important for the Sandinistas as the battle over the revolution's future intensified.[4] Anxious that a military escalation in Central America could result in the

FIGURE 8. Album cover of the record *April in Managua: The Central American Peace Concert*. The record was produced by Varagram and by the label Empresa Nicaragüense de Grabaciones Artísticas y Culturales (Enigrac), the latter sponsored by the Sandinista government and founded by the singer Luis Enrique Mejía Godoy in 1979. Solidarity activists in Europe and the Americas sold this record to raise money for the FSLN.

revolution's collapse, the FSLN intensified its efforts to mobilize international audiences for its cause. Whereas in the early 1980s the focus was primarily on anti-intervention and the long history of U.S. imperialism in Central America, the FSLN now sought to present the international community with an enchanting image of the revolution by organizing peace festivals, highlighting Sandinista cultural practices, and giving activists the opportunity to visit Nicaragua and participate in the revolutionary process. The success of the Sandinistas' diplomacy on this front frustrated officials in the Reagan administration, who were unable to convince Western audiences that they were being deceived by the revolutionaries, despite launching a multimillion-dollar propaganda campaign to counter the Sandinista message.

Yet, after the United States successfully invaded the island of Grenada in October 1983, it became clear to the FSLN that public sympathy alone might not be enough to ensure the revolution's survival. The invasion was a massive blow to the Sandinistas' sense of security, and fears that Reagan was planning something similar in Central America convinced the nine FSLN comandantes of the relevance of Western European and Latin American governmental involvement in regional affairs. In the aftermath of Grenada, the FSLN made significant concessions to reach out to these governments, which—despite active lobbying from pro-Sandinista activists—were not always supportive of the revolutionary project. To meet their critics halfway, the FSLN agreed to organize Western-style democratic elections, supported peace proposals, and embarked on a dialogue with the opposition, including the Catholic Church, the editors of *La Prensa*, and the Coordinadora Democrática Nicaragüense (Democratic Coordinating Committee, CDN). By widely publicizing these reforms to governments and audiences in Europe and the Americas, the FSLN hoped to eliminate the pretexts used by Washington to justify its military campaign against the revolution.

This chapter analyzes the strategic shifts that occurred after the United States' invasion of Grenada in October 1983, arguing it was a turning point in the international history of the Nicaraguan Revolution. Not only did the invasion put the Sandinistas on the defensive, pushing the FSLN toward a more conciliatory foreign policy, but the military might on display by U.S. occupation forces in Grenada also resulted in a change in Western European foreign policies. While EC countries had previously failed to agree on a common policy toward Central America, concerns about military escalation in the region, which would have had dangerous Cold War consequences, convinced EC governments of the necessity of collective action. The Western European and Latin American collaboration to deescalate tensions in Central America had significant consequences for the FSLN's revolutionary diplomacy, which had to be adapted accordingly.

## HOSTILITIES, NEGOTIATIONS, AND PEACE CONCERTS

In early 1983, the Reagan administration intensified its military, economic, and political campaign against the Sandinista Revolution. The U.S.-backed counterrevolutionaries, operating from their base camps in neighboring Honduras, launched the first of many military offensives on Nicaraguan territory in March 1983, when more than one thousand Contras infiltrated the country and attacked towns and hamlets in the northern province of Matagalpa. On 23 April 1983, Reagan criticized the Nicaraguan government in a combative speech, dramatically accusing the Sandinistas of spreading violence to El Salvador, destabilizing the Western Hemisphere, burning the villages and crops of indigenous Miskito Indians living on the country's Atlantic Coast, and imposing a totalitarian dictatorship.[5] On 9 May 1983, the U.S. administration also reduced Nicaragua's sugar export quota by 90 percent. According to Sandinista officials, who described Reagan's decision as a clear violation of international law, the reduction meant an annual loss of more than $54 million for the Nicaraguan government.[6]

In this context, the Nicaraguan economy and societal infrastructure started to deteriorate, making it impossible for the Sandinistas to successfully pursue their ambitious plans to improve Nicaraguans' standard of living. Food production for export and domestic consumption declined, particularly in the war zones, and—after a brief period of improvement in the revolution's early years—the FSLN struggled to provide poor Nicaraguans with equal access to basic foodstuffs. By 1984, the Sandinistas were dealing with a "shortage economy" in which essential foods (such as grain, sugar, and corn) were rationed and there was a consistent lack of products such as salt, chicken, eggs, and soap, leaving Nicaraguans frustrated and agitated.[7] This situation seemed likely to have damaging consequences for the revolution's future. Indeed, after visiting Nicaragua in February 1984, a group of specialists from the Council for Mutual Economic Assistance, the economic organization of socialist countries led by the Soviet Union, produced an alarming report about the state of the economy, noting that U.S. hostilities and unfavorable international exchange rates made the financial situation in Nicaragua "exceptionally complex and tense." The most concerning conclusion of the mission's findings, Cuban officials wrote to their foreign minister, Isidoro Malmierca, was that the difficult economic situation in Nicaragua "threatens the future of the revolution [as it was linked to] the FSLN's prestige, its alliance with the working class, the poor campesinos, the progressive intellectuals, and the socioeconomic transformation of the country."[8]

Moreover, in the eyes of Sandinista officials, Reagan's hostile rhetoric and the growing strength of the anti-FSLN insurgents were part of a U.S.-coordinated imperialist plan to create the necessary conditions and "prepare" domestic and international audiences for an upcoming "military intervention" in Central America. The Cold War hardliner desperately wanted to overthrow the Sandinista government before the U.S. electoral campaign in 1984, Nicaraguan diplomats believed, since "a victory over international communism would secure his presidential re-election."[9] The impending attack against the revolution, as Julio López, the head of the DRI, explained to Dutch solidarity activist Hans Langenberg on 19 July 1983, would probably be launched from Honduras. More than fourteen thousand Latin American mercenaries, Honduran soldiers, and former members of Somoza's National Guard were already stationed there, López elaborated, and they were supported by the American warships that were circling the shore and blockading Nicaraguan harbors.[10] Reagan was just waiting for a border incident between the Ejército Popular Sandinista and the Honduran army, Sandinista diplomats predicted, as this would provide his administration with a reason to send in the U.S. Marine Corps.[11]

Amid these rising tensions, the FSLN leadership proclaimed that the Sandinista army would not be easily defeated, hoping that the prospect of a long and bloody war in Central America would dissuade U.S. officials from launching a military attack. As Sandinista comandante Henry Ruiz told East German leader Erich Honecker during a visit to Berlin in February 1983, the FSLN was doing "everything" it could to avoid war, but it also needed to demonstrate that it was "prepared" to fight for the revolution.[12] Indeed, Nicaraguan diplomat Antonio Jarquín told Dutch solidarity activists in Managua in May 1983, the Americans needed to understand that a regional war in Central America, similar to the devastating struggle for Vietnam, would take on its own dynamics, becoming impossible to control.[13] Capitalizing on the so-called Vietnam syndrome, the Sandinista government made clear to Western audiences and politicians that a war against Nicaragua would take many years, cause thousands of innocent people to suffer, and negatively impact the West's position in the global Cold War.[14]

To prepare for the possibility of war, the Nicaraguan government sought to further increase the amount of weaponry it received from the socialist countries, requesting new helicopters, ammunition, rocket launchers, and armored vehicles. In April 1983, Daniel Ortega visited East Germany and the Soviet Union to ask for new military equipment and specialized training for Sandinista soldiers. Not wanting to provoke Western criticism, Ortega made sure to wear "civilian clothes" and requested that there be "no reports" of his trip in the "mass media."[15] Unfortunately, we still know little about the exact results of these and similar visits by Sandinista leaders to the socialist countries in the mid-1980s. According to historian Danuta Paszyn, socialist military aid to Nicaragua was worth around $100 million in 1983—double the amount of the previous year—and rose to at least $150 million in 1984.[16] United States officials operating in the 1980s worked with higher numbers. A CIA report from 1988 estimated that Nicaragua received $160 million in military aid from the Eastern bloc in 1982, $260 million in 1983, and $320 million in 1984.[17] Despite these quantitative differences, what is salient from both estimations is that there was clearly a significant increase in socialist military aid to Nicaragua during this period.

Notwithstanding war preparations in the East, the FSLN's priority was to avoid further military escalation. To achieve this, the revolutionaries looked toward the West, building on earlier propaganda, solidarity, and diplomatic campaigns to influence public opinion and government policies. As we have seen in the previous chapter, the anti-intervention movement in the early

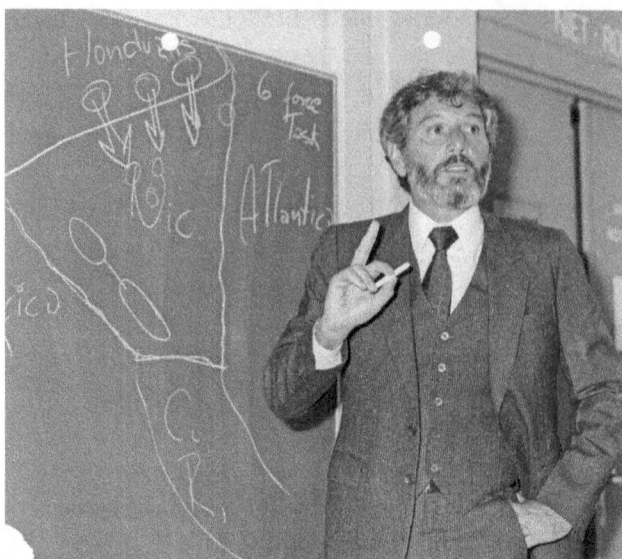

FIGURE 9. The mayor of Managua, Samuel Santos López, gives a lecture at the University of Amsterdam, the Netherlands, on 21 April 1983. As the improvised map on the blackboard shows, the talk focused on the Contra War, but Santos López also discussed Sandinista efforts to improve the standard of living in Managua, a fresh perspective that the audience appreciated. Photo: *NRC Handelsblad*, 22 April 1983, Spaarnestad Photo.

1980s had been successful in undermining the legitimacy and popularity of Reagan's foreign policy toward Central America. Yet, due to the campaign's focus on U.S. imperialism and the guerrilla struggle in El Salvador, the accomplishments of the Sandinista revolutionaries themselves had been somewhat absent from its narrative. While solidarity committees did publish information about the remarkable advances that had taken place in health care, education, and the fight against malnutrition, their focus had primarily been on denouncing Reagan. And as hostilities against the Sandinista government intensified, this narrative became slightly problematic for the FSLN, which wanted the country to be seen as a beacon of peace and social justice in a violent region. From 1983 onwards, then, the FSLN set out to shift the limelight back onto the accomplishments of the revolution itself. Speeches by the mayor of Managua, Samuel Santos López, who visited The Hague and Amsterdam in April and October 1983, were reflective of this change in the Sandinistas' revolutionary diplomacy (figure 9). While Santos did speak to his audience about the Contra war and U.S. foreign policy, he focused primarily on a grassroots project to improve access to clean water in Managua's poorest neighborhoods, as well as efforts to increase women's participation in the revolution. Dutch audiences appreciated this shift in focus, solidarity activists later reported, as it provided a fresh perspective on the "concrete improvements" to everyday life that the revolution had brought.[18]

Next to changing the narrative, the FSLN also took diplomatic steps to demonstrate its commitment to peace. The Nicaraguan government adopted a positive attitude toward the efforts of Mexico, Panama, Venezuela, and Colombia to facilitate a regional dialogue between the Central American governments of Guatemala, El Salvador, Honduras, Nicaragua, and Costa Rica. This so-called Contadora initiative was launched on 9 January 1983 after a summit at the Panamanian island of Contadora, when the participants announced that they would collaborate to find "Latin American solutions to Latin American problems."[19] To encourage dialogue and diplomacy as a means to end Central America's violent and externally-funded civil wars, the Contadora Group organized a number of conferences and summits for Central American foreign ministers and heads of state.[20] Western European governments supported the negotiations, seeing them as a welcome alternative to the threat of further military escalation and U.S. intervention, about which more below.

For the Sandinistas, Contadora was an important counterweight to U.S. foreign policy in Central America, and a way to present revolutionary Nicaragua in a positive light to the international community. It was crucial to keep the regional negotiations "active and alive", diplomats from Nicaragua's Ministerio del Exterior wrote in May 1983, as Contadora prevented international "isolation" and could be used as an "instrument" against the Reagan administration's "politics of aggression" in Central America, as well as the "complicity" of neighboring Honduras, which allowed Contra insurgents to operate from within its territory. Indeed, Nicaraguan diplomats wrote, the "support of European and Latin American countries for a negotiated solution in the region presents a limitation to the military solution that Reagan pursues."[21] The opinions of Western Europeans, most notably the United Kingdom and France, Sandinista officials argued privately, could certainly have a "major impact" on Reagan's foreign policy.[22] In this vein, the FSLN tried to make sure that Nicaragua was not "perceived as a disruptive factor" in the Contadora process, as this would damage the country's image as "flexible and in search of peace."[23] The Sandinistas' support for

Contadora was thus a pragmatic move, designed to strengthen Nicaragua's position in the international arena and isolate the Reagan administration.[24]

To provide further evidence of their commitment to peace and diplomacy, the FSLN officials and their allies sought to capitalize on the popularity of the Western European peace movement, organizing several peace concerts, benefits, and lectures in the Americas and Europe.[25] In speeches and interviews, Sandinistas and solidarity activists argued that Nicaraguans and Western Europeans were all victims of the United States president, whose dedication to winning the Cold War put the lives of millions of people at risk. The Reagan administration's ideological extremism, junta member Sergio Ramírez explained in an interview with Colombian-German journalist Carlos Rincón in August 1983, not only affected the people of Central America, but also "its own allies in Western Europe." The insistence that the U.S. should "impose the installation of missiles in the European countries" was driven by the same "mental insanity" that caused the bloodshed in Central America, Ramírez told the sympathetic journalist.[26] Solidarity activists in Western Europe echoed this sentiment. A poster produced by solidarity and peace activists in Amsterdam, for instance, called on citizens to participate in a demonstration against Reagan's foreign policy with the headline "Midden-Amerika Vrij, Europa Kernwapenvrij" (Central America Free, Europe Nuclear Free).[27] While the revolutionaries shifted the perspective toward the gains of the Nicaraguan Revolution, they were also careful to make clear that these were under severe threat due to the United States' policy of aggression.

As alluded to in the chapter's introduction, the festival in Managua in April 1983 was one of the highpoints of the FSLN's peace campaign, effectively using music to garner support for the Sandinista Revolution and to foster bonds of solidarity between visitors, international audiences, and Nicaraguan revolutionaries. Due to the work of solidarity activists, who acted as intermediaries between the FSLN and prominent leaders of the Western European peace movement, the festival in Managua also mobilized many peace activists for Nicaragua's revolutionary cause. At the invitation of the Nicaragua Komitee Nederland and the Sandinista government, for instance, the Interkerkelijk Vredesberaad (Dutch Interchurch Peace Council, IKV), a key player in the Western European peace movement, sent a large delegation to attend the festivities in Nicaragua, which included representatives from the United Kingdom, the Netherlands, West Germany, France, the United States, and the Catholic peace organization Pax Christi International.[28] After returning from Managua, Laurens Hogebrink, the head of the international section of the IKV, described the concert as the perfect opportunity for Western European peace organizations to learn more about "liberation struggle" in Central America.[29] Hogebrink agreed with Ramírez's comments, arguing that that events in Central America and the global campaign for disarmament were "obviously linked."[30] In July 1983, as part of a speech entitled "No Pasarán: No Contras, No Missiles," Hogebrink reiterated this view, declaring that Western European activists and Nicaraguan revolutionaries shared the same goal of building a future with no war, no interventions, and no nuclear weapons.[31] The timing of the peace concert in Managua worked out well for the Sandinistas, too. In 1983, Western European peace organizations were already developing an interest in promoting Third World causes as their own movement was losing momentum because of its inability to prevent the deployment of nuclear missiles on Western European soil.[32] It was due to the efforts of the FSLN and its allies that peace activists shifted their attention to the Nicaraguan Revolution, rather than to other countries in the Global South.

In Western European towns and cities, solidarity committees used the prospect of the peace festival to raise money for the FSLN and propagate the Sandinista cause. On 24 April 1983, responding to a telex from DRI diplomat Luis Caldera, activists organized demonstrations in front of United States embassies and consulates, celebrating the Concierto and carrying banners with the slogan "Peace in Central America: No Intervention!"[33] Moreover, the organizers of the concert, most notably Ernesto Cardenal, de Rooy, and Langenberg, turned the festival into a political and financial success for the Sandinista revolutionaries. To organize and record the concert, the Nicaraguan authorities received more than $600,000 in financial and material assistance from the Dutch and Greek governments, public broadcaster IKON (Interkerkelijke Omroep Nederland, Dutch Interchurch Broadcaster), development organization Novib, and the Thomas Kirche Gemeinde, a West German Protestant group. In addition to funding the festival, Langenberg and de Rooy made a documentary about the Nicaraguan Revolution that was broadcast in fifteen countries. This documentary, as the director of IKON, Jan Greven, explained to several Dutch journalists, demonstrated that problems in Latin America were not caused by the Cold War, as American propaganda wanted people to believe, but rather by poverty and social injustice.[34] The popular commercial record of the festival, *April in Managua*, was successfully sold by solidarity committees around Western Europe, making a significant financial profit for the FSLN.[35]

Despite the obvious propaganda benefits of collaborating with the peace movement, several Western European solidarity activists pointed out that supporting "peace" was very different from supporting "armed resistance" in Central America.[36] Indeed, there existed—exaggerated, it would turn out—fears that "hardline pacifists" in the peace movement would cause trouble for the solidarity committees, as they might not want to support armed revolution in Central America. Another concern was that the much larger peace movement would overshadow the individual message and propaganda of the Nicaraguan campaigns.[37] Nevertheless, for the majority of the Sandinistas' supporters, the benefits of cooperation with peace groups far outweighed the potential costs, particularly since the peace movement provided the FSLN with a new platform in Western Europe. The British Nicaragua Solidarity Campaign, to name one example, handed out twenty thousand leaflets about the accomplishments of the Nicaraguan Revolution during a large Campaign for Nuclear Disarmament demonstration in London, where they also sold over eight hundred copies of their magazine *Nicaragua Today*.[38] Indeed, the West German activist Hermann Schulz, one of the leaders of the Western European solidarity movement, explained to those who were hesitant to collaborate with the peace movement, solidarity committees simply had to make clear that "revolutionary violence" in Central America was of a "defensive" character, which would ultimately contribute to world peace.[39]

Among the peace activists, there existed some initial doubts about their movement's alliance with the Sandinistas, which some peace groups considered to be too closely aligned to the Soviet Union. Even though protesters mostly targeted NATO, most peace organizations did not want to be seen as pro-Soviet. Officially, the peace movement campaigned against the bipolar Cold War framework and rejected "domination" by both superpowers.[40] The Nicaraguan organization CONIPAZ, however, had close ties to the Moscow-led World Peace Council (WPC). Furthermore, peace activists noted, many participants at the Concierto in Managua represented communist organizations from the Eastern bloc and the Global South. This worried and irritated some Western activists, who wanted to bring across a different and what they described as a "more nuanced" message. IKV representative Wim Bartels, for instance, described the conference as "disappointing" due to the pro-Moscow speeches of the participants. Bartels complained about WPC president Romesh Chandra, the former leader of the Indian Communist Party, arguing that he had given an extremely anti-American and pro-Soviet speech that apparently "even shocked" the Eastern bloc representatives. Fortunately for the Sandinistas, Nicaraguan officials succeeded in convincing Western European representatives that the FSLN was not a communist organization, and truly wanted to be nonaligned in the Cold War. Sandinista comandante Carlos Núñez openly distanced himself from Chandra's pro-Soviet speech and, Bartels noted with relief, made an impressive case for "political pluralism and economic diversification" in Nicaragua.[41]

Overall, changes to the FSLN's revolutionary diplomacy worked in the Sandinistas' favor. By participating in regional negotiations and organizing festivals, Sandinistas and solidarity activist made the revolution appear attractive, progressive, and peaceful. The strategy of combining cultural activities with pro-Sandinista messaging significantly broadened the appeal of the solidarity movement. The British solidarity campaign, which had been relatively small in the late 1970s and early 1980s, started to thrive in 1983, rapidly evolving into one of the largest and more effective movements in Western Europe. Indeed, John Bevan of the NSC remembers, a successful benefit concert on 13 February 1983 in Shaftesbury Theatre entitled "An Evening for Nicaragua" was a turning point for the solidarity movement.[42] This popular event in London, hosted by actor Andy de la Tour and aired by new national television network Channel 4, featured performances by Daniel Viglietti, the band Pookiesnackenburger, and singer-songwriter Charlie Dore. In addition to cultural entertainment, a speech by the Nicaraguan ambassador Francisco d'Escoto, who had left his post in the United States in 1981, reminded audiences "of the reason" why the gathering was taking place, asking people "to remember those Nicaraguans who have fallen in combat trying to preserve the gains of the Nicaraguan revolution against U.S.-inspired aggression."[43] The wide appeal of the Sandinistas' revolutionary diplomacy, as the next section demonstrates, angered U.S. officials, who embarked on their own propaganda campaign to counter the Sandinista message.

## KISSINGER MEETS THE SANDINISTAS

As the FSLN's revolutionary diplomacy started to pay off, U.S. officials grew irritated with their inability to shape the public narrative. The domestic and international press was not giving "fair coverage" to "our true goals" in Central America, Reagan complained to Thatcher in the Oval Office on 29 September 1983; she agreed that Western countries were "losing the propaganda battle in Europe."[44] Reagan's frustration was not just a question of vanity; U.S. officials knew that public support could make or break the administration's Central America policy. Indeed, as one U.S. diplomat wrote on 16 July 1983, "much of what we would like to do, we cannot do now because of Congressional and public opinion concerns."[45] U.S. policymakers also regarded the insistence of Western European leaders that socioeconomic inequalities, rather than Soviet and Cuban interventions, lay at the root of Central America's unrest, as naïve and highly problematic. On 29 June 1983, Secretary of State George Shultz sent a letter to West German foreign minister Hans-Dietrich Genscher, stating that he was "concerned that our views do not coincide as closely as they might." Shultz was particularly upset by a recent statement by EC foreign ministers that blamed the "current uncertainty in the region primarily on long-term socio-economic consequences, with no mention of outside interference."[46]

Frustrated with the attitude of EC governments, as well as with the fact that the FSLN was clearly winning the battle for hearts and minds, the Reagan administration developed an ambitious propaganda campaign. Launched in June 1983, the project was led by Cuban-American Otto Juan Reich, who was made responsible for all "foreign and domestic efforts" to gain support for policies toward Latin America as a whole, and Central America in particular.[47] Reich's newly created Office of Public Diplomacy for Latin America and the Caribbean, as it was called, received interagency support, as well as covert CIA assistance, to coordinate a global network of individuals and organizations to amplify and lend credibility to Reagan's anticommunist message. Reich relied on a variety of strategies to influence public and congressional opinion, including conferences, lecture series, and media briefings.[48] He also brought anti-Sandinista speakers, such as Faith Ryan Whittlesey, Miguel Bolanos, Richard Stone, and Jeane Kirkpatrick into contact with media outlets, labor unions, business leaders, church groups, government officials, Rotary clubs, academics, politicians, human rights organizations, and foreign affairs groups.[49] Finally, in cooperation with the State Department and the CIA, the office edited and distributed a range of papers and pamphlets, lecturing people on the dangers of Nicaragua's military buildup, Cuban and Soviet infiltration of Central America, and the "broken promises" and human rights violations of the Sandinistas.[50]

A key element of the propaganda campaign against the FSLN was the establishment of the National Bipartisan Commission on Central America and the Caribbean, chaired by former Secretary of State Henry Kissinger, in July 1983. The purpose of the so-called Kissinger Commission, as one U.S.

policymaker admitted, was to "provide a rationale" for the Reagan administration's foreign policy.[51] To prepare the report, Kissinger and his companions toured Central America, visiting Managua in October 1983 and demanding to speak to Sandinistas and opposition leaders. Reluctantly, Daniel Ortega and foreign minister Miguel d'Escoto decided it would damage the Sandinistas' public image too much if they refused to meet with the U.S. representatives. However, they had no faith in the commission's intentions, objectivity, or bipartisanship. In the eyes of Nicaraguan leaders, Kissinger's commission was simply a propaganda tool to legitimize Reagan's illegal crusade against the revolution. What is more, they decried Kissinger leading such a project, given his past role in U.S. interventions in Chile during the early 1970s. The Sandinista newspaper *Barricada*, for example, declared that "Reagan is sending us the man who killed Allende."[52] Kissinger's commission members, the Nicaraguan foreign ministry predicted, would refuse to listen, behave in a "provocative" manner, and simply shout accusations at the Sandinistas. The only reason the American representatives did not exclude Nicaragua from their Central America tour, Sandinista officials believed, was to "project an image" of credibility and objectivity to the outside world.[53]

Unsurprisingly, given that each side had already made up its mind about the other's intentions, the private meetings went badly. As predicted by the Nicaraguans, U.S. representatives asked d'Escoto critical questions about religious freedom, democracy, censorship, and the presence of Cuban advisers in Nicaragua. Why were all of Nicaragua's Central American neighbors, even peaceful and democratic Costa Rica, so worried about Nicaragua's military buildup? When would the FSLN finally organize elections? The government clearly must be doing something wrong, commission member John Silber insisted, if even West German social democrats, the Sandinistas' former allies, now talked about how the Nicaraguan Revolution had been "betrayed." The Sandinistas, on the other hand, maintained that Reagan was the real aggressor in Central America and refused to talk about anything else. When asked about press freedom, d'Escoto attacked the "hypocrisy" of the U.S. government, pointing out that the White House "never showed any interest in the liberty" of Nicaraguans when Somoza was in power. Instead of lecturing the Sandinistas about freedom and censorship, he recommended that the members of the commission talk to the mothers and widows of those Nicaraguans killed because of Reagan's foreign policy.[54]

Nicaraguan records show that Kissinger's meeting with Daniel Ortega on 15 October 1983 occurred in a similarly unfriendly atmosphere. The former

Secretary of State barely spoke during the entire session, while Ortega lectured him about the history of the Sandinista Revolution and denounced Reagan's policies. Nicaragua, the comandante concluded his monologue, was simply a small country trying to defend itself from aggression and imperialism. After listening to Ortega's speech, Kissinger solemnly declared that he resented the Nicaraguan leader's attitude and arguments, felt disinclined to respond to his allegations, and left the room.[55] Publicly, Kissinger later warned the Nicaraguan government that the United States "should not be asked to choose between peace and democracy."[56] The Nicaraguans fired back. Sandinista comandante Omar Cabezas announced that Kissinger had behaved "with the arrogance of a Roman consul" and had refused to engage in any meaningful conversation, solely demanding that the FSLN start a dialogue with the Contras.[57] This was an insult, as the Sandinistas considered the Contras to be U.S.-funded mercenaries rather than an independent force that could engage in meaningful negotiations.

The FSLN did not have much time to come up with an elaborate response to Kissinger's accusations, though, as more pressing issues presented themselves to the revolutionaries less than two weeks later. Kissinger's painful visit to Managua was soon overshadowed by the invasion of the small Caribbean island of Grenada, which served as a reminder of the capacity and willingness of the U.S. government to resort to military means to achieve its Cold War objectives.

## GRENADA AND BRIGADES

On 25 October 1983, the United States attacked the republic of Grenada. Within weeks, U.S. Marines were in control of the small island and its hundred thousand inhabitants. The swift and successful military occupation of Grenada, codenamed Operation Urgent Fury, significantly boosted the confidence of the hardliners in the Reagan administration. Grenada had been under a left-wing government since Maurice Bishop seized power in a coup in March 1979, and the island received significant Cuban support. For the White House, therefore, the overthrow of what it called a "Marxist military dictatorship" in Grenada was a small but significant victory in the global Cold War.[58] In particular, Cold War ideologues saw the invasion as proof that direct military action was the most effective method in the international fight against communism. And although not all Americans backed the use of overt military force, Congress and the media were generally supportive of the invasion, which was thought to bring back order and democracy to the island.

Unsurprisingly, the FSLN observed Operation Urgent Fury with alarm. Sandinistas, and many other critics of Reagan's foreign policy toward Central America, were shocked by the invasion and feared that the occupation of Grenada was, in fact, a prelude to a much larger military intervention with the purpose of destroying the Nicaraguan Revolution. The editors of *Revista Envío*, a pro-FSLN journal, wrote in November 1983 that "the invasion of Grenada created a precedent and may also have created political momentum inside the White House for another invasion."[59] Meanwhile, activists and revolutionaries in Western Europe and Nicaragua responded by organizing "emergency" demonstrations, carrying banners with the slogan "First Grenada, then Nicaragua?"[60] The possible implications of the invasion of Grenada for the Nicaraguan Revolution were also debated in Western European parliaments. On 26 October 1983, to give one of many examples, Labour Party politician Denis Healey argued that there was "a grave danger" that the Reagan administration, inspired by Grenada, would use the same questionable methods to defend "freedom" in Nicaragua.[61] The invasion also caused further frustration and anxiety about Reagan's foreign policy among Western European governments, who had not been informed in advance of the plans to attack Grenada (a member of the British Commonwealth). In the weeks following the invasion, officials in London and Bonn, although skeptical that Reagan would take such a risk, had in-depth discussions about the effect that direct United States military action against Nicaragua would have on the transatlantic alliance and the Cold War system.[62]

After the fall of Grenada, the increasingly hostile tone adopted by U.S. officials and in anti-Sandinista propaganda reflects the deteriorating relationship between the two countries. On 10 May 1984, Constantine Menges, a member of Reagan's National Security Council, praised the U.S.-funded military actions in Nicaragua to British diplomat David Thomas. To the astonishment of the British representative—who was certainly no admirer of the Sandinistas himself—Menges described the "mining of harbors," which took place in early 1984, as "arguably one of the most humane ways of reducing Nicaragua's offensive capability."[63] Defected Sandinista guerrilla Miguel Bolanos, too, used confrontational language when he told journalists from the Heritage Foundation, a right-wing think tank, that Sandinista leaders were "more repressive than Somoza" and that Nicaragua was "the base of operations for the spread of international communism in the Western

Hemisphere." Based on these alarmist and distorted claims, Bolanos called for more U.S. support for the insurgents.[64]

In this tense and hostile context, the Kissinger Commission published its findings. Released on 11 January 1984, the 132-page report predictably concluded that Soviet interference in Central America threatened the United States' security. Pleased with this endorsement of his Central America policies, the Reagan administration used the report to influence Western European governments. When Shultz visited London on 15 January 1984, he handed Thatcher a copy of the report, which included policy recommendations such as cutting off aid to the Nicaraguan government and increasing support to El Salvador.[65] The Western Europeans had "significant" security interests in Central America and the Caribbean, Kissinger wrote, "since the ability of the United States to fulfil its commitments to the Western Alliance would be adversely affected by developments in Central America." If the situation in Central America escalated further, he warned, the United States would be forced to redeploy troops that were currently based in Western Europe to Central America. These security concerns were not "well-appreciated," Kissinger complained, adding that "some European governments and organizations have taken actions inimical to U.S.—and indeed, to European—security, such as supporting the Sandinista government or the Salvadoran insurgents."[66]

The Sandinistas were lucky that the Western Europeans were unimpressed by Kissinger's conclusions. The British Foreign and Commonwealth Office criticized the report for its "confrontationalist tone," its implication that Western Europe should "toe the American political line," and the "exaggerated perception of Soviet designs" in Central America.[67] The West Germans, too, believed that the contents of the report, especially the negative description of Western European foreign policies, were "controversial."[68] With regard to the Nicaraguans, European officials agreed that Kissinger's proposals, such as assisting the Contras, as well as demanding that the Sandinistas break their ties to Cuba, were "unrealistic" and "disappointing."[69] His insistence that Nicaragua should no longer benefit from Western European economic aid was also seen as counterproductive by those countries that believed financial support could keep Nicaragua nonaligned, as well as by those who supported a regional approach to Central American affairs. Finally, highlighting the impact of the FSLN's revolutionary diplomacy on government policy, diplomats complained that the report failed "to deal fairly with the real pressure on European governments from public opinion."[70]

The negative Western European response to the Kissinger report is emblematic of the United States' inability to mobilize support for its foreign policy in the aftermath of Grenada. Despite a multimillion-dollar propaganda campaign, public and governmental opinion remained dismissive. In January 1984, an anonymous CIA officer concluded that, "despite the Department's efforts to increase the flow of information and high-level visitors to European capitals, attitudes generally remain critical of U.S. policies in the region."[71] Another official added that, at the state level, "the most the United States can hope for from its allies is a sort of pained silence." Western Europeans had certainly no sympathy for the counterinsurgents, who failed to obtain any "significant funds from either Western European officials or private sources" despite several sponsored visits from Contra leaders Alfonso Robelo (the former junta member) and Adolfo Calero. On the contrary, in January 1984, nearly six hundred parliamentarians from the Netherlands, France, West Germany, the United Kingdom, Italy, Austria, and Denmark signed a letter to Tip O'Neill, the Speaker of the House, asking Congress to "oppose new CIA funds against Nicaragua" and declaring that they rejected the "economic isolation of Nicaragua."[72]

Even though it was clear that the Western Europeans would not endorse a military attack against Nicaragua, the military might on display in Grenada convinced the FSLN of the urgency of a strong military defense, hence the increase in Soviet military aid discussed in the previous section. Moreover, the FSLN hoped to complement its increase in military spending by boosting the solidarity movement, which they hoped could function as a nonmilitary means of defense. Less than two months after the invasion, the Sandinista government thus launched another high-profile campaign to increase public interest in the revolution.

On 20 December 1983, the comandantes made an important announcement, inviting tens of thousands of international volunteers to come to Nicaragua and assist with the harvest of the country's "all-important coffee crop."[73] Their call for international solidarity did not go unanswered. Despite the high financial costs (around $800 per person), potential danger, and long journey, thousands of curious people in the United Kingdom, West Germany, and the Netherlands enthusiastically sent in their applications to the recruiting solidarity committees.[74] On 21 December 1983, the first of many coffee-picking brigades from Western Europe arrived in Managua, where they were received by the minister of culture, Ernesto Cardenal, himself.[75] In Nicaragua, the brigadistas—working in groups of around twenty to thirty people—spent around four weeks picking

FIGURE 10. In December 1986, a Nicaragua Solidarity Campaign coffee brigade is seen off by Chris Smith, a Labour Party MP for the constituency Islington South and Finsbury, United Kingdom. The practice of sending brigadistas to Nicaragua was an effective tool to defend and popularize the Nicaraguan Revolution. Photo: Nicaragua Solidarity Campaign, London.

coffee on state farms and then another two weeks "travelling around the country and learning in greater depth about the Sandinista Revolution."[76] After the harvest season in 1983/1984, the practice of sending solidarity brigades to Nicaragua increased still further, as it proved to be an effective way of attracting people to the Sandinista cause (figure 10). In 1984, for instance, the London-based NSC sent more than 120 brigadistas to visit Nicaragua, "the vast majority for the first time."[77] Coffee-picking and building brigades were soon complemented with shorter "study tours," which lasted only two weeks and often had a specific theme, such as health care, women's rights, education, and labor unions in revolutionary Nicaragua. As part of these tours, Western European visitors traveled around the country to witness the tangible benefits of the revolution and speak with a range of representatives of Nicaraguan grassroots and mass organizations, such as the Sandinista women's association Asociación de Mujeres Nicaragüense Luisa Amanda Espinoza (Luisa Amanda Espinoza Association of Nicaraguan Women, AMLAE).[78]

While the solidarity committees were responsible for the recruitment of brigadistas in Western Europe, the FSLN decided what happened when the activists arrived in Nicaragua. Specifically, the Comité Nicaragüense de Solidaridad con los Pueblos (Nicaraguan Committee for People's Solidarity, CNSP), the part of the DRI that was responsible for managing the FSLN's relations with the solidarity movement, coordinated the brigades on a national level, deciding where the activists were going to work, sleep, and eat.[79] The CNSP also ensured that the coffee-pickers and other brigadistas would leave with a positive impression of the country, developing a political, educational, and touristic program that functioned as an introduction to life in revolutionary Nicaragua.[80] Ana Patricia Elvir, the General Secretary of the CNSP in the 1980s, remembers that she would often give seminars to newly-arrived brigadistas, telling them about the country's economic and military situation, and explaining the "importance of international volunteers" to Nicaragua.[81]

The work of the CNSP was complemented by the efforts of the Western European solidarity activists who resided in Nicaragua. These activists visited brigadistas at their place of work, providing information, materials (such as medicine and clothing), and pastoral care. The activities of Nicaragua-based solidarity activists were important for the brigades' functioning, as these Western Europeans usually had a good understanding of their compatriots' expectations and concerns, which made it easier for them to provide emotional and practical support. David Thomson from Dundee, Scotland, for example, was the "man in Managua" for the British and Irish brigadistas.[82] It was his job, Thomson remembers, to welcome the new arrivals, "calm their fears about going into a war zone," and keep up morale by bringing the activists letters from home and "food that wasn't gallo pinto [rice and beans]" or tortilla.[83]

The Western Europeans who participated in the brigades came from a range of different backgrounds, but all had a sympathetic attitude toward the Nicaraguan Revolution. Brigadistas were members of left-wing political parties, anti-imperialist organizations, the peace movement, labor unions, feminist groups, and religious movements attracted to the Sandinistas' version of liberation theology.[84] Latin American exiles in Western Europe, too, signed up to join the brigades. Indeed, the Dutch committee noted in 1984, brigades would ideally consist of people from different socioeconomic and political backgrounds.[85] While most of those who traveled to Nicaragua were relatively young (between eighteen and twenty-five years old), the NSC wrote in a newsletter in 1986 that the ages of people who picked coffee on a state farm near the northern town of Matagalpa ranged "from 18 year old Julian Ford to 60 year old Jim Stafford."[86] Thomson similarly remembers that he worked with "kids from the ages of 16 and 18 through people in their 50s."[87] We lack official data about the numbers of men and women who traveled to Nicaragua but based on images, anecdotal evidence, and descriptions from brigadistas, more men than women signed up. Of the 162 West Germans who left for Nicaragua on 20 December 1983, for instance, only 34 were women.[88]

The purpose of solidarity brigades went beyond building schools or helping with the coffee harvest. To be sure, volunteers could certainly make valuable contributions to local Nicaraguan communities, especially if they were trained construction workers, medical specialists, or teachers. Moreover, since coffee was Nicaragua's most important export product, the embattled Sandinistas were in desperate need of extra labor to make the harvest a success. Particularly in the parts of the country that were most affected by the Contra war, such as Matagalpa and Jinotega in the northern highlands, the FSLN consistently relied on the work of volunteers to ensure that enough coffee was being produced. In these dangerous areas in the mid-1980s, as historian José Luis Rocha writes, more than 30 percent of the coffee-pickers were volunteers, which included Nicaraguan students and public-sector workers as well as international visitors and solidarity activists.[89]

The propagandistic value of having hundreds of foreign activists working in Nicaragua, however, was arguably more important than their practical contributions. International brigadistas were not allowed to join the Sandinista army or to fight against the Contras (even though many of them wanted to) because the FSLN feared that Western governments would try to place the blame on the Sandinistas if any foreign nationals died in the war zones.[90] Yet the FSLN certainly hoped the presence of Western European and North American solidarity activists in Nicaragua's most vulnerable and dangerous regions would function as an "element of containment" against Contra raids and potential military strikes by the United States.[91] West German solidarity committees made a similar point, declaring that, by being physically present in Nicaragua's border areas, the brigades lent "practical, political, and moral support" to the everyday struggle of Nicaraguan campesinos against U.S. aggression.[92] Richard Owen, the British ambassador to Costa Rica, too, suggested that solidarity brigades functioned as a valuable "propaganda tool" in the Contra war. Indeed, he wrote after running into a group of British brigadistas in Managua, imagine "the rumpus that would ensue if one or more brigadistas were wounded or killed in the course of a Contra attack."[93] Building on the Left's long tradition of internationalism, the Sandinista decision to invite brigadistas to Nicaragua was an excellent way to ensure the Sandinista Revolution's survival, which seemed increasingly vulnerable after Grenada.

In Western Europe, returned brigadistas contributed to the FSLN's revolutionary diplomacy by sharing their personal insights and experiences in Nicaragua with the public. According to the NSC, which carried out a survey among former brigadistas in the United Kingdom, testimonies by those who traveled to Nicaragua received extensive media coverage. Local newspapers were particularly keen to publish interviews with activists, but some also appeared on television or were interviewed on the radio. Almost all brigadistas gave multiple talks about their experiences in revolutionary Nicaragua, speaking at local branches of the Labour Party, church groups, schools, and events organized by organizations such as Oxfam and War on Want. Crucially, the NSC pointed out, many brigadistas mentioned in the survey that "talking to friends, family, and work colleagues in an informal situation" about their experiences with the Sandinistas allowed them to reach people "who would not normally hear or think about Nicaragua." Traveling to this revolutionary country, the British activists concluded, was "absolutely essential" to keeping the solidarity movement alive, visible, and active.[94] Calculating that the testimonials of public figures would carry even more weight than those of normal citizens, the building and coffee-picking brigades were complemented by tours for prominent Western European journalists, politicians, and artists. Already in August 1982, for instance, Sandinista leaders including Daniel Ortega and Ernesto Cardenal extended a warm welcome to a West German delegation that included the famous novelist Günther Grass, left-wing politician Johann Strasser, and Christian Democratic journalist Franz Alt. Impressed by the revolution and the accessibility of FSLN officials, the West Germans contributed to the Sandinistas' revolutionary diplomacy by disseminating positive stories about Nicaragua and criticizing Reagan's foreign policy.[95]

On a more personal level, brigades, visits, and study tours were a tool to create affective connections between solidarity activists and the people who, in the eyes of the activists, embodied the revolution. After working, eating, and living side by side with Nicaraguan farmers, schoolchildren, teachers, and construction workers, many of whom were negatively affected by the Contra war, solidarity activists felt a deep sense of responsibility and emotional attachment to the revolution, the country, and its inhabitants. Because they had learned "at first hand of the sacrifices made by Nicaraguans," British coffee-pickers later wrote about their experience, they left the country "with a compelling obligation to become more involved in solidarity work."[96] John Allan, who worked for a British labor union and visited Nicaragua in 1984, wrote that he was "enormously impressed by everything [he] saw in Nicaragua." The "enthusiasm of the people so long oppressed by the brutal Somoza dictatorships," Allan concluded, needed "to be seen to be understood."[97] Personal connections between Nicaraguans and brigadistas lived on after the activists returned to their home countries. When a group of Dutch activists received news that "their" coffee farm had been destroyed by Contras, the ex-brigadistas raised money to rebuild the community that they felt part of.[98] The practice of organizing brigades and inviting visitors to Nicaragua worked out well for the Sandinistas, as it made the everyday reality of the revolution more tangible and attractive to Western European audiences.

To be sure, some international volunteers—sometimes mockingly described as "rucksack revolutionaries"—were disillusioned by their experience in Nicaragua.[99] Helping the FSLN achieve its ideals in such a "concrete way" sounded very "romantic" at first, one Dutch activist commented, but the reality on the ground turned out to be very different. Coffee-picking was difficult, painful, and mind-numbing work. The beautiful and tranquil mountain region also had its downsides, brigadistas admitted after spending several weeks in the countryside, noting that the daily practice of eating frijoles (beans) at the farmhouse had become rather boring.[100] A minority experienced the brutality of the Contra war up close, as Nicaraguan friends were killed, raped, or kidnapped by counterrevolutionary forces. It could also be dangerous for the activists themselves, although it needs to be stressed that Western activists were in a much more privileged position than the Nicaraguans, as the Sandinistas—and their own governments—tried to keep them out of harm's way as much as possible. Despite these precautions, on 17 May 1986, fifteen Nicaraguan farmers and twelve West German brigadistas who had been working at an agricultural cooperative in southern Nicaragua were abducted by Contras. While four of the activists managed to escape from their kidnappers, the campesinos and other eight brigadistas (four women and four men) were held captive for more than three weeks.[101] After their release, which was brought about by heavy pressure from West German officials, including foreign minister Genscher, and mediation efforts by the prominent social democrat Hans-Jürgen Wischnewski, the activists told journalists how scared they had been, noting that "they were never certain they would emerge from their ordeal alive."[102] Astrid Stelter, one of the kidnapped West Germans, remembers being exhausted and anxious, noting that the Contras "kept constantly on the move and at times shot over the heads of the Germans if they moved too slowly."[103]

The potential dangers and disadvantages of spending time in Nicaragua, however, did not stop Western Europeans from traveling to the country and contributing to the FSLN's revolutionary diplomacy. While it is difficult to determine to what extent solidarity brigades were a key factor in mobilizing new audiences for the Sandinista cause, activists in Western Europe described the brigades and study tours as an enormous success, noting that at least 70 percent of the returning brigadistas became active members of the solidarity movement.[104] British diplomats, too, believed that many Western Europeans had taken up "the Nicaraguan cause" because "they had been the guests of the Nicaraguan government."[105] The new strategy of using emotional connections and personal experiences to popularize the Nicaraguan Revolution in Western Europe certainly worked in the Sandinistas' favor.

## THE EC AND CONTADORA

Despite the growing strength and popularity of the solidarity movement, the FSLN calculated that popular support alone was not enough to ward off a U.S. military intervention. Ultimately, by influencing public opinion the FSLN hoped to positively shape the foreign policies of Western European governments, as the revolutionaries craved further legitimacy and financial support. Of course, the Sandinistas appreciated the fact that Western European leaders rejected Reagan's Central America policies, but this rejection was not the same as an endorsement of the revolution. Moreover, as we have seen in the previous chapter, Western European governments had failed to agree on a proactive foreign policy toward the region in 1982, thereby limiting their ability to influence the situation in Central America. Furthermore, as the political landscape in Western Europe shifted from the left to the right in the early 1980s, the Nicaraguan government's foreign policy fell onto increasingly barren ground. In particular, the fact that Nicaragua was excluded from the European Community's special aid package in 1982 weakened the Sandinistas' standing in the international community. Therefore, when Western European governments, fearful of another Cold War conflict and worried that the Contadora process was on the brink of collapse, stepped up their involvement in Central America, the FSLN comandantes were keen to use these developments to the Nicaraguan Revolution's benefit.

In early 1984, Western European officials noted that the threat of military escalation in Central America had drastically increased in the months following the Grenada invasion. First, as regional leaders were unable to make progress in their negotiations, one British official wrote to his French colleague that the Contadora countries appeared to be "reaching the point of considering abandonment of their efforts."[106] This possibility worried European policymakers, who calculated that without the Contadora process, the balance could easily tip in favor of the Reagan administration's preferred methods, namely a military struggle.[107] Indeed, British diplomats warned their European colleagues on 27 April 1984 that the implosion of the Contadora process would make the situation in Central America "much less hopeful."[108] Second, even though Reagan publicly claimed to support Contadora, Western European leaders lost faith in his administration's willingness to pursue a diplomatic solution in March 1984 when they found out that the CIA, in collaboration with the counterrevolutionaries, had mined several Nicaraguan harbors, damaging at least one British merchant vessel.[109] The French government, in particular, took a strong stance against the illegal mining, even offering to help the Sandinista government sweep the mines from their ports.[110]

In this context of heightening tensions and militarization, an intra-European consensus about a regional policy toward Central America could finally emerge. In view of the "difficulties the Contadora-initiative is facing," the West German foreign office concluded on 4 May 1984, "joint European support is needed more than before."[111] Genscher, collaborating closely with the Costa Rican president Luis Alberto Monge, was the driving force behind the new Western European initiative.[112] In May 1984, Genscher successfully proposed a regional cooperation agreement between the EC and the Central American countries, designed to give momentum and political legitimacy to the Contadora negotiations as well as provide Central American states with increased (but still limited) financial aid and a forum to discuss their grievances. Unlike the situation before the Grenada invasion, Genscher was able to convince his European colleagues that Nicaragua should be included. Failing to pursue an inclusive regional approach, he argued successfully, would undermine "both the Contadora-initiative, as well as efforts by the EC to encourage regional integration in Central America."[113]

Genscher's plans to stabilize Central America through political dialogue culminated in a historic summit between Latin American and Western European officials in San José, Costa Rica, on 28 and 29 September 1984. The conference's final joint communiqué, signed by the EC countries, Spain and

Portugal (both of whom were on the threshold of EC membership), the Contadora states, and the Central American governments, encouraged regional actors to "bring the Contadora process rapidly to final fruition."[114] The summit also marked the beginning of the so-called San José dialogue, which took the form of yearly meetings between European and Central American ministers and diplomats (see chapter 6). At the time, the historic and political significance of the San José conference was clear to all involved; this was the first time that EC foreign ministers came together in an official capacity outside of Western Europe, and they chose to do so in Central America, a region seen as firmly placed within the United States' sphere of influence. Indeed, the fact that Western European leaders found it necessary to become collectively involved in Central American affairs at all—despite the absence of traditional ties and without the lubricant of extensive trade links—highlights how remarkably important the region had become in the mid-1980s.

The San José meeting, and the fact that Shultz was not invited, offered the Nicaraguan revolutionaries an excellent opportunity to present their country as a symbol of peace, contributing to the delegitimization of Reagan's foreign policy.[115] In speeches and declarations, Sandinista leaders emphasized that EC involvement in the region demonstrated that revolutionary Nicaragua had international backing, while the United States stood isolated and alone. By gathering in the traditional "backyard" of the United States, the editors of *Revista Envío* concluded, the European Community "challenged the Monroe Doctrine" that was at the core of Reagan's approach toward Central America. Triumphantly, the editors referred to the words of French foreign minister Claude Cheysson, who responded to a question about U.S. efforts to influence the proceedings in San José by asking: "What does Reagan have to do with this? As far as I understand, he is not part of the EC, the Contadora group, or the Central American group."[116] Nicaragua's participation in the Western European initiative served as a powerful illustration of Reagan's international isolation following the invasion of Grenada.

On 21 September 1984, the Sandinista government further capitalized on the upcoming conference by announcing that Nicaragua was willing to sign the revised Contadora Act, presented on 7 September 1984 to the Central American countries, without any modifications. The Sandinistas thereby agreed to several concessions, such as limiting the number of Eastern bloc advisers in Nicaragua, reducing the size of its army, and ending its support for the FMLN guerrillas in El Salvador. This was worth it, the FSLN calculated, if these concessions would also force the Reagan administration to give up its support for the Contras. To that end, the Nicaraguan government demanded that the United States immediately sign an "additional protocol" to the revised Act, promising to "cease immediately all the acts of aggression against Nicaragua."[117]

The Nicaraguan decision to sign the Acta de Contadora, made official just one week before the San José conference, was a strategic and cleverly timed move, challenging a key argument of Reagan and his allies. In the weeks leading up to the summit, the U.S. administration had accused Nicaragua of obstructing the Contadora process, specifically citing the Sandinistas' refusal to sign the revised Act. On 7 September 1984, Shultz sent a letter to the EC foreign ministers, "strongly" urging them to ensure that the San José summit would "not lead to increased economic aid or any political assistance to the Sandinistas." Unlike the Reagan administration and the governments of Costa Rica, El Salvador, Guatemala, and Honduras, who all considered the revised Contadora Act an "important step forward" in the peace process, Shultz told his Western European colleagues, Nicaragua "has rejected key elements of the draft," including a reduction "in arms and troop levels."[118] By suddenly agreeing to cooperate, then, the FSLN had turned the tables on the U.S. administration. Indeed, as journalist Stephen Kinzer wrote in *The New York Times*, the Sandinista offer was "a propaganda victory for Nicaragua and it caught the United States by surprise."[119]

Despite the propaganda victory, Nicaragua's willingness to sign the revised Contadora Act failed to push the Reagan administration toward a less militaristic foreign policy. On the contrary, after the surprise announcement, the administration, already committed to the overthrow of the Sandinista regime, became, in the words of the British ambassador in Washington, "extremely keen" to block the Contadora Act.[120] In Western Europe and Central America, U.S. officials immediately contacted their colleagues, arguing that the Nicaraguan revolutionaries were trying to use the peace process to their own advantage by pushing through an agreement that was naturally unacceptable to the United States and its regional allies, as it lacked adequate control and verification mechanisms. Reagan and anticommunist Central American leaders such as Salvadoran president José Napoleón Duarte urged EC foreign ministers to refrain from publicly supporting the revised Act at the San José conference, warning them that the Sandinistas were unlikely to keep their promises.[121]

Less than a month after the Nicaraguan declaration, it was clear that Reagan's diplomatic offensive against the Contadora Act had succeeded. The governments of El Salvador, Costa Rica, and Honduras, suspicious of the Sandinistas' intentions and under heavy pressure by U.S. officials, changed their position and insisted that the draft needed to be changed. "Following intensive US consultations with El Salvador, Honduras, and Costa Rica," CIA officers concluded on 30 October 1984, "we have effectively blocked Contadora Group effort to impose the second draft of a Revised Contadora Act."[122] As a result, Western European leaders, unwilling to side with revolutionary Nicaragua over the other Central American countries (as this would clash with their regional approach), refrained from publicly backing the Act in San José, deciding to declare support for the Contadora *process* instead.

Moreover, the declaration that Nicaragua was willing to sign the Contadora Act failed to bring about a radical change in opinion in the right-wing governments of West Germany, the United Kingdom, and the Netherlands, which remained skeptical of the Sandinistas' motivations. Western European governments—particularly those led by conservative and Christian Democratic politicians—regarded the declaration as a tactical move, designed to strengthen the Sandinistas' international image and win a propaganda victory over the United States, the counterrevolutionaries, and the other Central American countries. After the San José conference, British officials concluded that, in the previous months, the Western European tendency to give Nicaragua "the benefit of the doubt" had diminished.[123] West German diplomats, too, continued to perceive what they saw as Nicaraguan stubbornness as the primary reason for Contadora's failure. Instead of blaming the shifting position of El Salvador or U.S. pressure for the failed peace talks, West German officials pointed to the fact that Sandinista leaders did not accept the proposed changes to the *revised* Contadora Act in October 1984.[124]

The harsh condemnation of the Sandinistas stood in stark contrast to the way Western European governments responded to the violence in other Central American countries, notably El Salvador. The Salvadoran government, under the leadership of the Christian Democrat Duarte, was not seen as responsible for the murders committed by its military—such as the infamous Atlácatl Battalion, which committed the 1981 El Mozote massacre—or the disappearances carried out by anticommunist death squads. Rather, most Western European governments adopted the attitude that, despite his good intentions, Duarte was unfortunately unable to prevent the violence from taking place. The British government, for instance, believed Duarte's democratic government was under "authoritarian pressure from the left and right."[125] Similarly, the West German government believed that Duarte should be supported in his efforts to "end the violence" and "consolidate democracy through social reforms." Indeed, after meeting Duarte in Bonn in July 1984, Genscher agreed with the Salvadoran president that Nicaragua's support for the Salvadoran guerrillas was the primary "obstacle" to the Contadora process.[126]

How then, from the Sandinistas' perspective, can we assess the heightened level of Western European state involvement in Central America in the aftermath of Grenada? On the positive side, the public position of EC governments functioned as a valuable deterrent against both a potential U.S. invasion and further military support for the Honduras-based Contras. Moreover, the Sandinista government welcomed EC involvement in Central America due to Western Europe's economic and material contributions to Nicaragua, which was now included in the EC's regional aid package. Aid from the European Commission to Nicaragua, consequently, more than doubled from $6.9 million in 1983 to $14.7 million in 1984. The FSLN desperately needed this extra support, as due to the debt crisis financial aid from Latin America decreased from $220 million in 1983 to $120 million in 1984.[127] Of course, the EC increase did not make up for the drastic decrease in Latin American aid, but at a time when the only other possible source of money was the Soviet Union, the FSLN was relieved that the Western Europeans continued to provide them with some financial backing. On the other hand, the importance of Western European public and governmental opinion for the survival of the Nicaraguan Revolution meant that the Sandinista comandantes needed to accommodate governments and organizations ideologically different from the FSLN and, in some cases, highly critical of the Nicaraguan leadership. Western European governments, for instance, criticized the Sandinista government's attitude toward Contadora, its support for the Salvadoran guerrillas, its press censorship, human rights violations, and the lack of political pluralism. Citing these concerns, the United Kingdom and West Germany postponed or further reduced their levels of bilateral aid to Nicaragua in 1984–85.[128]

In other words, as regional tensions heightened in the aftermath of the Grenada invasion, Western European involvement in Central America became a necessary inconvenience for the Sandinista comandantes. To survive, Nicaragua needed to demonstrate that Western European states and politicians, who were perceived as more moderate and neutral parties in the Central American conflict than the United States, were on their side. To do so, the FSLN comandantes were sometimes forced to make concessions they otherwise might not have approved. In this context, as the next section further demonstrates, the Sandinista government had few other options than to yield to international pressure.

## THE 1984 ELECTIONS

The most important step the Sandinista government took to appease its international critics following the overthrow of Maurice Bishop's government in Grenada was making a commitment to organize democratic elections, which took place on 4 November 1984, two days before people in the United States went to the polls to re-elect Ronald Reagan. As contemporary commentators, the Sandinista leadership, and Western European solidarity committees had predicted, the FSLN, with Daniel Ortega and Sergio Ramírez on the ballot, won the election in a landslide.[129]

For the Sandinistas, these elections were a "tactical" concession, forced on them by the realities of war and international pressure.[130] Since coming to power in 1979, the FSLN had consistently rejected calls by domestic and foreign critics to create what the revolutionaries and their allies described as a "bourgeois democracy" in Nicaragua.[131] Elections, the FSLN told its allies and opponents, would only be organized once the "power structures" in the country had been transformed so that previously marginalized groups, including workers and campesinos, could fully participate in the country's democratic process. In the meantime, placards around the country reminded Nicaraguans of the sacrifices made during the armed struggle, proclaiming that "the people have already made their choice with blood."[132] For the revolutionaries, it was possible to have democracy without elections. The "democratic character" of the revolution was perfectly visible to everyone who visited Nicaragua in the early 1980s, Ernesto Cardenal reflects in his memoirs, as Nicaraguan people participated in mass gatherings, town assemblies, and radio interviews with Sandinista leaders to openly discuss the revolution's strengths and weaknesses.[133] Solidarity activists echoed these views, telling Western European audiences that the connection between elections and democracy was not as straightforward as it might appear. In the past, the NSC reminded readers in a booklet on the Nicaraguan elections, "Central Americans had no shortage of elections but precious little democracy."[134] Rather than the beginning of a democratic process, then, the Sandinistas and their allies saw the elections as the revolution's final seal of approval, a confirmation of what most Nicaraguans already knew.

Sandinistas thus had a very different understanding of democracy and elections from most Western politicians. The purpose of the electoral process in Nicaragua, according to MINEX officials, was the international legitimization of a revolutionary process that benefited the Nicaraguan people as a whole. This process, Sandinistas argued, was under threat from forces outside of the country, most notably the aggressive "imperialism" of the United States and its capitalist allies.[135] Democratic elections in capitalist countries were different, they believed, because capitalist elections only existed to "strengthen the interests" of one particular domestic group, while Nicaragua's electoral process aimed to improve the entire society.[136] In other words, the electoral process in Nicaragua was up against foreign opposition (namely the efforts of the anticommunist countries to undermine the legitimacy of the revolution), while democracy in the West was designed to neutralize domestic opposition. Taking these contrasting perceptions of democracy into account, it is not surprising that, in the weeks leading up to polling day, the FSLN candidate for the Estelí constituency, Rosario Antuñez, rather than campaigning in Nicaragua, chose to travel through Western Europe to convince government officials, activists, and politicians of the "pluralistic nature" of Nicaragua's electoral process.[137]

As such, a crucial part of the electoral struggle took place in the international arena. First and foremost, the Sandinista leadership needed the elections to bring international legitimacy to the revolution. By holding elections, the FSLN planned to demonstrate to the rest of the world that accusations that Nicaragua was an oppressive, communist, and "totalitarian state" were false. This, in turn, would diminish support for what Sandinistas described as the U.S. "policy of aggression against the Sandinista People's Revolution."[138] Regarding Western Europe, MINEX officials speculated optimistically that the electoral process would not only "boost and deepen the economic cooperation between Western Europe and Nicaragua" but also lead to a renewed influx of expressions of political solidarity from Western European politicians and activists. In particular, the Sandinistas hoped the elections would repair their uncomfortable relationship with the Socialist International, which had pressured the FSLN about democracy and political pluralism for years. While the aspiration of the SI to "put its own stamp on the Sandinista People's Revolution," as Nicaraguan diplomats phrased it, irritated Sandinista government officials, they recognized it was crucial to maintain the support of social democrats.[139] Thus, as Sergio Ramírez writes in his memoirs, for the United States, as well as for the Sandinistas, the 1984 elections "were part of the war strategy."[140]

With international legitimacy as the ultimate prize, public opinion and perceptions once again became powerful weapons in the struggle for Nicaragua's future. Before and after the elections, the White House and the Sandinistas, relying on a combination of diplomacy, propaganda material, and transnational support networks, each aimed to convince international audiences that the elections were, respectively, a "Communist-style sham" or a celebration of democracy.[141] The United States government distributed what it described as a "resource book" on the undemocratic nature of the elections, in which they argued that the FSLN would never willingly give up power.[142] Meanwhile, solidarity committees embarked on a campaign to publicize the positive aspects of Nicaragua's transition toward democracy.[143] They published posters and leaflets explaining that the elections were "designed to extend popular participation" and that—despite claims by critics—all parties had equal access to the media in the run-up to the elections.[144] After the FSLN's triumph, activists wrote to Thatcher that "Nicaragua has recently held the first meaningful, democratic elections in its history," adding that "several hundred independent witnesses from governments and political bodies throughout the world were able to attend the polling, and their reports reflect an overwhelming consensus that the elections were free and fair."[145] Noticing that statements from prominent social democrats would carry a lot of weight in the international debate, both the FSLN and Reagan administration specifically targeted SI members. Sandinista officials encouraged social democrats to disseminate positive information about the openness of the Nicaraguan electoral process.[146] Similarly, the United States embassy in Bonn asked the West German social democrat Willy Brandt to put out a negative statement about Sandinista harassment of opposition parties, which Brandt refused to do.[147]

Already before the elections had taken place on 4 November 1984, however, it was clear that the process would fail to bring the Sandinista government the international approval it sought. In his memoirs, Ramírez writes that the FSLN only "partially" gained legitimacy by organizing elections.[148] Alejandro Bendaña, too, concedes that the Nicaraguan government lost the electoral battle for external legitimacy, noting that the 1984 elections "were called Soviet sham elections, even though by historical standards, or Central American standards, they weren't that bad." Indeed, he added, even though a number of opposition candidates boycotted the elections (about which more below), Nicaragua simply did not look like Cuba or the Soviet Union because the country had "opposition newspapers, 18 different parties, [and] a Constitution which looked more like the Constitution of Costa Rica than of Cuba."[149] Not all reports about the elections were negative, but an international consensus about the nature of the elections was not reached. The Netherlands, the only EC country to send an official observer team to the Nicaraguan elections, produced a generally positive report about the elections, which concluded that "there were no irregularities during polling or in the count" and conceded that the FSLN had won the elections with a "clear majority."[150] Dutch foreign minister Hans van den Broek, however, at a European Political Cooperation meeting in November 1984, made the rather vague statement that this did not actually mean that the Sandinista government was "representative" of the Nicaraguan people.[151] The British government, too, dismissed positive reports about the elections. On 9 November 1984, Foreign Secretary Geoffrey Howe presented his views of the elections in the House of Commons, and these largely backed the Reagan administration's position. To the frustration of many Labour MPs, Howe declared that there had been "no possibility of a genuinely free and fair contest, ... however orderly the polling may have appeared to visitors who spent the last few days in Nicaragua."[152]

The main reason why Western Europeans were skeptical of the validity of the elections was that a couple days before the vote, Arturo Cruz, the leader of the Coordinadora Democrática Nicaragüense, the main opposition party, declared that he had been forced to withdraw his candidacy. In a televised interview on *CBS News Nightwatch*, Cruz argued that he was "excluded on purpose by the Sandinistas" and suggested that, if the elections had been truly free, his party could have easily defeated the Sandinistas in the polls, considering the "pervading disillusionment" with the "Marxist-Leninist" leaders of Nicaragua.[153] Conscious that the withdrawal of a prominent and respected opposition leader would raise doubts about electoral freedom and political pluralism, the U.S. public diplomacy office used it as proof of the Sandinistas' bad intentions.[154] In Western Europe, it became an often-heard argument to undermine the legitimacy of the Nicaraguan elections. Howe, for instance, told the House of Commons that opposition parties in Nicaragua had "decided to withdraw from the elections" since they were "effectively intimidated and often physically harassed by Sandinista mobs."[155]

Some controversy exists to this day about the exact reason for Arturo Cruz's withdrawal from the election campaign, but evidence has emerged that the United States government pressured Cruz and other opposition candidates into boycotting the elections. Bendaña, for instance, claims that "because the principal opposition candidates had been heavily pressured by the U.S. to withdraw," the elections failed to fulfill their promise.[156] In October and November 1984, *The New York Times* backed up this claim, reporting on several occasions that United States diplomats in Managua "pressured opposition politicians to withdraw from the ballot in order to isolate the Sandinistas and to discredit the regime."[157] In 1998, historian William M. LeoGrande, too, relying on secondary sources and interviews, concluded that the Reagan administration dissuaded opposition parties from running in order "to wreck the elections as completely as possible."[158] The refusal of opposition parties to participate in the elections was thus part of the White House's strategy to undermine the elections, as it confirmed the argument that Sandinista revolutionaries and genuine democracy were, in fact, mutually exclusive. Moreover, as an anonymous CIA agent noted, it left the FSLN "holding a near worthless hand" in the struggle for international legitimacy.[159]

It is important to note here that it is likely that governmental opinion about the nature of the elections would not have been radically different if Nicaraguan opposition parties had participated in the elections. Ideological preferences, as well as an effort to avoid unnecessarily antagonizing the Reagan administration, had a significant impact on how Western Europeans decided to assess the elections. Already on 8 July 1984, months before Cruz announced his boycott, Thatcher told Vice President George H. W. Bush that "no one should be under any illusions that the forthcoming elections in Nicaragua would be free."[160] Moreover, the fact that all EC countries but the Netherlands rejected the Nicaraguan invitation to observe the electoral process suggests that, in most cases, Western European officials had already made up their minds prior to Cruz's withdrawal.[161] It appears that the Western Europeans, particularly those with conservative and Christian Democratic governments, were far more likely to give the benefit of the doubt to El Salvador and—albeit to a lesser extent—Guatemala when it came to assessing elections, press freedom, and democratization processes. For example, the West German, British, and Dutch governments all agreed to observe the U.S.-backed 1984 electoral process in El Salvador, despite the fact that this took place in a context of civil war, human rights violations, and the FMLN's boycott of the elections.[162] Indeed, the victory of Duarte was applauded by Western European governments, who perceived him as a moderate politician sandwiched between the extreme Left, embodied by the Salvadoran guerrillas, and the extreme Right, embodied by the military and anticommunist death squads. Notably, Chancellor Helmut Kohl, also a Christian Democrat, warmly welcomed Duarte in Bonn in July 1984, and the West German government offered El Salvador $18 million in developmental aid.[163] Cold War binaries, therefore, did more to shape Western European government perspectives than the concrete actions the Sandinista government took to appease its critics, who continued to see the elections as little more than a show to legitimize the FSLN's hold on power and silence its opponents.


CONCLUSION

In the two years leading up to the 1984 elections, the FSLN's revolutionary diplomacy was creative and flexible, appealing to grassroots actors and local communities while at the same contributing to high-level multilateral negotiations with Latin American and Western European governments. Cultural events and personal connections with Western Europeans were crucial aspects of the revolutionaries' international strategy. Absent massive amounts of public sympathy and interest in the Nicaraguan cause, the Sandinistas realized, their revolution was unlikely to survive the Reagan administration's anticommunist assault. Indeed, it is unlikely that Western European governments would have adopted such a proactive role in Central America without the pressure of grassroots actors—including returning brigadistas—on policymakers. Increasingly, the Sandinistas' enemies reached a similar conclusion, launching a well-funded campaign to undermine the FSLN's message. By spreading anti-Sandinista propaganda and amplifying the conclusions of the Kissinger Commission, the Reagan administration sought to increase the legitimacy of U.S. foreign policy and support for the Contra forces. For the revolutionaries, this was a significant setback because—even though there was virtually no Western European support for the Contras—the U.S. campaign did influence the public debate on Nicaragua, as evidenced by the fact that no consensus was reached about the legitimacy of the 1984 elections.

The invasion of Grenada in October 1983 also pushed the FSLN toward adopting a more defensive and conciliatory foreign policy at the state level. As fears of a U.S. military invasion grew to unprecedented heights, Sandinista leaders decided to align themselves more publicly with Western European and Latin American governments and politicians. Diplomatic support from these countries for a nonmilitary solution to the Central American conflicts, the FSLN calculated, was ultimately more valuable than military support from the Soviet Union, even though the latter was obviously important for keeping the Contras at bay. Unwilling to be fully pushed into the arms of the Soviet Union, as had happened with the Cubans in the 1960s, the Sandinistas opted to make several concessions to accommodate governments in the Americas and Western Europe, most notably by participating in the Contadora process and organizing democratic elections.

Did this strategy work? Not as well as the Sandinistas hoped it would, but it certainly did not fail completely. The joint foreign policy initiative of the European Community, combined with the ongoing efforts of the Contadora countries to find a diplomatic solution to the Central American crises, provided the FSLN with a welcome opportunity to undermine and delegitimize the Reagan administration's objectives. Indeed, the concessions made by the Nicaraguan revolutionaries prevented the Contadora process from collapsing, which meant that the United States could not successfully claim that a military solution was the only option on the table for Nicaragua. In terms of discouraging the United States from launching an armed intervention, then, the Sandinistas' revolutionary diplomacy—combining multilateral negotiations with transnational activism—was remarkably successful. Indeed, considering Reagan's unwavering determination to get rid of the Sandinistas, it appears unlikely that the FSLN revolutionaries could have maneuvered themselves into a better position in 1984. In the next chapter, where the long-term consequences and aftermath of the Nicaraguan elections are discussed, we will see if it was enough.

# FIVE

# Fundraising for the Revolution, 1985–1986

IN MAY 1985, AS PART of a diplomatic tour through Western Europe, the recently elected vice president of Nicaragua Sergio Ramírez launched the Campaña Nicaragua Debe Sobrevivir (Nicaragua Must Survive Campaign, CNDS).[1] The purpose of the new fundraising campaign, which was coordinated by Ligia Vigil of the CNSP, was to increase the levels of financial and material aid Nicaragua received from the populations of Western Europe, Canada, and the United States.[2] Moreover, by channeling all the campaign's proceeds through one central body, the CNSP, the Sandinista government increased its control over the allocation and redistribution of the donated money and material. Indeed, as the campaign's coordinating committee reminded Western European solidarity activists, because the FSLN best understood the economic and political "needs" of the Nicaraguan people, they should also be the ones to decide on the distribution of the funds.[3] In contrast to previous solidarity campaigns, which primarily targeted international public opinion and state policies in Western Europe and the United States, the highly centralized Campaña Nicaragua Debe Sobrevivir had a clear economic orientation.

The financial focus of the campaign was reflective of the Sandinistas' wider preoccupation with stabilizing the economy, which came under further pressure in the mid-1980s. In April 1985, Mexican president Miguel de la Madrid told Sandinista comandante Henry Ruiz that Nicaragua, which was fully dependent on Mexican oil, would no longer be able to import petrol "on the favorable terms that had been in place up to now."[4] Moreover, on 1 May 1985, U.S. president Ronald Reagan, capitalizing on Nicaraguan president Daniel Ortega's visit to the Soviet Union, imposed an economically damaging trade embargo on the country, making it impossible for the

Sandinistas to export products such as bananas, coffee, and beef to the United States, as well as import much-needed manufactured goods, including spare parts for agricultural equipment.[5] Finally, as Latin American countries struggled to comply with the structural adjustment packages demanded by the IMF, regional aid to Nicaragua decreased from $120 million in 1984 to $80 million in 1985, and finally to a meager $40 million in 1986.[6]

These external developments, combined with the high costs of keeping the Contra fighters at bay, continued to make it difficult for the Sandinista revolutionaries to improve the country's standard of living. As the FSLN struggled to come up with viable solutions for Nicaragua's economic troubles, an increasing number of people complained of low salaries, rapid inflation, lack of consumer goods, and expensive basic foodstuffs as the government eliminated subsidies on basic consumption, and poor public transportation.[7] This growing dissatisfaction at home was a dangerous development for the Sandinistas, who relied on the support and participation of the Nicaraguan people to carry out their ambitious revolutionary program and ward off external threats. For the revolution's continued existence, it was crucial for the Sandinistas to find a way out of their predicament.

As this chapter shows, despite efforts to the contrary the Nicaraguan government largely failed to strengthen the country's economy or increase international pressure on the Reagan administration. Western European governments, citing the Sandinistas' alleged authoritarianism, human rights violations, and dependency on the Soviet Union, were unconvinced by the 1984 election results, and continued to treat the revolutionaries as troublemakers. Within the solidarity movement, too, there were signs of discontent. Nicaraguan attempts to centralize the solidarity movement to make it more effective encountered resistance from activists, who saw this as a patronizing strategy. Rather than distancing themselves from the Nicaraguan Revolution altogether, however, activists and local politicians searched for new ways to engage with the revolutionary project. By establishing twinning links with towns, schools, and local communities in Nicaragua, European sympathizers bypassed the Sandinistas' top-down bureaucratic system and opted for more personal, humanitarian, and small-scale activities. Levels of popular enthusiasm for the Nicaraguan Revolution in Western Europe remained relatively high, but the solidarity movement took on its own life, and it became impossible for the FLSN to control and effectively channel its activities. As solidarity activism became increasingly about the needs of the individual rather than the needs of the collective, the transnational aspect of the Sandinistas' revolutionary diplomacy became less effective.

This chapter seeks to understand why the Sandinistas reached a series of dead ends as they sought the economic, moral, and political support of Western European governments and peoples in 1985–86. Crucially, due to the changing international context, the FSLN could no longer present Nicaragua as nonaligned in the Cold War. As economic assistance from Latin America declined even further and the EC countries refused to increase their aid levels, the Nicaraguan revolutionaries had no other option than to rely on the Soviet Union and the Eastern bloc for material, military, and financial support. In doing so, however, they further alienated the West and provided Reagan with arguments to intensify his policy of undermining the Nicaraguan Revolution. Furthermore, transformations in Western European civil society and public opinion caused the revolutionary diplomacy of the FSLN to fall on less fertile ground than in the early 1980s. When Reagan and the new Soviet leader Mikhail Gorbachev started to engage in a superpower dialogue, the image of the U.S. president as a dangerous Cold War hawk, which had been so important for the Sandinistas' propaganda campaign and collaboration with the peace movement, started to lose its persuasive power. In sum, the FSLN's turn toward the Soviet bloc at a time when Reagan appeared to adopt a more reasonable stance in the Cold War had damaging consequences for its international standing, which the revolutionaries could not fully repair.

## CAUTIOUS OPTIMISM

The year 1985 started on a positive note. Even though the FSLN knew the elections had failed to bring about an international consensus on the legitimacy of Nicaragua's revolutionary government, it still believed the electoral victory could be a step in the right direction. In the early months of 1985, newly appointed officials, cautiously optimistic, reassessed the international situation and developed plans for Nicaragua's future. For a moment, there existed a glimmer of hope that its new government could end the counterrevolutionary war and come to a peaceful understanding with the Reagan administration.

The primary threat to the survival of the Nicaraguan Revolution, the potential military overthrow of the Sandinista government, appeared largely under control in early 1985. The U.S.-backed insurgents were slowly but steadily being pushed back to their base camps in Honduras and Costa Rica by the EPS.[8] To both the Sandinista comandantes and the Reagan administration, it was clear that without a new injection of foreign military aid, the Contras would not be able to continue their armed struggle for much longer. Miguel d'Escoto, who stayed on as foreign minister after the elections, wrote to Daniel Ortega in March 1985 that the Reagan administration had no chance of getting congressional approval for a proposed $14 million aid package for the Contras.[9] With regard to the possibility of a direct military intervention by the United States, documents from Nicaragua's Ministerio del Exterior demonstrate that government officials, taking into account U.S. domestic politics and the fact that there was virtually no Western European or Latin American support for such a radical move, believed that this option was no longer on the Oval Office table.[10]

For the revolutionaries, it thus seemed like the right time to start making amends with their opponents. Ortega's inauguration speech at the Plaza de la Revolución in Managua on 10 January 1985 certainly struck a conciliatory tone. As the country's new president, Ortega told an audience of around ninety thousand Nicaraguans and international delegates, he remained committed to political pluralism, a mixed economy, and a nonaligned foreign policy. According to Peter W. Summerscale, the British ambassador to Costa Rica who also attended the inauguration, Ortega's normally hostile references to the United States remained "relatively restrained" in his first presidential speech.[11] Ortega stressed that Nicaragua was not the "enemy" of the United States and described an ongoing dialogue between Nicaraguan and U.S. delegates that had been launched in late 1984 in the Mexican town of Manzanillo as a "magnificent opportunity" for the normalization of U.S.-Nicaraguan relations.[12] Furthermore, in a demonstration of the Sandinistas' willingness to bring the expensive and devastating Contra war to an end, Ortega offered a general amnesty to all counterrevolutionaries—including the formerly excluded Contra leaders—who were willing to lay down their arms and reintegrate into Nicaraguan society.[13] In sum, the key message of Ortega's speech was that his government would do everything within its power to bring peace to Nicaragua.

Despite Reagan pulling the plug on the Manzanillo talks three days before his second presidential inauguration on 21 January 1985, the Nicaraguan revolutionaries remained committed to improving their relationship with his administration. Nicaraguan diplomats actively lobbied for an indirect dialogue with the United States, hoping that the Mexican government could act as mediator.[14] Miguel d'Escoto, in particular, pushed for better relations with the Americans. In a letter to Daniel Ortega on 29 March 1985, the foreign minister argued that, if Nicaragua's new government seriously wanted to "deepen and consolidate the revolutionary process" by successfully implementing economic, social, and political reforms, peace was simply a necessary precondition.[15] And for the country to get to a state of peace, he continued, the FSLN needed to do more than bring about the military defeat of the counterrevolutionaries; they also had to find a way to get the U.S. president to "seriously consider the possibility" of living with the Sandinista movement in power in Nicaragua.[16] D'Escoto proposed several concrete steps that might push Reagan toward peaceful coexistence with the Sandinistas. For instance, he advised Ortega to send at least a hundred of the 786 Cuban military instructors that were based in Nicaragua back to Cuba.[17] While the Sandinista leader's immediate response to d'Escoto's message is unknown, one hundred Cuban military advisers did withdraw from Nicaragua in May 1985, demonstrating the FSLN's willingness to make certain concessions to accommodate the United States.[18] By 1985, the Sandinistas had clearly come to the conclusion that the continued survival of the revolution would be best served by reaching some sort of agreement with their ideological enemies, even if this might have been an unlikely scenario.

This is not to say that Nicaraguan officials were naïve about the Reagan's not-so-secret desire to undermine their revolutionary project. Indeed, even though the FSLN leadership believed the Reagan administration could be forced by Congress and international public opinion to give up its support for the counterrevolutionaries, and perhaps even accept the existence of the left-wing government in Central America, they knew it was much more likely that it would resort to different measures, such as the imposition of economic sanctions or a trade embargo.[19] In that knowledge, Nicaraguan leaders were constantly looking for ways to make their country's economy less dependent on trade with the United States. Already from 19 July 1979 onwards, as one CIA official noted, the FSLN had implemented "contingency plans to cut back its economic ties with the United States."[20] To an extent, the Sandinista government had succeeded in finding alternative markets for Nicaraguan export products such as bananas, seafood, tobacco, coffee, and beef. Between 1980 and 1984, exports to the United States had decreased from $214 million (30.4 percent of Nicaragua's total trade) to $58 million (14.9 percent of Nicaraguan trade), as the country increasingly exported to Latin America,

Asia, and Europe. Exports to the Soviet Union, too, increased from 1 percent of the country's total trade in 1980 to 15.4 percent in 1984.[21] If Sandinista officials were relatively hopeful about improving their relationship with the Reagan administration, they certainly made sure to have a backup plan in place.

With regard to Western European governments, in the first three months of 1985, Nicaraguan politicians and journalists also briefly observed a positive change in attitude.[22] In January 1985, Jürgen Möllemann, the West German vice minister of foreign affairs, included Nicaragua in his journey through Central America. This was a good sign, according to pro-Sandinista journals *Barricada*, *El Nuevo Diario*, and *Revista Envío*, which noted optimistically that Möllemann's visit increased pressure on the Reagan administration, strengthened the Contadora peace initiative, and suggested that West Germany was about to increase the levels of bilateral aid to Nicaragua, which been in decline.[23] In addition, in March 1985, Nicaraguan officials noted with satisfaction that Western European leaders were growing increasingly concerned about the "negative effects" that Reagan's Central America policy had on the unity of NATO.[24] Finally, on 20 February 1985, Sergio Ramírez wrote to Daniel Ortega that, despite the contested nature of the elections, Western European leaders no longer challenged the democratic legitimacy of the Nicaraguan government.[25] Indeed, Ramírez assured Ortega, the Sandinistas' decision to organize democratic elections had given the Nicaraguan government a "great political advantage" in Western Europe.[26] Ramírez also believed that EC leaders appreciated the Nicaraguan government's declaration of support for the Contadora process and its willingness to engage in bilateral talks with the U.S. administration, which stood in stark contrast to Reagan's confrontational attitude.[27]

Ramírez based his optimistic—and, considering the way the EC countries had initially responded to the 1984 elections, perhaps slightly naïve— arguments about a possible shift in the foreign policies of Western European countries on the experiences and conversations he had during a diplomatic visit to the United Kingdom, Spain, Ireland, and France in February 1985. During the trip, the members of Ramírez's delegation received a warm welcome from a wide variety of European organizations, politicians, and activists. The delegation included Nora Astorga from MINEX, as well as Pedro Antonio Blandón from the newly created Ministerio de Cooperación Externa (Ministry of External Cooperation), which was responsible for managing Nicaragua's economic relations and the soliciting of foreign aid.[28] In the

United Kingdom, too, things appeared to go well, at least on the surface. Ramírez conversed with Foreign Secretary Geoffrey Howe, gave a talk at the think tank Chatham House, appeared on *Newsnight*, got a standing ovation at Oxford University, was interviewed by *The Times*, met with John Bevan of the Nicaragua Solidarity Campaign, and had a friendly dinner with Neil Kinnock, leader of the Labour Party.[29] Furthermore, to the surprise of both Howe and Ambassador Summerscale, who deemed a Nicaraguan call on the prime minister not "appropriate," Margaret Thatcher, too, decided that she wanted to meet with the representatives.[30] Jonathan Steele of *The Guardian* noted optimistically that this decision marked "a significant change in her attitude towards the Sandinista Government."[31] And while Sergio Ramírez knew that Thatcher's sympathies lay with Reagan, he also detected changes in the British attitude. Indeed, the greatest "diplomatic success" of his Western European tour, Ramírez wrote to Ortega after his return to Nicaragua, was Thatcher's description of him as "the vice president of Nicaragua."[32] The prime minister's public admission that he was, in fact, the country's vice president, Ramírez argued, demonstrated that the British government had finally accepted the legitimacy of the Sandinista government.[33]

Nicaraguan speculation about a forthcoming change in British and West German foreign policy, however, was largely based on wishful thinking. In West Germany, the subject of aid to Nicaragua was not even raised in Ortega's meeting with Möllemann, which took place in Managua in January 1985.[34] And Ramírez's suggestion that Thatcher, swayed by the elections, now accepted the legitimacy of the Sandinista government was an overly optimistic reading of the British government's perspective. More than anything, FCO officials noted, she wanted to speak with Ramírez to give him "a piece of her mind" about the situation in Central America and to express concern about "the direction the Nicaraguan Revolution" was taking.[35] According to her private secretary Peter Ricketts, in advance of the meeting, Thatcher was particularly "anxious" to have a brief with "sharp concise points she could make to Ramírez about the undemocratic nature of Nicaraguan elections, the arms buildup, and the Marxist leanings of the Sandinistas."[36] Despite its earlier optimism, therefore, *The Guardian* covered the meeting with the headline "PM berates Nicaragua."[37] In addition to Thatcher's personal dislike of the Sandinistas, British diplomats also remained skeptical of the Nicaraguan government. Proposed concessions by Sandinista leaders, such as the abovementioned offer to withdraw Cuban military advisers, for instance, were described as "empty gestures" of little value.[38]

Nevertheless, the sense of anticipation in early 1985 was not entirely baseless. Overall, Ramírez's journey through Western Europe was a useful and important exercise, and it highlights that many Western Europeans—at least outside government—continued to see revolutionary Nicaragua as a symbol of hope. The trip was good for publicity, as well as the strengthening of relationships beyond the state level. Press coverage of the diplomatic mission, as Ramírez later wrote to Ortega, had been extensive and overwhelmingly positive.[39] British government officials, too, noted that the delegation had successfully adopted a high media profile during their trip.[40] The fact that Ramírez's visit to London coincided with the English publication of his novel *To Bury Our Fathers*, which narrated the early days of the Somoza dictatorship, contributed to an attractive portrayal of the Nicaraguan Revolution in the British media.[41] On a personal level, too, the Nicaraguans received a warm welcome from left-wing politicians, solidarity activists, and other European supporters. The Labour leader Neil Kinnock treated the Nicaraguans in a very "cordial and fraternal" manner, even promising Ramírez he would lobby France and Spain to send military equipment to Nicaragua (which never materialized).[42] Kinnock evidently felt very close to the Sandinistas, as he also attended Daniel Ortega's inauguration in January 1985, and later told *The Times* that he considered the Nicaraguan elections "a demonstration of the strength of the will and principles of Sandinism, with its emphasis on democracy and human rights."[43]

Moreover, the Sandinistas were more realistic about the situation they found themselves in than it might appear at first sight. Even though they did not give up on the possibility that Western European governments would adopt a more pro-FSLN stance after the elections, the revolutionaries were aware of the limits to Europe's potential role. True, with the obvious exception of the Thatcher government, Western Europeans, both at the grassroots and at the level of the state, considered Reagan's confrontational Central America policies to be extremist, dangerous, and ineffective.[44] Yet the Nicaraguans knew that this unanimous rejection of the Reagan administration's aggressive Central America policies was unlikely to translate into direct governmental or economic support for the Nicaraguan Revolution, or even into public criticism of U.S. foreign policy. In March 1985, MINEX officials concluded that the levels of economic and political support for the revolution were still to a large extent dependent on the electoral performance of left-wing parties.[45] And at a time when most Western European governments were ruled by centrist or right-wing governments, this was a sobering conclusion.

Furthermore, Nicaraguan officials noted that, while Western European states publicly supported the Contadora negotiations and rejected the option of a direct U.S. intervention in Central America, their position on the counterrevolutionaries was less clear. Some Western European leaders, including Dutch foreign minister Hans van den Broek, for instance, pushed the Nicaraguan government to engage in a dialogue with the Contra leaders, which the FSLN still categorically refused to do as they considered the insurgents not independent actors, but rather mercenaries under the Reagan administration's control.[46] To be sure, the Sandinistas' insistence on describing the Contra war as a proxy conflict between Nicaragua and the United States does not do justice to the war's indigenous and domestic origins, nor to the influential role that anticommunist countries like Argentina and Honduras played in training and setting up the Contra army in the early 1980s.[47] But the Sandinistas' refusal to negotiate with the Contra leadership without the presence and participation of U.S. officials certainly made sense, considering the influential role that Reagan and his allies—including private citizens such as the retired U.S. general John Singlaub—played in financing and coordinating the war throughout most of the 1980s.[48]

In early 1985, then, the Sandinista leaders were hopeful but not naïve about how the international context would influence the revolution's development in the months following the elections. Nicaraguan officials implemented plans that might lead to a peaceful agreement with the Reagan administration, but also took cautionary measures in case its adversarial foreign policy escalated. And while Sandinista leaders encouraged further political, cultural, and economic cooperation with EC countries and peoples, they realized that Western European governments would never throw their full weight behind the Nicaraguan Revolution.[49] Indeed, MINEX officials were forced to conclude in March 1985, despite their ambitious revolutionary diplomacy since Somoza's fall, the only region that unconditionally sided with the Revolución Popular Sandinista was the socialist bloc.[50]

## UNEXPECTED SETBACKS

Hopes that the FSLN's electoral victory would bring Nicaragua international legitimacy and stability were dashed within months. In April and May 1985, a series of setbacks and miscalculations led to a significant weakening of the country's economy and global standing, which, as former Sandinista diplomat Luis Caldera remembers, pushed Nicaragua's revolutionary government further "into the arms of the Soviet Union."[51]

The situation started to deteriorate on 15 April 1985, when FSLN comandante and planning minister Henry Ruiz received the unwelcome news, alluded to above, that Mexico would no longer supply the Sandinista government with cheap oil unless it paid 80 percent in advance, which the Nicaraguan state could not afford.[52] According to the Sandinistas, the Mexican government's decision was made under heavy U.S. pressure. Indeed, Daniel Ortega told Bulgarian leader Todor Zhivkov on 2 May 1985, the Reagan administration had used a combination of "blackmail" and "foreign debt" to pressure Mexican leaders "not to help Nicaragua."[53] Specifically, Ortega added, the Americans were using information about the illegal involvement of "very high-ranking people in the drugs trade" to force the Mexican government's hand.[54] Due to the limited availability of sources, it is difficult to know if Ortega's accusations regarding the drug trade had any truth to them. There is little doubt, however, that the Reagan administration welcomed the Mexican government's decision to, in the words of a CIA official, "give greater balance to its regional policies."[55]

The news that Nicaragua's petrol supply was no longer guaranteed shocked the Sandinista leaders, who realized they had no other option than to ask the Soviet Union and its allies for help in resolving the impending oil crisis.[56] Venezuela, the other petrol-rich country in Latin America, had already cut off oil supplies in July 1982, citing Nicaragua's inability to pay back its debts.[57] To avoid an economic disaster, the Nicaraguan government acted quickly, and the FSLN leaders were thankful "for the speed" with which the socialist leaders responded to their urgent "request for a meeting."[58] Already on 24 April 1985, less than ten days after Henry Ruiz's visit to Mexico City, the Telegraph Agency of the Soviet Union (TASS) announced that Daniel Ortega would travel to the Soviet Union "within a week."[59] Indeed, four days later, on 28 April 1985, a prominent Nicaraguan delegation consisting of Daniel Ortega, Henry Ruiz, Miguel d'Escoto, and the director of the FSLN's Departamento de Relaciones Internacionales, Julio López, arrived in Moscow. After visiting the Soviet Union, the delegates also spoke to officials in Bulgaria, Hungary, Poland, and Yugoslavia.[60] With regard to oil supplies, Ortega's trip to the Soviet bloc was certainly a success. On 30 May 1985, *Barricada Internacional* announced that, for the year 1985, Moscow had agreed to cover at least 80 percent of Nicaragua's petrol needs on "favorable" terms, while the remaining 20 percent would be supplied by Libya, Iran, and Algeria.[61]

Yet the timing of the visit could not have been worse. On 23 April 1985, one day before the TASS announcement, Miguel d'Escoto's prediction that Reagan would lose the congressional vote on the $14 million Contra aid package came true. U.S. politicians, to Reagan's disappointment, rejected the administration's foreign policy proposals for Nicaragua.[62] In this context, the news that Ortega would travel to Moscow led to a storm of angry responses, as Western European and North American commentators, initially unaware of the Mexican oil decision, described Ortega's journey as a blatant insult to the members of Congress who had just voted against Contra aid.[63] The Nicaraguan president's "pilgrimage to Moscow," the U.S. embassy in Managua wrote to the State Department, "drew criticism not only in the United States but also among Latin American and Western European states often inclined to side with the [Government of Nicaragua] in its dispute with the United States."[64] The ill-timed visit, according to the British ambassador in Costa Rica, was a watershed in U.S.-Nicaraguan relations, as it convinced the majority of Congress that the Sandinista regime was, in fact, "Marxist and Communist backed."[65] Even solidarity activists failed to understand the Nicaraguan decision and were frustrated by the lack of information on the rationale behind the trip they received from the DRI, which prevented them from defending Ortega's trip against critical Western media outlets.[66]

Aside from causing public outcry, Ortega's highly publicized trip to the socialist bloc strengthened the hand of the U.S. administration, as most of Congress no longer felt inclined to resist Reagan's policies toward Nicaragua. On 1 May 1985, citing "an unusual and extraordinary threat to the national security and foreign policy of the United States," Reagan capitalized on Ortega's visit and announced an economic embargo against Nicaragua.[67] Moreover, in June 1985, Reagan and his allies brought about "a major reversal" in congressional opinion, and obtained approval for $27 million in "humanitarian" aid to the Contras, such as medicine, clothing, and food.[68] Several months later, in February 1986, Reagan requested another $100 million in Contra aid, including $70 million for military equipment and training, which Congress approved on 25 June 1986.[69] In the year following the Nicaraguan visit to the Soviet Union, Reagan and his congressional allies pushed through foreign policy proposals for Nicaragua with relative ease.[70]

As soon as the Sandinistas realized that Ortega's trip to Moscow was having unforeseen and unwelcome consequences, they responded with a diplomatic offensive to limit the damage as much as possible, focusing primarily on Western Europe. As in previous years, the FSLN hoped to demonstrate their continued nonalignment in the Cold War, as well as provide the world with evidence of the alleged transatlantic split regarding the correct policy toward the Nicaraguan Revolution. To make clear that Reagan falsely portrayed the U.S.-Nicaraguan conflict as a struggle between East and West, Ortega immediately added several Western European stops to his journey to the Soviet bloc, including Paris, Rome, and Madrid. Sergio Ramírez, too, for the second time that year, traveled to Western Europe, visiting Austria, the Netherlands, and the FRG in May and June 1985.[71] During these trips, Sandinista leaders assured Western European politicians that their country's dependency on Soviet oil was only temporary, as they were actively seeking economic assistance to be able to pay their debts to Mexico.[72] Moreover, with the U.S. embargo in mind, they also tried to open up new markets for Nicaraguan export products. To obtain higher levels of financial aid, the FSLN argued that it continued to seek "economic diversification" to prevent "total" economic dependency on the Soviet Union.[73]

The visits had mixed results. None of the Western European leaders joined the economic embargo, but the EC countries could not agree on a common response to Reagan's economic escalation of the Central American conflict. When Greece and France pressured their allies for a joint EC declaration to denounce the embargo in May 1985, the United Kingdom, the Netherlands, and West Germany, unwilling to publicly damage the transatlantic alliance, blocked these proposals, arguing that the bilateral responses of individual Western European leaders had been sufficient.[74] It was better for Western Europeans to take a "low profile" in this situation, the West Germans stated privately, since there was no point in aimlessly attacking a foreign policy decision that was unlikely to be reversed.[75] As a result of these disagreements, the EC also failed to adopt a common position in the United Nations. On 17 December 1985, when the UN General Assembly adopted a resolution that criticized the trade embargo and invited the international community to "help reduce the negative effects" of the measures imposed against Nicaragua, the vote of the EC countries was split. France, Greece, Denmark, and Spain, voted in favor of the resolution while the rest, to avoid the possibility of "a three-way split" of the European Community, decided to abstain.[76]

Once again, then, ideological preferences and ideas about how to fight the Cold War influenced how Western European governments responded to the Nicaraguan Revolution. Greece and France both had socialist leaders, respectively Andreas Georgios Papandreou and François Mitterrand, who hoped that social democrats could keep Nicaragua out of the Soviet camp. Next to collaborating with their EC colleagues, both countries also pursued a relatively independent foreign policy toward Nicaragua in the 1980s, providing the FSLN with support and vocally rejecting Reagan's approach to Central America. By doing so, they also targeted audiences in their own countries, where solidarity activists actively lobbied for a pro-Sandinista foreign policy. For instance, in Greece, which officially joined the European Community in 1981, Papandreou successfully mobilized voters by delivering a "radical message of anti-imperialism, anti-establishment, and anti-Americanism." Support for revolutionary Nicaragua dovetailed nicely with Papandreou's image as a Cold War "troublemaker," and he made no secret of his pro-Sandinista attitude.[77] On one occasion in 1984, Sergio Ramírez recalls, the Greek prime minister even offered the FSLN weapons. By providing the Sandinista army with ten thousand G3 assault rifles (a weapon used by NATO troops), Ramírez noted, Greece "wanted to remove [Nicaragua] from the Cold War battlefield."[78] However, despite lending rhetorical and—to a lesser extent—financial backing to the Sandinistas, both countries were also members of NATO and remained careful not to antagonize the United States to the extent that it could hurt their own national security interests. Ultimately, as Sergio Ramírez put it in his memoirs, Western European social democrats would side with the United States, as they were "part of their system."[79]

Although some were hesitant to issue a joint declaration on the embargo, individual EC countries made clear that they found Reagan's decision to impose an embargo counterproductive. Van den Broek, for example, told Dutch parliamentarians that the Netherlands rejected any measures that could lead to the economic and political isolation of Nicaragua, including the imposition of an "economic boycott."[80] Hans-Dietrich Genscher, too, publicly declared that his government believed economic sanctions served no useful political purpose. Furthermore, at the G7 economic summit in Bonn, Western European leaders, backed by the Canadian government, privately explained to the Americans that they had serious concerns about Reagan's unilateral decision.[81] Roland Dumas, the new French foreign minister, told George Shultz that Nicaragua would only become more dependent on the Soviet Union if the European countries joined the U.S. embargo. Giulio Andreotti, the Italian minister of foreign affairs, after reminding everyone that the Sandinistas were not "simply emanations of the devil," made the point that economic sanctions were "rarely helpful."[82] In this case, Andreotti added, the FSLN could use the embargo as an excuse when the Nicaraguan economy, because of the Sandinistas' own "incompetence," inevitably collapsed. Finally, Genscher told Shultz that the embargo would primarily hurt the "independent part" of Nicaraguan society, namely the private sector.[83]

Apart from expressing concern, however, there was little Western European governments could do, or wanted to do, to alleviate the damage of the trade embargo. First, with regard to sanctions, the Reagan administration did not seem to care much about the concerns of its Western European allies. Shultz made it clear that he did not seek European permission. The Reagan administration had never expected the EC countries to "respond positively" to the embargo, Shultz told his colleagues in Bonn, and that was exactly why they had not lobbied for Western European support in the first place.[84] Either way, Shultz added, the opinions of EC leaders simply would not deter Reagan from implementing his foreign policy toward Nicaragua.[85] British officials came to a similarly sobering conclusion in September 1985, when they evaluated their approach to the U.S.–Nicaraguan conflict. The United Kingdom had "few means of influencing events" in Central America, David Thomas concluded, and there was "little evidence" that British statements, either public or private, had "any effect" on Reagan's confrontational approach toward the Sandinista revolutionaries.[86]

Furthermore, Ortega and Ramírez largely failed to win additional economic assistance and secure new export markets for Nicaraguan products. Except for some minor concessions from Sweden and Norway, the majority of the Western European leaders made clear that, while they rejected the U.S. embargo in principal, they would not compensate Nicaragua for the economic damage it caused.[87] The EC countries, in particular, were reluctant to pick a side in the Central American crises, and had a strong preference for a multilateral approach to the region as a whole, rather than a "fixation" on Nicaragua alone.[88] In June 1985, Van den Broek explained that the Dutch government would not give more financial aid to Nicaragua, since this would only undermine EC foreign policy objectives toward the Central American region. Furthermore, he added, Nicaragua already received significant amounts of aid through the EC regional development program.[89] With regard to West Germany, Sergio Ramírez's mission to obtain financial credit was doomed from the start. Helmut Kohl did not even want to see Ramírez, as the chancellor was insulted by Daniel Ortega's comments in East Berlin, where he stated that the West Germans were "accomplices in the U.S. attempt to exterminate the Nicaraguan people."[90] Instead, the vice president had a brief and tense conversation with Genscher about the emotional causes of Ortega's "unfortunate" remarks, and aid was not mentioned at all.[91] Aside from a handful of individual statements denouncing the U.S. embargo and some minor pressure on Reagan's policies, Ortega's and Ramírez's improvised journeys through Western Europe failed to have much of an impact.

It is useful to mention here that Western European reluctance to compensate for Nicaragua's economic damage in the aftermath of the embargo was symptomatic of an already existing trend, in which financial flows from individual countries to Nicaragua were slowly but steadily drying up.[92] Indeed, in addition to the British government, which had never made any significant financial contribution, France, West Germany, Spain, and the Netherlands were also cutting back on bilateral aid. In the case of West Germany and the United Kingdom, the Nicaraguan revolutionaries assessed, this was predominantly due to the Sandinistas' political differences with the British Conservatives and German Christian Democrats. In France, Spain, and the Netherlands, MINEX officials believed, the main cause for the discontinuation of aid was Nicaragua's inability to pay back its debts. According to Nicaraguan sources, the country's debt to France in March 1985 was more than $54 million. However, these states were also growing disillusioned with their inability to keep Nicaragua out of the Eastern bloc. Of the Western European states, only the Nordic countries increased their levels of aid to the Nicaraguan revolutionaries. Under the leadership of prominent social democrat Olof Palme, who had supported the FSLN since the late 1970s, Swedish financial aid to Nicaragua remained at a consistently high level throughout the decade.[93]

In this context of heightening international tensions and reduced aid flows, the FSLN comandantes cracked down internally to ward off opposition amid economic crisis and prolonged conflict, undoing many of the concessions they had made in the run-up to the elections in November 1984. On 15 October 1985, the Sandinista leadership announced the reintroduction of the State of Emergency (first imposed in March 1982 and all but lifted during the electoral campaign in 1984), once again suspending various civil rights, such as press freedom, the right to appeal, the right to strike, and the right to peaceful assembly.[94] Publicly, the FSLN and its allies argued that the emergency decree was "a direct response to the latest escalation of the U.S.-backed war against Nicaragua."[95] Yet, as international observers and Nicaraguan journalists correctly pointed out, this argument was hardly convincing since the "military situation" had actually improved in the months leading up to the emergency announcement.[96] East German diplomats in Managua noted privately, for instance, that Sandinista comandantes Humberto Ortega, Luis Carrión, and Jaime Wheelock had repeatedly argued that the Contras were "as good as defeated."[97] More likely, therefore, the East Germans reported, the reintroduction of the State of Emergency was a response to a considerable "lapse in confidence" among the Nicaraguan population in the FSLN leaders, who consequently felt the need "to strengthen their influence and authority" over the country, which suffered from growing international isolation, civil war, and an economic crisis.[98] Similarly, the Nicaraguan editors of *Revista Envío* speculated that the state of emergency was designed "to consolidate the recent military gains with political restraints and controls."[99]

The emergency decree came as an unwelcome surprise to many Western Europeans, both from the left and the right. Predictably, the U.S. State Department portrayed the Nicaraguan decision as evidence that the FSLN was, as Reagan had foreseen, "imposing a totalitarian regime on the people of Nicaragua."[100] The British government had a similar response.[101] In addition to the usual suspects, the suspension of political rights in Nicaragua was also criticized by left-wing parties, newspapers, activists, and the leaders of, among others, France, Spain, West Germany, and the Netherlands.[102] Notably, the immediate reaction of Western European solidarity committees was one of frustration, disbelief, and confusion. Not only were the national representatives irritated by the limited communication they had with the DRI about the state of emergency, but they also questioned if it was truly necessary to restrict civil liberties.[103] For example, one of the reasons the FSLN's Agencia Nueva Nicaragua gave for the measures was the growing strength of an "internal front" in Nicaragua that was allegedly backed by the CIA, sabotaged the economy, secretly assisted Contra guerrillas, and encouraged Nicaraguans to evade military conscription. However, solidarity activists noted, prior to the Sandinista decision they had never received any information about this so-called internal front.[104] Similar points were made by national representatives from, among others, Finland, West Germany, and the United Kingdom at the Western European solidarity conference in Portugal on 18, 19, and 20 October 1985. To a tense Silvia McEwan, the representative of the CNSP, they pointed out that they could not convincingly argue in favor of the FSLN's decision without up-to-date information about the situation in Nicaragua.[105]

Even though solidarity activists initially criticized the state of emergency, their public declarations defended the decision of the Sandinista comandantes. John Bevan of the London-based NSC sent out a press release asserting that the state of emergency was "a direct response to the latest escalation of the U.S.-backed war against Nicaragua."[106] By comparing the Nicaraguan restrictions on civil liberties to the measures that the United Kingdom adopted in the Second World War, the NSC hoped to convince the British people of the urgency of the Nicaraguan situation.[107] After recovering from the initial shock, then, Western European activists quickly came to terms with the state of emergency. The official—and rather dubious—assessment of the Dutch committee was that the measures primarily targeted the U.S.-sponsored "internal front" and that there would be no consequences for the "normal civilians" of Nicaragua.[108] With regard to the lack of press freedom, Dutch activists believed that, even though it was certainly important for the Nicaraguan people to receive information and read opinions from a variety of sources, the anti-Sandinista newspaper *La Prensa* was simply spreading "subtle lies" to undermine the revolution. Noting that the anticommunist newspaper *El Mercurio* had played a crucial role in the overthrow of Salvador Allende in Chile in 1973, solidarity activists deemed the Nicaraguan government's controversial decision to censor *La Prensa* fully justified.[109]

In contrast, social democratic politicians in Western Europe found it impossible to defend the state of emergency in public, notwithstanding their previous support for the revolutionaries. François Mitterrand's government responded to the announcement by releasing a statement declaring that France "deplored all measures" that restricted democratic liberties.[110] Furthermore, Kinnock, on behalf of his party, wrote a solemn letter to Daniel Ortega in which he greeted the news about the reintroduction of the state of emergency "with sadness and dismay." Even though he fully understood the "terrible problems" that Nicaragua encountered as a result of the United States' "support for the Contra terrorists," Kinnock wrote, he was forced to urge Ortega to "restore the provisions for safeguarding civil liberties" as soon as possible.[111] Dutch labor leader Joop den Uyl, too, declared in parliament that he "rejected" the Sandinista decision to limit civil rights.[112] In addition to providing critics of the FSLN with more material, therefore, the imposition of the state of emergency also alienated Western European social democrats, who were already under considerable pressure to break ties with the Sandinistas.

Rather than gradual improvement, then, the period following the elections brought new problems. When Daniel Ortega, upon his return from Europe, explained that the visit to the Soviet Union was necessary because the Mexican government had suspended oil supplies, most of the political damage had already been done. Clearly, the Sandinista comandantes had not expected such a powerful international backlash. Daniel Ortega's emotional comments in Berlin, as well as the fact that the government did not send a lower-ranking delegation to Moscow, suggest that the Sandinistas were surprised and disappointed by Reagan's ability to capitalize on Ortega's trip so soon after the 1984 elections. In this context, the controversial decision to impose a state of emergency in October 1985 might well have been caused by the Sandinista leaders' growing sense of disillusionment with what the international community, most notably the Western countries, could offer the Nicaraguan Revolution. Of course, we should not overlook domestic causes, but from the perspective of the FSLN comandantes, it must have seemed like there was little benefit to making concessions to domestic opponents regarding democracy, amnesties, and pluralism in Nicaragua, if it did not fundamentally alter the way Western European politicians treated the Sandinista government.

## FUNDRAISING AND TWINNING

Due to the country's economic and political crises, however, Nicaraguan leaders could not afford to give up on their revolutionary diplomacy. At a time when EC governments showed little sympathy for the Nicaraguan revolutionaries' financial troubles, the FSLN decided to turn to Western European people and NGOs for desperately needed material and financial support. Crucially, in May 1985, in a direct response to the U.S. economic embargo, the FSLN launched their centralized solidarity campaign, the CNDS, which targeted non-state actors in the Americas and Western Europe.

While the campaign title suggests that Nicaraguans were on the brink of starvation in 1985, most of the funds raised by the CNDS went toward the country's relatively well-off middle classes, including doctors, teachers, and engineers. After the embargo, the materials the FSLN received from the Soviet Union, as Luis Caldera remembers, were not enough to satisfy the needs of these mostly urban Nicaraguans, who were accustomed to buying products made in the United States such as sardines, boots, condensed milk, dolls, and clothing.[113] The purpose of CNDS, therefore, was to collect goods in Western Europe, Canada, and the United States that would be shipped to Nicaragua in containers and sold to the middle classes in government stores. The FSLN provided solidarity committees with detailed lists of products the government needed, which varied from nylon stockings for nurses to tools for mechanics. It was up to the solidarity committees to decide if they wanted to raise money and buy the products themselves or call on people to donate the requested materials.[114] From the financial profits of the sales, the Nicaraguan government could import more manufactured goods from neighboring Costa Rica, Panama, and Honduras, such as refrigerators and televisions.[115] The CNDS, therefore, was designed to neutralize opposition, prevent the middle classes from leaving the country, and keep the economy going in the aftermath of the economic embargo.

Although most Western European solidarity committees agreed to support the CNDS, they were skeptical. In essence, the Sandinistas' broad focus on economic development and fundraising clashed with the rather selfish desire of Western European activists to be personally involved in the revolutionary process, as well as with their conviction that solidarity activism should have a clear political component. The character of the Sandinistas' new campaign was simply too "apolitical" to be successful in Western European countries, Isabel Cárcamo of the Informationsbüro Wuppertal, the headquarters of the West German solidarity movement, wrote in October 1986. Because it was almost impossible to mobilize local solidarity activists for what was essentially a humanitarian cause, Cárcamo argued, the FRG solidarity movement had only raised around $100,000 for the Nicaraguan government in the last year.[116] Representatives of the NKN, too, argued that Dutch people were not interested in the CNDS because the campaign offered no "structural solutions" to the problems revolutionary Nicaragua was encountering as a result of Reagan's destabilization policies.[117]

Moreover, since the FSLN determined how the donations were distributed, solidarity activists and contributors had no way of finding out where in Nicaragua their money and materials ended up. This would damage the campaign's impact, the Danish and Greek solidarity committees predicted, as potential donors in Western Europe would only respond to a clear message and objective. People simply did not care about such an abstract concept as the economic "survival" of the Nicaraguan Revolution, they argued, and the fundraising campaign would be more successful if committees were allowed to raise money for specific causes in Nicaragua, such as a coffee cooperative, a hospital, or a community theater.[118] At a solidarity conference in Lisbon in October 1985, therefore, some national representatives pressured the Milan-based Nicaraguan consul-general Bergman Zuniga Perez, who was responsible for coordinating the CNDS in Western Europe, to provide the solidarity movement with better opportunities to trace their donations within

Nicaragua. John Bevan, for instance, wanted to make sure the money ended up with AMLAE.[119] Not everyone in the solidarity movement shared this point of view. According to Mary Timmerman, who represented the NKN in Managua in 1986–90, the most important thing was that the Nicaraguan people profited from the material aid. Did solidarity activists and donors really have to know, she asked rhetorically, if certain products came from Spain, Eastern Europe, or the Netherlands?[120]

If we look at the results of the campaign, however, it appears that Timmerman underestimated the importance of visible results and personal connections for effective solidarity work. In November 1986, at the Western European solidarity conference in Athens, national representatives presented the proceeds of the CNDS to FSLN representatives Vigil and Bergman Zuniga. The activists concluded that the campaign had been a relative success in some countries, such as the Netherlands, where solidarity committees collected around $120,000, and West Germany, where local activists eventually managed to raise around $130,000. This was not a bad result. However, compared to the literacy campaign of 1980, when Dutch solidarity activists raised more than $250,000, it was less than the activists had hoped for. Moreover, other countries, such as France and Denmark, decided to quit fundraising for the CNDS altogether and focus on lobbying their national governments and spreading political information about Reagan's economic aggression and support for the Contra war instead.[121]

Out of all the Western European countries, the British solidarity movement, which had since 1983 established fruitful relations with labor unions, the Labour Party, and charities such as War on Want, was the most successful. Indeed, in 1989 the NSC calculated that, since the launch of the campaign in June 1985, British committees had collected enough money to send fifteen containers filled with medical supplies, kitchen utensils, and educational material, costing around $900,000.[122] One reason for the NSC's success was its ability to connect "practical solidarity"—which was essentially the same as humanitarian work—with a "political" message in its propaganda materials.[123] In leaflets and posters, British activists documented the atrocities carried out during the Contra war, arguing that Nicaragua's "survival was in question" because the Sandinistas "rejected the tradition that the United States has the divine right to control that country" (figure 11).[124] Building on the anti-intervention message that the solidarity movement had shared with audiences in the early 1980s, the NSC successfully framed the CNDS as the latest chapter in Nicaragua's long struggle against U.S. destabilization

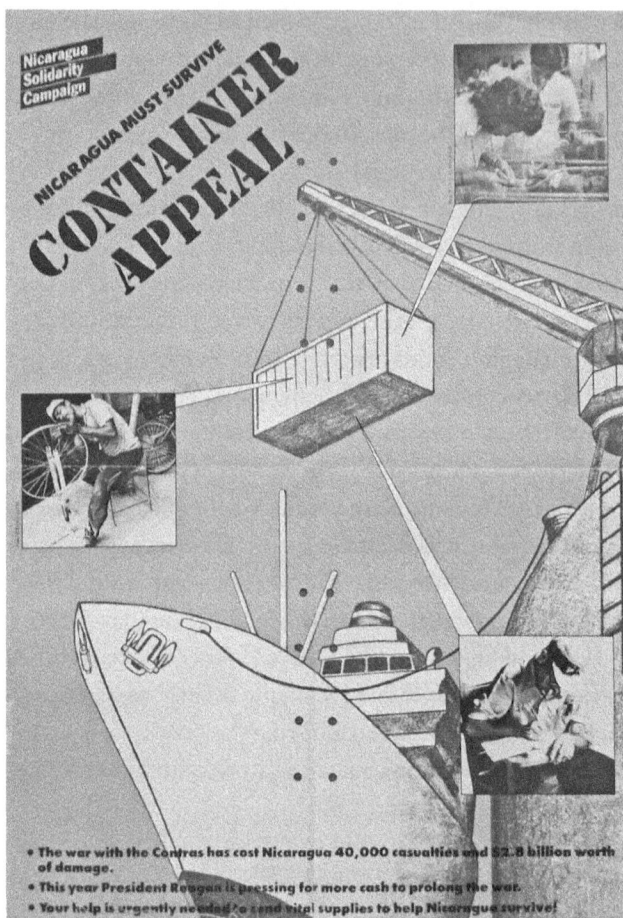

FIGURE 11. The Nicaragua Must Survive campaign was most successfully taken up by the Nicaragua Solidarity Campaign in the United Kingdom. From 1985 onwards, the British solidarity movement promoted the FSLN's international appeal for material support by combining political messaging about Reagan's foreign policy with imagery generally associated with humanitarianism and development. Photo: Nicaragua Solidarity Campaign, London.

policies, thereby significantly contributing to the FSLN's revolutionary diplomacy.

The mixed results of the Sandinistas' fundraising campaign must not be confused with a decline of interest in the Nicaraguan Revolution. On the contrary, popular interest in Central America remained high in the mid-1980s. Instead of collaborating with Nicaragua's central bureaucracy and raising money for the CNDS, however, solidarity activists moved in the opposite direction, focusing on more personal forms of solidarity activism and grassroots collaboration with Nicaraguan people. In addition to the fact that it was easier to mobilize Western Europeans for local development projects, such as helping with the harvest or the construction of a school, some activists were also frustrated by what they saw as the FSLN's tendency to undermine the independence of the Western European committees. As demonstrated by a letter that prominent activist Wim Jillings wrote to his friend Hans Langenberg, the Dutch national committee was particularly averse to well-intentioned efforts to centralize the solidarity movement. In May 1985, Jillings wrote to Langenberg that it was simply "astonishing" that Rafael Corea, the recently appointed head of the CNSP, had provided each national solidarity committee in Western Europe with a list of urgent tasks, which included buying "emergency plane tickets" in case Sandinista representatives needed to interrupt their travels to fly back to Nicaragua.[125] Seemingly unwilling to consider how these and similar proposals by Sandinista representatives could contribute to the effectiveness of the FSLN's revolutionary diplomacy, many activists simply chose to ignore them (the plane tickets were never bought) and opted for more intimate, personal, and flexible forms of solidarity work.

In addition to the continued popularity of solidarity brigades, discussed in the previous chapter, the most obvious example of this trend was the rapid growth of twinning links or sister-city relationships with Nicaraguan cities, towns, schools, and universities in the late 1980s. From 1984 onwards, more than a hundred Western European cities established formal or informal relationships with Nicaraguan municipalities.[126] In 1988, West Germany alone had forty-nine partnerships with Nicaraguan organizations, regions, and towns. Often, links were established because of active lobbying by solidarity committees and Nicaraguan representatives, such as the ambassador to the United Kingdom, Francisco d'Escoto.[127] Preferably, sister cities shared certain characteristic or interests. For example, Amsterdam, London, and Managua were national capitals, Oxford, Hamburg, Utrecht, and Léon were university cities, and Masaya and Leicester shared a sewing and clothing industry. Through the practice of twinning, solidarity activism with Nicaragua became more personalized and localized. As a result of the newly established partnerships, for instance, mayors from small Dutch towns traveled to Central America, German schoolchildren wrote letters to Nicaraguan pupils, murals about life and art in revolutionary Nicaragua were painted on buildings in British cities, and money was donated to the Nicaraguan sister cities to construct hospitals and community centers.[128] Like solidarity brigades, twinning offered Western Europeans an opportunity to personally experience the revolution. As a result of the link between Managua and Amsterdam, for instance, Dutch municipal workers Hans Ebberink and Luuk Weteling lived in Nicaragua for three years, working for the municipality of Managua. Between 1984 and 1987, Ebberink and Weteling were part of the Nicaraguan civil service, trying to improve infrastructure and housing in a context of civil war and economic chaos.[129]

The practice of setting up economic, political, and cultural links between towns and cities from distinct geographical areas was not new; it had existed in Western Europe since the end of the Second World War. Then, local councils and mayors had used twinning as a method to improve the relationships between former enemy states, such as the United Kingdom and Germany, and later to overcome the Cold War division of Europe.[130] Starting in the 1960s, city linking became increasingly focused on North-South cooperation and local development projects. French municipalities, for example, formed relationships with cities in their former colonies, in particular Senegal. In combination with a preference for direct and local forms of development cooperation, political activism and international solidarity were important driving factors behind the establishment of twinning links. For instance, in a clear example of so-called municipal internationalism in the final decade of the Cold War, dozens of Dutch cities built partnerships with black South African communities to support the fight against apartheid.[131] Through twinning, local activists and politicians could bypass their national governments to directly participate in international politics and contribute to development programs in the Global South. Indeed, according to the summary of a report on twinning with Nicaragua, "at the city-to-city level, the gap between the North and South can be bridged" and political solidarity could be effectively translated into tangible "acts or projects."[132]

Western European municipalities' decisions to establish twinning links with Nicaraguan cities were often driven by a combination of political factors, most notably sympathy for the Nicaraguan Revolution, anger with Reagan's foreign policy, and frustration with the approach of Western European governments to Central America. At a time when the Left had little influence on national foreign policies, twinning offered left-wing politicians, who often dominated in urban areas, an alternative foreign policy track. This was particularly true in West Germany, the United Kingdom, and the Netherlands, which were respectively governed by Christian Democrats, conservatives, and a center-right coalition. For example, on 1 October 1985, Labour councillor Colin Grundy chaired a town meeting to discuss plans to link Leicester with the Nicaraguan city of Masaya. At the public gathering, several local politicians, activists, and civil servants exchanged opinions and "enthusiastically" described their recent experiences as visitors in revolutionary Nicaragua. City Council worker John Perry, who was also a member of the Leicester Central America Support Group, explained how, due to the embargo and Reagan's "influence" on the Thatcher government, there were now "great shortages of imported goods" in revolutionary Nicaragua. And Rhys Evans, who was involved with the Nicaragua solidarity movement and had just returned from a visit to Masaya, declared "he remained convinced of the authenticity of the revolution" and stressed that it was important for British people to be "well informed" so that they could "argue in the Nicaraguans' favor." After noting that the Nicaraguans would perceive the partnership as an expression of "support for their country and the revolution," all those present at the meeting voted in favor of twinning with Masaya.[133] Other Western European cities were motivated by similar reasons, as is demonstrated by a joint declaration of Nijmegen, Leicester, Aken, and Dietzenbach in 1986, rejecting U.S. support for the Contras.[134]

As solidarity activism for the Nicaraguan Revolution took on a more personal and local character, the Sandinista government's conflict with the Reagan administration became increasingly embedded into local and domestic politics. In Western European town halls, universities, and community centers, politicians, activists, and students had heated, and in some cases violent, discussions about U.S. foreign policy, the Sandinistas' political program, and the possibility of West German and British support for the Contra fighters.[135] Opinions about the situation in Nicaragua were predictably split along party lines. Local Tories in Leicester, for example, accused the "loony Left" of wasting public money on projects in Masaya. If the citizens of Leicester realized "what a terrible regime there was in Nicaragua," Conservative councillor Michael Johnson stated to the local newspaper, they would refuse to pay another "penny" for the twinning program.[136] Similarly, Labour politician Ken Livingstone, leader of the Greater London Council, was ridiculed when he proposed to twin London with Managua as "a gesture of support" for the Sandinistas. Kenneth Baker, a Conservative MP and minister, declared that Managua and London had nothing in common, except for their "upwardly mobile Marxist politicians."[137]

Although politicians in West Germany and the Netherlands also used the Sandinista Revolution as a stick for beating their political and ideological enemies, the debate was most heated in Thatcher's highly polarized United Kingdom, where the Nicaraguan Contras had a small group of followers. In particular, the Federation of Conservative Students (FCS), which had also backed the U.S. invasion of Grenada in 1983, actively promoted the cause of the anti-Sandinista counterrevolutionaries, including by setting up the so-called Committee for a Free Nicaragua. Furthermore, on 6 and 7 December 1986, the FCS organized a pro-Contra conference at the Barbican center in London. In addition to Contra leader Arturo Cruz, the conference's program included anticommunist intelligence expert Brian Crozier, who spoke about "Central American and Soviet geopolitical design," and Republican congressman Robert Dornan, whose speech was entitled "Towards a Free Nicaragua."[138] According to the FCO, the Federation "evidently received considerable help and advice from their American contacts" to put together the conference, as the CIA and the U.S. State Department provided them with literature, financial assistance, and publicity material.[139] The FCS's activities were closely monitored by the NSC, which declared that the conservative group did not "represent anything more than a front for U.S. propaganda" and set up a picket in front of the Barbican.[140] As pressure on the revolution increased, then, Western European urban centers became another front in the international struggle for Nicaragua's future.

In sum, as state-level aid decreased, the FSLN once again tried to call on its transnational network of solidarity activists to alleviate Nicaragua's economic and political troubles. However, solidarity with the Nicaraguan Revolution took on a variety of new forms and meanings, losing much of its previous political radicalism. Solidarity committees continued to thrive in the mid-1980s, but the FSLN started to lose control over the movement's narrative, ideals, and practices. Sandinistas pushed for more fundraising and centralization, but local activists and politicians bypassed the FSLN and opted for more intimate forms of cooperation with towns, people, and organizations, working in a way that became very similar to the activities of charity groups. For many Western Europeans, participating in Nicaragua's revolutionary project no longer meant unconditionally supporting the FSLN's political program, but rather building emotional and practical connections with individual Nicaraguans and development projects. In other words, an individual's sense of participating in the revolution was increasingly prioritized over a more general financial contribution for the state or political party, which were no longer seen as trustworthy or capable enough to take care of the people. At its heart, this transformation of solidarity activism is illustrative of neoliberalism's triumph in the 1980s, as the individual's preference took precedence over the needs of the collective.

## THE INTERNATIONAL COURT OF JUSTICE

While local politicians, activists, and students fought each other over the question of who was to blame for the U.S.-Nicaraguan conflict, judges of the International Court of Justice (ICJ) in The Hague were confronted with a very similar question. On 9 April 1984, Carlos Argüello Gómez, the Nicaraguan ambassador to the Netherlands, filed an application to the court that accused the U.S. government of "responsibility for military and paramilitary activities in and against Nicaragua."[141] Rejecting several claims from U.S. representatives that the ICJ had no jurisdiction to intervene in this conflict, the court's fifteen judges decided on 26 November 1984 that the Nicaraguan case was admissible. On 27 June 1986, more than two years later, the court sided with Nicaragua and ruled that the Reagan administration had broken international law and violated Nicaraguan sovereignty by, among other activities, organizing, financing, and training the Contras, as well as mining the ports of El Bluff, Corinto, and Puerto Sandino. As a consequence, the court declared, the United States should from that moment on "refrain from all such acts" that violated international law. Crucially, the court ruled that the United States should pay Nicaragua reparations "for all injury caused."[142] To no one's surprise, the Reagan administration categorically refused to pay reparations, which were estimated at around $17 billion, and continued aiding the counterrevolutionaries. Indeed, as alluded to above, shortly after the court ruled in Nicaragua's favor, the U.S. House of Representatives decided to provide the Contras with another $100 million in aid, which included $70 million for military equipment.[143]

Despite the U.S. administration's refusal to comply with the court's decision, the Sandinista government described the ICJ ruling as its "greatest triumph" in the international arena in 1986.[144] The judgment of the court was important, not because Nicaraguan diplomats seriously believed the Reagan administration would actually start paying reparations or reconsider its foreign policy toward Nicaragua, but rather because the ICJ decision could strengthen the international position of the Sandinista government. In sharp contrast to the United States, one MINEX official wrote on 10 February 1986, a positive ruling of the ICJ demonstrated to the world that Nicaragua was a "respectable country" that abided by international law and the UN Charter.[145] On a less abstract level, this meant that the ICJ ruling could separate the Unites States from its Western European allies and further isolate the Reagan administration in international forums such as the United Nations. Furthermore, by declaring U.S. assistance to the Contras illegal, the court further delegitimized the struggle of the insurgents. Therefore, Nicaraguan diplomats sought to "internationalize" the decision of the court as much as possible.[146]

With regard to the solidarity movement, the ICJ ruling provided committees in Western Europe with new material to use in campaigns, demonstrations, and lobbying efforts. Naturally, solidarity committees used the ICJ ruling as evidence that Nicaragua, a small Central American country, was under illegal attack by the most powerful state in the world. The Dutch committee, for instance, mentioned the ICJ judgments in its advertisements for the Nicaragua Must Survive campaign. Citizens were invited to "condemn" U.S. aggression against Nicaragua, "just like the World Court had done."[147] In the United Kingdom, the NSC organized a demonstration in front of the U.S. embassy denouncing the Reagan administration for "breaching international law" (figure 12). The ruling of the ICJ, however, did not drastically alter the grassroots discussion about the U.S.-Nicaraguan conflict, nor did it figure prominently in the campaigns of the solidarity movement. Although the ruling was mentioned regularly, it was never more than a slogan. As John Bevan of the NSC remembers, "other than dropping [the court's ruling] now and again" into public attacks on U.S. foreign policy, the group did not really "know how to use the ICJ case" for the Nicaraguan Revolution's benefit.[148] Overall, the judgment of the court and the UN debates that followed were deemed too abstract to mobilize people at the grassroots level.

In the months after the ICJ ruling, then, Nicaraguan officials sought to capitalize on the judgment through international institutions, most notably the United Nations. Nicaraguan ambassador to the United Nations Nora Astorga, for instance, introduced several resolutions at the Security Council and General Assembly that called on the United States to comply with the court's judgment.[149] In the General Assembly, a large majority of countries voted for the Nicaraguan resolutions. On 3 November, the Assembly adopted a resolution (94 to 3) that emphasized the obligation of states "not

FIGURE 12. The Nicaragua Solidarity Campaign organized a protest outside the U.S. embassy in London, denouncing the Reagan administration's refusal to comply with the International Court of Justice's verdict in 1986. The protest was attended by the actress and comedian Maggie Steed (pictured on the right), who also helped to organize the successful 1983 benefit concert *An Evening for Nicaragua* at the Shaftesbury Theatre. The actor Alfred Molina (in the middle) was also present and would continue to promote several other NSC actions in the late 1980s, such the yearly London to Oxford Bike Ride. On the left is a lawyer (name unknown to the author). Photo: Julio Etchard, Nicaragua Solidarity Campaign, London.

to intervene in the internal affairs of other states" and urgently called "for full and immediate compliance" with the ICJ judgment.[150]

The Security Council was less forthcoming. While most of its member states (eleven out of fifteen), including the United States' allies Australia and Denmark, voted in favor of Nicaragua's proposal, the United States used its veto power.[151] According to U.S. ambassador Vernon Walters, his government had to veto the Sandinista resolution because the Nicaraguan government would have exploited its acceptance "as a blanket endorsement of its military and domestic policies."[152] Astorga, on the other hand, denounced it as "a vote against the fundamental principles and norms of this organization, ... a vote against international peace and security, and a vote for war, intervention and the use of force."[153] Furthermore, the Nicaraguans were frustrated that the United Kingdom, France, and Thailand abstained. The British representative—using rather warped logic—explained his country's vote by declaring that the resolution failed "to acknowledge that Nicaragua [had] largely brought its troubles upon itself."[154] Even a ruling by the ICJ, the Sandinistas were forced to acknowledge, could not fully isolate the United States from its European allies.

The decision-making process behind the Security Council vote on 28 October 1986, however, shows that the court's ruling did put the transatlantic relationship under strain. In particular, the United Kingdom was expected to vote in favor of the Nicaraguan resolution since it had always presented itself as a standard-bearer of international law. It would be highly damaging for their international standing and credibility, British officials believed, if they did not vote in favor of a resolution that simply asked for an ICJ judgment to be respected. FCO official David Joy, for instance, noted that a vote in favor of the resolution would "clearly underline, in a high profile way, our wish to be seen to be upholding international law."[155] And Richard Wilkinson, who worked at the British embassy in Mexico, concluded that the Nicaraguans had "tried hard" and eventually succeeded in putting on the table a resolution that "any country which accepts the compulsory jurisdiction of the ICJ would find hard not to vote for."[156] Foreign Secretary Geoffrey Howe came to the same conclusion. The resolution, he told Thatcher, was entirely in accordance with the ruling of the court and there were "no legal grounds on which [the United Kingdom] could object to the text."[157] Nicaraguan officials, keenly aware of the British predicament, constantly reminded the Thatcher government of its well-known position on international law. In October 1986, for instance, ambassador Francisco d'Escoto pointed out that Thatcher had recently told Ortega that "the support that Her Majesty's Government [gave] to international law [could not] be questioned."[158] By contrast, the French government experienced much less pressure than the United Kingdom, as France did not accept the jurisdiction of the court.

The British government's eventual decision to sidestep international law and abstain on the Nicaraguan resolution was partly the result of U.S. pressure but mostly due to a personal intervention from Thatcher, who overruled the Foreign Secretary. American officials were certainly lobbying hard to get the British to vote against the resolution, or at a minimum abstain. On 31 July 1986, Shultz wrote a personal letter to Howe stressing that he was "very concerned" that the ICJ ruling would bring the two countries "into diametric opposition in the Security Council." If the United Kingdom voted in favor of the resolution, Shultz threatened, it would be "detrimental to Alliance solidarity" and embolden critics of U.S. foreign policy "at home and abroad."[159] The FCO, however, were unfazed and continued to push for a British vote in favor. Noting that there was "little doubt that the U.S. . . . had engaged in actions contrary to the rule of international law" by supporting the Contras, British policymakers argued that the international community would perceive the United Kingdom as a U.S. puppet if it did not stick up for international law.[160] While "the Americans may huff and puff," policymaker

Derek Thomas wrote, the United Kingdom should take this opportunity to express "a clear and distinct British point of view."[161] Howe agreed and told Thatcher's private secretary, Charles Powell, that the American arguments were hypocritical. The United States, he pointed out, "voted against [the United Kingdom] on the Falklands issue in the General Assembly for several years and will no doubt do so again in a month's time."[162] In sum, the FCO took the position that—at least in this specific case—unbiased support for international law should trump political considerations.

To the disappointment of most British officials, Thatcher disagreed and ordered an abstention. She regarded the Nicaraguan resolution as a "blatantly political and propagandist exercise." The Nicaraguans, she noted, were "manipulating a legal judgement to make political capital" and embarrass the United States, an important Cold War ally.[163] Furthermore, Powell reminded the Foreign Secretary, in the grand scheme of things, Nicaragua simply did "not matter" to the United Kingdom, while the U.S. mattered "very much." That being the case, Powell wondered, then "how on earth" could the United Kingdom find itself in a position of voting for Nicaragua and against the United States, particularly in such an important body as the Security Council?[164] For Thatcher, in the case of the U.S.-Nicaraguan conflict, there was no such thing as objective support for international law.

Thatcher's intervention in the Security Council demonstrates that it was difficult, if not impossible, for the Sandinistas to overcome Cold War alliances and ideologies in the mid-1980s. Even beyond America's backyard, the FSLN could not escape U.S. global power and its ability to influence international institutions and European foreign policies. The U.K. and France showed themselves unwilling to publicly oppose the U.S. government, even though—behind the scenes—they believed Nicaragua was probably in the right. If the Sandinistas wanted to use Western Europe to put pressure on the Reagan administration, they thus had to look for alternative methods and channels.

CONCLUSION

Overall, in the period 1985–86, the Sandinistas failed to achieve the goals set out in their revolutionary and electoral programs. True, the FSLN was still in power, and it was not likely that they would be overthrown through military means any time soon. However, because of the Contra war and the deteriorating economic situation, the Sandinistas were forced to let go of many of their ambitions to improve health care, spread literacy, empower workers, and bring social justice to the country. This was a dangerous development, as it meant the FSLN leadership was at risk of losing the support of the Nicaraguan population.

Furthermore, as Western European and Latin American economic assistance to Nicaragua decreased, the Sandinistas had become increasingly dependent on Cuba and the Soviet Union, something they had not initially wanted as it undermined their nonaligned image. In 1980, the Soviet bloc and Cuba provided only $45 million in economic aid, while the OECD countries and Latin America provided $290 million. In 1986, however, due to the economic embargo and costs of the war, Nicaragua needed more money than the OECD countries could and wanted to offer. So the socialist countries provided Nicaragua with $582 million in 1986, while the Latin Americans and Western Europeans only gave $113 million. Economic assistance from the Netherlands, for example, went down from $24 million in 1983 to $15 million in 1986. Meanwhile, West Germany scaled down to only $3 million in bilateral economic assistance in 1986. Aid from multilateral institutions also declined, from $121 million in 1981 to $35 million in 1986.[165]

As this period in the revolution's history made painfully clear, the struggle for Nicaragua was more than a direct military conflict between the Sandinistas and the U.S.-backed contras. The country's future and revolutionary trajectory were, to a crucial extent, shaped by perceptions and popular ideas about modernity, democracy, development, freedom, and (social) justice. In the mid-1980s, in contrast to the decade's early years, the Sandinistas were no longer in an advantageous position when it came to the international battle for hearts and minds. As Cold War tensions between the United States and the Soviet Union started to decline, peace movements failed to prevent the stationing of missiles in Europe, and Western European governments moved increasingly toward the right, the FSLN found it difficult to argue that the revolution was representative of the wave of the future. Rather, during the second half of the 1980s, a significant number of Western European politicians, civil servants, and journalists compared the Sandinista government to the aging socialist regimes of the Eastern bloc, arguing that Nicaraguan leaders needed to reform and democratize to survive. Even though there were still many Western Europeans who rejected Reagan's bullying and sympathized with the Nicaraguan plight, the optimism of the revolution's early years had disappeared. In this context, the Sandinistas were confronted with the difficult task of using their limited room for maneuver to ensure the continued survival of the revolution.

# SIX

# Peace and Elections, 1987–1990

ON 7 AUGUST 1987 IN GUATEMALA CITY, the presidents of Nicaragua, Costa Rica, El Salvador, Guatemala, and Honduras signed a historic peace treaty known as the Esquipulas II Peace Accords. After hours of intense negotiations, the five Central American presidents declared to the international community that they had taken up "the historical challenge of forcing a peaceful destiny for Central America." They agreed on an ambitious document that included promises to implement amnesty decrees, the organization of free elections, and processes of national reconciliation and democratization. Acknowledging that foreign intervention had exacerbated the region's armed conflicts, the treaty also called on governments from outside the region to terminate the provision of any "military, logistical, financial, or propaganda support" to "irregular forces or insurrectionist movements." At the regional level, the Central American leaders committed to the "non-use of territory to attack other states," which meant they would no longer allow foreign guerrilla or counterinsurgent groups to operate from within their territories.[1]

For the Nicaraguan revolutionaries, the Esquipulas II Accords offered the only way out of a difficult and dangerous situation. By 1987, Sandinista leaders were desperate to bring an end to the Contra war and fix the spiraling economy. They realized that measures taken in previous years, such as the CNDS, were no longer sufficient to ensure the survival of the revolution in the face of growing international pressure and isolation. A major setback for the FSLN in the late 1980s was a shift in the Soviet Union's foreign policy toward the Third World. As Nicaraguan vice president Sergio Ramírez found out on a trip to the Eastern bloc in June 1987, despite its sympathy for the Sandinista cause the Soviet Union was not willing to protect the Nicaraguan

Revolution at any cost. Rather, the new leader Mikhail Gorbachev wanted the Sandinistas to reach an agreement with their Central American neighbors and, crucially, to obtain economic and material aid from the West rather than the East. Declining superpower tensions in the late 1980s, then, pushed the FSLN comandantes toward concessions that had been unthinkable in previous years, including negotiations with the insurgents and strict austerity measures.

In this context, Western Europe once again became a key area for the Sandinistas' revolutionary diplomacy. The FSLN, fearing that the United States would try to sabotage the peace negotiations, worked hard to drum up Western European political support for the Esquipulas accords and, more specifically, sought to demonstrate that Nicaragua, unlike the other Central American countries, was making a genuine effort to stick to its promises. There was an obvious financial element to this strategy. Arguing that it would be unfair to keep withholding aid now that Nicaragua was doing everything it could to accommodate the wishes of the Western countries, including organizing democratic elections for the second time since coming into power, the Sandinistas and solidarity activists lobbied for increased economic and material support from Western European governments and financial institutions. Beyond ending the Contra war, the FSLN reasoned, participation in the peace process could also help solve the country's financial crisis.

In the Western European arena, however, the Sandinistas ran into obstacles that they found difficult to overcome. Somewhat ironically considering Gorbachev's insistence that the FSLN should turn to the West, the Soviet retreat from Central America meant that European governments felt even less pressure to support the revolutionaries financially. After all, the primary reason for giving aid to Nicaragua—preventing the country from becoming too dependent on the Soviet Union—had largely disappeared by the late 1980s. Moreover, there was little that solidarity activists could do to change their governments' position on developmental aid to Nicaragua, mostly because levels of public sympathy for the Nicaraguan Revolution were in decline. As Eastern Europeans revolted against state socialism and global audiences grew disenchanted with communism, pro-Sandinista activists struggled to present revolutionary Nicaragua as a beacon of hope, social progress, and popular democracy. Strategies to change the tide, including focusing on "practical" rather than overtly "political" and radical forms of solidarity activism, largely failed due to the lack of public interest and critical news coverage of the chaotic situation in Nicaragua.[2] As the Cold War came to an end, space for maneuver in the international environment was quickly narrowing.

Tracing how the FSLN sought to overcome these obstacles, this chapter discusses the dwindling ability of the Sandinistas to implement their revolutionary diplomacy as the post-Cold War order started to take shape in the late 1980s. Although the FSLN sought to make concessions to its ideological critics, its efforts to appease the international community while at the same time maintaining control at home were not enough to ensure the survival of the Nicaraguan Revolution. Hoping for a Sandinista defeat at the polls, Western European leaders withheld financial aid until after elections had taken place, which meant that the Nicaraguan economy could not recover or even stabilize. In the United States, the newly installed George H. W. Bush administration also made it clear that the insurgents would only demobilize until after the elections. In this volatile context, many Nicaraguans opted for change and, on 25 February 1990, voted the FSLN out of power, thereby ending the country's decade-long revolutionary experiment.

## THE ROAD TO THE ESQUIPULAS II PEACE ACCORDS

When the Costa Rican president Óscar Arias first presented his peace plan at a Central American presidential summit in San José on 15 February 1987, very few believed it had the potential—or even the ambition—to end the region's conflicts. It seemed unlikely the Nicaraguan government would accept proposals from Arias, who was known as a staunch anticommunist and critic of the Sandinista leadership. Indeed, due to Arias's claim that "democracy" was a necessary precondition for an end to the region's hostilities, his peace proposal appeared specifically designed to isolate Nicaragua, reject the FSLN's claims to democratic rule, and pressure the Sandinistas into implementing domestic reforms.[3] Unlike his Salvadoran and Guatemalan colleagues, Nicaraguan president Daniel Ortega was not even invited to the summit in San José where Arias first announced his plans, on the grounds that he was not fully committed to democracy. An annoyed and suspicious Ortega described the meeting as a "U.S.-inspired" maneuver, while his foreign minister Miguel d'Escoto declared that it was "totally unacceptable" for other countries "to draw up recipes" for Nicaragua's internal affairs.[4] Private comments from U.S. Assistant Secretary of State Elliott Abrams also demonstrate that the Reagan administration hoped and expected the Nicaraguan revolutionaries to reject Arias's peace plan. A couple days before the San José summit in February 1987, Abrams told Günther van Well, the West German ambassador to Washington, that the Nicaraguan government would "certainly reject" Arias's proposals, commenting that Reagan planned to use this refusal to further isolate and "score propaganda points" against the Sandinistas.[5] And yet, even though Nicaraguan officials initially dismissed the plan as "made in the U.S.A.," their perspective shifted drastically in the weeks leading up to the summit in Guatemala City. By August 1987, the FSLN's National Directorate had reversed its position and concluded that going along with a—somewhat modified—version of Arias's proposal was the right way forward for Nicaragua's revolutionary project.

To understand this change in the Sandinista position, we need to zoom in on the FSLN's increasingly precarious situation in 1987, while at the same time assessing how these developments intersected with the growing international legitimacy and popularity of the Costa Rican president and his regional peace plan. First, Sandinista officials were under heavy pressure to find a diplomatic solution to the Contra war. As a result of the shift in U.S. congressional opinion on 25 June 1986, when Congress approved a $100 million aid package for the counterrevolutionary forces, the armed conflict between the EPS and the U.S.-backed Contra fighters grew more violent, costly, and deadly in early 1987. Aside from forcing the Nicaraguan government to spend exorbitant amounts of money on the military, the war had a devastating impact on everyday life in Nicaragua.[6] Newspapers in Central America, Europe, and the Americas chronicled the many atrocities inflicted on Nicaraguan people living in the war zones, giving examples of abductions, torture, rape, and murder.[7] And while both the Sandinista army and the counterrevolutionaries were accused of excessive violence and human rights violations, there was little doubt that the tactics of the insurgents caused most of the human suffering.[8] International human rights organizations such as Human Rights Watch reported that Contras were "major and systematic violators" of human rights and committed all sorts of abuses, including "launching indiscriminate attacks on civilians, selectively murdering non-combatants, and mistreating prisoners."[9] After years of armed conflict, it was clear that the war could not be brought to an end through military means. Although the Contras could not defeat the Sandinista army, they were also unlikely to be vanquished, since the insurgents could simply retreat to their base camps in Honduras and Costa Rica if the Sandinista army advanced. So long as the United States provided funding and military training, Central American states allowed the Contras to operate from their territories, and Nicaraguans—even if it was only a small number—were willing and able to take up arms against the Sandinista government, the war would most likely continue.[10]

Sandinista leaders were also increasingly open to making concessions in 1987 because they desperately needed to fix the country's chaotic financial situation, which consistently undermined the popularity and legitimacy of the revolutionary project. Despite earlier attempts to manage the economy by seeking international aid and introducing market-oriented reforms to boost production, Nicaragua's economic situation had not improved since it started to decline in 1983. State finances were stretched to the limit, as the U.S. economic embargo was still in place and the Contra war used up most of the country's resources. In 1988, the Nicaraguan government spent more than 60 percent of its budget on the military.[11] This, in combination with devastating natural disasters that destroyed significant parts of the country's arable land, the refusal of international banks and lending agencies to provide the Nicaraguan government with new loans, and the United States' pressure on its allies to cut off all support to Nicaragua, resulted in economic chaos.

Indeed, as Sandinista comandante Bayardo Arce told a group of Western European ambassadors in Managua, the state of the Nicaraguan economy was "disastrous."[12] As inflation skyrocketed, average incomes plummeted, and exports declined further still, the government was unable to pay off its debts.[13] At the grassroots level, Nicaraguans were struggling: there were empty stores, hunger, energy shortages, long lines, and regular power cuts.[14] Dutch solidarity activists living in Managua such as Mary Timmerman wrote about the "dire food situation" they and their Nicaraguan friends experienced, noting that there was little rice, no beans, and that almost all restaurants had closed.[15] In December 1987, the government declared a "national food emergency," as the average calorie intake was lower than it had been in the 1950s.[16] Daniel Ortega, according to West German officials, admitted to his Guatemalan counterpart Vinicio Cerezo Arévalo in April 1987 that the country was economically "exhausted." And while Ortega stressed that the Sandinistas would never "surrender" the revolutionary project, he also confessed his willingness to "make concessions" to other Central American leaders at the upcoming summit in Guatemala City.[17]

Changes in the international Cold War context, particularly the Soviet Union's desire to reduce tensions with the United States and reform the

Soviet economy, also pushed the Sandinista leaders toward accepting Arias's peace plan. Between 8 and 22 June 1987, Nicaraguan vice president Sergio Ramírez travelled through the Soviet bloc, where he visited the Soviet Union, Czechoslovakia, Poland, and the German Democratic Republic, hoping to secure much-needed economic, political, and material support, most notably oil supplies. Instead of providing Nicaragua with the necessary assistance, however, socialist leaders wanted to talk about the Sandinistas' contribution to the peace process. As Ramírez later wrote to Ortega, Eastern European officials were very critical of Nicaragua's public rejection of the Arias Plan, and it took quite some time and effort to defend the Sandinista government's position. Even after a "detailed" explanation from the Nicaraguan delegation, Ramírez noted, the socialist leaders maintained that the Sandinista comandantes should make a more serious effort to improve their relations with the other Central American states.[18]

According to Ramírez, whose claims are backed up by recent literature on the topic, the principal factor behind the decline of Soviet support for the Nicaraguan revolutionaries was the desire of Gorbachev to pursue a "policy of détente" with the United States, so that he could focus on reforming the economy and raising the "standard of living" in the Soviet Union instead. For financial reasons, then, Gorbachev preferred diplomatic solutions to expensive regional Cold War conflicts. Indeed, Ramírez informed Ortega at the end of his trip, the Soviet Union was urging its ideological allies to search for "quick negotiated solutions" to their problems with U.S.-backed neighbors.[19] Gorbachev's reformist ambitions thus had a direct impact on Central American affairs, as they pushed the Sandinista leaders toward adopting a more cooperative and pragmatic attitude in the Esquipulas negotiations of August 1987.[20]

At the same time as international, military, and economic pressure on the Nicaraguan government intensified, Arias's peace plan started to gain momentum and legitimacy.[21] After announcing his peace proposal, the Costa Rican president traveled around the world, drumming up significant support. In May and June 1987, Arias visited Western Europe, where he spoke with, among others, West German chancellor Helmut Kohl, British prime minister Margaret Thatcher, Spanish prime minister Felipe González, French president François Mitterrand, and former French foreign minister Claude Cheysson, the European Commissioner responsible for North-South relations. While some Western European leaders, such as Thatcher, were hesitant to throw their weight behind the peace plan without first consulting the Reagan administration, the response was overwhelmingly positive.[22]

Cheysson, for instance, declared in a joint press conference with Arias that the European Commission fully supported his proposal, adding that he was "sure" the twelve individual EC members would soon do the same.[23] And on 5 August 1987, on the eve of the Guatemala summit, Western European leaders issued a joint declaration, encouraging the Central Americans to come to an agreement and stating that Arias's peace plan represented "an original and constructive contribution to the establishment of peace through political means and to the consolidation of democracy in Central America."[24]

In the eyes of EC leaders, the Arias Plan represented an opportunity to breathe new life into the Central American peace process, which had stagnated in previous months, and supporting it simply made sense. After all, since 1984 the Western Europeans' official position had been that a workable solution to Central America's problems could only come from "political solutions springing from the region itself."[25] Furthermore, since the Arias Plan targeted the region as a whole, demanding democratic reforms and compliance from all five Central American countries, Western European politicians from different sides of the political spectrum could draw on a variety of reasons to get behind it. Sympathizers with the Sandinista Revolution, on the one hand, were happy with the aspects of Arias's proposal that criticized the Contra war, such as the request to the international community to terminate all assistance to irregular forces and insurrectionist movements. Western European conservatives and Christian Democrats, on the other hand, were more interested in the parts that dealt with domestic reforms and democratization, hoping that a successful peace agreement could strengthen the anti-Sandinista opposition in Nicaragua. Notably, the West German ambassador to Nicaragua, Josef Rusnak, told foreign minister Hans-Dietrich Genscher in April 1987 that the Europeans should back Arias's proposal, not only because it had the support of Nicaraguan opposition parties, but also because the Sandinista government, weakened as a result of the Contra war, was in no position to reject it.[26] British officials, too, were primarily interested in the extent to which the Nicaraguan government's "tactical concessions" on democratization could lead to "further dilution of Sandinista control."[27]

Of the EC member states, the West German government was the most dedicated to the Arias Plan, hoping it would boost the Nicaraguan opposition and bring peace to the region. In the run-up to the Guatemala City summit, West German officials lobbied actively for the proposal. Kohl and Genscher encouraged their allies to openly back the Costa Rican president, tried to assuage Reagan's concerns about the possibility that the Sandinistas could abuse and manipulate the peace process, and pushed the president of El Salvador, José Napoleón Duarte, who complained the proposal did not mention "Nicaraguan and Cuban aid" to the FMLN guerrillas, toward a more cooperative attitude.[28] In conversations with U.S. officials, West German diplomats promoted the Arias Plan by capitalizing on the Reagan administration's embrace of "democracy promotion" and human rights (not including social and economic rights) as a tool to fight the Cold War.[29] For instance, Genscher explained to Secretary of State George Shultz at the Venice Economic Summit in June 1987 that the West German government's principal reason for supporting Arias's proposal was that it forced the Sandinista regime to "show its true colors to the world" on issues such as pluralism, freedom of speech, and democratization. Genscher also told Shultz that the Arias Plan put the question of democracy at the center of the political debate on Central America's crises.[30]

It is important to note here that Reagan's criticism of the Arias Plan in 1987 had less of an impact on Central American decision-making than, for instance, his efforts to undermine the Contadora process in 1984. In fact, Óscar Arias's peace plan was able to gain strength and momentum, not only due to Latin American and Western European diplomatic support, but also because the Reagan administration's Central America policy was under severe strain due to the Iran-Contra affair. This scandal broke in October 1986, when Nicaraguan soldiers shot down a Contra supply plane and captured Eugene Hasenfus, a U.S. citizen who claimed to be working on direct orders from the CIA. In the following months, it emerged that the U.S. government, using a complex covert network of private funds, transnational agencies, and third parties, had secretly channeled profits from illegal arms sales to Iran to the Nicaraguan insurgents. As a result of the Iran-Contra affair, Sandinista officials noted optimistically, Reagan's foreign policy, particularly with regard to Central America, had lost all international legitimacy and congressional support.[31] Costa Rican officials, too, believed that the Reagan administration was in a position of "weakness" in the months leading up to the Guatemala City summit.[32]

Due to the outbreak of the Iran-Contra affair, then, the summit in August 1987 was more likely to produce a positive outcome. With the United States' influence in the region temporarily weakened, political space opened for the five Central American presidents, with the diplomatic support of the European Community and Contadora countries, to work out a peace agreement they could all agree on. By doing so, Central American leaders undermined U.S. diplomacy, which sought to isolate the Sandinistas from the four so-called "democracies" in the region.[33] Even at the height of the Iran-Contra scandal, though, it still was not easy for the five presidents to exclude the Reagan administration from the negotiating table and create a temporary regional bloc. According to former MINEX official Alejandro Bendaña, Reagan's phone calls "to get the whole thing sabotaged" constantly interrupted the negotiations in Guatemala City. To solve the issue of U.S. interference, Bendaña remembers that "the five Central American presidents [decided to] shut themselves off in a room with no advisers there, nobody taking phone calls, especially from Washington, until they hammered out a document called the Esquipulas II [Accords], or the Arias Plan."[34]

For the Sandinistas, the peace process that came out of the Arias Plan was both an irritating necessity and a welcome opportunity. On the one hand, precarious domestic, regional, and international circumstances forced the FSLN comandantes toward concessions on greater press freedom, a dialogue with domestic opposition parties, and a promise to organize democratic elections. Faced with regional isolation—a diplomatic disaster that could easily be exploited by the Sandinistas' enemies—the Nicaraguan government had no other choice than to go along with Arias's proposals once they gained international legitimacy and support, particularly from the Western Europeans. On the other hand, the Esquipulas II Accords presented the nine FSLN comandantes with a unique opportunity to end the Contra war, avoid regional isolation, and undermine U.S. foreign policy. Moreover, they calculated that if they played their cards right in the following months, the FSLN could potentially use the peace process to resolve the country's economic problems and once again promote Nicaragua as an international symbol of peace and democracy. In short, the peace process was the revolutionaries' only option, but it was not necessarily a bad one.

## CONTROLLING THE PEACE PROCESS

Having decided that the Esquipulas II Accords were the only possible way out of a dangerous situation, the Sandinistas put the peace process at the core of their revolutionary diplomacy in the months following the Guatemala City summit. By showcasing Nicaraguan compliance and contributions to Esquipulas II, the FSLN hoped to boost Nicaragua's international image, obtain much-needed economic aid from Western European countries, and increase pressure on the United States and Honduras to cut ties with the counterrevolutionaries. The Sandinista comandantes were particularly worried about U.S. efforts to obstruct the peace process and hoped that, by mobilizing international support for the accords, Reagan could be forced into adopting a more accommodating attitude.[35] As Bayardo Arce told the East German leader Erich Honecker in March 1988, the Sandinista government was convinced that "international pressure [was] absolutely crucial to get the United States to accept the sovereign decision of the Central American presidents to commit to the peace process."[36]

The Nicaraguans were not wrong about the U.S. administration's antipathy toward the Esquipulas II Accords. In the eyes of the Reagan administration, revolutionary Nicaragua remained part of the Soviet bloc and therefore a fundamental threat to the United States and its "political and security interests in the [Western] hemisphere."[37] By allowing for the possibility that the FSLN would remain in power, the accords failed to assuage Reagan's concerns about this Cold War threat. In a combative radio speech on 12 September 1987, Reagan announced that his administration "welcomed" the Esquipulas II Accords but that the treaty was fatally flawed. In particular, the president noted, since there was absolutely no guarantee that the Sandinistas would keep their promises regarding democratization, the treaty fell short of the necessary "safeguards for democracy and our national security." Reagan continued to believe that the presence of armed counterrevolutionaries was a necessary precondition for democracy in Nicaragua, and he told the nation that in the next couple of weeks, his administration planned to ask Congress to support another funding request of $270 million in Contra aid. Indeed, he concluded, there should be "no uncertainty" about his "unswerving commitment to the Contras."[38] In the period following the Guatemala City summit, as British diplomats correctly noted, the U.S. administration's real objective in Central America "remained quite clearly the removal from power rather than the containment of the Sandinistas," even though they continued to give public support to a negotiated solution.[39]

To counter Reagan's narrative, the Sandinistas and their supporters published reports on Nicaragua's many contributions to the peace process, which they contrasted with the uncooperative attitude of the Reagan administration and, albeit to a lesser extent, the other Central American countries (figure 13). British Foreign Secretary Geoffrey Howe lamented privately in 1987 that "not a day went by without media reports of new Nicaraguan concessions" with regard to the peace process.[40] In private meetings with

FIGURE 13. In the late 1980s, Sandinistas and solidarity activists published widely on Nicaragua's cooperative attitude in the peace process. This issue of *Nicaragua Today*, the bulletin of the London-based Nicaragua Solidarity Campaign, contrasts the Sandinistas' willingness to negotiate with the Contra leadership about a ceasefire with the Reagan administration's insistence on continuing the war. Photo: Nicaragua Solidarity Campaign, London.

Western European officials, Nicaraguan diplomats focused on the steps the Sandinista government had taken to implement the Esquipulas II Accords. On 12 August 1987, MINEX official Javier Chamorro Mora told EC diplomats in Managua that his government had already invited the eleven registered opposition parties to participate in a national dialogue mediated by Cardinal Miguel Obando y Bravo, a well-known critic of the FSLN.[41] Ortega and Miguel d'Escoto made similar points to Dutch Minister for Development

Cooperation Piet Bukman in October 1987, pointing out that Nicaragua was the first Central American country to create a reconciliation commission, and that they had effectively ended censorship by allowing opposition newspaper *La Prensa* and critical radio station *Radio Católica* to reopen. Meanwhile, they declared solemnly, Reagan was still sabotaging the peace process by refusing to give up on the Contras.[42]

The European-Central American dialogue, launched after the 1984 summit in San José (chapter 4), provided the Sandinista government with a useful platform to mobilize Western European leaders for the peace process. The yearly meetings gave Nicaraguan and other Central American officials an opportunity to share their views of the peace process with high-ranking EC officials. In the period following the Guatemala City summit, British officials noted, the "level of contact" between EC diplomats and Central American governments "increased substantially" because the "Central Americans continue to attach great importance to the political influence of the Twelve which they see as a means of counterbalancing the influence of the United States."[43] At a meeting in New York on 25 September 1987, for example, Nicaraguan diplomat Victor Hugo Tinoco was part of a Central American delegation that underlined to EC representatives Genscher, Tindemans, and Cheysson the crucial importance of "continued political support from the Twelve" for the Esquipulas II Accords.[44] The fact that the Nicaraguan government was able to bring across its pro-Esquipulas message as part of a Central American regional bloc contributed to the impact, visibility, and legitimacy of its diplomatic campaign.

As in previous years, the FSLN worked with solidarity committees to strengthen its revolutionary diplomacy. On 24 August 1987, Hernán Estrada from the FSLN's Departamento de Relaciones Internacionales asked solidarity activists living in Managua to inform the Western European public about the many advances of the peace process.[45] At a Western European solidarity conference in Helsinki in December 1987, DRI representative Ana Patricia Elvir stressed the vital importance of the solidarity movement's contribution to the Esquipulas II Accords, and encouraged solidarity committees to lobby their governments and mobilize public opinion in support of the initiative.[46] In response, solidarity committees published pamphlets and booklets urging EC leaders to support the peace process, put pressure on the Reagan administration, and praise the proactive role of Nicaragua. In the Netherlands, activists published an advert in left-wing newspaper *De Volkskrant*, declaring that the revolutionaries had taken the lead in the peace process and therefore "deserved support" from the international community.[47] In another booklet, the solidarity committees called on EC leaders to work harder so that the Central American peace process could succeed, even "if that means taking a stance against the United States."[48]

Fortunately for the FSLN, the Nicaraguan government and its allies were not alone in their conviction that the Esquipulas II Accords deserved international support. Aside from the Reagan administration, the entire international community appeared willing to throw its weight behind it. Most notably, in October 1987, Óscar Arias was awarded the Nobel Peace Prize for his contribution to the peace process in Central America.[49] In addition, Western European governments, the Socialist International, and the Organization of American States issued multiple declarations of support. And even though the twelve EC countries refrained from publicly criticizing the U.S. role in Central America, Western European declarations were clearly designed to push the Reagan administration toward a more cooperative attitude. In November 1987, the Twelve issued a joint declaration urging "the international community and, in particular, countries with links to and interest in Central America, to contribute to the region's effort to achieve peace, democracy, and economic development."[50]

While the FSLN appreciated international support for the peace process, believing it would end the Contra war and thus pave the way for consolidating their regime, the revolutionaries hoped for more than that. Nicaragua's suffering economy remained "the Achilles heel" of the revolution, Ortega told Honecker in Moscow on 3 November 1987, because food shortages, hyperinflation, and growing unemployment significantly weakened the Sandinistas' domestic support base. The growing discontent among the Nicaraguan population because of the war and the economic crisis, Ortega disclosed, was particularly worrying now that the comandantes had been forced to open "political space" at home to demonstrate their commitment to the peace process. The "counterrevolutionary" opposition, Ortega recognized, could use the new measures with regard to press freedom and a national dialogue to spread false propaganda and weaken the FSLN's position. Nevertheless, he added optimistically, the Sandinista leaders were convinced that Western European and Scandinavian countries would be more forthcoming with economic and development aid now that Nicaragua had taken concrete steps to implement the Esquipulas II Accords.[51]

In public declarations and private meetings, FSLN officials thus linked the promise of peace in Central America to the necessity of economic assistance to the region, and Nicaragua in particular. Sergio Ramírez, before traveling to Western Europe and Latin America in search of financial assistance on 18 August 1987, announced that "a country without relative economic normality cannot fully commit to the peace process."[52] Solidarity activists and left-wing politicians in Western Europe, too, argued that the Nicaraguan government should be rewarded with increased developmental aid for its proactive contribution to the Esquipulas process. To give one example, the leader of the West German Social Democratic Party, Hans-Jürgen Wischnewski, argued in a Bundestag debate in September 1987 that the Sandinista leaders had taken positive steps to implement the peace accords' requirements and that, in response, the West German bilateral aid program to Nicaragua should be resumed immediately.[53]

Unfortunately for the revolutionaries, however, Western European governments refused to provide the Nicaraguan government with more bilateral aid until it had "fulfilled all the requirements of the Guatemala City summit."[54] Nicaraguan officials, such as vice minister Pedro Antonio Blandón, who visited West Germany on 16 December 1987, tried to counter these Western European demands by pointing out that it was unfair to push Nicaragua toward compliance while the other Central American countries experienced much less diplomatic pressure, even though they were less forthcoming than Nicaragua in their efforts to make the peace process a success. The government of Honduras, Sandinista officials noted quite correctly, had made no effort to close the Contra bases. And in El Salvador, the government was unable to prevent left-wing activists, politicians, and priests from being murdered by extreme right-wing forces.[55]

To the frustration of the FSLN and its supporters, the Nicaraguan claim that the Sandinistas were under much more scrutiny than the other Central American states failed to have a significant impact on the policies of Western European governments toward Nicaragua. On the contrary, the levels of aid of individual EC member states to Nicaragua continued to decline after the Esquipulas II Accords were signed, and Nicaragua's economic situation did not improve. Even the Dutch and French governments, which had provided Nicaragua with significant amounts of aid throughout most of the 1980s, announced they would cut back on their bilateral assistance in favor of a regional aid program that targeted Central America as a whole.[56] Only the Swedish government, as Bayardo Arce told a group Western European ambassadors in Managua, deserved "praise" for its continued efforts to support the Nicaraguan people.[57]

While bilateral levels of aid declined, Nicaragua continued to receive aid from the European Commission as part of its regional aid package for Central America, which was launched after the 1984 San José conference. In 1987, 1988, and 1989, the commission allocated respectively $100, $120, and $120 million to the Central American countries, prioritizing support for small businesses, cooperatives, health initiatives, education, and regional integration. And to the frustration of Western Europe's conservative governments, Nicaragua received significantly more aid than the other Central American countries. It is important to note here, though, that Nicaragua's numbers were boosted by the high levels of food aid that were sent in response to poverty and natural disasters, such as drought, floods, and hurricanes. Honduras, in contrast, received the highest amount of financial and technical aid.[58]

Nicaraguan officials were not wrong when they stated that the Sandinista government was held to a different standard than the other Central American states for ideological reasons. As British diplomats noted in May 1989, "the West" was clearly "demanding of Nicaragua a level of immediate democratization that [it did] not demand simultaneously from El Salvador, Honduras, and Guatemala."[59] The problem was that, in the late 1980s, state officials in the Netherlands, the United Kingdom, and West Germany were convinced that the ideology of the Sandinista comandantes was inherently undemocratic, because it left no space for the possibility that, at some point in the future, Nicaragua might not be a revolutionary country. As the Dutch consul in Managua concluded in May 1988, the freedom and potential influence of opposition parties in Nicaragua was bound to be limited since the Sandinista leadership considered the FSLN to be the only political organization capable of carrying out Nicaragua's "revolutionary process."[60] Therefore, in the eyes of these Western European diplomats, the widely publicized democratic opening in revolutionary Nicaragua was no more than window dressing, designed to consolidate Sandinista rule in the face of international pressure and economic chaos. Louise Croll from the FCO's Mexico and Central America Department, for example, concluded that Nicaraguan compliance with Esquipulas was a purely pragmatic decision to end the Contra war, and that the Sandinista "determination" to stay in power at all costs gave little hope for "genuine democratization."[61] West German government officials, too, treated the Nicaraguan domestic reforms in the context of Esquipulas with suspicion, and constantly worried about the possibility that Ortega would go back on his promises if the international community did not keep up its diplomatic and economic pressure on the Sandinistas.[62] There was little, it seemed, that the revolutionaries could do to shift the political tide in their favor.

On 15 and 16 January 1988, when the five Central American presidents came together for another summit to discuss the future of the peace process in Alajuela, Costa Rica, the Nicaraguan government thus still found itself in a weak position. The country's economic and military situation had not improved, and even though the FSLN leaders had gained some political capital from their attitude toward the Esquipulas II Accords, they clearly had failed to convince the international community that Nicaragua was the most peaceful, democratic, and cooperative of the Central American countries. Certainly, Arias, winner of the Nobel Peace Prize, remained a much more popular and less controversial figure internationally than ex-guerrilla Daniel Ortega. In January 1988, the Nicaraguan government also desperately needed to make a good impression because the U.S. Congress was scheduled to vote on a new Contra aid package on 4 February. International observers and FSLN officials speculated that were the Central American peace talks to collapse at the Costa Rican summit, Reagan was significantly more likely to obtain the congressional support he needed to continue the counterrevolutionary war against Nicaragua, as he could blame the Sandinistas for the failure of the peace process. More than any of the other Central American states, then, the Nicaraguan government needed the summit to be a success.

At the Alajuela meeting, the four other Central American governments were able to benefit from the Sandinistas' predicament. When Ortega demanded compliance from his Central American colleagues, the leaders of Honduras, Costa Rica, El Salvador, and Guatemala threatened him with a "joint statement condemning Nicaragua for obstructing the peace process" unless he gave in and made further concessions. Faced with the unwelcome prospect of regional isolation and conscious of the upcoming U.S. congressional vote on Contra aid, the Nicaraguans had to agree to their opponents' demands. And after a "tense" and "ill-tempered" summit, Ortega announced that he had agreed to immediately suspend the state of emergency and start direct negotiations with the Contra leaders about a ceasefire.[63] The latter was a particularly awkward concession, as the Sandinista comandantes had previously categorically refused to negotiate with the Contra leadership, seeing the counterrevolutionaries as merely "delegates from the North American government."[64] Indeed, Bendaña remembered, before the Esquipulas process, the FSLN's position on a direct dialogue with the Contras had consistently been that "we don't talk to the monkeys, we talk to the zookeepers."[65] The other Central American states were under much less pressure during the Alajuela summit. According to an analysis by the British ambassador in El Salvador, Duarte "achieved his prime objectives of concentrating the heat on Nicaragua" and, consequently was spared the "embarrassment" of having to take "further measures to comply with the spirit of Esquipulas II."[66]

While the summit had been a painful demonstration of the Sandinistas' regional isolation and lack of alternatives, Ortega's concessions to ensure the survival of the peace process had not been in vain. On 4 February 1988, Congress rejected Reagan's proposed Contra aid package of $36.3 million. Reagan's defeat, the Dutch solidarity committee announced in a press release, was "an important victory for the people and government of Nicaragua."[67] What is more, the fact that Reagan could no longer provide the Contras with military assistance gave an impulse to ceasefire negotiations between the Sandinistas and the insurgents, and these progressed surprisingly quickly in the subsequent weeks. After days of intense negotiations in the small Nicaraguan border town of Sapoá, on 23 March 1988, Sandinista defense minister Humberto Ortega and the three Contra leaders Adolfo Calero, Aristedes Sánchez, and Alfredo César signed a temporary ceasefire agreement in which the Sandinista government, among other things, promised a general amnesty, freedom of speech, and compliance with the Esquipulas II Accords. In return, the Contras agreed to retreat their fighters to mutually agreed-upon "zones" and to participate in a national dialogue, thereby accepting the fact that—until elections were held—the Sandinistas were legitimately in power.[68] To be sure, the Sapoá agreement did not bring an end to the war, as the Contras did not demobilize and the threat of further violence loomed, but it was an important step toward peace and, at the very least, it gave the Sandinista government and the Nicaraguan people some breathing space. In March 1988, as U.S. journalist Stephen Kinzer put it, "a nation torn by war slowly stopped bleeding."[69]

Ultimately, then, the signing of the Sapoá accords and the congressional vote against Reagan's Contra aid package were positive developments for the Sandinistas, who considered the war one of the main threats to the revolution.[70] However, U.S. politicians did not vote in favor of the FSLN's revolutionary project. Rather, the vote on 4 February 1988 represented a rejection of Reagan's militaristic foreign policy and an endorsement of the Esquipulas II Accords. This is an important distinction to make because, as the Central American summit in Alajuela clearly demonstrated, the Sandinistas had very little influence on how the Esquipulas process was implemented and perceived. This meant that, at the beginning of 1988, the nine FSLN comandantes found themselves in a position of weakness, but also at the center of a regional peace process with strong international backing. The international actors who supported the Esquipulas II Accords, such as the West German, British, and Dutch governments, used the process to demand concessions from the Nicaraguan government that could, in the eyes of the Sandinista leaders, potentially weaken the revolutionary process. Until March 1988, when the ceasefire with the Contras was signed, the FSLN leaders calculated that concessions with regard to domestic policy, such as allowing for greater press freedom, were necessary to appease the international community and end the Contra war. As we shall see in the following section, however, the Sandinistas were not always able to successfully juggle their domestic and international politics.

## DOMESTIC CONTROL AND INTERNATIONAL DISAPPOINTMENT

With the military threat curtailed and a temporary ceasefire in place, the Nicaraguan revolutionaries still had to resolve the country's other pressing problems, most notably economic chaos and growing social tensions. As Arce told Honecker in March 1988, the situation in Nicaragua had grown more "complicated" in the preceding months because the disastrous economic situation "undermined the social basis of the revolution." Moreover, as a result of the Esquipulas II Accords, Arce admitted, the anti-Sandinista opposition was in a better position than ever to exploit the growing discontent among the Nicaraguan population.[71] International observers and newspapers also reported on how the economic situation, combined with concessions made during the peace process, had weakened Sandinista rule in Nicaragua. Journalists wrote about surprisingly large anti-government demonstrations, hunger strikes by construction workers, and frustrated doctors who demanded higher wages to cope with inflation and food shortages.[72] Solidarity activists living in Nicaragua, too, noted the increasing tension and polarization resulting from the war and economic crisis. On 15 February 1988, British activist Naomi Cohen wrote about a demonstration she had witnessed in Masaya—historically a Sandinista stronghold—where young Nicaraguans protested the Servicio Militar Patriótico (SMP), a military draft obliging all Nicaraguan men to serve for two years in the Sandinista army.

According to Cohen, in this volatile situation, anti-government groups "were easily able to manipulate the feelings" of the Masayan population and, as a result, "an anti-government and specifically anti-SMP demonstration marched through the [city's] center." Later that evening, she noted, "in response to the opposition" there were "fortunately" many "spontaneous mobilizations" in favor of the Sandinista government and the military draft.[73] Cohen's views were reflective of a wider sentiment among pro-FSLN solidarity activists, who tended to view anti-Sandinista protests primarily as evidence of foreign intervention or manipulation.

In previous years, when the domestic situation had proved difficult to manage for the Sandinista leaders, they had been able to turn to the international community for financial support and diplomatic backing. These international campaigns were not always a massive success, but the FSLN could usually count on a decent level of sympathy and solidarity. Yet, in 1988, as we have seen, the international context no longer favored the Sandinista project. True, the Soviet Union remained an important financial donor but, as Ramírez had already realized during his visit to the Eastern bloc in June 1987, socialist leaders had their own economic and social problems to deal with, and Gorbachev was seeking to resolve regional Cold War conflicts through diplomatic channels. In 1988 and 1989, therefore, Gorbachev—without first consulting Cuba or Nicaragua—negotiated an end to the interference of the Soviet Union in Central American affairs, agreeing with the United States that he would suspend arms deliveries to the Sandinistas.[74]

Fidel Castro, in contrast, remained willing to support the revolutionaries as much as he could. Yet Cuba itself was dependent on the Soviet Union for economic and military aid and, as Gorbachev made clear during a visit to the island in April 1989, the time of Soviet generosity had come to an end. Ultimately, Cuban aid alone was not enough to keep the Nicaraguan economy afloat and the Sandinista military strong.[75] Moreover, the potent combination of the Latin American debt crisis, Central American skepticism, and the U.S. embargo meant that the FSLN had little prospect of obtaining extra financial aid or material support from other countries in the Americas. And in Western Europe, the EC countries remained firmly committed to their regional policy toward Central America and were not inclined to give the Sandinistas preferential treatment, despite the exceptionally bad state of the Nicaraguan economy.

At the non-state level, the situation was not much better. The Nicaraguan solidarity movement was rapidly losing members, popular support, and political influence. At the fourteenth solidarity conference in Rome on 29 and 30 October 1988, Western European representatives from countries such as Greece, the Netherlands, France, the United Kingdom, Norway, Ireland, and Italy reluctantly concluded that, despite their hard work, the solidarity movement was in decline. While the domestic situation differed slightly in each country, the overall trend was clear: politicians avoided the topic, there were not enough volunteers to organize events and publish material, and money was short.[76] In the Netherlands, a group of Dutch activists observed at a small gathering in July 1988 that the public was no longer concerned with Central American affairs, concluding that the "unconditional sympathy" that the Nicaraguan revolutionaries had enjoyed in the early 1980s had clearly disappeared.[77]

Western European activists came up with various explanations for this downward trend, but they found it hard to decide on a definitive answer. Dutch activist Gerrit Vledder, for instance, concluded in February 1989 that the reasons for the negative "atmosphere surrounding Nicaragua [were] difficult to grasp."[78] One explanation solidarity committees offered for the shift in public opinion was the "rebirth" and growing popularity of right-wing ideologies in Western Europe, which made it easier for anti-FSLN and pro-Contra groups to spread "reactionary information" among the population, most notably through what activists described as the "multinational press."[79] Sandinista leaders echoed this sentiment. As Sergio Ramírez told Ed van Thijn, the mayor of Amsterdam, who visited Nicaragua as part of the Managua-Amsterdam twinning program in November 1988, a "conservative mentality" had somehow taken hold of Western Europe and consequently "double standards" were applied to Nicaragua.[80] The solidarity activists who came together in Rome, too, argued that "biased" media coverage limited the effectiveness of their work, most notably since committees were forced to spend most of their time and money on "defending" the Nicaraguan government from unfair accusations, rather than on spreading information about the complex peace process and the positive aspects of the Sandinista Revolution like the literacy campaigns, improvements in health care, and agricultural reforms.[81] Unsurprisingly, the Sandinistas and their allies also blamed U.S. pressure for what they saw as Western Europe's unfair treatment of the Nicaraguan revolutionaries. Ramírez notably told Van Thijn that the negative attitude could "certainly" be explained by the fact that Nicaragua was in the "backyard" of the United States.[82]

For all their frustration with the changing intellectual and political environment they encountered in Western Europe, left-wing politicians and solidarity activists did not seem to realize that they were also participating in this trend. In the late 1980s, a growing number of solidarity activists and revolutionary sympathizers voiced their criticism and disillusionment with the FSLN's domestic policies, which often ran counter to Western perceptions of democracy that prioritized elections and press freedom. At a national meeting on 9 July 1988, the NKN concluded it had become very difficult to maintain a "positive attitude towards the FSLN considering the current situation" in Nicaragua, as the revolutionaries were making "mistakes" by not doing things the "Western way."[83] And while left-wing politician Van Thijn agreed with Ramírez that many of the accusations against Nicaragua were "unjust," he added that the Sandinistas should nonetheless work harder to improve their human rights record and prevent the possibility of becoming "politically isolated" in Western Europe.[84] The Consejo Nicaragüense de Amistad, Solidaridad y Paz (CNASP), the new division of the DRI responsible for managing the transnational solidarity network, also noticed the growing sense of disillusionment amongst its supporters. FSLN officials were careful to underline that this was not a structural problem. In the words of the CNASP, "cultural differences" and a lack of proper communication between the Sandinistas and individual Western European committees were to blame for the fact that some solidarity activists misunderstood the Nicaraguan reality.[85] The simple solution to this problem, in the eyes of the CNASP, was to improve the lines of communication and provide better information about the complex situation in Central America to the activists.

Even so, Nicaragua's domestic situation was clearly negatively impacting the FSLN's ability to implement its revolutionary diplomacy. The practice of inviting Western European visitors to Nicaragua, in particular, started to backfire, as the Sandinistas had little influence—at least not at an individual level—on the conversations and experiences of the brigadistas, and thus on the stories they brought home. And by the late 1980s, some brigadistas concluded that the Sandinistas were not as popular as they had initially believed. Heleen, a Dutch woman who joined a building brigade in 1987, acknowledged that her expectations about the revolution were not met. The Nicaraguans she met in Managua and Granada, she noted with surprise, did not show much "enthusiasm" for the Sandinistas, as they were frustrated about the "military draft, . . . the lack of food, [and] the economic situation as a whole."[86] Adriën, too, who worked in the small town of Santa Teresa in July 1987, shared her sense of disillusionment with how the revolution was treating Nicaraguan women, noting that they "still do all the housework:

cooking, cleaning, taking care of the children." She quoted a woman selling refresco [soft drinks] in Managua, who told her: "Sandinistas or not, us women always come last."[87]

Moreover, as a new ideological climate took shape in Western Europe, the Sandinista government made certain decisions in 1988 that, according to former FSLN diplomat Luis Caldera, were simply "indefensible" to European audiences, even though they were made in an atmosphere of polarization, despair, and economic chaos.[88] The most notorious example was the police crackdown on protesters in the small town of Nandaime on 10 July 1988. The demonstration was organized by the opposition alliance the CDN and, according to Dutch diplomat Erik Klipp, the number of participants was somewhere between two and fifteen thousand.[89] Clashes between the Sandinista police and the protesters broke out during a speech of conservative leader Miriam Arguello Morales, as police officers fired tear gas grenades and arrested more than forty demonstrators, including Arguello Morales, labor leader Carlos Huembes of the Central de Trabajadores de Nicaragua (Nicaraguan Worker's Center), and Agustín Jarquín of the Social Christian Party. In the days following the Nandaime demonstration, the Nicaraguan government, which argued that the U.S. embassy had encouraged the protesters to provoke the Sandinista police, expelled U.S. ambassador Richard Melton and seven other American diplomats, shut down *Radio Católica* indefinitely, and prohibited *La Prensa* from appearing, although only for fifteen days. The Reagan administration immediately retaliated, and ordered Nicaraguan envoy Carlos Tünnerman Bernheim, together with seven colleagues, to leave the United States.[90]

The violence in Nandaime—despite being on a far smaller scale than the brutal atrocities carried out by neighboring governments—cost the Sandinistas dearly in terms of international support. According to a public document written by several Latin American solidarity committees in the Netherlands, because of the developments in Nandaime, the revolutionaries—"in one fell swoop"—had lost all the sympathy of the Western world.[91] Western European governments were quick to denounce the Sandinista government for its response to the opposition demonstration. FCO junior minister Tim Eggar stated in the House of Commons that the United Kingdom "deplore[d] these Nicaraguan actions" and considered them "further evidence of Nicaraguan failure to comply with its obligations to democratization under the Esquipulas II agreement."[92] In the West German Bundestag, Irmgard Schwaetzer from the AA declared that the Sandinista government's violations of the "spirit of the peace process" during and in the aftermath of the Nandaime protest were "incomprehensible and disappointing" to everyone that wanted peace.[93] At the initiative of the FRG, moreover, the twelve EC countries joined forces and sent a troika—a diplomatic delegation composed of representatives from the current, previous, and upcoming EC presidencies—to Managua to express "concern" about the "recent closing of *La Prensa* and *Radio Católica* and the imprisoning of opposition politicians after the Nandaime demonstration" to Miguel d'Escoto.[94] The twelve EC leaders, then, were united in their criticism of the Sandinista government's actions against the country's opposition parties and critical media in July 1988.

At the grassroots level, activists tended to see the events in Nandaime in a different light. Despite their criticisms of the FSLN, solidarity campaigners shared the Sandinista view that the anti-FSLN opposition movement in Nicaragua was little more than the "domestic manifestation" of Reagan's foreign policy objectives in Central America. On 15 July 1988, Dutch activists discussed the situation in Nandaime and concluded that the U.S. administration was desperately trying "to get rid of the Sandinistas" while Reagan was still in office.[95] Specifically, the FSLN and its allies believed the U.S. administration, annoyed by the Sandinista ceasefire with the Contras, had developed a new strategy to undermine the Nicaraguan Revolution. According to the FSLN, Melton, abusing the political opening in Nicaragua, was trying to destabilize the Sandinista government from within by financing and encouraging the right-wing opposition to organize strikes and demonstrations, which would hopefully provoke a violent response from the Sandinista police. As a result, they speculated, Nicaragua would enter a "downward spiral of strife" and the revolution would be weakened. During the Nandaime events, the NKN argued in a press release on 21 July 1988, the international community had seen this so-called "Plan Melton" in action.[96]

Undoubtedly, solidarity activists and the FSLN were right when they argued that the U.S. embassy in Nicaragua had become "part of the anti-Sandinista political movement."[97] This was even admitted by Jim Wright, the Democratic Speaker of the U.S. House of Representatives, who announced in a press conference that he had received testimony from the CIA about attempts to provoke the Sandinistas "into taking repressive measures, that would undermine support for the government."[98] Nevertheless, by publicly reproducing the Sandinista government's war rhetoric and siege mentality, in which you could only be with the revolution or against it, solidarity activists failed to connect with their intended audiences, nor did they accurately reflect Nicaragua's complex reality. From Managua, Naomi Cohen described this dilemma in one of her letters to the solidarity group in Leicester. In the United Kingdom, she wrote, it is important to "argue your case calmly and tolerantly" to get people to support the revolution. However, she continued, "living here and seeing the determination of people, the sacrifices made, the achievements of the Revolution and what the war is doing—how it's affecting everything and everyone—makes me burst with indignation and anger."[99]

There is little doubt that 1988 was an incredibly difficult year for the Sandinistas. Confronted with a hostile international environment and a fragile domestic situation, the FSLN struggled to implement its revolutionary diplomacy. When asked about this period, many Nicaraguans also mention Hurricane Joan, one of most devastating storms in their country's history. In late October 1988, this powerful hurricane destroyed many towns along the Atlantic Coast, taking the lives of around 150 people. In addition to having to deal with more chaos and destruction, the slow and inadequate reaction of the international community to the hurricane served as a painful reminder for the Sandinistas that they had become even more isolated in the previous months. Indeed, while some countries such as Cuba and other "unexpected" donors such as the United Kingdom were quick to send some emergency aid, the overall response was meager and there was little effort to help the Nicaraguan government with the reconstruction project.[100]

## PLAN DE SANDINO A SANDINO

In 1989, the Sandinistas made one final push to save the revolution from economic collapse, international condemnation, and political isolation. On 14 February 1989, after a Central American presidential summit at Tesoro Beach in El Salvador, Daniel Ortega announced that democratic elections in Nicaragua would take place on 25 February 1990. In the run-up to these elections, he guaranteed, there would be freedom of expression, international observers, equal access to state television and radio for all political parties, and a process of "national reconciliation." The other Central American leaders had made no such pledge, even though they were also required to organize elections in the framework of the peace process. In exchange for Ortega's concessions, however, they had agreed to draw up a "joint plan for the voluntary demobilization, repatriation or relocation . . . of members of the Nicaraguan resistance and their families." In addition, they called on the international community, and particularly the Western Europeans, to "support the social and economic recovery process of the Central American nations."[101] Similar to 1984, then, the FSLN leaders hoped that elections could "secure and strengthen" the revolution in the face of an unfriendly international environment, as well as finally bring an end to the Contra war.[102]

The nine Sandinista comandantes set out their strategy for the electoral process in a document entitled "Plan de Sandino a Sandino," which they shared with a small number of MINEX and DRI officials in early 1989.[103] This strategy, as FSLN leader Henry Ruiz explained to East German officials in Berlin on 24 April 1989, was developed in close collaboration with Cuba and the Soviet Union.[104] At its core, the plan recognized that legitimate elections were the only way to resolve Nicaragua's conflict with the United States and, by extension, ensure the survival of the revolution. To neutralize the threat of renewed military escalation and further economic hostility, the National Directorate argued, Nicaragua would have to comply with the promises made by Ortega at Tesoro Beach.[105] Indeed, they speculated, if the government adopted a cooperative attitude toward the Esquipulas process and the Tesoro Beach agreements, the newly inaugurated U.S. president George H.W. Bush—who replaced Reagan on 20 January 1989—would no longer be able to "deny the legitimacy" of the revolution. Therefore, the comandantes concluded, the electoral process, which would naturally have to result in an "overwhelming" triumph for the FSLN, was the country's "one single priority."[106]

The Plan de Sandino a Sandino combined domestic and international components, focusing primarily on the Contra war, the economy, and international public opinion. To ensure victory, the comandantes reasoned, the government needed to "accelerate the defeat" and "demobilization" of the Contras, bringing an end to more than a decade of violence and civil war.[107] They also needed to improve the economic situation. Arguably, Ruiz explained to his East German hosts, the latter was even more urgent than ending the war, because the insurgents were already on the brink of collapse.[108] To "reactivate" the country's production process, then, the FSLN launched an economic readjustment program, which it combined with lobbying in Western Europe to obtain aid.[109] At the same time, the comandantes warned, the Nicaraguan population should be shielded as much as possible from "the negative effects" of the austerity and anti-inflationary measures, as further deprivation could alienate voters from the FSLN.[110] Finally, since a Sandinista electoral victory would be worthless without the international seal of approval, the FSLN launched a publicity campaign to project "the

FIGURE 14. In the run-up to 25 February 1990, the NSC raised money for the FSLN's electoral campaign and lobbied the Bush administration to accept the election's outcome. Like most solidarity activists, the NSC did not seriously consider the possibility of the UNO defeating the FSLN in the polls. Photo: Nicaragua Solidarity Campaign, London.

fairness and honesty" of the elections, targeting audiences and governments in "the United States, Western Europe, and the rest of the international community."[111]

The FSLN understood that the views of Western European governments and people mattered greatly for the success of the Plan de Sandino a Sandino. By convincing Europeans of the validity of the electoral process, the FSLN calculated, pressure on the Bush administration to demobilize the Contras and accept the results of the elections would increase. And by demonstrating that Nicaragua was taking meaningful steps toward democratization and economic stabilization, the FSLN hoped to receive much-needed economic aid. As part of this effort, the Sandinistas asked solidarity committees to widely spread positive information about the elections, as well as raise money for the FSLN's electoral campaign (figure 14).[112] Moreover, in April and May 1989, Daniel Ortega, accompanied by Miguel d'Escoto, went on an extensive Western European tour, meeting with politicians, civil servants, solidarity activists, artists, students, and journalists in France, Belgium, Greece, Italy, West Germany, Spain, the United Kingdom, Sweden, Norway, and Ireland.[113] Aside from showcasing Nicaragua's democratization process, Ortega's journey was designed to push Western European governments toward participating in an upcoming donor conference in the Swedish capital of Stockholm, where the Nicaraguan government hoped to raise $250 million for its economic recovery program.[114]

The results of the Sandinistas' revolutionary diplomacy in the run-up to the elections were mixed. On the one hand, Ortega received positive press coverage and a warm welcome from his Western European followers. Hundreds of enthusiastic solidarity activists and politicians attended a public lecture by the Nicaraguan president in Brussels. Here, the audience praised the revolution's accomplishments and path toward democracy.[115] In the United Kingdom, famous playwright Harold Pinter threw Ortega a soirée at his London home, which was attended by artists, activists, and intellectuals such as Graham Greene, Bianca Jagger, Ian McEwan, and Peter Gabriel.[116] On the other hand, Western European governments generally preferred to adopt a wait-and-see attitude before making any commitments regarding long-term financial aid, statements supporting the elections, or pushing for Contra demobilization. After all, with the Soviet Union poised to pull out of Central America, the primary reason for Western European governments to send financial aid to revolutionary Nicaragua was no longer relevant. West German officials, therefore, while welcoming the Nicaraguan decision to organize elections, told Ortega that West Germany would only increase its bilateral aid "after demonstrably free and fair elections" had taken place in February 1990.[117] The British government was even more dismissive. While Thatcher agreed to meet with Ortega in May 1989, she merely told him that Nicaragua's economic problems were of the country's own making and that there had been little progress toward democracy.[118] Tellingly, at $50 million in donations from the governments of Spain, Norway, Sweden, Finland and Denmark, the results of the Stockholm conference—although not inconsiderable—were significantly lower than the Nicaraguan government needed for an economic revival.[119] Similarly, the Bush administration prevented the demobilization of the Honduras-based Contras, arguing that the Sandinistas "would not go forward at all with democratization" if the rebel army was completely disbanded before the elections had taken place.[120]

Naturally, the reluctance of the Western European governments to give Nicaragua the benefit of the doubt in the run-up to the elections was frustrating to the revolutionaries. After Ortega's disappointing meeting with Thatcher, for instance, one British observer reported on a conversation he overheard between Miguel and Francisco d'Escoto while the two brothers were walking "glumly to their car." "The problem is," Francisco said about Thatcher's dismissive attitude toward the Nicaraguan elections, "they seem not to have read the electoral and media laws." "No," Miguel apparently muttered back, "it wouldn't make a difference if they did: they're determined not to believe anything we say."[121] Similarly, on 8 May 1989, Miguel d'Escoto was unable to hide his annoyance about the double standards that Western European governments applied to Central America during a meeting with Geoffrey Howe. Unlike El Salvador and Guatemala, he commented, Nicaragua "had nothing to hide" when it came to the country's human rights situation, noting that the Sandinistas had welcomed "specialized agencies and others whose professional task it was to assess situations in many countries." Yet, he continued bitterly, "countries with flagrant human rights abuses were being canonized as democracies."[122]

Despite the suspicious attitude of some Western European governments, the international community was increasingly convinced that the Nicaraguan elections would be democratic and transparent. The official position of the British government in December 1989, for example, was to "welcome" the decision to hold "free and fair elections" in Nicaragua. The Thatcher government even accepted the Nicaraguan invitation to send an official observer to the elections, something it had refused to do in 1984.[123] West Germany, Spain, France, Italy, and the Netherlands, too, adopted a cooperative attitude and provided the Nicaraguan government with technicians, money, training, observers, and computers for electoral registration.[124] Indeed, arguing publicly that it was "preferable to be invaded by observers to an electoral process in which we have nothing to hide than to confront an invasion of U.S. troops with all its consequences," the Sandinista comandantes welcomed around two thousand observers from Europe and the Americas.[125] Among those observers were prominent figures such as former U.S. president Jimmy Carter, the Secretary General of the Organization of American States João Baena Soares, and Elliot L. Richardson, a former U.S. Attorney General who led the team of United Nations observers. This impressive number of international visitors further contributed to the election's legitimacy.

One of the reasons for the existence of this—somewhat fragile—international consensus was that critics of the Sandinistas increasingly believed that the main opposition party in Nicaragua, the Unión Nacional Opositora (National Opposition Union, UNO), had a decent chance of beating the FSLN at the ballot box. Arias, for instance, told Bush on 27 July 1989 that the Sandinistas were doing "very badly" according to the polling data he had seen (official polls were not allowed in Nicaragua).[126] On 26 July 1989, British officials reported on a private opinion poll, commissioned by *La Prensa* and carried out by a Costa Rican company, which showed that UNO opposition candidate Violeta Chamorro (a former member of the first revolutionary junta from 1979–80) would obtain more than 46 percent of the vote, while only 26 percent of the population would side with Ortega.[127] Rather than trying to undermine the legitimacy of the elections as they had done in 1984, therefore, anti-Sandinista groups focused on funding, supporting, and assisting Chamorro. Indeed, behind the scenes, the Bush administration and its allies worked hard to make a Chamorro victory possible, even though officials were careful "not to smother [the UNO] with a U.S. embrace."[128]

On the other side of the political spectrum, the Sandinistas and their supporters also wanted clean elections, as they were convinced of an easy FSLN victory. The people would never vote for the UNO, West German solidarity activists argued, as everyone in Nicaraguan realized that the opposition alliance was no more than a U.S.-backed group of Contra leaders.[129] Dutch solidarity activists agreed with their German colleagues, and declined to discuss the possibility of a Sandinista defeat at the 1989 national conference, arguing that this was simply not a "realistic" scenario.[130] As Managua-based Mary Timmerman wrote to local solidarity committees in the Netherlands, even though the UNO was funded and "directed" by the United States, the FSLN, with Ortega and Ramírez on the ballot, would certainly win the elections.[131] Similarly, Leonel Urbino Pérez from the Cuban Communist Party's Americas Department remembers that Havana's leaders expected the FSLN to defeat the UNO in February 1990.[132] Soviet officials, too, counted on a Sandinista triumph. They were a bit more cautious than their Cuban allies, warning that "one should not overlook the strengthening of the position of opposition parties" in recent months.[133]

The solidarity movement's unanimous dismissal of Chamorro as a U.S. puppet, however, did not automatically translate into public support for the FSLN. Unlike in the United Kingdom, where solidarity committees openly backed the Sandinistas, some Dutch activists were hesitant. Gerrit Vledder, who replaced Wim Jillings as the main coordinator of the solidarity movement in 1989, remembers that most activists, such as Hans Langenberg, believed that the NKN should only support the democratic *process* in Nicaragua. Indeed, Vledder recalls, the NKN had selected him to lead the organization precisely because he was seen as a rather moderate social democratic figure and therefore capable of further "broadening" the appeal of the solidarity movement. Before joining the NKN, Vledder had worked for the Evert Vermeer Stichting, a developmental organization linked to the center-left Dutch Labor Party. As such, he originally supported proposals to invite Nicaraguan opposition leaders to the Netherlands to discuss and promote the elections. After several rounds of heated discussions, however, the Dutch committee eventually abandoned these plans. Vledder personally changed his mind after a visit to Managua, where Sandinistas and solidarity activists, including Mary Timmerman, attacked the Dutch committee's new strategy and convinced him that a solidarity committee should never try to be "politically neutral."[134] While the NKN reversed its position at the last minute, this episode highlights the Sandinistas' declining ability to implement their revolutionary diplomacy in Western Europe at the end of the Cold War. The willingness of solidarity activists to adopt the seemingly apolitical language of democracy—even if it was mostly a strategic decision to appease Western European critics—clearly put their relationship with the FSLN at serious risk.

For the Sandinistas themselves, these discussions ultimately made little difference, as the Plan de Sandino a Sandino failed to safeguard the Nicaraguan Revolution. On the morning of 26 February 1990, to the surprise and shock of the Sandinistas and their supporters, the Supreme Electoral Council announced that, with 60 percent of the vote counted, the UNO had obtained 54 percent and the FSLN 41 percent of the popular vote. After a decade of revolutionary change and hardship, the Sandinistas had lost the support of the Nicaraguan population.[135] Daniel Ortega immediately conceded defeat, promising that the FSLN and the Nicaraguan government were going to "respect and obey the popular mandate coming out of the vote in these elections."[136] For the solidarity activists in Western Europe, Chamorro's victory was devastating news and a massive blow to their political legitimacy. Critics of the Sandinistas mockingly asked Dutch activists if they were planning to raise funds for the UNO. After all, commentators pointed out, the solidarity movement had previously claimed to support the "Nicaraguan people" and these people had clearly sided with the anti-Sandinista movement.[137] In the United Kingdom, too, the right-wing *Daily Mail* was happy to point out that the "well-heeled Left" had once again picked the wrong side. Unfortunately for Ortega, journalist Paul Johnson commented gleefully, "his voters do not live in Hampstead but in Central America."[138]

Two months after the FSLN's defeat, on 25 April 1990, Violeta Chamorro was inaugurated as Nicaragua's president (figure 15). The Bush administration subsequently lifted the embargo and offered a $300 million aid package,

FIGURE 15. On 25 April 1990, Violeta Chamorro was sworn in as Nicaragua's first female president. Under the UNO government, which was in charge until 1997, a neoliberal economic model was implemented, the Contra War ended, and relations with the United States improved. The international community, which had already started to turn its gaze away from Nicaragua in the late 1980s, quickly lost interest in Nicaragua's internal affairs. Photo: Fundación Violeta Chamorro, Creative Commons.

while also assisting with the demobilization of the Contras. The EC countries, like the IMF and the World Bank, also lifted their restrictions on financial aid to Nicaragua. To be sure, it took several years before some form of peace could return to the impoverished and war-torn country. Nevertheless, with the end of the Revolución Popular Sandinista, a new period in the country's history had begun.

## CONCLUSION

In the late 1980s, the Sandinista government realized that their country's participation in the Esquipulas peace process was necessary to ensure the continued survival of the Nicaraguan Revolution. At home, the FSLN was confronted with an economic crisis and an externally funded civil war, both of which threatened to undermine the social basis of the Revolución Popular Sandinista. In the international arena, they were faced with continued U.S.

hostility and the declining global reach of the Soviet Union, as Mikhail Gorbachev made clear that Nicaragua should come to an agreement with its neighbors. In this context, the peace process, which was backed by many Western European and Latin American governments, provided the Nicaraguan government with a much-needed way out of an impossible situation. Through the Esquipulas process—at least if everything went according to plan—the FSLN could terminate the Contra war, avoid regional isolation, obtain economic aid from Western Europe, undermine U.S. foreign policy toward the revolution, and stay in power.

Of course, the problem was that, with the Soviet Union out of the picture, the FSLN had no other alternatives to the peace process, which greatly limited Nicaragua's ability to influence the outcome of the negotiations. As a result, the Sandinistas were pushed toward further concessions regarding democratic elections, press freedom, and negotiations with the Contras, while the other Central American countries faced no such pressure. The insurgents, for instance, were not forced to demobilize, even though this was officially required by the Esquipulas II Accords. Moreover, because Western European countries were no longer preoccupied with Nicaragua's possible alignment to the Soviet bloc, they decided to withhold further economic aid until the Sandinistas had fulfilled their promise of democratic elections in February 1990. As the post-Cold War international order started to take shape, the FSLN's ability to use its revolutionary diplomacy to strengthen the Nicaraguan Revolution was drastically reduced.

From an ideological perspective, too, the message of the Sandinistas had lost its appeal and capacity to mobilize Western Europeans for the Nicaraguan Revolution. In the eyes of many Western Europeans who were closely following the protests and democratic transitions in Eastern Europe in the late 1980s, the Sandinistas represented a failed and old-fashioned ideology. In this context, solidarity activists who continued to support the FSLN struggled to present the revolution in a positive light, as audiences were increasingly confronted with news about Sandinista human rights violations, police repression in Nandaime, and economic chaos. Interestingly, then, as the Cold War in Europe came to an end, audiences appeared much more willing to criticize the Nicaraguan Revolution, while at the same time ignoring the—generally more violent—situation in other Central American countries, most notably El Salvador and Guatemala. In part, the singling out of Nicaragua should be understood as an unintended consequence of the Sandinistas' own revolutionary diplomacy, which sought to raise Western

European interest in the revolution. Yet it also reflects the rise of more conservative and right-wing forces in the region, as audiences were increasingly keen to point out the flaws of left-wing governments.

While the FSLN focused on convincing the international community that the Nicaraguan government was making genuine efforts to comply with the peace agreements, they lost the support of the domestic population. In 1989, Sandinista officials calculated that for the revolution's survival the FSLN leadership needed to terminate the war, improve the economy, and organize elections that the international community would recognize. Yet, in the international environment of the late 1980s, the Sandinistas were only able to accomplish the last of these objectives, as the economy continued to spiral and the Contra war—even with a temporary ceasefire in place—could have been reignited at any moment. Indeed, after years of civil war and economic decline, the situation in Nicaragua on the ground contrasted sharply with the hopes and promises made by the Sandinistas revolutionaries more than a decade earlier. In this context, most of the Nicaraguan people decided to vote for the U.S.-approved opposition, which appeared to be the best bet for improving the country's standard of living and terminating the externally funded civil war.

# Conclusion

IN DECEMBER 1990, SEVERAL MONTHS after the FSLN's electoral defeat on 25 February 1990, Sandinista diplomat Augusto Zamora praised the revolutionaries' foreign strategy in a lengthy interview with *Revista Envío*. One of the Nicaraguan Revolution's key accomplishments, Zamora argued passionately, was the development of an international policy that went "beyond, far beyond, its limitations, as well as the small geographical space that Nicaragua occupies on this planet."[1] Other Sandinistas shared his view. Five months earlier, in July 1990, comandante Jaime Wheelock, the former minister of agrarian reform, also commended the FSLN's revolutionary diplomacy as he spoke to Western European solidarity activists living in Managua. In the late 1980s, Wheelock reflected, the Sandinistas had managed to end the Contra war and forced the United States to accept the legitimacy of the elections, thereby successfully bringing peace to Central America. Of course, there was only one "small flaw" in this strategy, he admitted, and that was the unfortunate fact that the FSLN had lost the elections, thereby jeopardizing the revolution's accomplishments.[2]

The FSLN's revolutionary diplomacy in the late 1970s up until 1990 was indeed remarkable in its scope, creativity, and impact. It propelled Nicaragua into the global limelight, bringing its inhabitants into close contact with state and non-state actors who otherwise might not have been able to locate the country on a map. Foreign leaders, prominent intellectuals, and popular cultural figures from across the globe traveled to Nicaragua to see for themselves how and with what consequences the revolution was unfolding on the ground. Some stayed only for a couple days, speaking to the accessible Sandinista leaders about contentious international politics and ambitious domestic reforms, generally leaving the country with a positive impression of the FSLN's revolutionary project. Other visitors, most of them solidarity activists from the Americas and Western Europe, remained in the country for weeks or even months. Invited by the FSLN to contribute to the revolution's survival, thousands of brigadistas assisted Nicaraguans with the coffee or sugar harvests, education projects, and vaccination campaigns. For many, working and living so closely with Nicaraguans for an extended period was an unforgettable experience that continued to shape their lives long after they returned to their home countries. Enchanted by the revolution's promises, a small number decided to stay in Nicaragua permanently. Jan Kees de Rooy, for example, who organized the Central American Peace Concert in 1983, chose to relocate to Managua, where he continued to work as a movie producer and director.[3] The Sandinistas' outreach to the wider world transformed Nicaragua into a major hub of the transnational Left, where solidarity activists, campesinos, feminists, revolutionaries, politicians, journalists, and artists intermingled and exchanged ideas.

By mobilizing public opinion and coordinating a transnational solidarity network, the FSLN also managed to shape the foreign policies of other countries. In the late 1970s and early 1980s, Western European governments put pressure on the Somoza regime, provided financial and political support to the revolutionary junta, and tried to have a moderating influence on the aggressive foreign policy of the anticommunist Reagan administration. Undoubtedly, policymakers were influenced by the unusually high levels of public sympathy for the revolutionaries that existed in Western European countries. This pushed them toward developing a proactive approach toward a country they most likely would have ignored otherwise, considering it to be part of a region dominated by the United States. Beyond public pressure, Cold War concerns also impacted Western Europe's approach to Nicaragua, as policymakers—once their interest was sparked—wanted to prevent the revolutionaries from becoming regionally isolated and dependent on the Soviet Union. The Sandinistas strategically played into these concerns, and the FSLN's ability to convince policymakers of the revolution's malleability was a vital aspect of the benevolent attitude to Nicaragua that Western Europe subsequently adopted.

After the invasion of Grenada in 1983, the ability of the FSLN to directly influence Western European diplomacy declined. Fearing further military escalation and U.S. intervention in the Central American civil wars, Western Europe's foreign policy took on a distinctly regional character. Rather than siding with the FSLN or the Reagan administration, the European

Community backed Latin American solutions to the Central American crises, most notably the Contadora and Esquipulas processes. Within these multilateral frameworks, there was little space for preferential treatment for the revolutionaries. Nevertheless, the FSLN continued to encourage Western Europe's involvement in Central America, as it posed a challenge to U.S. regional hegemony. By dismissing the Reagan administration's foreign policy as unnecessarily violent and ineffective, the EC tipped the inter-American power balance in favor of the Latin Americans. The isolation of the United States provided the FSLN with crucial room for maneuver to ensure the revolution's continued survival, although it came at the cost of making domestic concessions to its ideological enemies. The Sandinistas might have had little influence on the way peace processes developed, but their ability to keep the negotiations alive and Western Europeans involved in the Western Hemisphere speaks to the necessity of their revolutionary diplomacy.

Ultimately, the story of the FSLN's international outreach is obviously not one of success. As superpower tensions declined and Latin America "returned to democracy [and] neoliberalism" in the late 1980s, the FSLN struggled and ultimately failed to adapt its foreign policy to the new post–Cold War environment.[4] In Western Europe, politicians and journalists turned their backs on the Nicaraguan Revolution and looked toward other causes, varying from Eastern Europe's democratic revolutions to apartheid in South Africa or humanitarian disasters and developmental projects in the Global South. Furthermore, as Cold War ideologies lost their persuasive power, solidarity activists moved away from utopian revolutionary ideals and grand designs, opting to work for more intimate and less ambitious grass-roots projects instead. To the Sandinistas' own surprise, after almost eleven years in power they lost the 1990 elections to an opposition coalition led by a former member of their own revolutionary junta.

Yet, despite Nicaragua's small size, economic dependency, and proximity to the United States, the Sandinista Revolution survived for much longer than Salvador Allende's attempt to bring about "a peaceful democratic revolution in Chile" from 1970–73.[5] And in the 1980s, the United States launched two successful military interventions in Central America and the Caribbean, overthrowing Maurice Bishop's left-wing government in Grenada in 1983 and the controversial Panamanian dictator Manuel Noriega in 1989. Did the Sandinistas' revolutionary diplomacy prevent a similar fate for Nicaragua? It is difficult to say, but we should be careful not to dismiss the revolution's longevity and resilience as mere luck. Policymakers in the United States certainly believed the FSLN's global outreach—and particularly its impact on Western public opinion—limited their options in Central America, making a direct intervention and increased military aid for the Contra fighters highly controversial. With regard to Western Europe, it is unlikely that EC governments would have wanted to play such a prominent role in Central America if it was not for the FSLN's revolutionary diplomacy. As journalists wrote headlines, solidarity activists organized festivals, and Sandinista diplomats traveled across the world, it was simply not an option for Western European leaders to treat the region in the same way as they had done in the past. Despite the FSLN's ultimate demise, one of this book's core arguments is that the Sandinistas' revolutionary diplomacy made a difference, shaping everyday life, international politics, and the revolution's own trajectory.

. . .

The history of the FSLN's revolutionary diplomacy can only be uncovered by blending transnational and diplomatic approaches, revealing the many overlapping ways that states and non-state actors interacted with one another. The protagonists in this story, therefore, cannot be reduced to the separate realms of either international or domestic politics. Rather, as was characteristic of many Latin Americans' Cold War experience, they acted and lived "in both at the same time."[6] As we have seen, in the international struggle for Nicaragua's future the Sandinistas' foreign policy not only targeted governments and international organizations, but also involved grassroots actors, cultural diplomacy, and transnational relationships. It was a battle of ideas and perceptions, hearts and minds, ideologies and values, music and literature, demonstrations and donations. And while the FSLN's revolutionary diplomacy was unique in its scope and ambition, the participation of non-state actors in international politics was certainly not. Rather than treating grassroots actors as separate from—or complementary to—the more important practice of state diplomacy, this book shows that international relationships were often defined by both. The hybrid methodology of diplomatic and transnational history, then, is not only useful to make sense of the Nicaraguan Revolution's international history, but will also allow future historians to uncover the many overlooked histories that gave shape and meaning to the global Cold War.

Beyond revealing the FSLN's creativity in the international arena, this study of the Sandinistas' revolutionary diplomacy has implications for how we understand the place of the Global South in the Cold War system. By paying attention to state-level diplomacy, transnational networks, and multilateral negotiations, *Nicaragua Must Survive* seeks to highlight the pivotal role that the Global South played in international politics during the second half of the twentieth century. Indeed, while much of the literature on the topic might have us believe otherwise, it was not just the Global North or the superpowers that successfully pursued diplomacy and statecraft to achieve their Cold War objectives. Revolutionary and postcolonial states in the Global South, as recent scholarship on countries such as Cuba, Vietnam, Chile, Mexico, and Algeria demonstrates, were doing exactly the same thing, with significant international consequences.[7] The task of uncovering these multilayered international histories is vital to our understanding of the Cold War and its legacies. After all, as Jeremy Friedman writes, to make sense of the post-Cold War world, we need to acknowledge that it is "as much a creation of the losing side in the Cold War as of the winning side."[8] Ultimately, the alternative future the Sandinistas pursued so ambitiously did not come to fruition, but their revolutionary diplomacy did transform international politics and civil societies in the charged atmosphere of the late Cold War, giving shape to the world we live in today.

Another striking aspect of the FSLN's revolutionary diplomacy was that it was truly global in scope. While this book focuses mostly on the Sandinistas' outreach to Western Europe, it also reveals how their strategy was part of a bigger plan to create a new international order, thereby safeguarding the Nicaraguan Revolution from ideological enemies around the world. Beyond the United States and Western Europe, the FSLN's foreign policy involved actors and international organizations based in the Soviet Union, Latin America, Africa, the Middle East, and beyond. The world, as seen from Nicaragua in late 1970s and 1980s, was not neatly organized according to a bipolar Cold War logic. Rather, it was a complex and interconnected whole, involving countries from both the Global North and South, that could be navigated and used for the revolution's benefit. In other words, the history of the Sandinistas' revolutionary diplomacy invites us to move beyond a regional and bipolar understanding of the Cold War, and instead adopt a global lens, paying attention to the multipolarity of the international order. Without downplaying the importance of U.S. interventions and Cuban foreign policy, therefore, future histories of the Cold War in Latin America can be enriched by seriously considering the involvement of actors beyond the inter-American system. By doing so, historians will be able to reveal the impact of the wider world on Latin America, and vice versa.

The FSLN's revolutionary diplomacy should also encourage us to reconsider the end of the Cold War in Latin America, and Central America's place within it. Looking back at Latin America's twentieth-century history, it might make sense to understand the Sandinista project and the Central American civil wars as outliers in the region's Cold War history. After all, like their counterparts in the Southern Cone before them, Central America's revolutionary dreams were ultimately crushed by counterinsurgent violence, neoliberal projects, and democratic reforms. And yet, the Sandinistas certainly did not feel like anomalies, believing at the time that they were turning the tide in the global struggle against capitalism and imperialism. Both the Sandinistas' backers and their ideological opponents shared this dramatic view, as is evidenced by the amount of attention the country received in the late 1970s and 1980s. Indeed, the sheer magnitude of the violence carried out in Central America in the name of anticommunism and—albeit to a significantly lesser extent—revolutionary ideals contrasts sharply with the idea that the Cold War in Latin America was on its way out by the time the FSLN came to power. From this perspective, the Cold War was far from over. On the contrary, it appeared to be in its most transformative and consequential phase.

This is not to say that the Cold War in Latin America only ended when the Sandinistas lost power. Rather it demonstrates that, if we study Latin America's experience in the 1980s from a global perspective, it looks as if the Southern Cone—and not Central America—was the exception to the general chronology of the Cold War, especially in the first half of the decade. As superpower détente broke down in the late 1970s and early 1980s, Cold War tensions were intensifying rapidly, and fears of military confrontations in the Global South increased. The escalation of the Central American civil wars in the aftermath of the Nicaraguan Revolution was representative of this wider trend. Furthermore, events like the Iranian Revolution, the Soviet invasion of Afghanistan, and the Polish crisis suggested that Western countries were at risk of losing this global ideological battle, which resulted in anxious debates between the United States and its European allies. Taking this global context into consideration, the international history of the Nicaraguan Revolution epitomizes rather than defies the tensions that characterized the highly charged atmosphere of the late Cold War.

Finally, by studying transnational activism within the framework of the FSLN's revolutionary diplomacy, this book zoomed in on the shifting power dynamics, contrasting motives, and practical problems that defined the solidarity movement. On the surface, the Sandinista revolutionaries and Western

FIGURE 16. This mural in Nicaragua was painted by brigadistas from England, Wales, and Scotland. The slightly altered version of Gioconda Belli's saying "la solidaridad es la ternura de los pueblos" (solidarity is the tenderness of the people) would have appealed to those Nicaraguans sympathetic to the revolution. The inclusion of the slogan "no poll tax aqui" (no poll tax here), however, was clearly not meant for a Nicaraguan audience. The reference to Margaret Thatcher's controversial tax reform is revealing of the factors that drove solidarity activism. For many, Nicaragua represented an escape from the political situation within their own countries, especially when they were governed by conservative or right-wing governments. Photo: Nicaragua Solidarity Campaign, London.

European activists worked toward a common goal, namely the advancement and survival of the Nicaraguan Revolution. And to be sure, their collaboration resulted in many successes, including the isolation of the Somoza regime, a powerful anti-intervention movement, and profitable cultural events. Yet sympathy for the Sandinista cause was only one of the reasons that caused solidarity activists to join the movement, as they were also motivated by personal ambitions and ideas, desire for revolutionary change and adventure, and frustration with Western European politics (figure 16). This had significant consequences for the FSLN's revolutionary diplomacy, as the Sandinistas were forced to engage with the activists' criticism, hesitancy, and sometimes outright rejection of their plans. In particular, Sandinista efforts to raise money and materials—desperately needed to alleviate Nicaragua's suffering economy—were often obstructed by the solidarity activists, who considered direct participation in the revolution to be much more appealing than the rather boring practice of fundraising. These findings should encourage historians to move beyond mere celebrations of transnational connections and solidarity activism, and toward a critical interrogation of their strengths, weaknesses, and processes for operating and resolving problems.

. . .

As the Sandinista Revolution came to an abrupt halt in 1990, the amount of international attention that Nicaragua received—already in decline since the late 1980s—went down to virtually zero. While some activists, academics, and journalists continued to write about the country's social and political developments under the Chamorro government, the vast majority shifted their interest to other causes. Western Europeans did not forget that the Sandinistas had once captured their imaginations, but they seemed to operate on the assumption that Nicaraguan history had ended with the FSLN's electoral loss. Former activists' descriptions of their experiences in Central America were steeped in nostalgia, as they looked back with amusement at their own youthful optimism and dedication to the revolutionary cause. Rather than being a real country with problems, hopes, and ambitions, Nicaragua became a place that was only remembered, no longer existing outside of the public's mind.

Of course, Nicaragua did continue to exist and the people who had developed and implemented the Sandinistas' revolutionary diplomacy did not suddenly disappear off the face of the earth. Following the electoral defeat, the FSLN embarked on a difficult period of internal reflection and debate, which resulted in a split within the party. Describing the chaotic atmosphere within the FSLN in the early 1990s, Alejandro Bendaña—who ended up working for the United Nations—recalls how "tensions that had simmered for over a decade boiled over [and] Sandinista rank and file rebuked leaders for the mistakes and abuses of the previous decades."[9] In 1995, Sergio Ramírez, Dora María Téllez, and Luis Carrión left the FSLN and created the Movimiento Renovador Sandinista (Sandinista Renovation Movement, MRS). Envisioning Sandinismo as a more social democratic political movement, as well as arguing against "street credibility" and confrontations with the Chamorro government, the former revolutionaries hoped to win the 1996 elections on a rather moderate platform.[10] Despite having the support of prominent Sandinista intellectuals, the MRS was never a serious challenge to the FSLN, which remained under the firm control of Daniel Ortega and his ally Tomás Borge, who declared their continued commitment to revolutionary activism and governing "from below." After a contested and highly irregular electoral process in 1996, however, even the FSLN could not defeat the Liberal leader and former Somoza official Arnoldo Alemán, who won with 51 percent of the popular vote.[11]

Similarly, the political violence and economic problems that the Sandinistas struggled with in the 1980s did not come to a sudden end with the collapse of the Nicaraguan Revolution. It took several years before all the Contra fighters demobilized, and their repatriation and resettlement was a difficult and sometimes violent process, particularly since land ownership was highly contested. During the Chamorro years, it is estimated, armed clashes between former Sandinista soldiers and Contras caused around three hundred deaths per year.[12] The situation of the Nicaraguan poor, who had suffered most during the revolution's final years, did not improve under the Chamorro government, which promoted trade liberalization, austerity measures, and privatization. The reestablishment of friendly relations with the United States brought the Nicaraguan economy some relief, as the country could now count on a significant increase in financial aid from U.S. administrations and international financial institutions such as the IMF, but this had virtually no impact at the grassroots level.[13] Moreover, with the Soviet Union no longer looming large in the minds of North American and Western European policymakers, they had little incentive to help with reconstruction in Nicaragua. The United States, as Stephen Kinzer writes, "turned its back on the country where it had sowed so much pain."[14]

In 2018, Nicaragua was propelled back into the international headlines when a wave of protests broke out against the government, which responded with excessive violence, the imprisonment and silencing of political opponents, and a crackdown on the press. The situation seemed eerily similar to Nicaragua's insurrectional culture of the 1970s, but this time the protesters targeted not Somoza, but the FSLN. Under Ortega's increasingly authoritarian style of leadership, the Sandinistas had returned to power more than a decade earlier, in 2007, promising the continuation of the Nicaraguan Revolution. For the protesters, however, the FSLN in the post–Cold War world had little in common with the group of young guerrillas who were willing to sacrifice their lives for radical revolutionary change in the late 1970s. Chanting the slogan "Ortega, Somoza, son la misma cosa," the opposition movement accused the FSLN of simply implementing a new form of Somocismo, continuing the former dictator's personalistic, corrupt, and violent governing style.[15] In 2018, the opposition alliance was not strong enough to defeat Ortega, and debates about how to bring change to Nicaragua continue until the present day, with some calling for U.S. intervention and revolutionary violence, while others attach more value to elections, economic pressure, and peaceful resistance.

The transformation of the FSLN into a repressive political movement, as well as Daniel Ortega's ruthless consolidation of power since 2007, has impacted how the Nicaraguan Revolution's history is remembered and written about. Disillusioned Sandinista comandantes have adopted a more self-critical approach to their policies and behavior during the country's revolutionary decade. A "dramatically new" aspect in the speeches of former Sandinistas, one journalist wrote in 2019, was "the amount of responsibility they placed on their own shoulders" for everything that went wrong in Nicaraguan history.[16] Former Contra leaders, in contrast, have become more vocal, dismissing claims that they were merely U.S.-funded mercenaries by arguing that the Contra fighters were a "massive social movement."[17]

All of this should serve as a warning not to rewrite history to fit the exigencies and context of contemporary events. The Nicaraguan Revolution should not be studied as a zero-sum game of heroes and villains, and critically interrogating the policies of the Sandinista revolutionaries should not automatically result in an exoneration of the Contra movement or the Reagan administration. Nor should we fall into the teleological trap of seeing the violence of 2018 as the inevitable result of the Sandinista triumph in 1979, or perhaps even of the cyclical nature of Nicaraguan history, in which the country is predestined for dictatorial rule. When the revolutionaries took power on 19 July 1979, there were many paths they—and the revolution—could have taken. What happened in Nicaragua after that moment was the result of a combination of structural factors, contingency, and human agency, involving a range of domestic and international actors. With this book, I hope to have contributed to a more nuanced understanding of that complex history.

# NOTES

## ABBREVIATIONS IN NOTES

| | |
|---|---|
| AA | Politisches Archiv des Auswärtiges Amt, Berlin, Germany |
| AAPD | Akten zur Auswärtigen Politik der Bundesrepublik Deutschland |
| ABP | Ángel Barrajón Private Archive, Managua, Nicaragua |
| ABPA | Alejandro Bendaña Private Archive, Managua, Nicaragua |
| AEI | Electronic Archive of European Integration |
| BZ | Archief Ministerie van Buitenlandse Zaken, The Hague, The Netherlands |
| CFP | Central Foreign Policy Files |
| CREST | Central Intelligence Agency Records and Search Tool |
| DOS | Department of State |
| FCO | Foreign and Commonwealth Office (United Kingdom) |
| FRUS | Foreign Relations of the United States |
| HI | Hoover Institute, Stanford, United States |
| IHNCA | Instituto de Historia de Nicaragua y Centroamérica, Managua, Nicaragua |
| IISG | Internationaal Instituut voor Sociale Geschiedenis, Amsterdam, the Netherlands |
| INW | Informationsbüro Nicaragua Wuppertal Collection |
| MACD | Mexico and Carribbean Department |
| MINEX | Ministerio de Relaciones Exteriores de Nicaragua |
| MINREX | Centro de Gestión Documental del Ministerio de Relaciones Exteriores, Havana, Cuba |

NA          Nationaal Archief, The Hague, The Netherlands

NKA         Archief Nicaragua Komitee Amsterdam

NKN         Archief Nicaragua Komitee Nederland

NSC         Private Archive, Nicaragua Solidarity Campaign, London, the United Kingdom

PHM         People's History Museum, Manchester, United Kingdom

PUL         Princeton University Library, New Jersey, United States

RL          Ronald Reagan Presidential Library, Simi Valley, United States

SA          Stadsarchief, Amsterdam, The Netherlands

SAPMO       Stiftung Archiv der Parteien und Massenorganisationen der DDR im Bundesarchiv, Berlin, Germany

SHL         Senate House Library, London, the United Kingdom

SI          Socialist International Archive

TNA         The National Archives, Kew, the United Kingdom

## INTRODUCTION

1. Alejandro Bendaña, interviewed by James S. Sutterlin, 29 July 1997, Yale-UN Oral History Project, https://digitallibrary.un.org/record/498540.

2. Brown, *Cuba's Revolutionary World*.

3. See, for recent works on the Cold War in Central America, García Ferreira and Taracena, eds., *La guerra fría y el anticomunismo en Centroamérica*; Chávez, *Poets and Prophets of the Resistance*; Chávez, "The Cold War"; Vrana, *This City Belongs to You*; Gibbings, *Our Time Is Now*.

4. See Brands, *Latin America's Cold War*; Harmer, "The Cold War in Latin America"; Iber, *Neither Peace nor Freedom*; Rabe, *The Killing Zone*. A recent exception is Pettinà, *Historia mínima*.

5. Kruijt, "Revolución y contrarrevolución," 56.

6. Armony, "Transnationalizing the Dirty War"; Avery, "Connecting Central America to the Southern Cone"; and Burke, *Revolutionaries for the Right*.

7. I explore this further in Van Ommen, "The Nicaraguan Revolution's Challenge to the Monroe Doctrine."

8. See Gutman, *Banana Diplomacy*; Kagan, *A Twilight Struggle*; Walter LaFeber, *Inevitable Revolutions*; LeoGrande, *Our Own Backyard*.

9. Nye, "Public Diplomacy and Soft Power," 94.

10. Long, *Latin America Confronts the United States*, 14–16.

11. Crump and Erlandsson, eds., *Margins for Manoeuvre*.

12. Nye, "Public Diplomacy and Soft Power," 95.

13. Chong, "Small State Soft Power Strategies," 386.

14. Chamberlain, *The Global Offensive*; Connelly, *A Diplomatic Revolution*; Nguyen, *Hanoi's War*.

15. Sargent, *A Superpower Transformed*, 1.

16. Sargent, *A Superpower Transformed*, 5–6.

17. See Klimke, *The Other Alliance*; Nehring, *Politics of Security*; Stites Mor, ed., *Human Rights and Transnational Solidarity*; and Harmer, *Beatriz Allende*.

18. See Marino, *Feminism for the Americas*; Marchesi, *Latin America's Radical Left*; Vrana, *This City Belongs to You*; Markarian, *Uruguay, 1968*; and Stites Mor, *South-South Solidarity*.

19. Slobodian, *Foreign Front*, 3.

20. Kelly, *Sovereign Emergencies*.

21. There exists a rich, although slightly scattered, body of scholarship on solidarity with the Nicaraguan Revolution. See, for example, Christiaens, "Between Diplomacy and Solidarity"; Sánchez Nateras, "¡Nicas y mexicanos solidarios como hermanos!"; Helm, *Botschafter der Revolution*; Ágreda Portero, "Internacionalistas, Activistas y Brigadistas"; Apelt, "Between Solidarity and Emancipation"; Peace, *A Call to Conscience*; and Perla, *Sandinista Nicaragua's Resistance to US Coercion*.

22. Sobocinska, *Saving the World*, 4.

23. Helm, "'The Sons of Marx Greet the Sons of Sandino.'"

24. Bowen, "Taking in the Broad Spectrum," 643.

25. Schmidli, "Rockin' to Free the World," 713.

26. Moyn, *Not Enough*, 173.

27. A recent exception is Field, Krepp, and Pettinà, eds., *Latin America and the Global Cold War*.

28. Harmer and Álvarez, "Introduction: Globalizing Latin America's Revolutionary Left," 6.

29. These recent works include Johnson Lee, *The Ends of Modernization*; Schmidli, *Freedom on the Offensive*; Jarquín, "The Nicaraguan Question"; Sánchez Nateras, "La última Revolución"; Snyder, "Internationalizing the Revolutionary Family"; and Vázquez Olivera and Campos Hernández, eds., *México ante el conflicto centroamericano*.

30. Some exceptions here are Yordanov, "Outfoxing the Eagle"; Ferrero Blanco, "Daniel Ortega y Mijail Gorbachov"; Paszyn, *The Soviet Attitude*.

31. AAPD, 1981, Document 265, Gespräch zwischen Genscher und Haig, 22 September 1981.

32. There is virtually no scholarship on the EC's relations with Latin America. A recent edited volume on the topic does not include Latin America. See Krotz, Patel, and Romero, eds., *Europe's Cold War Relations*.

33. Jarquín, "The Nicaraguan Question," 599.

34. Grandin, as quoted in Joseph and Spenser, eds., *In from the Cold*, 4; Joseph, "Border Crossings," 142.

35. Harmer, *Beatriz Allende*, 4.

36. See Agudelo Builes, *Contramemorias*; Berth, *Food and Revolution*; Francis, ed., *A Nicaraguan Exceptionalism*; Gould, *To Lead as Equals*; Martí i Puig, *La*

*revolución enredada*; Rocha, "La década de los años 80"; Rueda, *Students of Revolution*; Sierakowski, *Sandinistas: A Moral History*; Zimmerman, *Sandinista*.

37. A point made regarding U.S. foreign policy by Bessner and Logevall in "Recentering the United States."

38. Manela, "International Society as a Historical Subject."

39. Westad, *The Global Cold War*.

40. Keeley, *Reagan's Gun-Toting Nuns*; Peace, *A Call to Conscience*; Perla, *Sandinista Nicaragua's Resistance to US Coercion*.

## CHAPTER 1. INTERNATIONALIZING STRUGGLE, 1977–1979

1. TNA, FCO 99/187, Minter to Perceval, 1 November 1978.

2. TNA, FCO 99/187, Flyer, CAHRC, 27 October 1978.

3. Rueda, *Students of Revolution*, 207.

4. Lawson, *Anatomies of Revolution*, 8.

5. The first communiqués signed by the FSLN appeared in 1963, but several anti-Somoza organizations preceded these publications. See Zimmerman, *Sandinista*, 73.

6. For more on Sandino, see Bendaña, *Sandino*; Gobat, *Confronting the American Dream*; McPherson, *The Invaded*.

7. Borge, *The Patient Impatience*, 138.

8. Rueda, *Students of Revolution*, 143.

9. Borge, "Realmente tuvimos paciencia," in Baltodano, ed., *Memorias de la lucha Sandinista. Tomo 1*.

10. Zimmerman, *Sandinista*, 98. In the late 1960s, it is estimated that the FSLN did not have more than one hundred members.

11. Zimmerman, *Sandinista*, 165.

12. Kruijt, *Guerrillas*, 70.

13. Zimmerman, *Sandinista*,164.

14. Kruijt, *Guerrillas*, 70; Sánchez Nateras, "La última Revolución," 72.

15. "Interview with Henry Ruiz (Modesto)."

16. "Interview with Jaime Wheelock Roman."

17. Sánchez Nateras, "La última Revolución," 74.

18. Rueda, *Students of Revolution*, 155.

19. Sierakowski, *Sandinistas*, 195.

20. Gould, *To Lead as Equals*, 272–73.

21. Johnson Lee, *The Ends of Modernization*, 80.

22. FRUS, 1969–1976, Volume E-11, Part One, Mexico, Central America, and the Caribbean, 1973–1976, Doc. 249, Telegram 119 from the Embassy in Nicaragua to the Department of State, 9 January 1975.

23. García Márquez, "Sandinistas Seize the National Palace!"

24. Téllez, as cited in Arias, *Nicaragua: Revolución*, 163.

25. Téllez, "Tener ideales y luchar por ellos," as cited in Baltodano, ed., *Memorias de la lucha Sandinista. Tomo 2*.

26. "Interview with Daniel Ortega."

27. IHNCA, Folio 0049, Humberto Ortega Saavedra to Frente Norte "Carlos Fonseca Amador," 7 January 1979.

28. FRUS, 1977–1980, Volume XV, Central America, 1977–1980, Doc. 124, Memorandum from the Executive Secretary of the Department of State (Tarnoff) to the President's Assistant for National Security Affairs (Brzezinski), undated.

29. Johnson Lee, *The Ends of Modernization*, 94.

30. Johnson Lee, *The Ends of Modernization*, 92.

31. Ramírez, *Adiós Muchachos*, 81.

32. F. Cardenal, *Faith and Joy*, 75.

33. TNA, FCO 99/44, Translation of Statement by "The Twelve" as published in *La Prensa*, on 21 October 1977.

34. Ramírez, *Adiós Muchachos*, 85.

35. Mexico, Colombia, Venezuela, and Panama showed enthusiasm for the Sandinista cause and supported the Group of Twelve with money, material, and political backing. FRUS, 1977–1980, Volume XV, Central America, 1977–1980, Doc. 98, Memorandum from Robert Pastor of the National Security Council Staff to the President's Assistant for National Security Affairs (Brzezinski) and the President's Deputy Assistant for National Security Affairs (Aaron), 18 September 1978.

36. FRUS, 1977–1980; Volume XV, Central America, 1977–1980, Doc. 85, Memorandum of Conversation, 29 August 1978.

37. Tünnermann Bernheim, *Memorias de un Ciudadano*, 221.

38. Ágreda Portero, "Un acercamiento."

39. Interview with Tomás Arguello Chamorro, Managua, Nicaragua, 29 July 2016.

40. For more on Nicaragua's revolutionary culture, see Esch, *Modernity at Gunpoint*; Rueda, *Students of Revolution*; and Whisnant, *Rascally Signs*.

41. Bruno, "Speaking through the Body"; Belli, *The Country under My Skin*, 151.

42. Henighan, *Sandino's Nation*, 240.

43. E. Cardenal, *La revolución perdida*, 44.

44. TNA, FCO 99/186, Washington to FCO, 14 September 1978.

45. FRUS, 1977–1980, Volume XV, Central America, 1977–1980, Doc. 234, Telegram from the Embassy in Panama to the Department of State, 28 June 1979.

46. TNA, FCO 99/350, Note of Meeting, 2 July 1979.

47. "Nicaraguan Rebels Hobnob with Bankers," *The Washington Post*, 20 December 1978.

48. "Siege Gunman Fly out of Nicaragua," *The Times*, 25 August 1978.

49. Sánchez Nateras, "La última Revolución," 284.

50. Kruijt, *Cuba and Revolutionary Latin America*, 158–59.

51. MINREX, Nicaragua 1977, Ordinario, René Anillo to Isidoro Malmierca, 19 October 1977.

52. DOS/CFP, Telegram, AmEmbassy Panama to SecState, 22 March 1978.

53. DOS/CFP, Electronic Telegram, AmEmbassy Santo Domingo to SecState, 24 November 1978.

54. FRUS, 1977–1980, Volume XV, Central America, 1977–1980, Doc. 85, Memorandum of Conversation, 29 August 1978.

55. FRUS, 1977–1980, Volume XV, Central America, 1977–1980, Doc. 85, Memorandum of Conversation, 29 August 1978.

56. IISG, INW, Bericht und Ergebnisse des Europäische Treffens der Nicaragua Solidaritätskomitees, May 1979.

57. IISG, INW, Bericht und Ergebnisse des Europäische Treffens der Nicaragua Solidaritätskomitees, May 1979.

58. TNA, FCO 99/34, British Embassy San Jose to FCO, 5 December 1977.

59. ABPA, not catalogued, Barrajón to unknown, 1 December 1978.

60. TNA, FCO 99/187, CAHRC to David Owen, 8 November 1978.

61. TNA, FCO 99/187, Flyer, CAHRC, date unknown.

62. It is unclear from extant sources how much this financial support amounted to.

63. Belli, *The Country under My Skin*, 178.

64. For more on the Latin American response, see Sánchez Nateras, "The Sandinista Revolution."

65. Kruijt, *Guerrillas*, 83.

66. FRUS, 1977–1980, Volume XV, Central America, 1977–1980, Doc. 95, Minutes of a Special Coordination Committee Meeting, 12 September 1978.

67. Sánchez Nateras, "La última Revolución," 182–83.

68. BZ, Inventarisnummer 11838, Memorandum, 17 May 1979.

69. FRUS, 1977–1980, Volume XV, Central America, 1977–1980, Doc. 67, Telegram from the Embassy in Nicaragua to the Department of State, 8 February 1978.

70. As cited in Schmidli, "The Most Sophisticated Intervention," 80.

71. Henighan, *Sandino's Nation*, 129; Sabia, *Contradiction and Conflict*, 60.

72. TNA, FCO 99/187, Flyer, CAHRC, date unknown.

73. Interview with Ángel Barrajón, Managua, Nicaragua, 8 August 2016.

74. Enrique Schmidt Cuadra was killed in the Contra war on 4 November 1984. For more, see Hübner et al., eds., *Enrique Presente*.

75. Ágreda Portero, "Internacionalistas, Activistas y Brigadistas," 101.

76. Interview with Ángel Barrajón.

77. IISG, NKN, Box 17, Concept Dutch Viewpoint for the 10th European Conference in Brussels, 23 November 1984.

78. Van Ommen, "The Sandinista Revolution in the Netherlands," 5.

79. Langenberg, as cited in Hertogs, ed., *Nederlanders naast Nicaragua*.

80. Weidhaas, *See You in Frankfurt*, 129.

81. SA, NKA, Box 1, Annual Report, 1984.

82. NSC, not catalogued, George Black to Doris Tijerino, 30 October 1979.

83. TNA, FCO 99/188, MACD to Keith Hamylton Jones, 22 November 1978.

84. Interview with John Bevan, London, United Kingdom, 20 March 2017; interview with Ángel Barrajón.

85. Interview with Ángel Barrajón; IISG, INW, Bericht und Ergebnisse des Europäische Treffens der Nicaragua Solidaritätskomitees, May 1979.

86. *Leeuwarder Courant*, 12 June 1979.

87. See Helm, "Booming Solidarity."

88. NSC, George Black to Doris Tijerino, 30 October 1979.

89. ABP, not catalogued, Circular letter, Deutsche Solidaritätskomitees mit Nicaragua Göttingen, 20 November 1978.

90. NSC, George Black to Doris Tijerino, 30 October 1979.

91. IISG, INW, Bericht und Ergebnisse des Europäische Treffens der Nicaragua Solidaritätskomitees, May 1979.

92. ABP, Barrajón to Casteñeda, 28 February 1979.

93. Zimmerman, *Sandinista*, 215–16.

94. See Harmer, "The View from Havana"; Kelly, "The 1973 Chilean Coup"; and Perry, "With a Little Help."

95. Interview with Klaas Wellinga and Hans Langenberg, Utrecht, the Netherlands, 6 August 2014.

96. Interview with Klaas Wellinga and Hans Langenberg.

97. Interview with Klaas Wellinga and Hans Langenberg.

98. Interview with George Black, Skype, 21 November 2017; interview with John Bevan.

99. SA, NKA, Box 1, Annual Report, 1984; interview with Klaas Wellinga and Hans Langenberg.

100. Fairley, "La Nueva Canción," 107–8.

101. NSC, George Black to Doris Tijerino, 30 October 1979.

102. Perla, "Central American Counterpublic Mobilization," 168.

103. For more on the history of women's participation in the Central American civil wars see Kampwirth, *Women and Guerrilla Movements*.

104. "The Historic Programme of the FSLN," as published in Marcus, ed., *Sandinistas Speak*.

105. Apelt, "Between Solidarity and Emancipation," 175.

106. Cappelli, "Women of the Revolution," 6.

107. IHNCA, ASD 064, Carta de remisión de documentos a la Oficina de Seguridad Nacional de la Embajada de Nicaragua en Alemania, Mendoza to Stern, 20 October 1978.

108. For more information on the Socialist International and Latin America see Pedrosa, "La Internacional Socialista"; Pedrosa, *La otra izquierda*; Garavini, *After Empires*; and Rother, *Global Social Democracy*.

109. As quoted in Di Donato, "The Cold War," 196.

110. Garavini, *After Empires*, 236.

111. Pedrosa, "La Internacional Socialista."

112. Henighan, *Sandino's Nation*, 129.

113. DOS/CFP, Electronic telegram, AmConsul Vancouver to SecState, 4 November 1978; *NRC Handelsblad*, 6 November 1978.

114. DOS/CFP, Electronic telegram, AmConsul Vancouver to SecState, 4 November 1978; *NRC Handelsblad,* 6 November 1978.

115. At least nine Constituency Labour Parties wrote the British Secretary of State about the situation in Nicaragua. See, TNA, FCO 99/346.

116. TNA, FCO 99/346, Resolution, Labour Party, 20 December 1978.

117. Staten Generaal Digitaal, Handelingen Tweede Kamer, 20 November 1978.

118. Staten Generaal Digitaal, Handelingen Tweede Kamer, 5 October 1978.

119. IISG, INW, Klaas Wellinga to European Solidarity Committees, 15 June 1979.

120. For more on the SPD's involvement in Central America, see Mujal-Leon, "The West German Social Democratic Party."

121. TNA, FCO 99/350, Shakespeare to Hall, 26 June 1979.

122. TNA, FCO 99/350, Note of Meeting, 2 July 1979.

123. Rother, "Between East and West," 221.

124. AEI, Statement of the EEC Foreign Ministers, 29 June 1979. The nine member states were West Germany, France, Belgium, the Netherlands, Italy, Luxembourg, the United Kingdom, Denmark, and Ireland. Greece became a member state in 1981.

125. TNA, FCO 99/186, Hamylton Jones to MACD, 8 September 1978.

126. TNA, FCO 99/112, Shakespeare to Unwin, November 1978.

127. TNA, FCO 99/43, Embassy San Jose to MACD, 5 December 1977.

128. TNA, FCO 99/116, Record of conversation, 2 June 1978.

129. Apart from the abovementioned joint statement, Western European governments did not coordinate their foreign policies toward Nicaragua in the 1970s.

130. TNA, FCO 98/187, Brief for EPC Latin America Working Group meeting, 22 September 1978.

131. TNA, FCO 99/346, David Owen to MACD, 27 February 1979.

132. TNA, FCO 99/350, Brief for visit by David Owen to Washington, 31 January 1979.

133. AA, Zwischenarchiv 111.158, PP Bonn to AA, 21 February 1978.

134. TNA, FCO 99/350, Brief for visit by David Owen to Washington, 31 January 1979.

135. TNA, FCO 99/350, Brief for visit by David Owen to Washington, 31 January 1979.

136. AA, Zwischenarchiv 111.160, Gerta and Reinhard Kober to Genscher, 4 January 1978; Christliche Arbeiter-Jugend Diözesanverband Paderborn to Genscher, 10 April 1978; Amnesty International Deutschland to Botschaft der Bundesrepublik Deutschland in der Republik Nicaragua, 7 February 1978. For more letters, see AA, Zwischenarchiv 111.158.

137. TNA, FCO 99/186, Council of Churches to David Owen, 20 September 1978.

138. For these and more letters, see TNA files FCO 99/188 and FCO 99/186.

139. TNA, FCO 99/266, Brewster to Carrington, 19 June 1979.

140. TNA, FCO 99/266, Brewster to Carrington, 19 June 1979.

141. TNA, FCO 99/266, Brewster to Carrington, 19 June 1979.

142. TNA, FCO 99/266, Parsons to FCO, 28 June 1979.

143. BZ, Inventarisnummer 11838, Memorandum, DWH/NC to DWH, 19 June 1979.

144. AAPD, 1979, Document 207, Aufzeichnung des Ministerialdirektors Meyer-Landrut, 10 July 1979.

145. TNA, FCO 99/42, Hamylton Jones to FCO, 5 December 1977.

146. TNA, FCO 99/187, Overseas Information Department to FCO, 1 November 1978.

147. BZ, Inventarisnummer 11838, DWH/NC to DWH, 19 June 1979.

148. See Schulz and Schwartz, eds., *The Strained Alliance*; Sargent, *A Superpower Transformed*.

149. See Gilbert, *Cold War Europe*; Basosi, "Principle or Power."

150. See Spohr, *The Global Chancellor*.

151. Young, "Western Europe and the End of the Cold War."

152. AAPD, 1979, Document 207, Aufzeichnung des Ministerialdirektors Meyer-Landrut, 10 July 1979.

153. TNA, FCO 99/186, Hamylton Jones to MACD, 28 February 1978.

154. TNA, FCO 99/186, British Embassy in Washington to FCO, 14 September 1978.

155. TNA, FCO 99/266, Parsons to MACD, 28 June 1979.

156. TNA, FCO 99/340, Memorandum, MACD, 22 June 1979.

157. BZ, Inventarisnummer 11838, DWH/NC to DWH, July 1979.

CHAPTER 2. TRIUMPH AND CONSOLIDATION,
1979–1980

1. *The Guardian*, 20 July 1979; *De Volkskrant*, 19 July 1979; *The New York Times*, 20 July 1979; *El País*, 20 July 1979.

2. Interview with Eduardo Ramón Kühl, Selva Negra, Nicaragua, 1 August 2016; *The Economist*, 21 July 1979.

3. Colburn, *The Vogue of Revolution*, 6.

4. LeoGrande, for instance, in his book *Our Own Backyard*, dedicates only five pages to the period July 1979–December 1980, but more than two hundred to the period 1981–88. Gutman's book *Banana Diplomacy* only covers the Reagan presidency. An exception is Robert Pastor's *Condemned to Repetition*, which does deal with the postrevolutionary period and the Carter administration.

5. See Peace, *A Call to Conscience*; Perla, *Sandinista Nicaragua's Resistance to US Coercion*; and Christiaens, "Between Diplomacy and Solidarity."

6. See Berth, *Food and Revolution*; and Francis, ed., *A Nicaraguan Exceptionalism*.

7. Johnson Lee, *The Ends of Modernization*, 105.

8. "David resistió a Goliat: 10 años de politica exterior," *Revista Envío* 95 (July 1989).

9. "David resistió a Goliat: 10 años de politica exterior."

10. Ramírez, *Adiós Muchachos*, 94.

11. "The Historic Programme of the FSLN," as published in Marcus, ed., *Sandinistas Speak*.

12. Prashad, *The Darker Nations*, 209.

13. For more on the civil war in El Salvador, see Chávez, *Poets and Prophets of the Resistance*.

14. Political Declaration of the Sixth Conference of Heads of State or Government of Non-Aligned Countries in Havana, Cuba, from 3 to 9 September 1979, Middlebury Institute of International Studies at Monterey, http://cns.miis.edu/nam/documents/Official_Document/6th_Summit_FD_Havana_De claration_1979_Whole.pdf.

15. MINREX, Nicaragua 1979, Ordinario, Ernesto Alomá Sánchez, Nicaragua y el movimiento de paises no-alineados (exact date unknown).

16. For more on the NIEO and the NAM, see Gilman, "The New International Economic Order"; Prashad, *The Darker Nations*; Garavini, *After Empires*.

17. "David resistió a Goliat: 10 años de politica exterior."

18. Arce Castaño, "La intervención extranjera en Nicaragua."

19. MINREX, Nicaragua 1979, Ordinario, Ernesto Alomá Sánchez, Nicaragua y el movimiento de paises no-alineados (exact date unknown).

20. Gary Prevost writes that Nicaragua under Somoza was nearly 90 percent dependent on U.S. aid and trade ("Cuba and Nicaragua: A Special Relationship").

21. Berth, *Food and Revolution*, 70

22. Summerfield, "Health and Revolution," 845.

23. Rocha, "Agrarian Reform," 104.

24. Barraco, "The Nicaraguan Literacy Crusade," 342.

25. Arce, "La intervención extranjera."

26. For more on the consolidation of Sandinista power, see Ferrero Blanco, "El diseño de las instituciones en el Estado Sandinista"; Kruijt, "Revolución y contrarrevolución."

27. Ramírez, *Adiós Muchachos*, 73.

28. Ramírez, *Adiós Muchachos*, 73.

29. Interview with Victor Hugo Tinoco, Managua, Nicaragua, 17 August 2016; Peace, *A Call to Conscience*, 155.

30. Ramírez, *Adiós Muchachos*, 75.

31. FRUS, 1977–1980, Volume XV, Central America, 1977–1980, Doc. 298, Paper prepared in the White House, 30 July 1979.

32. FRUS, 1977–1980, Volume XV, Central America, 1977–1980, Doc. 298, Paper prepared in the White House, 30 July 1979.

33. TNA, FCO 99/350, Dublin to FCO, 25 July 1979.

34. TNA, FCO 99/350, Dublin to FCO, 25 July 1979.

35. Yordanov, "Outfoxing the Eagle," 876.

36. Paszyn, *The Soviet Attitude*, 31.

37. For more on Cuba's contributions to Nicaragua's foreign ministry, see Snyder, "Cuba, Nicaragua, Unidas Vencerán."

38. Wilson Center Digital Archive, Soviet Ambassador to Cuba Vorotnikov, Memorandum of Conversation with Raul Castro, 1 September 1979, https://digitalarchive.wilsoncenter.org/document/111249.

39. Wilson Center Digital Archive, Soviet Ambassador to Cuba Vorotnikov, Memorandum of Conversation with Raul Castro, 1 September 1979.

40. Email correspondence with Eduardo Kühl, 8 December 2016.

41. MINREX, Nicaragua 1980, Ordinario, Memorandum of Conversation, Bayardo Arce and Pelegrín Torras, 6 February 1980.

42. Arce, "La intervención extranjera."

43. Interview with Eduardo Kühl.

44. *El Nuevo Diario*, 19 May 2013.

45. Interview with Eduardo Kühl.

46. DOS/CFP, AmEmbassy Stockholm to SecState, 20 July 1979.

47. *El Nuevo Diario*, 19 May 2013.

48. Interview with Eduardo Kühl.

49. *De Volkskrant*, 23 July 1979.

50. AA, Zwischenarchiv 112.912, Bonn Coreu to Dublin Coreu, 18 September 1979.

51. TNA, FCO 99/350, Dublin to FCO, 25 July 1979.

52. TNA, FCO 99/350, Dublin to FCO, 25 July 1979.

53. TNA, FCO 99/351, JS Wall to BG Cartledge, 26 July 1979.

54. DOS/CFP, Electronic Telegram, AmEmbassy Bonn to SecState, 4 September 1979.

55. AA, Zwischenarchiv 112.912, Bonn Coreu to Dublin Coreu, 18 September 1979.

56. AA, Zwischenarchiv 112.912, Bonn Coreu to Dublin Coreu, 18 September 1979.

57. AA, Zwischenarchiv 112.912, Rom Coreu to All Coreu, 8 April 1980.

58. DOS/CFP, Electronic Telegram, AmEmbassy Bonn to SecState, 4 September 1979.

59. *El País*, 14 August 1979.

60. *De Waarheid*, 10 August 1979.

61. AEI, *Bulletin of the European Communities: Commission* 7/8 (1979); *The Courier: Africa-Caribbean-Pacific-European Community* 57 (1979).

62. H. Smith, *European Union Foreign Policy*, 60–61.

63. CREST, Directorate of Intelligence, Office of European Analysis, Western Europe and Central America, April 1979.

64. PHM, The Judith Hart Papers, File 05/58, Neil Marten to Judith Hart, 30 January 1980.

65. TNA, FCO 99/558, AJ Payne to FCO, 7 February 1980; CREST, Soviet Bloc and Cuban Military and Economic Assistance to Nicaragua, 27 January 1988. In fact, according to the CIA graph, the Soviet Union provided no economic assistance

to Nicaragua in 1979–1980. The rest of the Eastern bloc contributed $20 million in this period.

66. *Het Parool*, 4 August 1979.

67. *Trouw*, 21 July 1979.

68. IISG, INW, Klaas Wellinga, Hermann Schulz, and William Agudelo to Western European solidarity committees, 1 August 1979.

69. IISG, NKN, Box 17, Statement NKN for European Solidarity Conference in Vienna on 13–14–15 June 1980, date unknown.

70. *The Guardian*, 5 November 1979.

71. Helm, *Botschafter der Revolution*, 149.

72. IISG, NKN, Box 1, Record of NKN Meeting, 17 September 1979.

73. *De Waarheid*, 18 August 1979; *Leeuwarder Courant*, 23 July 1979.

74. *Der Spiegel*, 23 July 1979.

75. Interview with Tomás Arguello Chamorro, Managua, Nicaragua, 29 July 2016.

76. IISG, INW, Klaas Wellinga, Hermann Schulz, and William Agudelo to Western European solidarity committees, 1 August 1979.

77. IISG, INW, Klaas Wellinga, Hermann Schulz, and William Agudelo to Western European solidarity committees, 1 August 1979.

78. IISG, NKN, Box 1, Record of NKN Meeting, 17 September 1979.

79. IISG, INW, Zum Selbstverständnis der Nicaragua-Solidaritätskomitees nach dem Sturz Somozas, Diskussionspapier von Ernesto Medina, date unknown.

80. IISG, NKN, Box 1, Record of NKN Meeting, 17 September 1979.

81. IISG, NKN, Box 1, Record of NKN Meeting, 17 September 1979.

82. NSC, Informe preparado por George Black, John Bevan, Richard Furtado, 12 June 1980; IISG, NKN, Box 1, Standpunt van het Nicaragua-Komitee tav. het solidariteitswerk met Nicaragua.

83. Hans Langenberg, "Solidair vanaf het begin," in Hertogs, ed., *Nederlanders naast Nicaragua*.

84. Hans Langenberg, "Solidair vanaf het begin," in Hertogs, ed., *Nederlanders naast Nicaragua*.

85. NSC, not catalogued, George Black to Doris Tijerino, October 1979.

86. NKN, Box 17, Statement NKN for European Solidarity Conference in Vienna on 13–14–15 June 1980, date unknown.

87. Ulrike Hanemann, "Nicaragua's Literacy Campaign" (UNESCO, 2005), https://unesdoc.unesco.org/ark:/48223/pf0000146007.

88. "The Historic Programme of the FSLN," in Marcus, ed., *Sandinistas Speak*.

89. F. Cardenal, *Faith and Joy*, 132.

90. Black, *Triumph of the People*, 311.

91. F. Cardenal, *Faith and Joy*, 136.

92. F. Cardenal, *Faith and Joy*, 136.

93. For more on the literacy campaign, see Deiner, "The Nicaraguan Literacy Crusade."

94. For more on Freire and literacy, see Kirkendall, *Paulo Freire*.

95. Guerra, *Visions of Power in Cuba*, 158.

96. F. Cardenal, *Faith and Joy*, 132.

97. F. Cardenal, *Faith and Joy*, 132.

98. F. Cardenal and Miller, "Nicaragua: Literacy and Revolution."

99. F. Cardenal, *Faith and Joy*, 171.

100. TNA, FCO 99/424, Brief, Nicaragua Background: Foreign Policy, date unknown.

101. AA, Zwischenarchiv 127.452, Limmer to Staatssekretär, 25 March 1980.

102. TNA, FCO 99/562, Brown to Payne, 9 February 1980.

103. Sergio Ramírez, "Hasta 1985," as cited in Assman, ed., *Nicaragua triunfa en la alfabetización*.

104. F. Cardenal and Miller, "Nicaragua: Literacy and Revolution."

105. Ramírez, *Adiós Muchachos*, 101.

106. IISG, NKN, Box 72, Lausanne Comité de Solidarité avec le Nicaragua, "Alphabetisierung in Nicaragua," date unknown.

107. IISG, NKN, Box 72, Flyer, Nicaraguan Embassy in London, date unknown.

108. IISG, NKN, Box 72, Flyer, Nicaraguan Embassy in London; open letter, Tomás Arguello Chamorro to British Public, date unknown.

109. TNA, FCO 99/562, Record of ODA Meeting, Maradiaga Lacayo and Arguello Chamorro, 26 February 1980.

110. *De Waarheid*, 1 March 1980.

111. *The Daily Telegraph*, 10 December 1979.

112. TNA, FCO 99/562, Record of ODA Meeting, Maradiaga Lacayo and Arguello Chamorro, 26 February 1980.

113. F. Cardenal, *Faith and Joy*, 140.

114. SHL, ER320/PAM2, Christian Aid, "Nicaragua: Bienvenidos a Nicaragua libre," date unknown; ER320/PAM1, Report of First National Conference in Solidarity with the People of Nicaragua, London, 29 March 1980.

115. SHL, ER320/PAM2, Christian Aid, "Nicaragua: Bienvenidos a Nicaragua libre," date unknown.

116. IISG, NKN, Box 72, Lausanne Comité de Solidarité avec le Nicaragua, "Alphabetisierung in Nicaragua," date unknown.

117. SHL, ER320/PAM2, Christian Aid, "Nicaragua: Bienvenidos a Nicaragua libre," date unknown.

118. NSC, *Nicaragua Today*, 1980.

119. Black, *Triumph of the People*, 311–15.

120. "Discurso del Ministro de Educación al recibir el premio de UNESCO," 8 September 1980, as published in Assman, ed., *Nicaragua triunfa en la alfabetización*.

121. TNA, FCO 99/562, PJL Scott to GS Cowling, 8 April 1980.

122. *Trouw*, 29 March 1980.

123. TNA, FCO 99/562, Brown to ODA, 15 January 1980.

124. TNA, FCO 99/562, Background Brief, 14 January 1980.

125. TNA, FCO 99/561, Note of Meeting, Robelo and Ridley, 8 September 1980.

126. TNA, FCO 99/559, Cowling to Payne, 20 May 1980.

127. TNA, FCO 99/559, Brown to Trew, 9 April 1980.

128. F. Cardenal, *Faith and Joy*, 216.

129. CREST, National Intelligence Daily, 24 April 1980.

130. TNA, FCO 99/561, Record of Meeting, Gonzalo Murillo-Romero with FCO, 11 December 1980.

131. NSC, Informe preparado por George Black, John Bevan, Richard Furtado, 12 June 1980.

132. NSC, *Nicaragua Today*, 1981.

133. NSC, *Nicaragua Today*, 1980.

134. SHL, ER320 PAM/2, *Las Milicias en Acción*, 1982.

135. TNA, FCO 99/559, Communiqué by Nicaraguan Embassy in Washington, 26 April 1980.

136. TNA, FCO 99/559, Communiqué by Nicaraguan Embassy in Washington, 26 April 1980.

137. For more on this visit see AA, Zwischenarchiv 127.450.

139. AA, Zwischenarchiv 127.450, Vermerk, Besuch des AM von Nicaragua Miguel d'Escoto, 28 August 1980.

141. AA, Zwischenarchiv 127.450, Vermerk, Besuch des AM von Nicaragua Miguel d'Escoto, 28 August 1980.

142. For more see Armony, *Argentina, the United States, and the Anti-Communist Crusade in Central America*.

143. FRUS, 1977–1980, Volume XV, Central America, 1977–1980, Doc. 325, Memorandum of Notification prepared in the Central Intelligence Agency for the Special Coordination Committee, 5 December 1980.

144. CREST, National Intelligence Daily, 26 April 1980.

145. BZ, Inventarisnummer 11839, Brief, San Jose to BZ, 28 February 1980.

146. AA, Zwischenarchiv, 127.450, Zum Besuch des AM Von Nicaragua Miguel d'Escoto, 2 September 1980.

147. AA, Zwischenarchiv 127.450, Genscher to Muskie, 4 September 1980.

148. AA, Zwischenarchiv 127.450, Genscher to Muskie, 4 September 1980.

149. Hager and Snyder, "The United States and Nicaragua," 16.

150. TNA, FCO 99/559, Crabbie to FCO, 24 April 1980.

151. *Het Parool*, 24 April 1980.

152. This is reflective of a longstanding rivalry between Nicaraguan Christian Democrats and the FSLN, which both sought to lead the anti-Somoza opposition in the 1960s and 1970s. For more on Christian Democracy in Central America, see Véliz Estrada, "Más agresivos y más revolucionarios."

153. AA, Zwischenarchiv 127.450, Ottfried Hennig, Marxistische Revolutionäre als Muster der Demokratie: Genscher zeichnet falsches Bild von Nicaragua, 23 September 1980.

154. NSC, not catalogued, Informe preparado por George Black, John Bevan, Richard Furtado, 12 June 1980.

155. TNA, FCO 99/561, Trew to Payne, 22 July 1980.

156. IISG, NKN, Box 1, Ted van Hees and Hans Langenberg, on behalf of the Dutch solidarity movement, to the Western European solidarity committees, 11

June 1980; Box 17, Verslag vergadering ter voorbereiding Europees congres in Wenen, 8 June 1980.

157. IISG, NKN, Box 1, Ted van Hees and Hans Langenberg, on behalf of the Dutch solidarity movement, to the Western European solidarity committees, 11 June 1980.

158. IISG, NKN, Box 1, Ted van Hees and Hans Langenberg, on behalf of the Dutch solidarity movement, to the Western European solidarity committees, 11 June 1980.

159. IISG, NKN, Box 17-18, Informe Sobre el Encuentro a Nivel Europeo del Movimiento de Solidaridad con Nicaragua, 15 June 1980.

160. Kirkpatrick, as quoted in LaFeber, "The Reagan Administration," 1.


CHAPTER 3. THE REVOLUTION UNDER
ATTACK, 1981–1982

1. Interview with Klaas Wellinga and Hans Langenberg, Utrecht, the Netherlands, 6 August 2014.

2. NSC, *Nicaragua Today*, 1981.

3. IISG, NKN, Box 17, Verslag Encuentro Managua, 26–31 January 1981.

4. IISG, NKN, Box 17, Verslag Encuentro Managua, 26–31 January 1981.

5. Yeshitela and Waller, "The First Conference in Solidarity with Nicaragua."

6. See Prashad, *The Darker Nations*; Ogle, "State Rights against Private Capital"; Gilman, "The New International Economic Order."

7. For more on the debt crisis in Latin America, see Bulmer-Thomas, *The Economic History of Latin America*.

8. LeoGrande, *Our Own Backyard*, 54.

9. Jarquín, "Red Christmases," 136.

10. See Armony, *Argentina, the United States, and the Anti-Communist Crusade in Central America*.

11. *The New York Times*, 20 March 1982.

12. *Revista Envío* (April 1982).

13. Several historians have written about anti-intervention activism in the early 1980s. See Nepstad, *Convictions of the Soul*; C. Smith, *Resisting Reagan*; Peace, *A Call to Conscience*; Helm, *Botschafter der Revolution*.

14. See Sjursen, *The United States, Western Europe and the Polish Crisis*; Romano, "Re-Designing Military Security in Europe"; Patel and Weisbrode, eds., *European Integration and the Atlantic Community*; Gilbert, *Cold War Europe*.

15. Interview with Luis Ángel Caldera Aburto, Managua, Nicaragua, 24 August 2016.

16. Ronald Reagan, "Peace: Restoring the Margin of Safety," 18 August 1980, https://www.reaganlibrary.gov/archives/speech/peace-restoring-margin-safety.

17. See Kirkpatrick, "Dictatorships and Double Standards."

18. ABPA, Political Section (Michael Clark) to Rita Delia Casco, 9 January 1981.

19. ABPA, Francisco d'Escoto Brockmann to Miguel d'Escoto Brockmann, 17 February 1981.

20. ABPA, Casimero Sotelo, Saúl Arana, and Ramón Meneses to Miguel d'Escoto, Leonte Herdocia, Luis Vanegas, 27 November 1980.

21. ABPA, Political Section (Michael Clark) to Rita Delia Casco, 9 January 1981.

22. Francisco d'Escoto Brockmann to Miguel d'Escoto Brockmann, 17 February 1981.

23. ABPA, Casimero Sotelo, Saúl Arana, and Ramón Meneses to Miguel d'Escoto, Leonte Herdocia, Luis Vanegas, 27 November 1980.

24. Interview with Luis Ángel Caldera Aburto, 24 August 2016.

25. IISG, NKN, Box 17, Address by Commander Bayardo Arce Castaño, 26–31 January 1981.

26. IISG, NKN, Box 17, Report by UK representatives of international solidarity conference in Managua, 1981; Address by Commander Bayardo Arce Castaño.

27. IISG, NKN, Box 72, Records of European solidarity conference, Paris, April 1981; Box 17, Report by UK representatives of international solidarity conference in Managua.

28. IISG, NKN, Box 17-18, Records of European solidarity conference, Geneva, November 1981.

29. *Barricada Internacional*, 5 July 1981.

30. *Revista Envío* (June 1981).

31. IISG, INW, Übersetzung der in den Arbeitskommissionen erreichten und in der Vollversammlung verabschiedeten Beschlüsse und Empfehlungen, date unknown.

32. IISG, NKN, Box 101, Notulen van landelijke vergadering, 1 June 1986.

33. NSC, *Nicaragua Today*, 1981.

34. IISG, NKN, Box 17, Address by Commander Bayardo Arce Castaño, 26–31 January 1981.

35. IISG, NKN, Box 17, Text of final resolution Managua conference, 26–31 January 1981.

36. See, for instance, Oñate-Madrazo, "Insurgent Diplomacy"; Kruijt, *Guerrillas*.

37. Avery, "The Latin American Anticommunist International," 178.

38. Jarquín, "A Latin American Revolution," 138.

39. IISG, NKN, Box 17, "Address by Commander Bayardo Arce Castaño," 26 January 1981.

40. IISG, NKN, Box 17, Verslag Encuentro Managua, 26–31 January 1981.

41. "David resistió a Goliat: 10 años de politica exterior," *Revista Envío* 95 (July 1989).

42. CREST, Soviet Bloc and Cuban Military and Economic Assistance to Nicaragua, 27 January 1988

43. Interview with Luis Ángel Caldera Aburto, 24 August 2016.

44. Ramírez, *Adiós Muchachos*, 98.

45. SAPMO, DY30/69777, Vermerk über ein Gespräch im Staatlichen Komitee für wirtschafliche Zusammenarbeit der UdSSR zu Fragen spezieller Lieferungen nach Nikaragua, 25 January 1982.

46. SAPMO, DY30/69777, Vermerk über ein Gespräch im Staatlichen Komitee für wirtschafliche Zusammenarbeit der UdSSR zu Fragen spezieller Lieferungen nach Nikaragua, 25 January 1982.

47. Storkmann, "East German Military Aid," 64.

48. *The Washington Post*, 18 July 1981.

49. Storkmann, "East German Military Aid," 64.

50. IISG, NKN, Box 17, Report by UK representatives of international solidarity conference in Managua, 1981.

51. IISG, NKN, Box 17, Report by UK representatives of international solidarity conference in Managua, 1981.

52. IISG, NKN, Box 17, Verslag Encuentro Managua, 26–31 January 1981.

53. IISG, NKN, Box 17-18, Verslag van het vijfde congres van de Europese solidariteitsbeweging in Parijs, 18–20 April 1981.

54. IISG, INW, Report of meeting of Germany solidarity committees in Wolfsburg, 27–28 February 1982.

55. PHM, NSC, Box 77, Meeting to discuss coordination of Central America Work in Britain, 3 April 1981.

56. IISG, NKN, Box 17-18, Verslag van het vijfde congres van de Europese solidariteitsbeweging in Parijs, 18–20 April 1981.

57. IISG, NKN, Box 17-18, Verslag van het vijfde congres van de Europese solidariteitsbeweging in Parijs, 18–20 April 1981.

58. We still know little about the (lack of) solidarity with Guatemala. See Janssens, "Stumbling among Giants."

59. NSC, Summary of activities, February–April 1981.

60. IISG, INW, Informe de la Coordinadora Nacional en la RFA 'Informationsbüro Nicaragua e.V. Wuppertal' sobre el trabajo de solidaridad realizado en la RFA entre abril e octubre 1981.

61. NSC, Summary of activities, February-April 1981; Summary of activities, May-October 1981.

62. IISG, NKN, Box 53, Hans Langenberg, Informe sobre la caravana anti-intervencionista, date unknown.

63. IISG, INW, Hans Langenberg to European solidarity committees, 15 December 1981.

64. IISG, NKN, Box 17-18, Summary of Speech by Raúl Guerra, 18–20 Paris 1981.

65. TNA, FCO 98/1127, London to Coreu, 30 October 1981.

66. Ludlow, "The Unnoticed Apogee of Atlanticism?," in Patel and Weisbrode, eds., *European Integration and the Atlantic Community*, 18–19.

67. IISG, NKN, Box 17-18, Records of European solidarity conference, Geneva, November 1981.

68. IISG, NKN, Box 17-18, Verslag van het vijfde congres van de Europese solidariteitsbeweging in Parijs, 18–20 April 1981.

69. IISG, NKN, Box 53, Hans Langenberg, Informe sobre la caravana anti-intervencionista, date unknown.

70. NSC, Summary of activities, May-October 1981.

71. TNA, FCO 99/1265, FCO to Michael Brown, 1 April 1982.

72. IISG, SI, Nicaragua 1980, Press Release No. 21/80, 6 December 1980.

73. IISG, SI, Nicaragua 1980, Press Release No. 21/80, 6 December 1980.

74. NSC, *Nicaragua Today* 4. For more on the SI, see Di Donato, "The Cold War and Socialist Identity," and Rother, "Between East and West."

75. IISG, SI, Nicaragua 1980, Pierre Schori to the members of the International Committee for the Defence of the Nicaraguan Revolution, 18 December 1980.

76. IISG, SI, Nicaragua 1981, Reunión Comité de Defensa de la Revolucion Nicaragüense de la IS, 27 November 1981.

77. IISG, SI, Nicaragua 1981, Bernt Carlsson to Willy Brandt, February 1981.

78. *Barricada Internacional*, 5 July 1981.

79. Ramírez, *Adiós Muchachos*, 94–95.

80. For more on the FSLN's position on elections, see chapter 4.

81. IISG, SI, Nicaragua 1980, Pierre Schori to the members of the International Committee for the Defence of the Nicaraguan Revolution, 18 December 1980.

82. Wilson Center Digital Archive, Letter by the President of the Socialist International, Brandt, to the Chairman of the Committee of the SI for Defence of the Revolution in Nicaragua, González, 2 June 1981, https://digitalarchive.wilson center.org/document/112717.pdf?v=fc264a634cf8118458 6955102bec6d68.

83. Christopher Dickey, "Nicaraguan Divisions Grown After Businessman's Death," *The Washington Post*, 23 November 1980; Inter-American Commission on Human Rights, Report on the Situation of Human Rights in the Republic of Nicaragua, 30 June 1981, http://www.cidh.org/countryrep/nica81eng/chap.6.htm.

84. Wilson Center Digital Archive, Letter by the President of the Socialist International, Brandt, to the Chairman of the Committee of the SI for Defence of the Revolution in Nicaragua, González, 2 June 1981.

85. Ramírez, *Adiós Muchachos*, 95.

86. *Het Vrije Volk*, 5 May 1982.

87. Solórzano, ed., *The Nirex Collection*, Volume IV, Document 711; *Barricada Internacional*, 16 May 1982.

88. *Amigoe*, 6 May 1982.

89. TNA, FCO 99/1269, Call by Francisco d'Escoto on Day, 13 January 1982.

90. TNA, FCO 99/1270, Call by Francisco d'Escoto on Onslow, 29 June 1982.

91. AA, Zwischenarchiv 127.457, Vermerk: Arbeitsbesuch des AM von Nicaragua, Pater Miguel d'Escoto, 3 March 1982.

92. TNA, FCO 99/1267, Duncan to FCO, 21 July 1982.

93. TNA, FCO 99/768, Call by Francisco d'Escoto on Luce, 11 November 1981.

94. AAPD, 1982, Document, 140, Gespräch des Bundesministers Genscher mit dem nicaraguanische Arbeitsminister Godoy, 13 May 1982.

95. AA, Zwischenarchiv 127.453, Managua to AA, 24 August 1981.

96. Solórzano, ed., *The Nirex Collection*, Volume IV, Document 635; *Revista Envío* (August 1982).

97. TNA, FCO, 99/1267, Press Release, French Embassy in London, 12 January 1982.

98. TNA, FCO 99/1275, Adams to FCO, 14 May 1982.

99. ABPA, Francisco d'Escoto Brockmann to Miguel d'Escoto Brockmann, 17 February 1981.

100. RL, Executive Secretariat Meeting Files C1-10, National Security Council Meeting. Subject: Central America, 11 February 1981.

101. RL, Executive Secretariat Meeting Files C1-10, National Security Council Meeting. Subject: Central America, 11 February 1981.

102. AAPD, 1981, Document 49, Gespräch des Bundesministers Genscher mit dem designierter Abteilungsleiter im amerikanischen Außenministerium, Eagleburger, 20 February 1981.

103. TNA, FCO 99/792, Records of meeting, Eagleburger and Gilmour, 19 February 1981.

104. NA, Inventarisnummer 2.02.05.02, Omslag 3232, Notulen MR, 20 February 1981.

105. TNA, PREM 19/600, Record of meeting, Thatcher and Reagan, 26 February 1981.

106. TNA, FCO 99/792, Records of meeting, Eagleburger and Gilmour, 19 February 1981.

107. AAPD, 1981, Document 49, Gespräch des Bundesministers Genscher mit dem designierter Abteilungsleiter im amerikanischen Außenministerium, Eagleburger, 20 February 1981.

108. RL, Executive Secretariat, NSC, RAC, Box 3, Haig to Reagan, 3 June 1982.

109. "French Arms go to Nicaragua," *The New York Times*, 13 July 1982.

110. CREST, Mitterand's France: Near-Term Outlook, 21 March 1983.

111. TNA, FCO 99/769, FCO to Washington, 1 September 1981.

112. TNA, FCO 99/769, Record of meeting, Carrington and Haig, 23 September 1981, FCO 99/769, NA.

113. TNA, FCO 51/494, CIA Research Department, Human Rights in Nicaragua: The Case of the Miskito Indians, September 1982.

114. AAPD, 1982, Document 332, Gespräch zwischen Genscher und Shultz, 7 December 1982. The Salvadoran army and anticommunist death squads were engaged in a brutal counterinsurgency campaign throughout most of the 1980s. The El Mozote massacre of December 1981, when the military killed more than eight hundred civilians, was just one of the many atrocities carried out during the Salvadoran civil war.

115. Solórzano, ed., *The Nirex Collection*, Volume IV, Document 554; *Nicaraguan Perspectives*, Fall 1981.

116. TNA, FCO 99/1275, Croll to FCO, 21 July 1982.

117. *Het Vrije Volk*, 3 May 1982.

118. TNA, FCO 99/1269, Meeting with the Nicaraguan ambassador, Lic. Aldo Diaz Lacayo, 6 January 1982.

119. TNA, FCO 99/1265, Annual review: Nicaragua, 9 January 1982.

120. TNA, FCO 99/1281, Webb to Birrell, 9 September 1982.

121. TNA, FCO 99/653, Report by John Ure on his visit to Central America, 27 November 1981.

122. These numbers are based on data from the Instituto de Relaciones Europeo-Latinoamericanas and the CIA.

123. *Revista Envío* (December 1982).

124. AA, Zwischenarchiv 136.670, Vermerk, Besprechung beim Bundesminister über Lateinamerika am 12.01.1982, 14 January 1982.

125. Data based on reports from Instituto de Relaciones Europeo-Latinoamericanas, copies in author's possession.

126. BZ, Inventarisnummer 25202, DWH, Memorandum, 19 May 1982.

127. AA, Zwischenarchiv 136.670, Vermerk, Hilfsaktion der EG und EG-Mitgliedstaaten für Mittelamerika, 16 February 1982.

128. TNA, FCO 99/769, Cowling to Payne, 2 November 1981.

129. AAPD, 1982, Document 332, Gespräch zwischen Genscher und Shultz, 7 December 1982.

130. AAPD, 1981, Document 265, Gespräch zwischen Genscher und Haig, 22 September 1981.

131. *NRC Handelsblad*, 9 April 1984.

132. NA, Inventarisnummer 2.02.05.02, Omslag 3502, Notulen MR, 26 March 1982.

133. TNA, FCO 98/1425, Brussels to FCO, 23 March 1982. This meeting of the leaders of the ten EC member states took place at least twice a year.

134. AA, Zwischenarchiv 136.670, Vermerk, Hilfsaktion der EG und EG-Mitgliedstaaten für Mittelamerika, 16 February 1982.

135. TNA, FCO 98/1142, Brussels to FCO, 20 January 1982.

136. Hill and Smith, eds., *European Foreign Policy*, 429–30.

137. TNA, FCO 98/1432/2, MCAD, European Political Cooperation, Political Committee Copenhagen, 1 October 1982. The Mexico and Caribbean Department (MACD) was succeeded by the Mexico and Central America Department (MCAD) in 1982.

138. TNA, FCO 98/1432/2, MCAD, European Political Cooperation, Political Committee Copenhagen, 1 October 1982.

139. NA, Inventarisnummer 2.02.05.02, Omslag 3509, Notulen MR, 22 October 1982.

140. TNA, FCO 99/1281, Note, European Community Department, 14 October 1982.

141. TNA, FCO 99/1281, War on Want to Pym, 8 October 1982.

142. TNA, FCO 99/1281, Nicaraguan Embassy to FCO, 4 October 1982.

143. TNA, FCO 99/1281, Holmes to Hunter, 1 December 1982. "Mecu" stands for "million European currency units"—the internal European currency preceding the Euro.

144. TNA, FCO 99/1281, Brussels to FCO, 22 November 1982.

145. In 1981–1985, the European Commission's president was Gaston Thorn, the former Prime Minister of Luxembourg.

146. TNA, FCO 99/1281, Carberry to Crowe, 13 December 1982; Harrison to MCAD, 16 December 1982.

147. TNA, FCO 99/1281, Harrison to Baker, 23 November 1982.


CHAPTER 4. CREATIVE DEFENSE, 1983–1984

1. Esch, *Modernity at Gunpoint*, 121.

2. Gonzalez, "April in Managua," 247–49.

3. Interview with Jan Kees de Rooy, Managua, Nicaragua, 11 August 2016.

4. For more on the FSLN's use of culture and music, see Whisnant, *Rascally Signs*, and Esch, *Modernity at Gunpoint*.

5. Ronald Reagan, "Address on Central America," 27 April 1983, Miller Center, https://millercenter.org/the-presidency/presidential-speeches/april-27-1983-address-central-america. For a more nuanced appraisal of the Sandinista relationship with the Miskito Indians, see Hale, *Resistance and Contradiction*; Tijerino, "Conflicto étnico, geopolítica e identidad," 95–114; Bataillon, *Crónica sobre una guerrilla*.

6. *The New York Times*, 10 May 1983.

7. Berth, *Food and Revolution*, 107.

8. MINREX, Ordinario, Nicaragua 1984, Rodríguez to Malmierca, 7 May 1984.

9. ABPA, MINEX, Consenso general sobre la coyuntura actual. The exact publication date of this document is unknown but, based on the content, it was written between May and September 1983.

10. IISG, INW, Hans Langenberg to Western European solidarity committees, August 1983.

11. ABPA, MINEX, Consenso general sobre a la coyuntura actual.

12. SAPMO, DY30/43863, Bericht über die Gespräche mit einer Delegation der Nationalleitung der Sandinistischen Front der Nationalen Befreiung Nikaraguas [FSLN] unter Leitung des Genossen Henry Ruiz Hernandez, 16 February 1983.

13. IISG, NKN, Box 73, report of IKV trip to Nicaragua, April and May 1983.

14. ABPA, MINEX, Obstáculos que la administración tiene para implementar una intervención directa contra Nicaragua, date unknown.

15. Storkmann, "East German Military Aid," 60.

16. Paszyn, *The Soviet Attitude*, 49.

17. CREST, Soviet Bloc and Cuban Military and Economic Assistance to Nicaragua, 27 January 1988.

18. *NRC Handelsblad*, 22 April 1984.

19. Bagley, "Contadora: The Failure of Diplomacy," 2.

20. For more on Contadora, see Jarquín, "The Nicaraguan Question."

21. ABPA, MINEX, Obstáculos que la administración tiene para implementar una intervención directa contra Nicaragua.

22. ABPA, MINEX, Evaluación, Perspectivas y Planes—1984, date unknown.

23. ABPA, MINEX, Memorandum, 26 May 1983.

24. ABPA, MINEX, Evaluación preliminar de la ultima ronda de Contadora, date unknown.

25. For more on the peace movement, see Wittner, *The Struggle against the Bomb*; van Diepen, *Hollanditis*; de Graaf, *Over de Muur*; Nuti et al., eds., *The Euromissile Crisis*; Conze et al., eds., *Nuclear Threats*; Karamouzi and Chourchoulis, "Troublemaker or Peacemaker."

26. Sergio Ramírez, as quoted in Marcus, ed., *Nicaragua: The Sandinista People's Revolution,* 335–51.

27. IISG, poster collection, "Midden-Amerika Vrij," 1982, https://iisg.amsterdam /en/detail?id=https%3A%2F%2Fiisg.amsterdam%2Fid%2Fitem %2F844542.

28. IISG, NKN, Box 73, Report of visit of European and US Peace Movement Delegations to Nicaragua, 8 February 1983.

29. IISG, NKN, Box 73, Speech, Laurens Hogebrink, Amsterdam, July 1983.

30. IISG, NKN, Box 73, European and US Peace Movement Delegation to Nicaragua, 8 February 1983.

31. IISG, NKN, Box 73, Speech, Laurens Hogebrink, Amsterdam, July 1983.

32. Wettig, "The Last Soviet Offensive."

33. IISG, INW, Caldera to European Secretariat of the solidarity movement, 18 April 1983.

34. *Leeuwarder Courant*, 9 September 1983.

35. Interview with Jan Kees de Rooy, interview with Klaas Wellinga and Hans Langenberg, Utrecht, the Netherlands, 6 August 2014; interview with John Bevan, London, United Kingdom, 20 March 2017.

36. IISG, NKN, Box 17-18, Geneva conference, 1981.

37. IISG, NKN, Box 20, Background Document, 2 January 1984.

38. PHM, NSC, Box 77, Minutes of General Meeting, 6 June 1984.

39. IISG, NKN, Box 17-18, Geneva conference, 1981.

40. IISG, NKN, Box 73, European and US Peace Movement Delegation to Nicaragua, 8 February 1983.

41. IISG, NKN, Box 73, report of IKV trip to Nicaragua, April and May 1983.

42. Interview with John Bevan.

43. NSC, *Nicaragua Today*, 1983.

44. RL, Executive Secretariat, NSC: Subject Files, Memorandums of Conversations—President Reagan, Box 51, Reagan and Thatcher, 29 September 1983.

45. RL, Executive Secretariat, NSC: Meeting Files, Report on Central America, 16 July 1983.

46. AAPD, 1983, Document 192, Martius to Botschaft Washington, 29 June 1983.

47. RL, Raymond Walter Files, CentAm Meetings, Box 3, Memorandum, 7 July 1983.

48. Report of the Congressional Committees Investigating the Iran-Contra Affair, 17 November 1987, https://babel.hathitrust.org/cgi/pt?id=mdp.39015014635240&view=1up&seq=13.

49. RL, Executive Secretariat, NSC: Meeting Files 00081-00090, Box 9.

50. RL, Raymond Walter files, CentAm meetings, Box 3; CREST, Background Paper: Nicaragua's military buildup and support for Central American subversion, 18 July 1984.

51. As cited in LeoGrande, *Our Own Backyard*, 210.

52. *UPI*, 19 July 1983.

53. ABPA, MINEX, Comisión Kissinger, 15 October 1983.

54. ABPA, MINEX, Comisión Kissinger, 15 October 1983.

55. ABPA, MINEX, Comisión Kissinger, 15 October 1983.

56. *The Washington Post*, 16 October 1983.

57. *Het Vrije Volk*, 27 October 1983.

58. LeoGrande, *Our Own Backyard*, 345.

59. *Revista Envío* (November 1983).

60. *NRC Handelsblad*, 26 October 1983.

61. Hansard, House of Commons Debate, 26 October 1983, https://hansard.parliament.uk.

62. TNA, FCO 99/1743, Carrington and Shultz, 11 December 1984.

63. TNA, FCO 99/1741, Record of call by Mr David Thomas on Mr Constantine Menges, National Security Council, Washington DC, 10 May 1984.

64. "Inside Communist Nicaragua: The Miguel Bolanos Transcripts," 30 September 1983, The Heritage Foundation, http://www.heritage.org/americas/report/inside-communist-nicaragua-the-miguel-bolanos-transcripts.

65. Margaret Thatcher Foundation Archive, Record of a Conversation between the Prime Minister and the US secretary of State, 15 January 1984, https://www.margaretthatcher.org/archive.

66. Report of the National Bipartisan Commission on Central America, 10 January 1984, https://digitalcommons.law.ggu.edu/federal_documents/8.

67. TNA, FCO 99/1738, Memorandum, MCAD, Central America: European Involvement Proposed by Kissinger Report, 21 January 1984.

68. AA, AV Neues Amt 15.534, Memorandum Bericht der Kissinger-Kommission zu Zentralamerika und die Lage in dieser Region, 17 January 1984.

69. TNA, FCO 99/1738, Memorandum, MCAD, Kissinger Commission Report, 19 January 1984.

70. TNA, FCO 99/1738, Note, MCAD, Baker to Watt, 23 January 1984.

71. CREST, Intelligence Officer for Western Europe to the Director of Central Intelligence, 13 January 1984.

72. CREST, Intelligence Assessment, Western Europe and Central America: Influence but not Power, April 1984.

73. *The Times*, 20 December 1983.

74. See, for example, IISG, NKN, Box 41.

75. Informationsbüro Nicaragua, *Gemeinsam werden wir Siegen! Arbeitsbrigaden in Nicaragua*.

76. NSC, *Nicaragua Today*, 1986.

77. PHM, NSC, Box 77, Report on the Brigades for General Meeting, 12 June 1984.

78. SHL, ER230, PAM 5/19, "Work Brigades + Study Tours," 1990.

79. Officially founded in 1980 as an organization to support other Third World liberation movements, the CNSP took over the official responsibility for the FSLN's relations with the Western European solidarity movement in 1984. See Ágreda Portero, "Internacionalistas, Activistas, y Brigadistas," 121–22.

80. Helm, "The Sons of Marx Greet the Sons of Sandino," 157.

81. Roger Peace, "The Politics of Transnational Solidarity: Washington Versus Managua," *United States Foreign Policy: History and Resource Guide,* http://peacehistory-usfp.org/washington-vs-managua.

82. NSC, *Nicaragua Today,* Winter 1985/1986.

83. Deirdre Veldon, "The Coffee-Pickin' Irish," *The Irish Times,* 28 June 2014.

84. Helm, "The Sons of Marx Greet the Sons of Sandino," 154.

85. IISG, NKN, Box 17-18, Background paper on brigades, exact date unknown but c. fall 1984 (made in preparation for a Western European solidarity conference in November 1984).

86. NSC, *Nicaragua Today,* Spring 1986.

87. Veldon, "The Coffee-Pickin' Irish."

88. TNA, FCO 99/1779, Eastwood to Baker, "Nicaragua: International Volunteers," 5 January 1984.

89. Rocha, "La década de los años 80," 79.

90. NSC, *Nicaragua Today,* 1986.

91. Helm, "The Sons of Marx Greet the Sons of Sandino," 158.

92. IISG, INW, Pressemitteilung, 24 June 1984.

93. TNA, FCO 99/1779, San Jose to MCAD, 17 January 1984.

94. IISG, NKN, Box 46, Survey of the activity of ex-brigadistas upon returning from Nicaragua and their effect on the NSC, 1987.

95. Franz Alt, "Unvorstelbar, dass wir verlieren," *Der Spiegel* 37 (1982).

96. HI, Nicaragua Subject Collection, Box 5, NSC, Nicaragua Work Brigades/Study Tours 1988.

97. PHM, The Judith Hart Papers, Section 5, File 24, Report on NALGO visit, December 1984.

98. IISG, NKN, Box 17-18, Brigades, November 1984.

99. *The Christian Science Monitor,* 12 June 1986.

100. IISG, NKN, Box 46, Wim Jillings to NKN, 22 November 1984.

101. For more on the kidnapping of West German activists in 1986, see AA, AV Neues Amt, 15.495.

102. *The New York Times,* 13 June 1986; *Stuttgarter Zeitung,* 12 June 1986.

103. Filadelfo Aleman, "Kidnapped West Germans Released and Hospitalized," *Associated Press News,* 12 June 1986.

104. IISG, NKN, Box 17-18, Brigades, November 1984.

105. TNA, FCO 99/1911, Memorandum, MCAD, 7 December 1984.

106. TNA, FCO 98/2045, London Coreu to Paris Coreu, 27 April 1984.

107. BZ, Inventarisnummer 25292, Van den Broek to Paris Embassy, 18 June 1984.

108. TNA, FCO 98/2045, London Coreu to Paris Coreu, 27 April 1984.

109. TNA, CAB 128/78/13, Conclusions of a Meeting of the Cabinet, 29 March 1984; Ronald Reagan, "Address to the Nation on United States Policy in Central America," 9 May 1984, https://www.reaganlibrary.gov/archives/speech/address-nation-united-states-policy-central-america.

110. *Revista Envío* (May 1984); *The Washington Post*, 7 April 1984.

111. BZ, Inventarisnummer 25292, Bonn Coreu to All Coreu, 4 May 1984.

112. AAPD, 1984, Document 110, Ruhfus to AA, 17 April 1984.

113. AA, Zwischenarchiv 146.679, Vermerk, Allgemeiner Rat 20/21.2.1984; EG-Zentralamerika, 16 February 1984.

114. Hill and Smith, eds., *European Foreign Policy*, 430–32.

115. ABPA, MINEX Ayuda Memoria, 24 May 1984.

116. *Revista Envío* (October 1984).

117. Permanent Representatives of Nicaragua to the UN to President of the Security Council, 21 September 1984, United Nations Digital Library, https://digitallibrary.un.org/record/69318.

118. TNA, FCO 99/1774, Dublin Coreu to All Coreu, 7 September 1984.

119. *The New York Times*, 30 September 1984.

120. TNA, FCO 99/1773, Washington to FCO, 22 September 1984.

121. AA, Zwischenarchiv 178.891, San Salvador to Bonn, 27 September 1984.

122. CREST, CIA Background Paper for NSC Meeting, 30 October 1984.

123. TNA, FCO, 99/1742, Memorandum, 3 October 1984.

124. AA, Zwischenarchiv 136.331, Vermerk, 14 January 1985.

125. TNA, FCO 98/2045, Brief on Central America, for European Political Cooperation, Meeting of Foreign Ministers, Paris, 27 February 1984.

126. AAPD, 1984, Document 210, Aufzeichnung des Ministerialdirigenten Peckert, 20 July 1984

127. Data based on reports from Instituto de Relaciones Europeo-Latinoamericanas, copies in author's possession.

128. TNA, FCO 99/2141, Nicaragua: Annual Review for 1984, 4 January 1985; FCO 99/1906, Nicaragua: Annual Review for 1983, 2 January 1984.

129. *Revista Envío* (November 1984).

130. Ramírez, *Adiós Muchachos*, 75.

131. Black, *Triumph of the People*, 254.

132. Black, *Triumph of the People*, 254.

133. E. Cardenal, *La Revolución Perdida*, 381–82.

134. *Nicaragua: Elections; Fact or Fiction*.

135. ABPA, MINEX, Memorandum, Evaluación, Perspectivas y Planes—1984, date unknown.

136. ABPA, MINEX, Memorandum, 14 February 1984.

137. TNA, FCO 99/1779, MCAD, Memorandum, 18 October 1984.

138. ABPA, MINEX, Memorandum, Evaluación, Perspectivas y Planes—1984, date unknown.

139. ABPA, MINEX, Memorandum, 14 February 1984.

140. Ramírez, *Adiós Muchachos*, 101.

141. Ronald Reagan, "Remarks at the Welcoming Ceremony for President Jaime Lusinchi of Venezuela," 4 December 1984, https://www.reaganlibrary.gov/research /speeches/120484a.

142. CREST, USIA Public Diplomacy Activities on Central America, 2 November 1984.

143. IISG, NKN, Box 14, Nicaragua Komitee Nederland to Paul Bremer, 21 February 1984.

144. *Nicaragua: Elections; Factor and Fiction.*

145. TNA, FCO 99/1779, NSC to Thatcher, 2 December 1984.

146. ABPA, MINEX, Memorandum, 14 February 1984.

147. CREST, USIA Public Diplomacy Activities on Central America, 2 November 1984.

148. Ramírez, *Adiós Muchachos*, 102.

149. Alejandro Bendaña, interviewed by James S. Sutterlin, 29 July 1997, Yale-UN Oral History Project, https://digitallibrary.un.org/record/498540.

150. BZ, Inventarisnummer 25292, Map 18, Van den Broek aan Tweede Kamer, 19 December 1984.

151. TNA, FCO 99/1759, UKRep Brussels to Immediate FCO, "European Political Cooperation Ministerial Dinner: Central America," 13 November 1984.

152. Hansard, House of Commons Debate, 9 November 1984, https://hansard .parliament.uk.

153. CREST, USIA Public Diplomacy Activities on Central America, 2 November 1984.

154. CREST, Background Paper NSC Meeting on Central America, 30 October 1984.

155. Hansard, House of Commons Debate, 9 November 1984, https://hansard .parliament.uk.

156. Interview, Bendaña with Sutterlin.

157. *The New York Times*, 15 November 1984; 21 October 1984.

158. LeoGrande, *Our Own Backyard*, 319–21.

159. CREST, Background Paper NSC Meeting on Central America, 30 October 1984.

160. TNA, FCO 99/1742, Summary of Conversation Thatcher and Bush, 6 July 1984.

161. TNA, FCO 98/2024, MCAD, Memorandum, 11 September 1984.

162. For more on the role of the United States in the elections in El Salvador, see McCormick, "US Electoral Assistance to El Salvador and the Culture of Politics, 1982–1984."

163. AAPD, 1984, Document 210, Aufzeichnung des Ministerialdirigenten Peckert, 30 July 1984; James M. Markhan, "Duarte Thanks Bonn for Aiding El Salvador," *The New York Times*, 19 July 1984.

## CHAPTER 5. FUNDRAISING FOR THE REVOLUTION, 1985–1986

1. *Barricada Internacional*, 13 June 1985.

2. The CNSP was part of the foreign policy arm of the FSLN, the Departamento de Relaciones Internacionales.

3. IISG, NKN, Box 41, Balance anual de la Campaña Nicaragua Debe Sobrevivir en el año 1987, exact date unknown.

4. SAPMO, DY30/43863, Vermerk, Gespräch des Erick Honecker mit Henry Ruiz, 11 February 1983; Wilson Center Digital Archive, Minutes of Conversation, Todor Zhivkov and Daniel Ortega Saavedra on the Situation in Central America and Bulgarian Aid to Nicaragua, 2 May 1985, https://digitalarchive.wilsoncenter .org/document/minutes-conversation-todor-zhivkov-daniel-ortega-saavedra-situation-central-america-and. I want to thank Vesselin Dimitrov for kindly providing me with a translation of this document.

5. LeoGrande, "Making the Economy Scream," 338–39.

6. These numbers are based on reports from the Instituto de Relaciones Europeo-Latinoamericanas, copies in author's possession.

7. SAPMO, DY30/13771, Einige Bermerkungen zur aktuellen situation, July 1985; *Revista Envío* (October 1985, September 1986).

8. LeoGrande, *Our Own Backyard*, 349.

9. ABPA, Miguel d'Escoto to Daniel Ortega, 29 March 1985.

10. ABPA, Miguel d'Escoto to Daniel Ortega, 29 March 1985.

11. TNA, FCO 99/2138, Summerscale to FCO, 11 January 1985.

12. *De Volkskrant*, 12 January 1985. For more on Mexico's involvement in the Central America, see Vázquez Olivera and Campos Hernández, eds., *México ante el conflicto centroamericano*.

13. *The Guardian*, 12 January 1985; *Revista Envío* (February 1985).

14. ABPA, MINEX, Documento de Trabajo: Contadora, date unknown.

15. ABPA, Miguel d'Escoto to Daniel Ortega, 29 March 1985.

16. ABPA, Miguel d'Escoto to Daniel Ortega, 29 March 1985.

17. ABPA, Miguel d'Escoto to Daniel Ortega, 29 March 1985.

18. *The New York Times*, 3 May 1985.

19. ABPA, Miguel d'Escoto to Daniel Ortega, 29 March 1985; ABPA, MINEX Documento de Trabajo Contadora, date unknown.

20. CREST, CIA Report, Nicaragua: Initial Reaction to US Sanctions, 23 May 1985.

21. CREST, CIA Report, Nicaragua: Initial Reaction to US Sanctions, 23 May 1985; LeoGrande, "Making the Economy Scream," 339.

22. TNA, FCO 99/2153, San Jose to FCO, 31 January 1985.

23. *La Prensa*, 23 January 1985; *Barricada*, 1 February 1985; *El Nuevo Diario*, 23 January 1985; *Revista Envío* (February 1985).

24. ABPA, Memorandum, MINEX, 19 March 1985.

25. PUL, Sergio Ramírez Papers, Box 62, Folder 8A, Sergio Ramírez to Daniel Ortega, 20 February 1985.

26. PUL, Sergio Ramírez Papers, Box 62, Folder 8A, Sergio Ramírez to Daniel Ortega, 20 February 1985.

27. PUL, Sergio Ramírez Papers, Box 62, Folder 8A, Sergio Ramírez to Daniel Ortega, 20 February 1985.

28. The Ministerio de Cooperación Externa was officially created on 21 March 1985.

29. See TNA, FCO 99/2153 and PUL, Sergio Ramírez Papers, Box 62, Folder 8A.

30. TNA, FCO 99/2153, Telegram, Summerscale to FCO, 18 January 1985.

31. *The Guardian*, 29 January 1985.

32. PUL, Sergio Ramírez Papers, Box 62, Folder 8A, Ramírez to Ortega, 20 February 1985.

33. PUL, Sergio Ramírez Papers, Box 62, Folder 8A, Ramírez to Ortega, 20 February 1985.

34. TNA, FCO 99/2147, "Visit of Herr Moellemann to Nicaragua: 22–25 January," 1 February 1985.

35. TNA, FCO 99/2142, MCAD, Note, 30 January 1985.

36. TNA, FCO 99/2153, MCAD, Note, 29 January 1985.

37. *The Guardian*, 9 February 1985.

38. TNA, FCO 99/2145, Nicaragua: Statement by President Ortega of 26 February, 5 March 1985.

39. PUL, Sergio Ramírez Papers, Box 62, Folder 8A, Ramírez to Ortega, 20 February 1985.

40. See FCO 99/2147 and FCO 99/2142.

41. PUL, Sergio Ramírez Papers, Box 62, Folder 8A, Ramírez to Ortega, 20 February 1985; *The Guardian*, 25 January 1985.

42. PUL, Sergio Ramírez Papers, Box 62, Folder 8A, Ramírez to Ortega, 20 February 1985.

43. *The Times*, 12 January 1985.

44. PUL, Sergio Ramírez Papers, Box 62, Folder 8A, Ramírez to Ortega, 20 February 1985.

45. ABPA, MINEX, Memorandum, 28 March 1985.

46. ABPA, MINEX, Memorandum, 28 March 1985.

47. Jarquín, "Red Christmases," 106.

48. For more on transnational anticommunist support for the Contras, see Burke, *Revolutionaries for the Right*.

49. ABPA, MINEX Memorandum, 28 March 1985.

50. ABPA, MINEX Memorandum, 28 March 1985.

51. Interview with Luis Ángel Caldera Aburto, Managua, Nicaragua, 16 April 2018.

52. Grayson, *Oil and Mexican Foreign Policy*, 147–48.

53. Wilson Center Digital Archive, Todor Zhivkov and Daniel Ortega Saavedra, 2 May 1985.

54. Wilson Center Digital Archive, Todor Zhivkov and Daniel Ortega Saavedra, 2 May 1985.

55. CREST, Directorate of Intelligence, Nicaragua: Oil Problems and Prospects, May 1985.

56. Interview with Luis Ángel Caldera Aburto 16 April 2018; interview with Jaime Wheelock Román, Managua, Nicaragua, 18 April 2018.

57. CREST, CIA Report, Nicaragua: Oil Problems and Prospects, May 1985; *Barricada Internacional*, 30 May 1985.

58. Wilson Center Digital Archive, Todor Zhivkov and Daniel Ortega Saavedra, 2 May 1985.

59. *UPI*, 24 April 1985.

60. *El País*, 1 May 1985; *UPI*, 8 May 1985; *Barricada Internacional*, 9 May 1985.

61. *Barricada Internacional*, 30 May 1985.

62. Ronald Reagan, Statement on House of Representatives Disapproval of United States Assistance for the Nicaraguan Democratic Resistance, 24 April 1985, https://www.reaganlibrary.gov/research/speeches/42485c.

63. AA, Zwischenarchiv 136.368, Sachstand, Zentralamerika, 29 May 1985; Kinzer, *Blood of Brothers*, 359.

64. Digital National Security Archive, AmEmbassy Managua to SecState Washington, 5 May 1985.

65. TNA, FCO 99/2387, Nicaragua: Annual Review 1985, 9 January 1986; AmEmbassy Managua to SecState Washington, 5 May 1985; *The Times*, 29 April 1985.

66. IISG, NKN, Box 101, "Noodtoestand afgekondigd in Nicaragua, een aantal rechten teruggedraaid," October 1986.

67. Ronald Reagan, Executive Order 12513, Prohibiting Trade and Certain Other Transactions Involving Nicaragua, 1 May 1985, https://www.reaganlibrary.gov/research/speeches/50185a.

68. Report of the Congressional Committees Investigating the Iran/Contra Affair, 17 November 1987, https://babel.hathitrust.org/cgi/pt?id=mdp.3901501463 5240&view=1up&seq=13.

69. For more on U.S. aid for the Contras, see Hoekstra, "Helping the Contras."

70. LeoGrande, *Our Own Backyard*, 363–73.

71. *Barricada Internacional*, 30 May 1985.

72. BZ, Inventarisnummer 03795, BZ to San Jose, 4 June 1985.

73. BZ, Inventarisnummer 03795, BZ to San Jose, 4 June 1985; CREST, CIA Report, Nicaragua: Initial Reaction to US Sanctions, 23 May 1985.

74. AA, Zwischenarchiv 129.579, Sitzung der EPZ-AG Lateinamerika am 20 Mai in Rom, 22 May 1985; BZ, Inventarisnummer 02037, Ambassade Parijs naar BZ, 19 June 1985.

75. AA, Zwischenarchiv 129.579, Sitzung der EPZ-AG Lateinamerika am 20 Mai in Rom, 22 May 1985.

76. For more on the debate see TNA, FCO 99/2152. Officially, Spain only joined the EC on 1 January 1986, but the Spanish government already coordinated its foreign policy with its European allies before this date.

77. Karamouzi and Chourchoulis, "Troublemaker or Peacemaker, "51.

78. Ramírez, *Adiós Muchachos*, 110.

79. Ramírez, *Adiós Muchachos*, 95.

80. Staten Generaal Digitaal, Handelingen Tweede Kamer, 1 May 1985.

81. AAPD, 1985, Document 112, Gespräch der Außenminister der G-7 in Brühl, 3 May 1985.

82. TNA, FCO 99/2142, Minutes of Economic Summit in Bonn, Foreign Ministers' Meeting, 3 May 1985.

83. TNA, FCO 99/2142, Minutes of Economic Summit in Bonn, Foreign Ministers' Meeting, 3 May 1985.

84. It is likely that the attitudes of EC and U.S. officials regarding the embargo were rooted in the transatlantic conflict about the Euro-Soviet gas pipeline project, which the Reagan administration actively opposed. For more on this, see Ksenia Demidova's chapter in Patel and Weisbrode, eds., *European Integration and the Atlantic Community*.

85. AAPD, 1985, Document 112, Gespräch der Außenminister der G-7 in Brühl, 3 May 1985.

86. TNA, FCO 99/2145, David Thomas to MCAD, 18 September 1985.

87. Staten Generaal Digitaal, Buitenlandse Zaken, Verslag van een Mondeling Overleg, 2 September 1985.

88. *Het Vrije Volk*, 6 June 1985.

89. Staten Generaal Digitaal, Buitenlandse Zaken, Verslag van een Mondeling Overleg, 2 September 1985.

90. AA, Zwischenarchiv 136.368, Sachstand: Zentralamerika, 29 May 1985; TNA, FCO 99/2147, Bonn to FCO, 5 June 1985.

91. AAPD, 1985, Document 139, Gespräch des Bundesministers Genscher mit dem nicaraguanischen Vizepräsidenten Ramírez, 28 May 1985.

92. ABPA, MINEX, Memorandum, 28 March 1985.

93. ABPA, MINEX, Memorandum, 28 March 1985.

94. Normas Jurídicas de Nicaragua, Decreto No. 128, Estado de Emergencia Nacional, 15 October 1985, http://legislacion.asamblea.gob.ni/normaweb.nsf/($All )/5D721BC989D4B071062570A10057E24E?OpenDocument.

95. PHM, NSC, Box 1, Press Release, date unknown; TNA, FCO 99/2385, Nicaraguan Embassy in London, Press Release on the State of Emergency, 17 October 1985.

96. *Revista Envío* (November 1985).

97. SAPMO, DY30/13771, Monatsbericht November 1985, 8 November 1985.

98. SAPMO, DY30/13771, Monatsbericht November 1985, 8 November 1985.

99. *Revista Envío* (November 1985).

100. TNA, FCO 99/2139, Washington to FCO, 17 October 1985.

101. TNA, FCO 99/2139, Coreu London to Coreu, 21 October 1985; FCO 99/2385, Budd to Addison, 1 April 1986.

102. *The Times*, 17 October 1985; TNA, FCO/2139, Statement French Foreign Ministry, 17 October 1985.

103. IISG, NKN, Box 101, Verslag van het Europees Congres in Lissabon, 20 October 1985.

104. IISG, NKN, Box 101, Noodtoestand afgekondigd in Nicaragua, een aantal rechten teruggedraaid, October 1986.

105. IISG, NKN, Box 101, Verslag van het Europees Congres in Lissabon, 20 October 1985.

106. PHM, NSC, Box 1, NSC Press Release, date unknown.

107. PHM, NSC, Box 1, NSC Press Release, date unknown.

108. IISG, NKN, Box 96-97, NKN to local solidarity committees, 17 October 1985. The causes and consequences on the ground of the State of Emergency are complex and—as far as I know—have not been covered in detail by historians. For a detailed contemporary analysis, see "Nicaragua: El país en Emergencia," *Revista Envío* (November 1985).

109. IISG, NKN, Box 101, "Noodtoestand afgekondigd in Nicaragua, een aantal rechten teruggedraaid," October 1986.

110. TNA, FCO 99/2139, Press Release, French Ministry for External Affairs, 17 October 1985.

111. PHM, The Judith Hart Papers, File 05/58, Kinnock to Ortega, 16 October 1985.

112. Staten Generaal Digitaal, Handelingen Tweede Kamer, 17 October 1985.

113. Interview with Luis Ángel Caldera Aburto, 16 April 2018.

114. IISG, NKN, Box 17-18, Coordinadora Europea de Comités Nacionales de Solidaridad con Nicaragua, 31 August 1985.

115. Interview with Luis Ángel Caldera Aburto, 16 April 2018.

116. IISG, NKN, Box 17-18, "Informe de la coordinación alemana-RFA correspondiente Nov 85–Nov 86," 23 October 1986.

117. IISG, NKN, Box 17-18, "Informe para el II Congreso Europeo del Comité de Holanda," date unknown.

118. IISG, NKN, Box 17-18, Danish Solidarity Committee, Balance del Trabajo de Solidaridad de Nov 85 a Sep 86.

119. IISG, NKN, Box 101, Records of European Solidarity Conference in Athens, 22–23 November 1985.

120. Hertogs, ed., *Nederlanders naast Nicaragua.*

121. IISG, NKN, Box 101, Records of European Solidarity Conference in Athens, 22–23 November 1986.

122. IISG, NKN, Box 146, "Campaña Británica de Solidaridad con Nicaragua: Monografía," July 1989.

123. NSC, Nicaragua Must Survive: Container Appeal. Guidelines for Donors (Revised edition), date unknown.

124. NSC, Leaflet, Nicaragua Must Survive: Container Appeal, 1987.

125. IISG, NKN, Box 41, Jillings to Langenberg, 29 May 1985.

126. Bontebal, *Cities as Partners*, 85–86.

127. See IISG, NKN, Box 17-18; Stichting Stedenband Nijmegen-Masaya, "Burgemeester Ortega van Masaya in Nijmegen," November 1986.

128. Hertogs, ed., *Nederlanders naast Nicaragua.*

129. Hertogs, ed., *Nederlanders naast Nicaragua*, 93.

130. See Vion, "Europe from the Bottom Up" and Clarke, "Town Twinning in Cold War Britain."

131. Bontebal, *Cities as Partners*.

132. IISG, NKN, Box 17-18, European Conference on city linking with Nicaragua: an example of North-South cooperation and dialogue, 26–28 May 1988.

133. Leicester Masaya Link Group Archive, Leicester, the United Kingdom, Leicester City Council, Public Meeting, Twinning with Nicaragua, 1 October 1985.

134. *De Gelderlander*, 1 December 1986.

135. Labour member Paul Gosling was assaulted at the public meeting about twinning Masaya with Leicester. The assailants, he later claimed, all wore Federation of Conservative Students badges.

136. *Leicester Mercury*, 14 February 1987.

137. *The Times*, 4 June 1985; *The Standard*, 6 June 1985; *The Sun*, 5 June 1985.

138. TNA, FCO 99/2390, Pamphlet, "Conference for a Free Nicaragua," 6 December 1986.

139. TNA, FCO 99/2390, Note on the Conference for a Free Nicaragua, 8 December 1986.

140. PHM, NSC, Box 1, NSC Policy towards the Committee for a Free Nicaragua, January 1987.

141. Military and Paramilitary Activities in and against Nicaragua (Nicaragua v. United States of America), Merits, Judgment, ICJ Reports 1986, 27 June 1986, https://www.icj-cij.org/en/case/70/judgments.

142. Military and Paramilitary Activities in and against Nicaragua.

143. *The Los Angeles Times*, 26 June 1986.

144. ABPA, MINEX, Balance Anual de Political Exterior Durante 1986, date unknown.

145. ABPA, MINEX, Balance Anual 1985 Relaciones Políticas Estados Unidos/Nicaragua, 10 February 1986.

146. ABPA, MINEX, Balance Anual 1985 Relaciones Políticas Estados Unidos/Nicaragua, 10 February 1986.

147. *Trouw*, 11 May 1984.

148. Correspondence with John Bevan, 22 February 2018.

149. Astorga, a former guerrilla, was one of only four women who represented their countries at the United Nations in 1986. See *The New York Times*, 28 September 1986.

150. UN General Assembly, 53rd Plenary Meeting, Judgment of the International Court of Justice of 27 June 1986 concerning military and paramilitary activities in and against Nicaragua: need for immediate compliance, 3 November 1986, https://digitallibrary.un.org/record/123967?ln=en.

151. In favor: Denmark, China, the Soviet Union, Bulgaria, Australia, Madagascar, Trinidad and Tobago, Congo, Ghana, Venezuela, the United Arab Emirates; Against (veto): the United States; Abstained: United Kingdom, France, Thailand.

152. *The Washington Post*, 1 August 1986.

153. *The Washington Post*, 1 August 1986.

154. TNA, FCO 99/2404, Telegram, FCO to New York, 27 October 1985.

155. TNA, FCO 99/2403, UN Security Council: US/Nicaragua and the ICJ, 30 July 1986.

156. TNA, FCO 99/2403, Security Council: Nicaragua and the ICJ, 7 August 1986.

157. TNA, PREM 19/2367, UN Security Council: Nicaragua/ICJ Decision, 23 October 1986.

158. TNA, FCO 99/2403, d'Escoto to Young, 20 October 1986.

159. TNA, FCO 99/2403, Shultz to Howe, 31 July 1986.

160. TNA, FCO 99/2403, UN Security Council: US, Nicaragua and the ICJ, 31 July 1986.

161. TNA, FCO 99/2403, UN Security Council: US, Nicaragua and the ICJ, 31 July 1986.

162. TNA, PREM 19/2367, United Nations Security Council: Nicaragua/ICJ, 24 October 1986.

163. TNA, PREM 19/2367, United Nations Security Council: Nicaragua/ICJ, 26 October 1986.

164. TNA, PREM 19/2367, Memorandum, 24 October 1986.

165. CREST, CIA Report, Nicaragua: Prospects for Sandinista Consolidation, August 1987.

## CHAPTER 6. PEACE AND ELECTIONS, 1987–1990

1. "Procedure for the establishment of a firm and lasting peace in Central America," 27 August 1987, https://peacemaker.un.org/sites/peacemaker.un.org /files/CR%20HN%20GT%20NI%2 0SV_8 70807_EsquipulasII.pdf.

2. IISG, NKN, Box 4, Met het oog op de toekomst: stuk ter voorbereiding op de KOKO-special van 10 en 11 feb. 1989, date unknown.

3. Dunkerley, *The Pacification of Central America*, 45–46; AAPD, 1987, Konferenz des Bundesministers Genscher mit Botschaftern in zentralamerikanischen Staaten in San José, 9 April 1987.

4. AAPD, 1987, Konferenz des Bundesministers Genscher mit Botschaftern in zentralamerikanischen Staaten in San José, 9 April 1987; *The Guardian*, 16 February 1987.

5. AAPD, 1987, Gespräche MR Dr. Teltschik in Washington am 11.2.1987, 14 February 1987.

6. CREST, Directorate of Intelligence, Nicaragua and El Salvador, Monthly Report, July 1987; TNA, FCO 99/2844, Nicaragua: Annual Review 1987, 20 January 1988. For more on everyday life in Nicaragua, see Nygren, "Violent Conflicts and Threatened Lives."

7. *The Los Angeles Times*, 24 June 1987; *The Chicago Tribune*, 10 January 1987; *Revista Envío* (January 1989).

8. *UPI*, 20 February 1986.

9. Human Rights Watch, *World Report*, 1989, https://www.hrw.org/reports/1989/WR89/Nicaragu.htm.

10. CREST, Directorate of Intelligence, Nicaragua: Assessment of Insurgent and Regime Capabilities in First Quarter 1988, 21 April 1988; Nicaragua: Assessment of Insurgent and Regime Capabilities in First Quarter 1988, 21 April 1988, 20 July 1988. According to these reports, urban support for the Contras in the period 1986–88 was nonexistent (they only operated in the border areas). The appeal of the Contra movement in Nicaragua as a whole, including the rural areas, was deemed "weak." The total number of Contra soldiers was estimated to be between fifteen and sixteen thousand.

11. CREST, Directorate of Intelligence, Nicaragua: Prospects for the Economy, 24 June 1988.

12. BZ, Inventarisnummer 03761, Memorandum, from OS/Managua to CDP/San José, 28 April 1988.

13. CREST, Directorate of Intelligence, Nicaragua: Prospects for the Economy, 24 June 1988.

14. BZ, Inventarisnummer 03026, Dienstreis Nicaragua, van 4 tot 18 November 1987, door L. P. M. van Geel; Berth, *Food and Revolution*, 164–72.

15. IISG, NKN, Box 97, Solidarity activists in Managua to NKN, 7 July 1986.

16. Berth, *Food and Revolution*, 146.

17. AAPD, 1987, Konferenz des Bundesministers Genscher mit Botschaftern in zentralamerikanischen Staaten in San José, 9 April 1987.

18. ABPA, Informe del viaje al Campo Socialista 8.6.1987/22.6.1987, Ramírez to Ortega, 25 June 1987.

19. ABPA, Informe del viaje al Campo Socialista 8.6.1987/22.6.1987, Ramírez to Ortega, 25 June 1987.

20. For more on this, see Paszyn, *The Soviet Attitude*, and Ferrero Blanco, "Daniel Ortega y Mijail Gorbachov."

21. See Travis, "Oscar Arias and the Treaty of Esquipulas."

22. TNA, FCO 99/2474, Memorandum MCAD, 24 April 1987.

23. *The Guardian*, 22 May 1987.

24. AEI, European Political Cooperation Documentation Bulletin, Statement on the Guatemala Summit, 5 August 1987.

25. Joint Communiqué of the Conference of Foreign Minister of the European Community and its Member States, Portugal and Spain, the States of Central America and the Contadora States, San José, Costa Rica, 28–29 September 1984, as published in Hill and Smith, eds., *European Foreign Policy*.

26. AAPD, 1987, Konferenz des Bundesministers Genscher mit Botschaftern in zentralamerikanischen Staaten in San José, 9 April 1987.

27. TNA, FCO 99/2844, Nicaragua: Annual Review 1987, 20 January 1988.

28. AAPD, 1988, Gespräch des Bundeskanzlers Kohl mit Präsident Duarte, 7 July 1988.

29. For more on the Reagan administration's embrace of democracy promotion and its impact on the Nicaraguan Revolution, see Schmidli, *Freedom on the Offensive*.

30. AAPD, 1987, Ministerialdirektor Freiherr von Richthoften z.Z. BM-Delegation, an das Auswärtige Amt. Betr.: Weltwirtschaftsgipfel, 11 Juni 1987.

31. ABPA, Evaluación Anual: Dirección de Norteamérica 1988, date unknown.

32. AAPD, 1987, Konferenz des Bundesministers Genscher mit Botschaftern in zentralamerikanischen Staaten in San José, 9 April 1987.

33. RL, Executive Secretariat, NSC, Meeting Files, Box 13, Meeting with the National Security Council, 5 May 1987; Reagan Library, National Security Planning Group Meeting, 20 February 1987.

34. Alejandro Bendaña, interviewed by James S. Sutterlin, 29 July 1997, Yale-UN Oral History Project, https://digitallibrary.un.org/record/498540.

35. ABPA, Alejandro Bendaña to Directores Generales y Directores, 13 January 1989.

36. SAPMO, DY30/13776, Über das Gespräch des Genossen Erich Honecker mit Genossen Bayardo Arce am 4 März 1988 im Hause des Zentralkomitees, 5 March 1988.

37. RL, Executive Secretariat, NSC: Meeting Files, Box 13, Memorandum by Frank C, Carlucci, Meeting with the National Security Council, 12 March 1987.

38. Ronald Reagan, Radio Address to the Nation on the Situation in Nicaragua, 12 September 1987, https://www.reaganlibrary.gov/archives/speech/radio-address-nation-situation-nicaragua-0.

39. TNA, FCO 99/2707, Coltman to Eggar, 13 January 1988.

40. TNA, FCO 99/2474, Record of meeting held by the Secretary of State to discuss policy on Central America, 28 September 1987.

41. AA, AV Neues Amt 16.917, Managua to Bonn, 13 August 1987.

42. Staten Generaal Digitaal, Bukman to Tweede Kamer, 10 December 1987.

43. TNA, FCO 99/2726, Background brief MCAD, 25 February 1988.

44. AA, Zwischenarchiv 145.031, Copenhagen Coreu to All Coreu, 29 September 1987.

45. IISG, NKN, Box 3, Mary (Managua Dependance) to NKN, 24 August 1987.

46. IISG, NKN, Box 145, Report solidarity conference in Helsinki, 6 December 1987.

47. *De Volkskrant*, 9 January 1988, 17 October 1987.

48. IISG, NKN, Box 117, Commentaar van het Guatemala Komitee Nederland, Het Nicaragua Komitee Nederland en de gezamelijke El Salvador Komitees op één jaar regiobeleid voor Midden-Amerika ten behoeve van begrotingsbehandeling 1988/89 van ontwikkelingssamenwerking, date unknown.

49. *The New York Times*, 14 October 1987.

50. AA, Zwischenarchiv 136.369, Declaration by the Twelve on Central America, 13 November 1987.

51. SAPMO, DY30/2385, Vermerk: Honecker und Ortega, 3 November 1987.

52. AA, AV Neues Amt 16.917, Managua to Bonn, 20 August 1987.

53. Deutsche Bundestag, 39. Sitzung, 12 October 1987, https://pdok.bundestag.de.

54. AA, Zwischenarchiv 136.369, Vermerk, 17 December 1987.

55. *The New York Times*, 10 January 1987.

56. RL, Raymond Walter Files, Central America, Box 2, AmEmbassy Paris to SecState WashDC, 28 February 1987.

57. BZ, Inventarisnummer 5029, OS/Managua to CDP/San José, 27 April 1988.

58. H. Smith, *European Union Foreign Policy*, 100. According to Smith, in the period 1976–88, Nicaragua received 172 ECU (European Currency Unit), Honduras received 100 ECU, Guatemala 51 ECU, El Salvador 42 ECU, and Costa Rica 35 ECU.

59. TNA, FCO 99/2969, Note, MCAD, 10 May 1989.

60. BZ, Inventarisnummer 5039, OS/Managua to Ambassador, 4 May 1988.

61. TNA, FCO 99/2844, Croll to FCO, 5 February 1988.

62. See AAPD, 1987, Konferenz des Bundesministers Genscher mit Botschaftern, 9 April 1987.

63. TNA, FCO 99/2685, San Jose to FCO, 16 January 1988.

64. TNA, FCO 99/2707, Francisco d'Escoto to Geoffrey Howe, 22 January 1988.

65. Interview, Sutterlin with Bendaña.

66. TNA, FCO 99/2707, San Salvador to FCO, 16 January 1988.

67. IISG, NKN, Box 23, Persbericht, 4 February 1988.

68. Acuerdo de Sapoá, 23 March 1988, https://peacemaker.un.org/sites /peacemaker.un.org/files/NI_880323_Acuerdo%20de %20Sapoa.pdf.

69. Kinzer, *Blood of Brothers*, 376.

70. ABPA, Alejandro Bendaña to Directores Generales y Directores, 13 January 1989.

71. SAPMO, DY30/44238, Bericht über den Besuch einer Delegation der Nationalleitung der FSLN Nikaraguas unter Leitung des Genossen Bayardo Arce, Stellvertratender Koordinator der Exekutivkommission der Nationalleitung der FSLN Nikaraguas, vom 2. bis 6. März 1988 in der Deutschen Demokratischen Republik, 8 March 1988.

72. Kinzer, *Blood of Brothers*, 378.

73. Leicester Masaya Link Group Archive, Naomi Cohen to Twinning group, 15 February 1988.

74. Ramírez, *Adiós Muchachos*, 110–11.

75. Kruijt, *Cuba and Revolutionary Latin America*, 176.

76. IISG, NKN, Box 145, Resultados y Conclusiones del 14 Congreso Europeo de Solidaridad con Nicaragua Celebrado en Rome el 29 al 31 de octubre de 1988.

77. IISG, NKN, Box 3, Notulen KOKO, 9 July 1988.

78. IISG, NKN, Box 4, Stuk ter voorbereiding op de KOKO-special, 10 February 1989.

79. IISG, NKN, Box 245, Resultados y Conclusiones del 14 Congreso Europeo de Solidaridad con Nicaragua Celebrado en Rome el 29 al 31 de Octubre de 1988.

80. BZ, Inventarisnummer 15035, Van Muyzert/Managua aan CDP/San José, 22 November 1988.

81. IISG, NKN, Box 145, XIV Congreso Europeo de Solidaridad con Nicaragua, Roma 29–39 October 1988.

82. BZ, Inventarisnummer 15035, Van Muyzert/Managua aan CDP/San José, 22 November 1988.

83. IISG, NKN, Box 3, Notulen KOKO, 8 and 9 July 1988.

84. BZ, Inventarisnummer 15035, Muyzert/Managua naar CDP/San José: Nicaragua, 22 November 1988.

85. IISG, NKN, Box 144, Documente Base del III Encuentro Internacional de los comites de solidaridad con Nicaragua, date unknown.

86. IISG, NKN, Box 40, Nieuwsbrief II, Bouwbrigade 1987.

87. IISG, NKN, Box 40, Nieuwsbrief II, Bouwbrigade 1987.

88. Interview with Luis Ángel Caldera Aburto, phone via Signal, 22 October 2018.

89. BZ, Inventarisnummer 15035, Codebericht, van San Jose aan Min van BZ, 2 August 1988.

90. *The New York Times*, 16 July 1988.

91. IISG, NKN, Box 117, Commentaar van het Guatemala Komitee Nederland, Het Nicaragua Komitee Nederland en de gezamenlijke El Salvador Komitees op één jaar regiobeleid voor Midden-Amerika, date unknown.

92. Hansard, House of Commons Debate, 14 July 1988, https://hansard .parliament.uk.

93. Deutscher Bundestag, 11. Wahlperiode, Schriftliche Fragen, 21 October 1988.

94. TNA, FCO 99/2710, Telegram, Managua to San Jose, 25 July 1988.

95. IISG, NKN, Box 3, Notulen van de KOKO, 15 July 1988.

96. IISG, NKN, Box 23, Press release, 23 July 1988.

97. Kinzer, *Blood of Brothers*, 381.

98. *The Washington Post*, 21 September 1988.

99. Leicester Masaya Link Group Archive, Naomi Cohen to Leicester Committee, 15 February 1988.

100. TNA, FCO 99/3103, Nicaragua: Annual Review 1988, 18 January 1989.

101. Letter dated 24 February 1989 from the representatives of Costa Rica, El Salvador, Guatemala, Honduras and Nicaragua to the United Nations addressed to the Secretary-General, 27 February 1989, https://digitallibrary.un.org/record /58245?ln=en.

102. ABPA, Plan de Sandino a Sandino, 23 May 1989.

103. ABPA, Josefina Vigil (despacho del Cmdt. Bayardo Arce) to Alejandro Bendaña, 3 August 1989.

104. SAPMO, DY30/44301, Gespräch Hermann Axen, Egon Krenz und Gerhard Schürer mit Henry Ruiz, 24 April 1989.

105. ABPA, Plan de Sandino a Sandino, 23 May 1989.

106. ABPA, Plan de Sandino a Sandino, 23 May 1989.

107. ABPA, Plan de Sandino a Sandino, 23 May 1989.

108. SAPMO, DY30/44301, Gespräch Hermann Axen, Egon Krenz und Gerhard Schürer mit Henry Ruiz, 24 April 1989.

109. ABPA, Plan de Sandino a Sandino, 23 May 1989.

110. ABPA, Plan de Sandino a Sandino, 23 May 1989.

111. ABPA, Plan de Sandino a Sandino, 23 May 1989.

112. IISG, NKN, Box 18, Report to BINLUK meeting, date unknown; Box 147, CNSAP to solidarity committees, 26 September 1989.

113. BZ, Inventarisnummer 9112, Bonn Coreu to Madrid Coreu, 12 May 1989; TNA, FCO 99/3119, March to Imrie, 3 May 1989.

114. SAPMO, DY30/44301, Gespräch Hermann Axen, Egon Krenz und Gerhard Schürer mit Henry Ruiz, 24 April 1989.

115. TNA, FCO 99/3119, March to Imrie, 26 April 1989.

116. *The Guardian*, 12 March 2017; IISG, NKN, Box 146, NSC report, July 1989.

117. TNA, FCO 99/3116, Brown to Webb, 25 August 1989.

118. "Ortega Requests Thatcher Help, Gets Lecture Instead," *The Los Angeles Times*, 8 May 1989.

119. TNA, FCO 99/3119, Falconer to San Jose, 15 May 1989.

120. George H. W. Bush Library, Telcon, Óscar Arias, 27 July 1989, https://bush41library.tamu.edu.

121. TNA, FCO 99/3119, Coltman to San Jose, 11 May 1989.

122. TNA, FCO 99/3119, Record of a call by Nicaraguan foreign minister on Secretary of State, 8 May 1989.

123. TNA, FCO 99/3105, Webb to Francisco d'Escoto, 5 December 1989.

124. TNA, FCO 99/3095, Managua to FCO, 10 August 1989.

125. *The Los Angeles Times*, 25 February 1990.

126. George H. W. Bush Library, Telcon, Óscar Arias, 27 July 1989, https://bush41library.tamu.edu.

127. TNA, FCO 99/3095, Brown to FCO, 26 July 1989.

128. George H. W. Bush Library, Memcon, Violeta Chamorro, 8 November 1989, https://bush41library.tamu.edu/files/memcons-telcons/1989-11-08—Chamorro.pdf.

129. IISG, NKN, Box 147, Llamamiento, Wuppertal, 23 September 1989.

130. IISG, NKN, Box 119, Aandachtspunten, date unknown.

131. IISG, NKN, Box 4, Timmerman to Dutch committees, 26 September 1989.

132. Interview with Leonel Urbino Pérez, Havana, Cuba, 5 April 2018.

133. Wilson Center Digital Archive, Excerpt from Protocol No. 179 of the Meeting of the Politburo CC CPSU, 17 February 1990, https://digitalarchive.wilsoncenter.org/document/excerpt-protocol-no-179-meeting-politburo-cc-cpsu-upcoming-elections-nicaragua.

134. Interview with Gerrit Vledder, Amersfoort, the Netherlands, 5 January 2018.

135. The exact causes of Chamorro's victory in 1990 are still being debated. See Vilas, "Especulaciones sobre una sorpresa"; Williams, "Elections and Democratization in Nicaragua"; Robinson, *A Faustian Bargain*; Castro and Prevost, eds., *The 1990 Elections*; Hernández Ruigómez, "La Nicaragua sandinista."

136. *The New York Times*, 27 February 1990.

137. IISG, NKN, Box 4, Rapport van de Uitgangspunten-commissie, date unknown.

138. *The Daily Mail*, 27 February 1990.

1. *Revista Envío* (December 1990).

2. IISG, NKN, Box 147, Informe over Encuentro van Europese solidariteit-skomitees, 28 July 1990.

3. Interview with Jan Kees de Rooy.

4. Brands, *Latin America's Cold War*, 224

5. Harmer, *Beatriz Allende*, 270

6. Keller, *Mexico's Cold War*, 5

7. Gleijeses, *Conflicting Missions*; Harmer, *Allende's Chile*; Byrne, *Mecca of Revolution*; Thornton, *Revolution in Development*; Nguyen, *Hanoi's War*; Luthi, *Cold Wars*.

8. Friedman, *Ripe for Revolution*, 7

9. Bendaña, "The Rise and Fall of the FSLN," 24.

10. Bendaña, "The Rise and Fall of the FSLN," 25.

11. Cruz Feliciano and Chaguaceda, "Los intelectuales públicos," 19–21.

12. Henighan, *Sandino's Nation*, 430.

13. Berth, *Food and Revolution*, 163

14. Kinzer, *Blood of Brothers*, 396

15. Johnson Lee, *The Ends of Modernization*, 174

16. Stephen Kinzer, "40 Years Later, Grappling with Regime Change in Nicaragua," *The Boston Globe*, 8 May 2019.

17. Kinzer, "40 Years Later."

# BIBLIOGRAPHY

## ARCHIVES

### Cuba

Archivo Central del Ministerio de Relaciones Exteriores de Cuba (Central Archive of the Cuban Ministry of Foreign Relations), Havana

### Germany

Bundesarchiv, Stiftung Archiv der Parteien und Massenorganisationen der DDR (Federal Archive of Parties and Mass Organizations of the GDR), Berlin-Lichterfelde

Politisches Archiv des Auswärtigen Amt, Ministerium für Auswärtige Angelegenheiten der Deutschen Demokratischen Republik (Political Archive of the Foreign Ministry), Berlin

### The Netherlands

Buitenlandse Zaken Archief (Foreign Affairs Archive), The Hague

Internationaal Instituut voor Sociale Geschiedenis (International Institute of Social History), Amsterdam

Nationaal Archief (National Archive), The Hague

Stadsarchief Amsterdam (Amsterdam City Archive), Amsterdam

### Nicaragua

Alejandro Bendaña Private Archive, Managua

Ángel Barrajón Private Archive, Managua

Instituto de Historia de Nicaragua y Centroamericana, Archivo Histórico (Institute for Nicaraguan and Central American History, Historical Archive), Managua

### United Kingdom

Leicester Masaya Link Group Archive, Leicester
The National Archives, Kew
Nicaragua Solidarity Campaign Archive, London
People's History Museum, Manchester
Senate House Library, London

### United States

Hoover Institution, Stanford
Princeton University Library, New Jersey
Ronald Reagan Presidential Library, Simi Valley

### Online

Access to Archival Databases, Central Foreign Policy Files. The National Archives. https://aad.archives.gov/aad/fielded-search.jsp?dt=2532&tf=X.
Archive of European Integration. University of Pittsburgh. http://aei.pitt.edu.
Central Intelligence Agency Records and Search Tool. https://www.cia.gov/readingroom/collection/crest-25-year-program-archive.
Margaret Thatcher Foundation Archive. https://www.margaretthatcher.org/archive.
Staten Generaal Digitaal. https://zoek.officielebekendmakingen.nl/uitgebreidzoeken/historisch.
UK Parliament. Hansard. https://hansard.parliament.uk.

### INTERVIEWS

Tomás Arguello Chamorro, Managua, Nicaragua, 29 July 2016.
Ángel Barrajón, Managua, Nicaragua, 8 August 2016.
Alejandro Bendaña, Managua, Nicaragua, 23 August 2016.
John Bevan, London, United Kingdom, 20 March 2017.
George Black, Skype, 21 November 2017.
Luis Ángel Caldera Aburto, Managua, Nicaragua, 24 August 2016; 16 April 2018; Signal, 22 October 2018.
Orlando Castillo, Managua, Nicaragua, 11 April 2018.
Rita Delia Casco, Managua, Nicaragua, 29 July 2016.
Giovanni Delgado Campos, Managua, Nicaragua, 15 August 2018; 11 April 2018.
Eduardo Ramón Kühl, Selva Negra, Nicaragua, 1 August 2016; Email, 8 December 2016.

Sergio Ramírez Mercado, 11 August 2016.
Jan Kees de Rooy, Managua, Nicaragua, 11 August 2016.
Victor Hugo Tinoco, Managua, Nicaragua, 17 August 2016.
Leonel Urbino Pérez, Havana, Cuba, 5 April 2018.
Gerrit Vledder, Amersfoort, the Netherlands, 5 January 2018.
Klaas Wellinga and Hans Langenberg, Utrecht, the Netherlands, 6 August 2014.
Jaime Wheelock Román, Managua, Nicaragua, 25 July 2016; 18 April 2018.
Helen Yuill, London, United Kingdom, 11 March 2016.

NEWSPAPERS

*Germany*

*Nicaragua Aktuell*
*Der Spiegel*
*Stuttgarter Zeitung*


*Ireland*

*The Irish Times*


*The Netherlands*

*Amigoe*
*De Gelderlander*
*Leeuwarder Courant*
*NRC Handelsblad*
*De Volkskrant*
*Het Vrije Volk*
*De Waarheid*
*Het Parool*
*Trouw*


*Nicaragua*

*Barricada*
*Barricada Internacional*
*Encuentro*
*El Nuevo Diario*
*La Prensa*
*Revista Envío*

*Spain*

*El País*

*United Kingdom*

*The Daily Telegraph*
*The Economist*
*The Guardian*
*The Leicester Mercury*
*Nicaragua Today*
*The Standard*
*The Sun*
*The Times*

*United States*

*Associated Press News*
*The Boston Globe*
*The Chicago Tribune*
*The Christian Science Monitor*
*The Los Angeles Times*
*The New York Times*
*United Press International*
*The Washington Post*

PUBLISHED WORKS AND DISSERTATIONS

Ágreda Portero, José Manuel. "Internacionalistas, Activistas y Brigadistas. La red transnacional de solidaridad con Nicaragua desde el Estado español, 1978–1991." PhD diss., Universidad de Santiago de Compostela, 2021.

———. "Un acercamiento al Comité de Solidaridad con Nicaragua en Zaragoza, España (1978–1990)." *Nuevo Mundo Mundos Nuevos* (2016). https://doi.org /10.4000/nuevomundo.69639.

Agudelo Builes, Irene. *Contramemorias: Discursos e imágenes sobre/desde La Contra, Nicaragua 1979–1989.* Managua: IHNCA, 2017.

Apelt, Friederike. "Between Solidarity and Emancipation? Female Solidarity and Nicaraguan Revolutionary Feminism." In Jan Hansen, Christian Helm, and Frank Reichherzer, eds., *Making Sense of the Americas: How Protest Related to America in the 1980s and Beyond.* Chicago: University of Chicago Press, 2015.

Arce Castaño, Bayardo. "La intervención extranjera en Nicaragua y el proceso de autodeterminación Nicaragüense. Aspecto militar." *Encuentro: Revista Académica de la Universidad Centroamericana* 15 (1980): 56–64.

Arias, Pilar. *Nicaragua: Revolución: Relatos de combatientes del frente sandinista.* Mexico City: Siglo Veintiuno Editores, 1980.

Armony, Ariel C. *Argentina, the United States, and the Anti-Communist Crusade in Central America, 1977–1984.* Athens: Ohio University Press, 1997.

———. "Transnationalizing the Dirty War: Argentina in Central America." In Gilbert M. Joseph and Daniela Spenser, eds., *In from the Cold: Latin America's New Encounter with the Cold War.* Durham, NC: Duke University Press, 2008.

Assman, Hugo, ed. *Nicaragua triunfa en la alfabetización: Documentos y testimonios de la Cruzada Nacional de Alfabetización.* Managua: Ministerio de Educación, 1981.

Avery, Molly. "Connecting Central America to the Southern Cone: The Chilean and Argentine Response to the Nicaraguan Revolution of 1979." *The Americas* 78, no. 4 (2021): 553–79.

———. "The Latin American Anticommunist International: Chile, Argentina and Central America." PhD diss., London School of Economics and Political Science, 2022.

Bagley, Bruce Michael. "Contadora: The Failure of Diplomacy." *Journal of Interamerican Studies and World Affairs* 28, no. 3 (Autumn 1986): 1–32.

Baltodano, Mónica, ed. *Memorias de la lucha Sandinista. Tomo 1: De la forja de la vanguardia a la montaña.* Berlin: Rosa Luxemburg Stiftung, 2011.

———. *Memorias de la lucha Sandinista. Tomo 2: El crisol de las insurrecciones: Las Segovias, Managua y León.* Berlin: Rosa Luxemburg Stiftung, 2011.

Barraco, Luciano. "The Nicaraguan Literacy Crusade Revisited: The Teaching of Literacy as a Nation-Building Project." *Bulletin of Latin American Research* 23, no. 3 (2004): 339–54.

Basosi, Duccio. "Principle or Power? Jimmy Carter's Ambivalent Endorsement of the European Monetary System, 1977–1979." *Journal of Transatlantic Studies* 8, no. 1 (2010): 6–18.

Bataillon, Gilles. *Crónica sobre una guerrilla: Nicaragua 1982–2007.* México City: Centro de Estudios Mexicanos y Centroamericanos/Centro de Investigación y Docencia Económicas, 2015.

Belli, Gioconda. *The Country under My Skin: A Memoir of Love and War.* New York: Anchor Books, 2003.

Bendaña, Alejandro. *Sandino: Patria y libertad.* Managua: Anamá Ediciones, 2016.

———. "The Rise and Fall of the FSLN." *NACLA*, 25 September 2007.

Berth, Christiane. *Food and Revolution: Fighting Hunger in Nicaragua, 1960–1993.* Pittsburgh: University of Pittsburgh Press, 2021.

Bessner, Daniel, and Fredrik Logevall. "Recentering the United States in the Historiography of American Foreign Relations." *Texas National Security Review* 3, no. 2 (2020): 38–55.

Black, George. *Triumph of the People: The Sandinista Revolution in Nicaragua.* London: Zed Books, 1981.

Bontebal, Marike. *Cities as Partners: The Challenge to Strengthen Urban Governance through North-South City Partnerships.* Utrecht: Eburon, 2009.

Borge, Tomás. *The Patient Impatience*. Willimantic, CT: Curbstone Press, 1992.

Bowen, Alyssa. "Taking in the Broad Spectrum": Human Rights and Anti-Politics in the Chile Solidarity Campaign (UK) in the 1970s." *Journal of Social History* 54, no. 2 (2020): 623–43.

Brands, Hal. *Latin America's Cold War*. Cambridge, MA: Harvard University Press, 2012.

Brown, Jonathan C. *Cuba's Revolutionary World*. Cambridge, MA: Harvard University Press, 2017.

Bruno, Elizabeth Casimir. "Speaking through the Body: The Eroticized Feminism of Gioconda Belli." PhD diss., University of North Carolina at Chapel Hill, 2006.

Bulmer-Thomas, Victor. *The Economic History of Latin America since Independence*. Cambridge: Cambridge University Press, 2014.

Burke, Kyle. *Revolutionaries for the Right: Anticommunist Internationalism and Paramilitary Warfare in the Cold War*. Chapel Hill: University of North Carolina Press, 2018.

Byrne, Jeffrey James. *Mecca of Revolution: Algeria, Decolonization, and the Third World Order*. Oxford: Oxford University Press, 2016.

Cappelli, Mary Louisa. "Women of the Revolution: Gendered Politics of Resistance and Agency in the Cultural Production of Margaret Randall." *Cogent Arts and Humanities* 4, no. 1 (2017). https://doi.org/10.1080/23311983.2017.1407020.

Cardenal, Ernesto. *La revolución perdida. Memorias III*. Buenos Aires: Fondo de Cultura Económica de Argentina, 2005.

Cardenal, Fernando. *Faith and Joy: Memoirs of a Revolutionary Priest*. Maryknoll, NY: Orbis Books, 2015.

Cardenal, Fernando, and Valerie Miller. "Nicaragua: Literacy and Revolution." *The Crane Bag* 6, no. 2 (1982): 64–70.

Castro, Vanessa, and Gary Prevost, eds. *The 1990 Elections in Nicaragua and Their Aftermath*. Lanham, MD: Rowman and Littlefield, 1992.

Chamberlain, Paul Thomas. *The Global Offensive: The United States, the Palestine Liberation Organization, and the Making of the Post–Cold War Order*. Oxford: Oxford University Press, 2012.

Chávez, Joaquín M. "The Cold War: Authoritarianism, Empire, and Social Revolution." In Robert H. Holden, ed., *The Oxford Handbook of Central American History*. New York: Oxford University Press, 2020.

———. *Poets and Prophets of the Resistance: Intellectuals and the Origins of El Salvador's Civil War*. New York: Oxford University Press, 2017.

Chong, Alan. "Small State Soft Power Strategies: Virtual Enlargement in the Cases of the Vatican City State and Singapore." *Cambridge Review of International Affairs* 23, no. 3 (2010): 383–405.

Christiaens, Kim. "Between Diplomacy and Solidarity: Western European Support Networks for Sandinista Nicaragua." *European Review of History* 21, no. 4 (2014): 617–34.

Clarke, Nick. "Town Twinning in Cold War Britain: (Dis)continuities in Twentieth-Century Municipal Internationalism." *Contemporary British History* 24, no. 2 (2010): 173–91.

Colburn, Forrest D. *The Vogue of Revolution in Poor Countries.* Princeton, NJ: Princeton University Press, 1994.

Connelly, Matthew. *A Diplomatic Revolution: Algeria's Fight for Independence and the Origins of the Post–Cold War Era.* Oxford: Oxford University Press, 2002.

Conze, Eckart, Martin Klimke, and Jeremy Varon, eds. *Nuclear Threats, Nuclear Fear and the Cold War of the 1980s.* New York: Cambridge University Press, 2017.

Crump, Laurien, and Susanna Erlandsson, eds. *Margins for Manoeuvre in Cold War Europe: The Influence of Smaller Powers.* Abingdon: Routledge, 2020.

Cruz Feliciano, Héctor, and Armando Chaguaceda. "Los intelectuales públicos y el Frente Sandinista en Nicaragua: presencia, desencuentros y actualidad (1990-2012)." *Cahiers des Amériques latines* 74 (2013). https://doi.org/10.4000/cal.3021.

de Graaf, Beatrice. *Over de Muur: De DDR, de Nederlandse kerken en de vredesbeweging.* Amsterdam: Boom, 2004.

Deiner, John T. "The Nicaraguan Literacy Crusade." *Journal of Reading* 25, no. 2 (1981): 118–25.

Di Donato, Michele. "The Cold War and Socialist Identity: The Socialist International and the Italian 'Communist Question' in the 1970s." *Contemporary European History* 24, no. 2 (May 2015): 193–211.

Dunkerley, James. *The Pacification of Central America: Political Change in the Isthmus, 1987–1993.* London: Verso Books, 1994.

Esch, Sophie. *Modernity at Gunpoint: Firearms, Politics, and Culture in Mexico and Central America.* Pittsburgh: University of Pittsburgh Press, 2018.

Fairley, Jan. "La Nueva Canción Latinoamericana." *Bulletin of Latin American Research* 3, no. 2 (1984): 107–16.

Ferrero Blanco, María Dolores. "Daniel Ortega y Mijail Gorbachov. Nicaragua y la URSS en los últimos años de la guerra fría (1985–1990)." *Hispania Nova. Revista de Historia Contemporánea* 13 (2015): 26–53.

———. "El diseño de las instituciones en el Estado Sandinista: La revolución como fuente de derecho." *Revista de Indias* 75, no. 265 (2015): 805–50.

Field, Thomas C., Stella Krepp, and Vanni Pettinà, eds. *Latin America and the Global Cold War.* Chapel Hill: University of North Carolina Press, 2020.

Francis, Hilary, ed. *A Nicaraguan Exceptionalism? Debating the Legacy of the Sandinista Revolution.* London: University of London Press, 2020.

Friedman, Jeremy. *Ripe for Revolution: Building Socialism in the Third World.* Cambridge, MA: Harvard University Press, 2021.

Garavini, Juliano. *After Empires: European Integration, Decolonization, and the Challenge from the Global South, 1957–1986.* Oxford: Oxford University Press, 2012.

García Ferreira, Roberto, and Arturo Taracena, eds. *La guerra fría y el anticomunismo en Centroamérica.* Ciudad de Guatemala: FLACSO, 2017.

García Márquez, Gabriel. "Sandinistas Seize the National Palace!" *The New Left Review* 111 (1978). https://newleftreview.org/issues/i111/articles/gabriel-garcia-marquez-sandinistas-seize-the-national-palace.

Gilman, Nils. "The New International Economic Order: A Reintroduction." *Humanity* 6, no. 1 (Spring 2015): 1–16.

Gibbings, Julie. *Our Time Is Now: Race and Modernity in Postcolonial Guatemala.* Cambridge: Cambridge University Press, 2020.

Gilbert, Mark. *Cold War Europe: The Politics of a Contested Continent.* Lanham, MD: Rowman and Littlefield, 2015.

Gleijeses, Piero. *Conflicting Missions: Havana, Washington, and Africa, 1959–1976.* Chapel Hill: University of North Carolina Press, 2003.

Gobat, Michel. *Confronting the American Dream: Nicaragua under U.S. Imperial Rule.* Durham, NC: Duke University Press, 2005.

Gonzalez, Mike. "April in Managua: The Central American Peace Concert." *Popular Music* 6, no. 2 (May 1987): 247–49.

Gould, Jeffrey. *To Lead as Equals: Rural Protest and Political Consciousness in Chinandega, Nicaragua, 1912–1979.* Chapel Hill: University of North Carolina Press, 1990.

Grayson, George W. *Oil and Mexican Foreign Policy.* Pittsburgh: University of Pittsburgh Press, 1988.

Guerra, Lillian. *Visions of Power in Cuba: Revolution, Redemption, and Resistance, 1959–1971.* Chapel Hill: University of North Carolina Press, 2012.

Gutman, Roy. *Banana Diplomacy: The Making of American Policy in Nicaragua, 1981–1987.* New York: Simon and Schuster, 1988.

Hager, Robert P., Jr., and Robert S. Snyder. "The United States and Nicaragua: Understanding the Breakdown in Relations." *Journal of Cold War Studies* 17, no. 2 (2015): 3–35.

Hale, Charles R. *Resistance and Contradiction: Miskitu Indians and the Nicaraguan State, 1894–1987.* Stanford, CA: Stanford University Press, 1994.

Harmer, Tanya. *Beatriz Allende: A Revolutionary Life in Cold War Latin America.* Chapel Hill: University of North Carolina Press, 2020.

———. *Allende's Chile and the Inter-American Cold War.* Chapel Hill: University of North Carolina Press, 2011.

———. "The Cold War in Latin America." In Artemy M. Kalinovsky and Craig Daigle, eds., *The Routledge Handbook of the Cold War.* Abingdon: Routledge, 2014.

———. "The View from Havana: Chilean Exiles in Cuba and Early Resistance to Chile's Dictatorship, 1973–1977." *Hispanic American Historical Review* 96, no. 1 (2016): 109–46.

Harmer, Tanya, and Alberto Martín Álvarez. "Introduction: Globalizing Latin America's Revolutionary Left: Historiography, Approaches, and Context." In Tanya Harmer and Alberto Martín Álvarez, eds., *Toward a Global History of Latin America's Revolutionary Left.* Gainesville: University of Florida Press, 2021.

Helm, Christian. *Botschafter der Revolution: Das transnationale Kommunikation-snetzwerk zwischen der Frente Sandinista de Liberación Nacional und der bundes-deutschen Nicaragua-Solidarität 1977–1990.* Oldenburg: De Gruyter, 2018.

———. "The Sons of Marx Greet the Sons of Sandino: West German Solidarity Visitors to Nicaragua Sandinista." *Journal of Iberian and Latin American Research* 20, no. 2 (2014): 153–70.

———. "Booming Solidarity: Sandinista Nicaragua and the West German Solidarity Movement in the 1980s." *European Review of History* 21, no. 4 (2014): 597–615.

Henighan, Stephen. *Sandino's Nation: Ernesto Cardenal and Sergio Ramirez; Writing Nicaragua, 1940–2012.* Montreal: McGill-Queen's University Press, 2014.

Hernández Ruigómez, Manuel. "La Nicaragua sandinista y las elecciones de febrero de 1990." PhD diss., Universidad Computense de Madrid, 2012.

Hertogs, Erik-Jan, ed. *Nederlanders naast Nicaragua, 10 jaar revolutie beleefd.* Utrecht: Nicaragua Komitee Nederland, 1990.

Hill, Christopher, and Karen E. Smith, eds. *European Foreign Policy: Key Documents.* Abingdon: Routledge, 2000.

Hoekstra, Quint. "Helping the Contras: The Effectiveness of U.S. Support for Foreign Rebels during the Nicaraguan Contra War (1979–1990)." *Studies in Conflict and Terrorism* 44, no. 6 (2021): 521–41.

Hübner, Hans, et al., eds. *Enrique Presente: Enrique Schmidt Cuadra—Ein Nicaraguaner Zwischen Köln und Managua.* Cologne: Schmidt von Schwind Verlag, 2004.

Iber, Patrick. *Neither Peace nor Freedom: The Cultural Cold War in Latin America.* Cambridge, MA: Harvard University Press, 2015.

Informationsbüro Nicaragua. *Gemeinsam werden wir Siegen! Arbeitsbrigaden in Nicaragua.* Wuppertal: Edition Nahua, 1984.

"Interview with Daniel Ortega." *Latin American Perspectives* 6, no. 1 (1979): 114–18.

"Interview with Henry Ruiz (Modesto)." *Latin American Perspectives* 6, no. 1 (1979): 118–21.

"Interview with Jaime Wheelock Roman." *Latin American Perspectives* 6, no. 1 (1979): 121–27.

Janssens, Joren F. "Stumbling among Giants: Europe's Frustrated Solidarity with Guatemala, 1979–1996." *Bulletin of Latin American Research* 39, no. 5 (November 2020): 598–613.

Jarquín, Mateo. "A Latin American Revolution: The Sandinistas, the Cold War, and Political Change in the Region, 1977–1990." PhD diss., Harvard University, 2019.

———. "The Nicaraguan Question: Contadora and the Latin American Response to US Intervention against the Sandinistas, 1982–86." *The Americas* 78, no. 4 (2021): 581–608.

———. "Red Christmases: The Sandinistas, Indigenous Rebellion, and the Origins of the Nicaraguan Civil War, 1981–82." *Cold War History* 18, no. 1 (2018): 91–107.

Johnson Lee, David. *The Ends of Modernization: Nicaragua and the United States in the Cold War Era.* Ithaca, NY: Cornell University Press, 2021.

Joseph, Gilbert M., and Daniela Spenser, eds. *In from the Cold: Latin America's New Encounter with the Cold War*. Durham, NC: Duke University Press, 2008.

Joseph, Gilbert M. "Border Crossings and the Remaking of Latin American Cold War Studies." *Cold War History* 19, no. 1 (2019): 141–70.

Kagan, Robert. *A Twilight Struggle: American Power and Nicaragua, 1977–1990*. New York: The Free Press, 1996.

Kampwirth, Karen. *Women and Guerrilla Movements: Nicaragua, El Salvador, Chiapas, Cuba*. University Park: Penn State University Press, 2002.

Karamouzi, Eirini, and Dyonysios Chourchoulis. "Troublemaker or Peacemaker? Andreas Papandreou, the Euromissile Crisis, and the Policy of Peace, 1981–86." *Cold War History* 19, no. 1. (2019): 39–61.

Keeley, Theresa. *Reagan's Gun-Toting Nuns: The Catholic Conflict over Cold War Human Rights Policy in Central America*. Ithaca, NY: Cornell University Press, 2020.

Keller, Renata. *Mexico's Cold War: Cuba, the United States, and the Legacy of the Mexican Revolution*. Cambridge: Cambridge University Press, 2015.

Kelly, Patrick William. "The 1973 Chilean Coup and the Origins of Transnational Human Rights Activism." *Journal of Global History* 8, no. 1 (2013): 165–86.

———. *Sovereign Emergencies: Latin America and the Making of Global Human Rights Politics*. Cambridge: Cambridge University Press, 2018.

Kinzer, Stephen. *Blood of Brothers: Life and War in Nicaragua*. Cambridge, MA: Harvard University Press, 2007.

Kirkpatrick, Jeane. "Dictatorships and Double Standards." *Commentary* (November 1979): 34–45.

Kirkendall, Andrew J. *Paulo Freire and the Cold War Politics of Literacy*. Chapel Hill: University of North Carolina Press, 2010.

Klimke, Martin. *The Other Alliance: Student Protest in West Germany and the United States in the Global Sixties*. Princeton, NJ: Princeton University Press, 2010.

Krotz, Ulrich, Kiran Klaus Patel, and Federico Romero, eds. *Europe's Cold War Relations: The EC towards a Global Role*. London: Bloomsbury, 2019.

Kruijt, Dirk. *Cuba and Revolutionary Latin America: An Oral History*. London: Zed Books, 2017.

———. *Guerrillas: War and Peace in Central America*. London: Zed Books, 2013.

———. "Revolución y contrarrevolución: El gobierno Sandinista y la guerra de la Contra en Nicaragua,1980–1990." *Desafíos* 23, no. 2 (2011): 53–81.

LaFeber, Walter. *Inevitable Revolutions: The United States in Central America*. New York: Norton, 1993.

———. "The Reagan Administration and Revolutions in Central America." *Political Science Quarterly* 99, no. 1 (Spring 1984): 1–25.

Lawson, George. *Anatomies of Revolution*. Cambridge: Cambridge University Press, 2019.

LeoGrande, William M. "Making the Economy Scream: US Economic Sanctions against Sandinista Nicaragua." *Third World Quarterly* 17, no. 2 (1996): 329–48.

———. *Our Own Backyard: The United States in Central America, 1977–1992.* Chapel Hill: University of North Carolina Press, 1998.

Long, Tom. *Latin America Confronts the United States: Asymmetry and Influence.* Cambridge: Cambridge University Press, 2015.

Luthi, Lorenz M. *Cold Wars: Asia, the Middle East, Europe.* Cambridge: Cambridge University Press, 2020.

Manela, Erez. "International Society as a Historical Subject." *Diplomatic History* 44, no. 2 (2020): 184–209.

Marchesi, Aldo. *Latin America's Radical Left: Rebellion and Cold War in the Global 1960s.* Cambridge: Cambridge University Press, 2017.

Marcus, Bruce, ed. *Nicaragua: The Sandinista People's Revolution: Speeches by Sandinista Leaders.* New York: Pathfinder Press, 1985.

———. *Sandinistas Speak: Speeches, Writings, and Interviews with Leaders of Nicaragua's Revolution.* New York: Pathfinder Press, 1982.

Marino, Katie. *Feminism for the Americas: The Making of an International Human Rights Movement.* Chapel Hill: University of North Carolina Press, 2020.

Markarian, Vania. *Uruguay, 1968: Student Activism from Global Counterculture to Molotov Cocktails.* Oakland: University of California Press, 2017.

Martí i Puig, Salvador. *La revolución enredada. Nicaragua 1977–1996.* Madrid: Los Libros de la Catarata, 1997.

McCormick, Evan D. "US Electoral Assistance to El Salvador and the Culture of Politics, 1982–1984." In Robert Pee and William Michael Schmidli, eds., *The Reagan Administration, the Cold War, and the Transition to Democracy Promotion.* Cham: Palgrave Macmillan, 2019.

McPherson, Alan. *The Invaded: How Latin Americans and Their Allies Fought and Ended U.S. Occupations.* New York: Oxford University Press, 2014.

Moyn, Samuel. *Not Enough: Human Rights in an Unequal World.* Cambridge, MA: Harvard University Press, 2018.

Mujal-Leon, Eusebio. "The West German Social Democratic Party and the Politics of Internationalism in Central America." *Journal of Interamerican Studies and World Affairs* 29, no. 4 (1988): 89–123.

Nehring, Holger. *Politics of Security: British and West German Protest Movements and the Early Cold War, 1945–1970.* Oxford: Oxford University Press, 2013.

Nepstad, Sharon Erickson. *Convictions of the Soul: Religion, Culture, and Agency in the Central America Solidarity Movement.* Oxford: Oxford University Press, 2005.

Nguyen, Lien-Hang. *Hanoi's War: An International History of the War for Peace in Vietnam.* Chapel Hill: University of North Carolina Press, 2012.

*Nicaragua: Elections; Fact or Fiction.* London: Nicaragua Solidarity Campaign, 1984.

Nuti, Leopoldo, Frédéric Bozo, Marie-Pierre Rey, and Bernd Rother, eds. *The Euromissile Crisis and the End of the Cold War.* Stanford, CA: Stanford University Press, 2015.

Nye, Joseph S., Jr. "Public Diplomacy and Soft Power." *The Annals of the American Academy of Political and Social Science* 616, no. 11 (2008): 94–109.

Nygren, Anja. "Violent Conflicts and Threatened Lives: Nicaraguan Experiences of Wartime Displacement and Postwar Distress." *Journal of Latin American Studies* 35, no 2. (2003): 367–93.

Ogle, Vanessa. "State Rights against Private Capital: The 'New International Economic Order' and the Struggle over Aid, Trade, and Foreign Investment, 1962–1981." *Humanity* 5 (Summer 2014): 211–23.

Oñate-Madrazo, Andrea. "Insurgent Diplomacy: El Salvador's Transnational Revolution, 1970–1992." PhD diss., Princeton University, 2016.

Pastor, Robert A. *Condemned to Repetition: The United States and Nicaragua.* Princeton, NJ: Princeton University Press, 1987.

Paszyn, Danuta. *The Soviet Attitude to Political and Social Change in Central America.* London: Palgrave Macmillan, 2000.

Patel, Kiran Klaus, and Kenneth Weisbrode, eds. *European Integration and the Atlantic Community in the 1980s.* Cambridge: Cambridge University Press, 2013.

Peace, Roger. *A Call to Conscience: The Anti–Contra War Campaign.* Amherst: University of Massachusetts Press, 2012.

Pedrosa, Fernando. "La Internacional Socialista y la Guerra de Malvinas." *Latin American Research Review* 49, no. 2 (2014): 47–67.

———. *La otra izquierda. La socialdemocracia en América Latina.* Buenos Aires: Capital Intelectual, 2012.

Perla, Héctor. "Central American Counterpublic Mobilization: Transnational Social Movement Opposition to Reagan's Foreign Policy toward Central America." *Latino Studies* 11, no. 2 (2013): 167–89.

———. *Sandinista Nicaragua's Resistance to US Coercion: Revolutionary Deterrence in Asymmetric Conflict.* Cambridge: Cambridge University Press, 2017.

Perry, Mariana. "With a Little Help from My Friends: The Dutch Solidarity Movement and the Chilean Struggle for Democracy." *European Review of Latin American and Caribbean Studies* 101 (April 2016): 75–96.

Pettinà, Vanni. *Historia mínima de la Guerra Fría en América Latina.* Ciudad de México: El Colegio de México, 2018.

Prashad, Vijay. *The Darker Nations: A People's History of the Third World.* New York: The New Press, 2008.

Prevost, Gary. "Cuba and Nicaragua: A Special Relationship?" *Latin American Perspectives* 17, no. 3 (1990): 120–37.

Ramírez, Sergio. *Adiós Muchachos: A Memoir of the Sandinista Revolution.* Durham, NC: Duke University Press, 2012.

Rabe, Stephen. *The Killing Zone: The United States Wages Cold War in Latin America.* New York: Oxford University Press, 2012.

Rocha, José Luis. "Agrarian Reform in Nicaragua in the 1980s." In Hilary Francis, ed., *A Nicaraguan Exceptionalism? Debating the Legacy of the Sandinista Revolution.* London: University of London Press, 2020.

———. "La década de los años 80: Revolución en Nicaragua, revolución en la caficultura Nicaragüense." *Anuario de Estudios Centroamericanos* 29, no. 1–2 (2003): 69–99.

Romano, Angela. "Re-Designing Military Security in Europe: Cooperation and Competition between the European Community and NATO during the Early 1980s." *European Review of History* 24, no. 3 (2017): 445–71.

Rother, Bernd. "Between East and West—Social Democracy as an Alternative to Communism and Capitalism: Willy Brandt's Strategy as President of the Social-ist International." In Leopolde Nuti, ed., *The Crisis of Détente in Europe: From Helsinki to Gorbachev, 1975–1985*. London: Routledge, 2008.

———. *Global Social Democracy: Willy Brand and the Socialist International in Latin America*. London: Lexington Books, 2020.

Robinson, William I. *A Faustian Bargain: US Intervention in the Nicaraguan Elec-tions and American Foreign Policy in the Post–Cold War Era*. Boulder, CO: Westview Press, 1992.

Rueda, Claudia. *Students of Revolution: Youth, Protest, and Coalition Building in Somoza-Era Nicaragua*. Austin: University of Texas Press, 2019.

Sabia, Debra. *Contradiction and Conflict: The Popular Church in Nicaragua*. Tusca-loosa: University of Alabama Press, 1997.

Sánchez Nateras, Gerardo. "La última Revolución: La insurrección sandinista y la Guerra Fría interamericana." PhD diss., El Colegio de México, 2019.

———. "'¡Nicas y mexicanos solidarios como hermanos!': El movimiento mexicano de solidaridad con Nicaragua (1974–1979)." *Secuencia* 108 (2020). https://doi.org/10.18234/secuencia.v0i108.1840.

———. "The Sandinista Revolution and the Limits of the Cold War in Latin America: The Dilemma of Non-intervention during the Nicaraguan Crisis, 1977–78." *Cold War History* 18, no. 2 (2018): 111–29.

Sargent, Daniel, *A Superpower Transformed: The Remaking of American Foreign Relations in the 1970s*. Oxford: Oxford University Press, 2015.

Schmidli, William Michael. *Freedom on the Offensive: Human Rights, Democracy Promotion, and US Interventionism in the Late Cold War*. Ithaca, NY: Cornell University Press, 2022.

———. "'The Most Sophisticated Intervention We Have Seen': The Carter Admin-istration and the Nicaraguan Crisis, 1978–1979." *Diplomacy and Statecraft* 23, no. 1 (2012): 66–86.

———. "Rockin' to Free the World? Amnesty International's Benefit Concert Tours, 1986–88." *Diplomatic History* 45, no. 4 (2021): 688–713.

Schulz, Matthias, and Thomas A. Schwartz, eds. *The Strained Alliance: U.S.-European Relations from Nixon to Carter*. Cambridge: Cambridge University Press, 2010.

Sierakowski, Robert. *Sandinistas: A Moral History*. Notre Dame, IN: University of Notre Dame Press, 2020.

Sjursen, Helene. *The United States, Western Europe and the Polish Crisis: International Relations in the Second Cold War*. New York: Palgrave Macmillan, 2003.

Slobodian, Quinn. *Foreign Front: Third World Politics in Sixties West Germany.* Durham, NC: Duke University Press, 2012.

Smith, Christian. *Resisting Reagan: The U.S. Central America Peace Movement.* Chicago: University of Chicago Press, 1996.

Smith, Hazel. *European Union Foreign Policy and Central America.* Basingstoke: Macmillan Press, 1995.

Snyder, Emily. "'Cuba, Nicaragua, Unidas Vencerán': Official Collaborations between the Sandinista and Cuban Revolutions." *The Americas* 78, no. 4 (2021): 609–37.

———. "Internationalizing the Revolutionary Family: Love and Politics in Cuba and Nicaragua, 1979–1990." *Radical History Review* 136 (2020): 50–74.

Sobocinska, Agnieszka. *Saving the World? Western Volunteers and the Rise of the Humanitarian-Development Complex.* Cambridge: Cambridge University Press, 2021.

Solórzano, Porfirio R., ed. *The Nirex Collection: Nicaraguan Revolution Extracts; Twelve Years, 1978–1990.* Austin, TX: Litex, 1994.

Spohr, Kristina. *The Global Chancellor: Helmut Schmidt and the Reshaping of International Order.* Oxford: Oxford University Press, 2016.

Stites Mor, Jessica. *South-South Solidarity and the Latin American Left.* Madison: University of Wisconsin Press, 2013.

———, ed. *Human Rights and Transnational Solidarity in Cold War Latin America.* Madison: University of Wisconsin Press, 2013.

Storkmann, Klaus. "East German Military Aid to the Sandinista Government of Nicaragua, 1979–1990." *Journal of Cold War Studies* 16, no. 2 (Spring 2014): 56–76.

Summerfield, Derek. "Nicaragua: Health and Revolution." *The Lancet* 335, no. 8693 (1990): 845.

Thornton, Christy. *Revolution in Development: Mexico and the Governance of the Global Economy.* Oakland: University of California Press, 2021.

Tijerino, Frances Kinloch. "Conflicto étnico, geopolítica e identidad: El caso de las comunidades miskitas del río coco en Nicaragua." *Estudios Fronterizos* 40 (1997): 95–114.

Travis, Philip. "Oscar Arias and the Treaty of Esquipulas." *Oxford Research Encyclopaedia of Latin American History* (2017).

Tünnermann Bernheim, Carlos. *Memorias de un Ciudadano.* Managua: Hispamer, 2016.

van Diepen, Remco. *Hollanditis: Nederland en het kernwapendebat 1977–1987.* Amsterdam: Bert Bakker, 2004.

van Ommen, Eline. "The Nicaraguan Revolution's Challenge to the Monroe Doctrine: Sandinistas and Western Europe, 1979–1990." *The Americas* 78, no. 4 (2021): 639–66.

———. "The Sandinista Revolution in the Netherlands: The Dutch Solidarity Committees and Nicaragua (1977–1990)." *Naveg@merica: Revista electrónica editada por la Asociación Española de Americanistas* 17 (2016). http://revistas.um.es/navegamerica.

Vázquez Olivera, Mario, and Fabián Campos Hernández, eds. *México ante el conflicto centroamericano. Testimonio de una época*. Ciudad de México: Universidad Nacional Autónoma de México, 2016.

Véliz Estrada, Rodrigo. "Más agresivos y más revolucionarios": Los límites y el agotamiento de la "revolución democristiana" en América Central, 1961–1974." *Hispanic American Historical Review* 101, no. 4 (2021): 657–87.

Vilas, Carlos M. "Especulaciones sobre una sorpresa: Las elecciones en Nicaragua." *Desarrollo Económico* 30, no. 118 (1990): 255–76.

Vion, Antoine. "Europe from the Bottom Up: Town Twinning in France during the Cold War." *Contemporary European History* 11, no. 4 (2002): 623–40.

Vrana, Heather. *This City Belongs to You: A History of Student Activism in Guatemala*. Oakland: University of California Press, 2017.

Westad, Odd Arne. *The Global Cold War: Third World Interventions and the Making of Our Times*. Cambridge: Cambridge University Press, 2005.

Weidhaas, Peter. *See You in Frankfurt! Life at the Helm of the Largest Book Fair in the World*. New York: Locus Publishing, 2010.

Wettig, Gerhard. "The Last Soviet Offensive in the Cold War: Emergence and Development of the Campaign against NATO Euromissiles, 1979–198." *Cold War History* 9, no. 1 (2009): 79–110.

Whisnant, David E. *Rascally Signs in Sacred Places: The Politics of Culture in Nicaragua*. Chapel Hill: University of North Carolina Press, 1995.

Williams, Philip J. "Elections and Democratization in Nicaragua: The 1990 Elections in Perspective." *Journal of Interamerican Studies and World Affairs* 32, no. 4 (1990): 13–34.

Wittner, Lawrence S. *The Struggle against the Bomb: Toward Nuclear Abolition; A History of the World Nuclear Disarmament Movement, 1971 to Present*. Stanford, CA: Stanford University Press, 2003.

Yeshitela, Omali, and Joseph Waller. "The First Conference in Solidarity with Nicaragua." *The Black Scholar* 12 (1981): 25–35.

Yordanov, Radoslav. "Outfoxing the Eagle: Soviet, East European and Cuban Involvement in Nicaragua in the 1980s." *Journal of Contemporary History* 55, no. 4 (2020): 871–92.

Young, John. "Western Europe and the End of the Cold War, 1979–1989." In Melvyn P. Leffler and Odd Arne Westad, eds., *The Cambridge History of the Cold War*. Cambridge: Cambridge University Press, 2010.

Zimmerman, Matilde. *Sandinista: Carlos Fonseca and the Nicaraguan Revolution*. Durham, NC: Duke University Press, 2000.

# INDEX

Note: Pages in *italics* refer to illustrations.

National Guard. *See* Guardia Nacional (National Guard)

National Literacy Crusade, 54, 72–80. *See also* human rights; social justice movement

National Palace occupation, 40–41

NATO (North Atlantic Treaty Organization), 5, 128, 159, 166

Netherlands, 10, 40, 68, 101, 111–13, 126–28, 213–14. *See also* EC; Western Europeans

*New Left Review* (publication), 24

*New York Times, The* (publication), 109, 144, 151

*Nicaragua Libre* (publication), 71

Nicaragua Must Survive campaign. *See* CNDS

*Nicaragua: Patria Libre o Morir* (film), 40

*Nicaragua Today* (publication), 81, 88, 128

NIEO (New International Economic Order), 57, 89

Nine (EC group), 45, 49, 66, 236n124. *See also* EC; EPC; Western Europeans

NKN (Nicaragua Komitee Nederland), 36, 37, 39, 68, 78–79, 85, 126, 172–73, 205, 207, 213–14

non-alignment, 56, 83, 97, 104, 107, 110, 116, 157, 164–65, 184

Noriega, Manuel, 220

Northampton Labour Party, 77

*Novedades* (publication), 69

Novib, 81, 127

NSC (Nicaragua Solidarity Campaign; United Kingdom): base in Managua, 17; benefit concerts by, 84, 129; brigades by, 136, 139; on British interest, 99, 102–3; campaigns by, 128, 169–70, 173, 180, 181; on Nicaraguan democracy, 81, 147; 1990 election fundraising by, 210

Nuñez, Carlos, 60, 129

OAS (Organization of American States), 21, 91, 92, 197

Obando y Bravo, Miguel, 81, 195

*Observer, The* (publication), 115

Ochoa, Amparo, 119

Oduber Quirós, Daniel, 43

Office of Public Diplomacy for Latin America and the Caribbean, 130. *See also* United States

OID (Overseas Information Department), 48

oil, 154, 163–65, 190

Operation Urgent Fury, 132–33. *See also* Grenada

Ortega, Daniel: about, 23, 59; in Dirección Nacional, 60; elections and, 147, 161, 208; peace process and, 157, 187, 189, 210–11; on post-FSLN work, 225–26; revolutionary diplomacy by, 107, 123, 131–32; on tercerista strategy, 25, 29

Ortega Saavedra, Humberto, 22–23, 25, 63, 168, 201

Owen, David, 46

Owen, Richard, 138

Oxfam, 77, 139

Palestine Liberation Organization (PLO), 7

Palme, Olof, 42, 64, 103, 168. *See also* Sweden

Panama, 29, 30, 92, 125, 172, 220

Pancasán operation (1967), 22

Papandreou, Andreas Georgios, 165. *See also* Greece

Parsons, Anthony, 47

Pastora, Edén, 24, 28, 29–30

Paszyn, Danuta, 62

Pax Christi International, 126

Payne, Alan, 67–68

peace concerts, 18, 40, 68, 78, 119, 120, 126, 127–29, 219. *See also* cultural expression; concerts

peace movement, 90, 93, 102, 126–29, 137, 156, 184. *See also* human rights; social justice movement; transnational solidarity

peace process, 185–87, 215–17; control of, 193–202; domestic and international response to, 202–8; lead-up to Esquipulas II accords, 187–93; Plan de Sandino a Sandino on, 208–15. *See also* Contadora process; Esquipulas II Peace Accords (1987)

*Pedagogy of the Oppressed* (Freire), 73

Founded in 1893,
UNIVERSITY OF CALIFORNIA PRESS
publishes bold, progressive books and journals
on topics in the arts, humanities, social sciences,
and natural sciences—with a focus on social
justice issues—that inspire thought and action
among readers worldwide.

The UC PRESS FOUNDATION
raises funds to uphold the press's vital role
as an independent, nonprofit publisher, and
receives philanthropic support from a wide
range of individuals and institutions—and from
committed readers like you. To learn more, visit
ucpress.edu/supportus.